Voices of the
U.S. Latino Experience

Voices of the U.S. Latino Experience

VOLUME 3

Edited by Rodolfo F. Acuña and Guadalupe Compeán

GREENWOOD PRESS
Westport, Connecticut • London

Library of Congress Cataloging-in-Publication Data

Voices of the U.S. Latino experience / edited by Rodolfo F. Acuña and Guadalupe Compeán.
  p. cm.
  Includes bibliographical references and index.
  ISBN 978–0–313–34020–8 (set : alk. paper)—ISBN 978–0–313–34021–5 (v. 1 : alk.
paper)—ISBN 978–0–313–34022–2 (v. 2 : alk. paper)—ISBN 978–0–313–34023–9 (v. 3 :
alk. paper)
  1. Hispanic Americans—History—Sources. I. Acuña, Rodolfo. II. Compeán, Guadalupe.
  E184.S75V65 2008
  973′.0468—dc22   2007046170

British Library Cataloguing in Publication Data is available.

Library of Congress Catalog Card Number: 2007046170
ISBN: 978–0–313–34020–8 (set)
      978–0–313–34021–5 (vol. 1)
      978–0–313–34022–2 (vol. 2)
      978–0–313–34023–9 (vol. 3)

First published in 2008

Greenwood Press, 88 Post Road West, Westport, CT 06881
An imprint of Greenwood Publishing Group, Inc.
www.greenwood.com

Printed in the United States of America

The paper used in this book complies with the
Permanent Paper Standard issued by the National
Information Standards Organization (Z39.48–1984).

10 9 8 7 6 5 4 3 2 1

To Our Angela and Her Shadow

Contents

VOLUME 2

Part XI Push and Pull   337

Part XII The Gateway to the Americas   421

PART XVIII
Latinos in the 1960s

The 1960s were crucial to Latinos living in the United States. Because of their isolation they were not fully part of American society and were separate nationalities within a dominant nationality that affected their identity. The large scale migration of Puerto Ricans, Boricua, Borinquen, or borincano brought about differences within the community; although 95 percent identified as Puerto Rican the second generation often had different priorities. A slightly different pattern emerged; in the decade of the 50s 470,000 Boricua migrated to the United States slowing down in the 1960s to 214,000. In 1940, 88 percent of Puerto Ricans lived in New York City; by 1970, 59 percent lived there. The population of the island was 2.3 million versus 892,513 on the mainland that meant the second generation assumed a greater role in forming a mainland Puerto Rican identity. The younger generation lived and struggled amidst African Americans and other Latinos. Television and the radio played a big part in their lives. Puerto Ricans still felt the presence of the island but English was now more prevalent. Though Puerto Ricans had always been militant, the size of youth groups such as the Black Panthers would be more dramatic.

As a result of the Cuban Revolution many Cubans joined the Puerto Rican community, although most early Cubans migrated to the Miami area. Even though large sectors of this migration were middle-class and white, many were working class and were victims of the racist tradition toward Latinos. Trickles of other Latinos escaping a worsening economic situation in Latin America came to the United States hoping to live the life portrayed in the movies and in trade magazines. Not only Caribbean folk came but larger numbers of South Americans. As with the Puerto Ricans, the larger younger generation was attuned to domestic issues such as poverty, the lack of equal education, the civil rights movement, and the Vietnam War. In places like Milwaukee, they came together in the flurry of protests during 1968.

The 1960s highlighted the civil rights traditions of the Puerto Rican and Mexican communities. History took on new importance—Pedro Albizu Campos died on April 21, 1965. His body was taken to the Old San Juan Cemetery by over 75,000 Puerto Ricans. The New York chapter of the Young Lords Organization (YLO) was founded on July 26, 1969, to fight for the rights of the Puerto Rican community. Latinos coalesced and joined the wave of protests of that and following years. The Cuban American community for the most part diverged from these interests. Their focus was Cuba and they joined conservatives in the United States who supported their political agenda and interests. However, they remained united with other Latinos on cultural and linguistic issues. Most retained their Latin American identity.

Dominicans were not strangers to the United States. Small numbers had trickled in since the nineteenth century and there was a recorded number in New York City in the 1930s. Larger numbers migrated to the United States in the 60s when economic and political unrest push them to areas such as the United States. The United States had invaded and then occupied the Dominican Republic from 1916 to 1924 and in 1965. They did not come in larger numbers because of distance and the cost of transportation. Unlike Puerto Ricans they were not citizens and were not brought in large numbers to the United States by labor contractors. Dominicans were important in forming the musical fusion of Caribbean beats along with the Puerto Ricans and Cubans. Events were also shaping up in Central America that would bring in large numbers of Nicaraguans, Salvadorans, and Guatemalans.

316. Excerpts from Frances Negrón-Muntaner, "Feeling Pretty: *West Side Story* and Puerto Rican Identity Discourses," 2000

As with most people living in the United States, the question of identity has been important to Latinos and Puerto Ricans in particular. Although Puerto Ricans use the term Latino in the cultural sense, they generally identify themselves as Puerto Rican, Boricua, Borinquen, or borincano, which comes from the Taíno name for the island. The Taíno Indians were the first inhabited Puerto Rico. In the 1960 Census, over 95 percent identified as Puerto Rican. Immigration to the U.S. mainland slowed down—during the decade from 1950 to 1960, 470,000 Boricua left the island; in the 1960s only 214,000 would leave. There were other patterns affecting identity: in 1940, 88 percent of mainland Puerto Ricans lived in New York City; by 1970 only 59 percent lived there. In the 1960s, Puerto Ricans were the second largest Spanish-speaking group in the United States, second only to Mexican Americans. Nearly 2.3 million Puerto Ricans living on the island and 892,513 on the mainland. In the 1960s the second generation of immigrants to the mainland was now larger. More and more youth were influenced by Black Americans and they attempted to construct an identity for the U.S. Boricua community. Other Spanish-speaking people lived amongst them but they had not reached a critical mass and remained "more immigrant," looking to their home country for identity. While Puerto Ricans continued to look to the island they were building a unique group identity. Over time many had become Nuyoricans.

The Puerto Rican island itself was at the meeting point of the English-speaking and Spanish-speaking Americas and was greatly affected by the anti-colonial rhetoric of the day. Part of this identity discourse was portrayed in movies and through expressions of racism in the greater society. This discourse would influence other Spanish-speaking groups sharing physical and, finally, cultural space, which saw the fusion of Puerto Rican music with other Caribbean peoples, especially with the Cubans and Dominicans. Many Latinos credit the music with helping maintain the disparate groups' identity and unity. New York was the center of much of this fusion, although in the 1960s Chicago had begun to rival it. The following excerpts are from a critical review of *West Side Story*, a Broadway musical that was also a 1961 film criticized by Puerto Ricans and other Latinos because it used a white actress in the main role and stereotyped Puerto Ricans. *West Side Story* was billed as a Puerto Rican Romeo and Juliet in which the white guy gets the girl.

There is no single American cultural product that haunts Puerto Rican identity discourses in the United States more intensely than the 1961 film, *West Side Story*, directed by Robert Wise and Jerome Robbins. Although neither the first nor last American movie to portray Puerto Ricans as gang members (men) or as sassy and virginal (women), hardly any Puerto Rican cultural critic or screen actor can refrain from stating their very special relationship to *West Side Story*. Jennifer López, the highest paid Latina actress in Hollywood today, recalls that her favorite movie was *West Side Story*. "I saw it over and over. I never noticed that Natalie Wood wasn't really a Puerto Rican girl. I grew up always wanting to play Anita [Rita Moreno's Oscar-winning role], but as I got older, I wanted to be María. I went to dance classes every week." Journalist Blanca Vázquez, whose editorial work in the publication *Centro* was crucial in creating a space for critical discourse on Latinos in media, comments: "And what did the 'real' Puerto Rican, Anita, do in the film? She not only was another Latina 'spitfire,' she also sang a song denigrating Puerto Rico and by implication, being Puerto Rican.... I remember seeing it and being ashamed." For Island-born cultural critic Alberto Sandoval, the film became pivotal in his own identity formation: "'Alberto, I've just met a guy named Alberto.' And how can I forget those who upon my arrival would start tapping flamenco steps and squealing: 'I like to be in America?' As the years passed by I grew accustomed to their actions and reactions to my presence. I would smile and ignore the stereotype of Puerto Ricans that Hollywood promotes."

Without a touch of irony, Leonard Bernstein has written about the extent to which he researched Puerto Rican culture in New York before writing the score: "We went to a gym in Brooklyn where there were different gangs that a social organization was trying to bring together. I don't know if too much eventually got into *West Side Story*, but everything does help." The "superficiality" of the way that Puerto Ricans were represented in the book made one of the original *West Side Story* producers, Cheryl Crawford, insist that "the show explains why the poor in New York, who had once been Jewish, were now Puerto Rican and black...." When someone said the piece was a poetic fantasy, not a sociological document, she replied, "You have to rewrite the whole thing or I won't do it." Hence, if *West Side Story* was never intended to be "real" and doesn't feel real to Puerto Rican spectators, what accounts for its reality effects?

For many Puerto Rican spectators who identify with the narrative, *West Side Story* is a morality play about "our" everyday problems: racism, poverty, and the destructiveness of violence. An example of this pedagogical reading is exemplified by Actor's Playhouse, a Miami-based theater group that recently staged the musical to a group of "at risk" young adults who were mostly Latinos. The purpose was "to show them the devastating consequences of associating with gang members who use violence as their primary way of solving differences. This benign view of the film, however, was not shared by the government officials who pulled *West Side Story* out of the Brussels World's Fair "on the grounds that it was bad publicity for America." Hence, far from the homogeneous reading some critics have given the film as a piece of racist propaganda against Puerto Ricans, *West Side Story* endures in part due to the many discursive uses and "real" identifications it allows.

Several key discourses and histories of Puerto Rican–American representation coalesce in this text. First, the film—although not an entirely predictable Hollywood musical ... perseveres in a long tradition of representing Latinos as inherently musical and performative subjects, ready to wear their sexualized identity for a white audience at the drop of a hat. Consistent with this history, the "Puerto Rican music" found in *West Side Story* is an American-made fusion of a wide range of rhythms with no discernible or specific national origin. In this sense, despite *West Side Story*'s dramatic elements, Latinos are doing exactly what they are expected to do, particularly at a time of significant racial and social unrest in the United States: singing and dancing the night away.

Source: Frances Negrón-Muntaner, "Feeling Pretty: *West Side Story* and Puerto Rican Identity Discourses," Social Text 63, Vol. 18, No. 2, Summer 2000, pp. 84–85. Reprinted with permission of Duke University Press.

317. Al Burt, "Miami: The Cuban Flavor," 1971

In the case of most revolutions, the elites leave the country. It happened to the Mexicans in 1913, when massive numbers left Mexico after the overthrow of Mexican dictator Porfirio Díaz (1830–1915). After Fidel Castro took over Cuba in 1959, many wealthy Cubans, many of whom were supporters of Cuban dictator Fulgencio Batista (1901–1973), sent thousands of Cuban children to the United States in the early 1960s in a U.S.-sponsored operation known as Pedro Pan. Operation Peter Pan (Operación Pedro Pan) was initiated by the U.S. government, the Roman Catholic Church, and anti-Castro Cuban dissidents from December 26, 1960, to October 23, 1962. The mass exodus of 14,000 unaccompanied children from the Caribbean island nation was touted as a save-the-children operation that would take youngsters away from Communists. These children were followed by thousands of political refugees. While Cubans migrated to New York and elsewhere, their capital became Miami, which was about 90 miles from Cuba and shared the same climate. The first wave of immigrants comprised professionals, the better educated, and mostly white people. They received government support and were soon able to dominate the city's life. Miami became the exiles' center of anti-Castro activity. The following *Nation* article discusses Cuban Americans in the 1960s and the formation of a Cuban American community.

Miami, more renowned in the past for a brassy exterior than a loving heart, is undergoing a Cuban transplant that may change that image. The city has been Latinized, and there is, loose on the streets and in the bistros, the famous quality that prompted tourists visiting pre-Castro Cuba to marvel at what "good" people Cubans were.

Last spring, a Cuban exile robbed a secondhand clothing store, beat up a woman clerk (also Cuban), took $20, and fled into a Cuban neighborhood. He did not find the cover he expected. In minutes, the word spread and 300 angry Cubans gathered to help the pursuing police. When the man was dragged out of a vacant rooming house, the Cubans cheered and applauded. Then, emotionally carried away, they charged upon the robber. Police hustled him into their car, but some of the crowd beat on the roof and windows until it pulled away.

That incident tells much about the Spanish-language community (some 90 percent Cuban) in the Miami area. It numbers an estimated 318,000 in a city population of 1.3 million and is expected to reach 428,000 within five years. The instincts of this group are winningly human, but its brakes could be improved. In the case of the clothing-store robber, he offended the Cuban sense of honor, not for stealing but by beating a woman. He had to be caught and punished and the Cubans were eager to help with both jobs. In all human affairs, the Cubans' multifaceted impact on Miami has ranged from the beautiful to something less.

They have given Miami a flavor it lacked. Their gift for living whether they are rich or poor, seems both more festive and more real than the native style. Theirs is a mixture of pleasure seeking, understanding for human frailty, pride, devotion to church and family that are being lost in the computer age. Practice may fall short of the ideals, but human weaknesses are shrugged off, when not enjoyed.

To the motorist on the street with a flat tire or with a stalled car, or in any number of other fixes that focus notice on the individual in distress, the Cuban can be a cheering sight. The chances are that he will be more sympathetic than the native, more willing to inconvenience himself for the sake of a stranger.

The Cubans have done well in most areas—business, education, politics—with the major exception of their efforts against Fidel Castro, the man who sent them into exile. While most everything else they have touched has prospered (their annual earning power is estimated at nearly $600 million), the anti-Castro movements have foundered.

In the peak days of 1964, there were more than 300 active and militant anti-Castro exile groups in Miami, but they have dwindled to a handful. Those that are left still picket, demonstrate, and protest, but they also tend to bicker among themselves. With a few heroic exceptions, their efforts have sputtered out on the shores of Florida rather than in Cuba.

The Cubans cluster, perhaps because their orientation toward tradition is not understood in the larger community. They stress inherited custom and law and order. Police say that, except in traffic offenses, they are more law-abiding than the average Miamian. The exile community has been embarrassed, though, by increasing involvement of a few Cubans in narcotics traffic, particularly cocaine. After some forty Cubans had been arrested in Miami as part of a nationwide attack on drug smuggling, one federal narcotics officer announced that there was a Cuban Mafia. He described it as exceptionally violent.

Most Cubans will tell you that the one great political lesson of their lives was taught them by Castro. To them, it was a lesson of betrayal and it has left them highly suspicious of liberal thought and devoted to a kind of evangelical anti-communism. In a local election, some Cubans grumbled because one candidate had a travel agency that did business with Aeroflot, the Russian airline, and that another was unsuitable because a peace symbol hung on his office wall. The John Birch Society and similar conservative groups have recruited among Cubans with some success, limited, however, because most Cubans believe in a cradle-to-grave government care that enrages conservatives.

During the early days of the Cuban influx, when droves of uprooted professionals and technicians were trying to find outlets for their skills, a "clandestine" system of service developed. A wide variety of unlicensed or nonunion Cubans, from barbers to carpenters to doctors, quietly peddled their trades at bargain prices to fellow Cubans in need. Today, the signs of Cuban success are numerous. Rather than Miami's downtown core degenerating into a shell of empty stores and "for rent" signs, as has happened in other cities, Cubans have moved in. There and in nearby neighborhoods they have created Little Havana, not as boisterous and attractively sinful as pre-Castro Havana but with a touch of the same style.

A walk down the Tamiami Trail, or through parts of the southwest section of the city, has the smell and flavor of Cuba. Street conversations are in Spanish; the signs are in Spanish; the food, coffee, and businesses are Cuban; the people read Spanish-language newspapers and listen to Spanish-language radio stations or watch Spanish-language television.

An estimated 6,000 Cuban businesses now operate in the area (current hard times may eliminate some), producing everything from hand-rolled cigars to shoes to boats and furniture. The Cuban labor force numbers more than 65,000 and is expected to reach 100,000 in less than five years. Some 35,000 Cuban children go to public schools. Cuban doctors (nearly 600 are now licensed in Florida) abound in the hospitals.

This vast bilingual pool has helped attract thirty regional Latin American offices to serve international corporations. Even so, some Cubans still complain that they have difficulty making the telephone operator at the fire station or police station understand them when they speak Spanish. The situation is being corrected.

One exception to the general rule of successful relocation, an exception to be found, perhaps, in any American community today, is the behavior of Cuban youth. To the despair of their parents and grandparents, many are adopting North American ways. It becomes a generation gap of extraordinary width, for as older Cubans try to maintain traditions at home, many of the young spend their time outside the home trying to acquire new customs.

An outstanding example has been a young Cuban football player at the University of Florida, Carlos Álvarez (refugee vintage: 1960). A sophomore pass receiver, Álvarez was chosen on most of the all-American teams. He was an instant hero. But when he became a U.S. citizen, let his hair grow stylishly long, and criticized the war in Vietnam, some Cubans felt that Álvarez was abandoning his heritage.

It is odd that, though the United States is conducting one of the most unusual refugee operations in history—an airlift which has brought 230,000 Cubans to this country—many Americans are not even aware of it. Until 1962, regular commercial flights were available from Cuba. After they were curtailed, some refugees arrived by small boat and via legal transit through Spain and Mexico. But most of those now in Miami have come since 1965, when President Johnson inaugurated the airlift as a humanitarian gesture to unite families separated by the revolution. These have received U.S.-paid transportation, federally supervised food and health care, plus their own welfare system, and job settlement.

It works as follows. Twice each day, a U.S. plane takes off from Miami International Airport, flies to Cuba, and returns home with a load of refugees. In Miami, this is called the Freedom Airlift. The arrivals, as might be expected, are both tearful and joyous, and moving even to a non-Cuban spectator. The planes bring in some 800 new Cubans each week, or between 3,000 and 4,000 a month. Some 230,000 have been flown from Cuba since the flights began in December 1965.

The United States charters the planes for $800,000 a year, and welcomes the refugees to these shores with a welfare program that will cost U.S. taxpayers $112 million in 1971. It is a program unique in this era, when more than 20 million refugees are shuffling across various borders, searching for a place to survive. But, of course, what the Cubans have done with this U.S.-subsidized new start may also be unique.

Castro has challenged the propaganda aspect of the airlift by declaring that if the United States made a like offer to people in northeast Brazil, as one example, the same outpouring would result. Others have suggested that the offer might also empty Harlem. Nor does there seem much doubt that the Haitian refugees who try to flee to the Bahama Islands, and are refused permission by U.S. authorities there to continue on to the United States, would welcome such an opportunity. Jamaican migrant workers who cut sugar cane in Florida and must return home at the end of the season (some try to "escape" and stay) would be receptive. The examples could go on and on, for the immigration quota of 120,000 for the Western Hemisphere has a long waiting list.

In local politics, Cubans have yet to realize their potential, partially because many have not yet become citizens but also because exile politics and the yearning for home have diverted their attention. So far, their influence has been mostly vocal, but that is sometimes considerable, because Cubans are skilled, through their anti-Castro experiences, in the arts of propaganda. However, politicians already are looking ahead to the day when the exiles may be 20 percent or more of the registered voters in the Miami area. That would give them a political edge over the black community, which is already 50,000 smaller.

Cuban views seldom mesh with those of the blacks, who have the same ambitions and feel much more frustrated. To Cubans, the blacks often seem suspiciously liberal. Rivalry between the two minorities is spurred by feelings among the blacks that the Cuban is a Johnny-come-lately who walked in (with white complexion, for the most part, and with better education) and skimmed the cream off whatever opportunity there was in Miami. Blacks have grumbled that Cubans were better received and that the federal umbrella of assistance extended to Cubans has been broader than that extended to them.

In some cases, this argument is more emotional than factual, but certainly the Cubans did benefit from a crash program of help and did find open arms in the community. For example, blacks do not have a job resettlement program enabling them to move to other parts of the country, as do the Cubans. The program was designed to spread the Cuban influx to the rest of the country. Federal officials cite a 70 percent resettlement figure. Nevertheless, the Cuban population in the Miami area has increased 100,000 in the last three years as the airlift has brought in from 105,000 to 120,000. These figures indicate that many resettled Cubans become dissatisfied in colder climates and return to Miami.

An unemployed but employable Cuban male head of family can still get $100 a month welfare, but the U.S. citizen in similar circumstances gets nothing. A riot in the Miami black community during the 1968 Republican National Convention brought on a presidentially appointed commission to study the causes. It found that black resentment toward Cuban welfare was one factor. Studies are now under way to determine exactly what welfare differences exist so that they may be corrected.

A recent county survey disclosed that the 1969 median income for blacks was $5,350; for Cubans, $6,550. By 1985, the Cuban income was projected to rise to $9,400; the blacks, $7,800. Other complicating factors are a housing shortage, questions about the security screening given arriving Cubans, and crowding in the schools.

Apparent inequities in welfare caught the eye last summer of William Clay, a young black Congressman from East St. Louis, and so angered him that, as a member of a House Subcommittee on Labor, he began a movement that almost ended not only the airlift but the Cuban Refugee Program as well. Rep. Clay contended there should be one welfare system for all. In a letter dated May 20, he asked President Nixon "to take immediate action to terminate the Cuban airlift operation and make a public announcement of our future posture toward Cuba and its citizens."

This did not go over well at the White House, where the prevailing attitude has been a desire to ignore Cuba (Vice President Agnew has called U.S. policy one of "benign neglect"). Exiles, once enthusiastic about candidate Nixon, have been openly disappointed about his failure as President to move against Cuba. Not wishing to estrange them still further, Nixon preserved the airlift.

But though Clay made no headway with the Administration, he continued the argument. "No longer can this policy be couched or obscured in 'refugee' terminology," he said. "The real refugees of Cuba left in the early 1960s when they had to flee for sanctuary. They were the ones who opposed Castro politically and who faced oppression and mistreatment at the hands of the Castro regime.... Though the United States does not recognize Castro, our government volunteers to handle his social and economic problems. Our policy to solve these problems is at the expense of and detriment to American citizens...."

Clay's attempt to stop the airlift came to a vote in the House and failed by 45 to 40 (attendance was not at its best that day). He vowed to continue the fight. One of his opponents, Rep. Otto Passman of Louisiana, made his feelings clear with this comment: "There is a lot of jealousy growing up because these Cubans are willing to work and it embarrasses some of those people who would rather live on a handout."

The common complaint about the airlift, as publicized by Clay, was gently and humorously explored in the 1969 movie, *Popi*. In it, a Puerto Rican slum dweller in New York City, working at three jobs, decided that the only way he could give his two sons a better life was to pass them off as Cuban refugees arriving in Miami. Then, the United States would be moved to help.

In any case, the airlift will eventually wind down because Cuba stopped accepting names for the waiting list in May 1966. A State Department official has estimated that the present list will require another four or five years of the airlift.

Also waiting in Cuba is an impatient group of 800 Americans and their families. When arrangements were made in 1965 to take care of Cubans who wished to leave, these Americans were forgotten. Cuba does not permit them to be part of the airlift, and only a few have been allowed to leave on special flights to Mexico. The United States sends some $15,000 a month in interest-free subsistence loans to those still in Cuba who need help.

Meanwhile Miami, already brimming with Cubans, gets a fresh batch every day on the airlift. They arrive to find a page out of their past coming alive again.

Source: Reprinted with permission from the March 8, 1971 issue of *The Nation*. For subscription information, call 1-800-333-8536. Portions of each week's *Nation* magazine can be accessed at http://www.thenation.com.

318. "Confidential Cabinet Meeting Decisions," October 6, 1960

Plans to sterilize Puerto Rican women took shape as early as 1900 as Euro-American nativists grew concerned about the growth of "less desirable" races. Sterilization was a program pushed by powerful financiers and industrialists who were influenced by social Darwinism. They believed that heredity, among other factors, determined intelligence. In the United States, they pushed for antimiscegenation laws and the sterilization of the "feeble minded." American social scientists and politicos were concerned with the growth of the island population, even though it was substantially below that of other Caribbean nations. William Moran, director of the U.S.-Puerto Rican Reconstruction Administration, testified before a 1965 U.S. Senate Population Crisis Hearing that the driving force behind the introduction of massive birth control programs in the colonial government's maternal child health services during the 1930s was unemployment and the Depression. One hundred and sixty private hospitals were open to exclusively or primarily deal with sterilizations. As a consequence, it was reported that by the mid 1960s just over a third of the Puerto Rican women of child bearing age had been sterilized—two-thirds were in their early 20s—most of them were poor. Sterilization programs were condoned by President John F. Kennedy's program for Latin America known as the Alliance for Progress. The following document is puzzling since these programs were well known and occurred since at least the 1930s. October 6, 1960, in a meeting between Puerto Rico's Gov. Luis Muñoz Marín and his cabinet Muñoz Marín was informed that some companies favored by the government would hire women only if they agreed to undergo surgical sterilization. The governor acted surprised and ordered a complete investigation. One does not get a sense of moral outrage. But the document does tie sterilization to economic policies of colonial government.

Prepare statistics on the government revenue collected by taxes with revenue from the decade of 1930–40, and also the savings resulting from when the Republicans lowered the salaries of teachers and other public functionaries.

Compare the 1940 budget made by the PER with the 1941 budget made under the PPD.

Sierra will write an explanation on the diverse methods of collecting statistics about unemployment and how the system used in Puerto Rico differs from that used in the United States.

Sierra will send facts about unemployment among 4th year graduates.

Cancio will report on the laws that cover sterilization.

[Department of] Health will report on what has been the practice and regulation of this issue [sterilization] and the ways to provide information on contraceptives, specifically on who to give it to.

The Department of Justice should prepare legislation prohibiting job discrimination against un-sterilized women.

[Department of] Justice will prepare an amendment to the Law about electoral funds so that rich candidates cannot spend their own funds in excess of $300.

Agriculture will send many facts to refute the allegation that the PPD has abandoned and persecuted agriculture.

Moscoso will send statements of experts to the sugar industry claiming negligence on the part of Puerto Rican sugar producers in not dedicating more funds to investigation efforts.

Following are some of the issues that arose or were mentioned in debate:

1. The argument of the PER that they did not have sufficient funds in their 8 years of governing.

The Governor indicated that the PER has been using this argument as an excuse for what happened during their time in government. The counterarguments are they had more money in special funds than they claim, and furthermore, they didn't collect what they could have from personal income taxes. He asked for statistics on the government revenue collected through said taxes and also about the savings resulting from when they lowered the salaries of teachers and other public functionaries.

As a demonstration of the way in which one could govern favoring economic development and protecting the poor, he mentioned that it would be interesting to compare the revenue made in 1940 by the PER and the 1941 revenue under the PPD.

2. Unemployment

Ferré alleges that there are currently 90,000 unemployed, and the Governor asked about the certainty of that number. Sierra said that allegation was false, and explained the many ways of collection statistics on unemployment and how the system used in Puerto Rico differs from the system used in the United States. The Governor asked him to write an explanation on this topic.

He also asked Sierra for facts about unemployment among 4th year graduates, because he had the impression that these young people had the least opportunities for work, and for that reason, they emigrate.

3. Sterilization

The Governor asked Moscoso about the allegation of Ferré that some of the industries of Cayey refused to employ women that were not sterilized. Moscoso informed him that the Industrial Association has proposed to respond to Ferré in the newspapers.

Independently of what the Industrial Association does, the Governor asked Cancio for a report on sterilization laws, and Salud for a report on the practice and regulation on this issue. Salud should also report on ways to gain information on.

Source: "Cabinet Meeting Decisions" (Puerto Rico). October 6, 1960. Women in World History, http://chnm.gmu.edu/wwh/modules/lesson16/lesson16.php?menu=1&s=12.

319. Excerpt from Harriet B. Presser, "Puerto Rico: The Role of Sterilization in Controlling Fertility," 1969

Sterilization was a controversial policy. Many Puerto Ricans claim it was a form of genocide, particularly when required by employers as a hiring prerequisite. Also claimed is that the overpopulation of the island was a result of the American occupation, and its failure to level the playing field socially, economically, and politically between the Puerto Rican population and the influx of industrialists from the United States. By most accounts, sterilization in Puerto Rico as a method of birth control began in the early 1930s as a result of an incessant campaign trumpeting that the island was overpopulated. In San Juan, several physicians in the hospital encouraged the practice of sterilization among their patients. In the late 1940s, an island-wide study revealed that about 7 percent of the women had been sterilized. Six years later this figure climbed to over 16 percent of the women in Puerto Rico. The following is an excerpt from a 1969 study on sterilization practices in Puerto Rico.

We have estimated that about one third of all Puerto Rican mothers aged 20 to 49 in 1965 were sterilized. This is twice as high as the estimate of its prevalence in the mid-1950s. Sterilized women in the 1965 sample became sterilized early in the reproductive span: the median age at time of sterilization is 26 and, for women in stable first marriages, the median number of years married when sterilized is 6. Over half of the sterilized women had only 2 or 3 births. The widespread prevalence and early timing of sterilization suggested that the impact of sterilization on fertility was substantial.

Source: Studies in Family Planning, Vol. 1, No. 45 (September 1969), p. 8.

320. Excerpts from Jorge Duany, "Caribbean Migration to Puerto Rico: A Comparison of Cubans and Dominicans," 1992

The Cold War dominated U.S. politics (1945–1989) and demands to invoke the 1823 Monroe Doctrine (warning that the Americas were for Americans and that the United States would not tolerate a foreign presence) were common during the 1960s. Americans clamored for intervention in Cuba and other states that were believed to be under the influence of the Soviet Union. After the failed 1961 Bay of Pigs invasion when U.S.-sponsored Cubans invaded Cuba, the Soviet Union placed missiles in Cuba to protect Cuba from further planned attacks by the United States. This encouraged two schools of thought in the United States justifying intervention: the old rationale was that intervention was justified by the Monroe Doctrine—the United States was protecting the Americas from Europe; the other concept was based on self-defense. Aside from Cuba, U.S. strategists were concerned with the Dominican Republic. The assassination of Dominican dictator Rafael Trujillo (1891–1961) in 1961 left the United States without a reliable ally while nationalism among Dominican students was sharply on the rise. Juan Bosch (1909–2001) was a politician, writer, and educator. He was the first democratically elected president after the assassination of Trujillo. However, Bosch was overthrown in 1963 by the military and conservatives who called him a Socialist. Two years later, the constitutionalists in support of Bosch launched a counterrevolution to overthrow the dictatorship. The United States intervened in the civil war and dispatched 42,420 troops to the island in Operation Powerpack (1965), preventing Bosch from taking the office to which he was constitutionally elected. The United States said it thought that Bosch's party was full of Communists, something that was never proven. The United States claimed that Bosch exercised a charismatic influence on young people. U.S. intervention led to the out migration of Dominicans and that impacted Puerto Rico. The following excerpts review the movement of Dominicans to Puerto Rico as a consequence of U.S. intervention.

Large numbers of people have moved from one Caribbean territory to another since the late eighteenth century. During the Haitian Revolution (1791–1803), more than 30,000 Haitian refugees settled in Cuba … the triumph of Fidel Castro's Cuban Revolution in 1959 and the assassination of Rafael Leonidas Trujillo, the dictator of the Dominican Republic, in 1961 [saw another exodus].… These events set into motion a complex series of socioeconomic forces leading to the migration of more than a million Cubans and half a million Dominicans to the United States over the past three decades.... The vast majority of Dominicans moved to Puerto Rico after 1961 and especially after the 1965 civil war in the Dominican Republic. According to the census, 82 percent of all Dominicans residing in Puerto Rico migrated between 1965 and 1980. Thus, the Dominican population of Puerto Rico doubled from 1970 to 1980.... Although relatively few in number, Caribbean immigrants are a highly visible segment of Puerto Rico's population. This visibility results from the extreme concentration of Cubans and Dominicans in the island's major urban centers.

Source: Jorge Duany, "Caribbean Migration to Puerto Rico: A Comparison of Cubans and Dominicans," *International Migration Review*, Vol. 26, No. 1 (Spring 1992), pp. 46, 47, 50, 52.

321. Classified U.S. State Department Documents on the Overthrow of Chilean President Salvador Allende, 1973

When Henry Kissinger (1923–), the U.S. secretary of state from 1973 to 1977, was U.S. National Security Advisor in 1970, he said of the fair election of Chilean President Salvador Allende, "I don't see why we need to stand by and watch a country go Communist due to the irresponsibility of its people." President Richard M. Nixon directed the CIA to prevent Allende's inauguration through a military coup which failed because of Allende's popular support. After the failed coup, Chilean Army Chief of Staff Gen. René Schneider (1913–1970) was assassinated, and many believed that the assassination was directed by Washington, D.C. However, Allende took office as scheduled and immediately initiated reforms, including the nationalization of great estates, which were turned over to peasants and small farmers. A military coup d'état directed by the U.S. Central Intelligence Agency (CIA) took place in 1973, in which Allende was either assassinated or committed suicide while defending his Socialist government. The right-wing military officers then initiated a reign of terror, assassinating cabinet ministers, placing the universities under martial law, and banning opposition parties. The military rounded up thousands of Chileans who were tortured and killed. The names of many of the victims had been provided by the CIA. The overthrow of Allende ushered in a long period of terror. As a result, many Chileans left their country to come to the United States. The following are two declassified documents that prove U.S. complicity in the overthrow of Allende.

NAVY SECTION

UNITED STATES MILITARY GROUP, CHILE
CASTILA 141-V
VALPARISO, CHILE

1 October 1973

SITREP #1 dated 26 February 1973 reported, "Chile is a revolution looking for a place to happen ... elastic of people's patience will snap with a bang!" Prediction became reality on 11 September. On that day of destiny for Chile, the Armed Forces and National Police, acting in close coordination, staged a coup d'etat against

President Allende's Marxist Government. Less than eight hours after the initiation of the coup, Allende was dead and a three-year experiment in Marxist joined him in the grave. There are few mourners for Allende or Marxism visible in Chile today.

DEAD END STREET

The Armed Forces decision to forcefully remove the Allende Government from power was made with extreme reluctance and only after the deepest soul-searching by all concerned. Even to we sideline observers, it was obvious the Chilean Military were extremely reluctant to destroy over 100 years of prideful tradition in support of their country's constitution without exhausting every other avenue of solution. Unfortunately there were no other avenues of solution. Chile was on a dead end street. Their rate of inflation was the worst in the history of the world, terrorists and weapons were being illegally introduced into Chile by the CUBANS for USE AGAINST CHILEANS, food resources were near total exhaustion, a nationwide transportation strike had paralyzed the country, numerous other professions were striking in sympathy with the transportation workers, the Armed Forces had been systematically infiltrated by saboteurs who carried not patriotism for Chile in their hearts, but rather fidelity to world Marxism, Chile's children had not been to school for over two months ... and so goes the incredible litany of tragedy that was Chile under Allende's Marxism. What perhaps history will ask in retrospect, is not "Why the overthrow of the Allende Government by the Armed Forces," but rather "Why the Armed Forces waited so long?"...

CHILEAN PAUL REVERE

My first responsibility was to warn the other U.S. families [Viña] to stay undercover and secondly, if possible, got an advisory type radio message off to the Panama Canal from whence evacuation help for U.S. dependents would come if deemed necessary by the U.S. Ambassador. Moving about the city even in military uniform, driving a diplomatic auto and flashing a Chilean Navy I.D. card wasn't easy. Roadblocks had been established at all key intersections, most were armed by nervous young soldiers/sailors with semi-automatic weapons, round in chamber and weapon OFF safe. They had been briefed to expect a violent combat reaction from Marxists forces and itchy trigger fingers were the rule rather then the exception. In my appointed rounds I used back alleys and side streets where possible—where not, maximum discretion coupled with an extremely friendly "Buenos Dios" in my best Irish brogue, managed to reach all but one American family before Russian Roulette game with roadblocks ran out of luck. Apparently final roadblock didn't "sabe" my Irish-Spanish. However, I clearly understood their pointed signals with Grease Guns, which in any language translated into: "Get going, Gringo." The hour was 0710.

ISSUE IN DOUBT

Chile's coup d'etat was close to perfect. Unfortunately, "close" only counts in horseshoes and hand grenades; consequently there were problems. H-hour was not in cement countrywide for 0600, but as often happens in such people-controlled operations, someone doesn't follow the script. For reasons too labyrinth to explain here, H-hour in Santiago was slipped to 0830.

Original plan called for President Allende to be held incomunicado in his home until the coup was a fait accompli. H-hour delay in Santiago permitted Allende to be alerted at 0730. Allende immediately dashed to the Moneda (palace) under escort of a heavily armed personal security force, Grupo de Amigos Personales [Group of Personal Friends] (GAP). At the Moneda he had access to radio communications facilities which permitted him to personally implore "workers and students, come to the Moneda and defend your Government against the Armed Forces." The hour was 0830.

Allende's hope was to surround the Moneda with thousands of Chilean students and workers on the supposition the Armed Forces would not shoot their way past unarmed citizens. A somewhat similar ploy had worked during the coup d'etat "rehearsal" on 29 June 1973. It didn't work this time. Military had all roads to Santiago blocked. Lid was on TIGHT inside city. Anyone on streets not wearing right color jersey stood an excellent chance of getting shot.

Allende managed to personally broadcast two "MAYDAY" type messages. The first, at 0830, sounded strong and confident as he summoned the workers and students. The second at 0945 sounded morose, almost as if he was preparing the eulogy for his dying government. It was his last broadcast as the Air Force soon located and rocketed his antennae. The hour was 1015.

PATRICK J. RYAN
Lieutenant Colonel, USMC

DEPARTMENT OF STATE

BRIEFING MEMORANDUM
SECRET—NODIS
TO: The Secretary
FROM: ARA—Jack B. Kubisch

Chilean Executions

On October 24 the Junta announced that summary, on-the-spot executions would no longer be carried out and that persons caught in the act of resisting the government would henceforth be held for military courts. Since that date, 17 executions following military trials have been announced. Publicly acknowledged executions, both summary and in compliance with court martial sentences, now total approximately 100, with an additional 40 prisoners shot while "trying to escape." An internal, confidential report prepared for the Junta puts the number of executions for the period September 11–30 at 320. The latter figure is probably a more accurate indication of the extent of this practice.

Our best estimate is that the military and police units in the field are generally complying with the order to desist from summary executions. At least the rather frequent use of random violence that marked the operations of these units in the early post-coup days has clearly abated for the time being. However, there are no indications as yet of a disposition to forego executions after military trial.

The Chilean leaders justify these executions as entirely legal in the application of martial law under what they have declared to be a "state of siege in time of war." Their code of military justice permits death by firing squad for a range of offences, including treason, armed resistance, illegal possession of arms, and auto theft. Sentences handed down by military tribunals during a state of siege are not reviewable by civilian courts.

The purpose of the executions is in part to discourage by example those who seek to organize armed opposition to the Junta. The Chilean military, persuaded to some degree by years of Communist Party propaganda, expected to be confronted by heavy resistance when they overthrew Allende. Fear of civil war was an important factor in their decision to employ a heavy hand from the outset. Also present is a puritanical, crusading spirit—a determination to cleanse and rejuvenate Chile. (A number of those executed seem to have been petty criminals.)

The Junta now has more confidence in the security situation and more awareness of the pressure of international opinion. It may be a hopeful sign that the Junta continues to stall on bringing to trial former cabinet ministers and other prominent Marxists—people the military initially has every intention of standing up before firing squads. How the military leaders proceed in this area from now on will be influenced to some degree by outside opinion, and particularly by ours, but the major consideration will continue to be their assessment of the security situation.

The Junta has announced that state of siege measures will remain in force for at least another eight months, but they have relaxed the curfew somewhat, removed on-the-spot executions, placed some restrictions on searches, and promised that persons charged with civil offenses committed before the coup will be prosecuted under standard civil procedures. Although the traditional parties are well represented on the commission charged with drafting a new constitution, there is growing apprehension among them that the Junta's "anti-political" orientation will close off normal political activity for a long time to come. Again ruling out any timetable for turning Chile back to the civilians, Junta President Pinochet reinforced these fears by placing much of the blame for the country's present state on politicians in general.

Source: Peter Kornbluh, Chile and the United States: Declassified Documents Relating to the Military Coup, National Security Archive Electronic Briefing Book No. 8, September 11, 1973, In National Security Archive, George Washington University, http://www.gwu.edu/~nsarchiv/NSAEBB/index.html.

322. Excerpts from Antonia Pantoja, *Memoir of a Visionary: Antonia Pantoja*, 2002

Due to factors such as the brutal suppression of the Puerto Rican nationalists during the 1930s and 1950s and the growth of the middle-class, the number of Puerto Ricans demanding independence from the United States declined. Many seemed resigned to remaining a colony within the United States. However, encouraged by the anti-colonial rhetoric of the time, many Puerto Rican youth took up the cause of independence and considered nationalists such as Pedro Albizu Campos (1891–1965) and Lolita Lebrón (1920–) role models and martyrs to the cause of freedom. Both had been imprisoned for their political beliefs and actions. Because they did not compromise their ideals, young Puerto Ricans identified more with the nationalists than with Puerto Rico's accommodationist former governor, Luis Muñoz Marín (1898–1980). Within this context, the status of Puerto Rico was debated. Moreover, the 1960s saw a surge in the second-generation Puerto Rican in the United States, and while inspired by Campos, Lebrón, and love for the island, their issues focused on the mainland. The following excerpts are from the memoirs of Antonia Pantoja

(1922–2002). Pantoja was the founder of one of the 1960s premier organizations for the empowerment, education, and leadership development of Puerto Rican youth, ASPIRA, a non-profit agency with offices in six states. The organization took its name from the Spanish word *aspira,* which means *aspire.* Pantoja was a Puerto Rican activist in the 1960s, and she is still remembered today. The following excerpts from her memoirs show the link between the "younger generation" of Puerto Ricans in the 1960s and their beloved island.

Our family was one of the many families that grew up poor in Puerto Rico, surrounded by a society where privilege, abundance, and opportunities existed for others. The families of Barrio Obrero, a workers' community, survived and enjoyed the benefits of a strong internal social structure of belonging and respecting one another. The struggles of living in this community, under these circumstances, affected me in both positive and negative ways. I was born in Puerta de Tierra, a slum of the Old San Juan city. San Juan is a walled city, and the wall had two doors: Puerta del Mar, which still exists, and the door to the land, Puerta de Tierra. These doors in the wall were made for people to escape in case an invader would win a battle and the inhabitants had to escape either by sea or by land. The land door does not exist anymore because the wall was demolished on that side as the city grew. Today, there is only a small piece of the wall where the door used to be. The people left behind as San Juan grew were poor families that rented railroad-type apartments in houses made of wood.

I must have been two or three years old when we left Puerta de Tierra and moved to Barrio Obrero. We were a poor family in a poor neighborhood. In Barrio Obrero, the streets were numbered from 1 to 17. Avenida Borinquen, the main avenue, had a plaza from streets 12 to 15. As you traveled away from Avenida Borinquen toward the water, called El Caño, the land became muddy, and when it rained, the waters flooded over the banks. The people who lived between Avenida Borinquen and Avenida A had sturdy houses. The first four houses were made of cement and the rest were made of wood. Houses below Avenida A did not have inside toilets or showers. They had outhouses. Barrio Obrero was built as a housing project for workers and their families who had lived in overcrowded areas. Other homes were built in the muddy areas by homeless, poorer people who had moved from rural areas.

Families living in Barrio Obrero did not pay rent. They paid taxes at the end of the year. This left us with the basic expenses of food, clothing, transportation, and medical care. In our family, we had a generous contributor to the food supply. We had a prolific breadfruit tree that fed us for years. You could add oil, vinegar, and codfish flakes to the breadfruit when there was money to buy luxuries. This tree was particularly important to us when Grandfather lost his job and after he died.

Barrio Obrero was a good neighborhood to grow up in. We all knew each other. There was a spirit of belonging, and we identified with one another. We knew of other neighborhoods, like Sunoco, but we always felt more united and proud of our own community. For other people, we were just a poor neighborhood, but we knew that we were more. Famous people were our neighbors. The Cortijos, a well-known family of musicians, lived in Barrio Obrero. Our neighbors were carpenters and cement workers who worked in the local factory.

Racial identity was not a major issue among the members of my neighborhood. We were a people of many colors and many shades. Some had straight hair; some had kinky hair, like mine; others had red or blond hair. This mixture was typical of the poor Puerto Rican neighborhoods. Although I would be considered a *grifra* (the name given to a person who has kinky hair, but has features associated with a Caucasian background), my mother was a black person with Negroid features, as were my grandmother and grandfather.

In the new home in Barrio Obrero, we had a place where we could have meetings. On some evenings, many men friends and coworkers of my grandfather would come to the house. They spoke loud, banged on the table, and used vulgar and dirty words and phrases. They were all workers who lived in the neighborhood. I would be put to bed and prohibited from coming to the parlor. However, I would get up and sit by the entrance of the living room to watch and listen. I was not allowed to participate or be seen. These men were angry at the tobacco factory owners. They wanted to get paid more money for their work. They wanted to form what was called a sindicato, a workers' union. My grandmother would bring coffee and large serving dishes full of serenta, slices of potatoes, tomatoes, yautfa, yuca, avocado, rings of white onions, red sweet peppers, and sliced codfish.

I did not realize that my work would be of such future historical importance to my community and to the city. It was only when I became the executive director of ASPIRA that I began to realize that our work would change the lives of many Puerto Rican youths and their families. As I write this book today, I continue to learn about the full impact of the work that we have had.

With the experience that the Forum gained in creating its first institution, the board began an examination of new problems that it could address. At the same time, a new public policy was announced by the federal government to designate funds for assisting the poor in establishing instruments for their own empowerment. Our board felt that we had the experience, knowledge, and philosophical understanding to work on a project that could address the community's poverty. We were an institution that had worked before anyone ever mentioned the War on Poverty. We had worked, placing our time, intelligence, energy, and personal funds together, to develop the organization. We had tested experience. We felt called upon to establish a citywide effort to assist all the existing Puerto Rican organizations in our community to develop the best War on Poverty effort in the city of New York. This commitment led the Forum to embark on its second project, the Puerto Rican Community Development Project in 1964.

ASPIRA, THE MOST IMPORTANT WORK OF MY LIFE

If you asked me, "What was the most important and impacting work that you have ever done?" I would reply, "The founding of ASPIRA." ASPIRA occupies a very special place in my heart. Trying to tell the story will be very difficult. Don Miguel de Unamuno, the Spanish philosopher and novelist, once said that a sheet of paper is dead and incapable of transmitting the emotions one wishes to convey. My words are clumsy in English and may be unable to capture the feelings that I wish to transmit. I will try, however.

The idea for a youth project began out of the early work of PRACA [Puerto Rican Association for Community Affairs] and its youth conferences. The conceptualizing of the idea continued throughout my education as a social worker and during [my] association with Puerto Rican youths while working at the Union Settlement

House. The ideas lived in my mind and on pieces of paper, the full implementation did not come about until Dr. Horne supported the effort through the Commission on Intergroup Relations. This … period actually spans over seven years, ending in 1961. As I reflect on it now, I had begun to consider many theories of group work and development when I was a student at the New York School of Social Work, but I had not begun to think of program ideas. When I graduated from the School of Social Work, I went out of my way to find a job in the Puerto Rican community commonly called "El Barrio" in East Harlem. I could not be employed in a Puerto Rican agency, since they were non existent. I opted for the best substitute in selecting the Settlement House on 104th Street between Third and Second Avenues. I was employed as the director of the adult program. There were only two Puerto Ricans on the staff. Although situated in the heart of El Barrio, the Settlement House did not attract many Puerto Ricans because they did not speak English.

While working at the Settlement, I continued to share an apartment with Helen, but we had moved to a small unit in a renovated apartment building on 97th Street, between Lexington and Third Avenues. While we lived there, I found myself relating more and more to the Puerto Rican community. Helen would accompany me to some of the activities, but most of the time I would attend alone. Our lives began to go in separate directions. After a big disagreement, we separated our lives, and I continued to live in the apartment until I applied to buy a cooperative apartment at La Salle and 125th Street. The meetings of PRACA could now be held comfortably in my new apartment, since it was big and beautiful. My house became the center of activity for the younger professionals in the Puerto Rican community. I began to be considered the center of the group.

The original idea that I presented to Dr. Horne was called "New Leaders in New York." It was to organize youths into clubs that would become the vehicles to encourage them to find their identity, learn leadership skills by working on problems that their communities suffered, complete high school, and enter college to pursue a career that would allow them to give back to their community. The idea had germinated in my mind as a result of various experiences that I had when I arrived in New York. The idea began to haunt my thoughts after having heard discussions from Puerto Rican high school students who attended the youth conferences that PRACA was holding. These conferences were organized and held by the youths themselves, who were the leaders and speakers telling us how powerless and insignificant they were made to feel by their classmates and teachers. The students discussed their fear of speaking in their classes, their shame because of their native language, their fear of the gangs from other ethnic groups, and their fear of the police. I was deeply concerned about what I was hearing.

The implementation of my ideas would not come easily. I had to pursue many different persons and approaches before I could succeed. At the Settlement House and through the activities of PRACA, I had become more deeply committed to a program of action that would change the lives of these young people. As I would walk to my job in El Barrio, I would see a group of Puerto Rican teenagers standing in front of the Settlement, engaging in what seemed to me a strange ritual: taking turns spitting. I would say, "Good afternoon." There would be no answer. One early evening as I prepared to visit the adult club meeting, I noticed a young man leaning against the wall in front of the door to my office. He seemed to be a member of the group that I had seen spitting in front of the building. I said hello and he responded.

I seized the opportunity to ask if he was a member of the youth program on the fourth floor. He replied no, but said that he had come to speak with me if I had the time. When I said that I had the time, he sat down and opened with a barrage of questions, one right after the other.

What was my position in the Settlement House? Since I had an accent, was I a Puerto Rican? Did I go to school in New York?

I answered the questions as he asked them. Then I asked one question, "What is the game that I see you and your friends playing outside? The spitting?"

"It's a contest. Whoever spits the farthest, wins." "Wins what?" I asked.

"Wins nothing."

We continued to talk about the fact that he lived in the Bronx, but came to East Harlem to visit his friends. He worked in a shoe factory downtown. His name was Eddie Gonzalez, and he was seventeen years old. He was one of fourteen children. He had dropped out of school to help support his family. The Gonzalez family was on welfare, but he had to supplement their income, since sixteen members needed his help. Eddie confessed that he was sorry that he had dropped out of school, but he considered it too late to return. I shared my experiences of going to night school and using vocational services to plan to complete college. I encouraged him to consider that he was young enough to return to school to complete his high school education at night and still continue to help his family. He argued that he was too old to return to school. I shared my experiences of attending night school with many adults who were his age or older.

I invited Eddie to join the group called HYAA. Later on, Eddie did complete his education and left his own impact on the city of New York by helping a whole generation of Puerto Ricans to obtain leadership positions in the labor unions. He developed a union leadership institute at Cornell University.

The experience with Eddie propelled me into writing the project for leaders of the new immigrants in the city. My idea was to pick up youth and provide a way for their "hanging out together" (the clubs), following a behavior that was natural to their age group. In the clubs, they would learn about their culture and the country of their parents, and also learn how to survive in the school and the neighborhood. The club would provide opportunities to develop feelings of self-worth and appreciation for their culture as they learned leadership skills to work in their communities. The clubs would substitute for the gangs that were already becoming popular protective groups for Italian, Polish, and black youths.

I worked on my idea of developing youth clubs by researching how the Jewish community had developed its youth programs. I also studied the literature on youth gangs and their origins. This information was becoming available through the city's newly organized agency, the Youth Board, an agency that had been formed to work mission, objectives, and a work plan. Everyone agreed that this new leadership program should not become a service agency; instead, in form and methods, it should be a movement. However, we all were wise enough to understand that it had to render some service if it was to be successful in raising funds.

The very important act of naming the project engaged the group in discussions that clearly indicated a philosophical position and a profound understanding that to work with youth we had to impart values, optimism, and the decision to succeed. We wanted an upbeat name, one word to express belief in one's self. The word *aspira* was finally selected. It was chosen because to aspire is upbeat. We all wished the meaning would be "I will aspire and I will attain." The Spanish command form ASPIRA, of the verb aspirar, was perfect.

We made fast progress in organizing ASPIRA. Dr. Horne's introduction to Mr. Sol Markoff, executive director of the New York Foundation, went a long way toward making our proposal more fundable. Horne introduced me to four other foundations. A couple of board members and I met with representatives of these foundations to present and defend the proposal. We were all novices in such matters, but we were able to obtain interviews with five funding sources: the New York, the Field, the Hofueimer, the Rockefeller Brothers, and the Taconic Foundations. Sol Markoff became our mentor and our facilitator during these interviews. All five foundations approved requests for funding. In fact, after a few months of functioning, we approached the Taconic Foundation. They suggested that I increase the amount requested, and funded us for three consecutive years, pending the positive evaluation of each year's work.

In the autumn of 1961, we received letters from the five foundations accepting our proposals and assigning funds. The Forum board called a meeting to discuss what to do, since we now had funds to start the project, but no one had ever had the experience of administering an institution. At the meeting, they all concluded that I should resign my position with the city of New York to come and direct ASPIRA. I postponed an answer until I had spoken with Dr. Horne. He agreed with the board: I should leave the Commission and become the first executive director of ASPIRA. He acknowledged that it was risky to leave the security of city employment, but he said that I was the only person who could get ASPIRA going. It must be understood that I had never directed an institution, but with the help of all my friends, I took the job. And I learned on the job as problems emerged and needed to be resolved.

The physical work and good social times were accompanied by long and arduous hours of discussion and decisions. We wanted to develop a program that would work with youths in groups because we believed that that way, it would be economically feasible to reach large numbers of young people. I had been a group worker, and I also knew that the adolescents would be most influential on each other. We planned for the groups or clubs to be organized in schools, in churches, on street corners, in billiard parlors, or wherever young people congregated. The youths would be asked to organize their own ASPIRA clubs, and by following a list of eight required steps, they would be accepted into a federation of clubs. Once the groups completed the eighth step, they would be initiated through a ceremony called *areyto*. The idea of the areyto had been borrowed from a ceremony of the native Taínos (the original inhabitants of the island of Puerto Rico who used the ceremony to celebrate their leaders).

From the beginning, ASPIRA adopted three major objectives in working with youth:

1. To organize a youth movement in the Puerto Rican community that would learn leadership skills, problem identification, and problem-solving skills, and to work through the clubs and the club federation in resolving the problems of the Puerto Rican community of New York.
2. To help club members study the history and the culture of Puerto Rico, as well as the history of their parents' immigration to New York, and to use this knowledge to develop a commitment to and positive identification with their community, in order to strengthen their participation in the life of their community.

3. To stay in high school, to graduate, and to identify a field, profession, or area of work in which the youths could earn a livelihood and acquire the skills to work as a leader in the community. The federation bylaws spelled out the number of youths allowed in each club, the naming of the club, the community projects to be selected for the club's work, the selection of career study areas, the assignment of a staff person, and the training and responsibilities of personnel to work with youth.

Our planning went very well. However, immediately upon opening our doors for service, a series of internal problems with the board and members of the community emerged. The members of our board had never served before on the board of directors of an institution. The Puerto Rican community of New York had never had an institution that offered services with a staff and formal offices. So, neither the board nor the community knew how to relate to their new institution.

An example of the kind of problem that I had to resolve with my own board came very early in the life of ASPIRA. At one of the early board meetings, the chairperson requested monies to establish a bar for the meetings. I would not approve the expenditures of grant funds for purchasing rum, beer, gin, ice, cheese, crackers, lemons, or mixers. I added that the idea was a good one, however, and I placed $20 as my donation to support the idea of the bar. I requested that board members do the same. I further requested that a proposition be introduced for a vote that would establish the policy that funds donated to ASPIRA could not be spent on activities or items for the benefit of the board, because it violated our tax-exempt status. A long and heated discussion followed with the board finally approving a policy that established the board's respect for donated funds and our responsibility to use funds only for the objectives of the specific donation. Even though I felt good about the end result of this first struggle, I was upset because it resulted in a tense relationship between the chair of the board and myself.

Problems that we encountered as we began to be known in the community were created by our community's lack of knowledge and experience in relating to an institution and in the feelings of some community members that felt they had a privileged status because they knew members of the board. For example, members of the community who considered themselves "important" would bring or send their children to request scholarships without belonging to or working in the clubs. In other instances, board members would send relatives or friends to obtain jobs for which they had no skills or for jobs that did not exist. The examples were numerous, but they always reflected a desire to obtain special privileges or resources. These problems and complaints were discussed at our board meetings, and were at times used by others to say that ASPIRA was not serving the community. I held firm in refusing to compromise our funding obligations and our mission and philosophy. As ASPIRA became better known, these problems diminished.

The most serious and destructive problems came from other youth and educational agencies and from non-Puerto Ricans. Very serious examples of these were hate letters, tapes, and recordings sent to me personally and to ASPIRA. Threats of violence were received whenever there was a news article announcing our receipt of a grant. I opened a file on these letters, following the advice of the police. Other less violent attacks came from people in the audiences at conferences where I was invited to speak. Members of the audience would angrily ask why we were segregating our youths into separate clubs and why we Puerto Ricans needed help in adjusting to the city when other newcomers had to make it on their own. Other youth-serving agencies attacked the idea of our setting up a separate new agency instead of bringing the funds and our youths into already existing programs. Fortunately, no physical attacks were ever made, only threats. From these experiences, I learned how to handle myself and to deflect the attacks. Sometimes I would respond directly and harshly. Other times, I thought it best to throw the questions back to those who challenged our work.

By far, the most difficult opposition came from the Board of Education, which wrote to ASPIRA saying our counselors would not be allowed to counsel the students because they were not licensed. I wrote back stating that we did not want the licensed counselors of the Board of Education to counsel our children because their advice was destructive to our youths' future. In the end, this was a function of ASPIRA that the board could not control, since our educational planning and counseling was conducted in the clubs at ASPIRA's offices. Later on when we had many clubs, they met at schools, but by then ASPIRA had enough strength to overcome the Board of Education's protests.

One of the really destructive acts of the Board of Education was not to allow the organizing of ASPIRA clubs in schools with high enrollments of Puerto Rican students unless a teacher was present at all times. This was fought vehemently by ASPIRA at the Board of Education level because it involved the attendance of teachers in meetings after school hours, for which they were not compensated. ASPIRA collected information on other student organizations, such as Hillel, NAACP [National Association for the Advancement of Colored People], Catholic and Protestant clubs, and other ethnic youth clubs, such as the Irish, Spanish, and Italian clubs. ASPIRA was able to win recognition for its clubs, but the issue of the presence of a teacher advisor to be present at all meetings remained. The youths were able to convince some teachers to fulfill this requirement.

The club programs grew to be very impressive in membership size, number, and impact. The ASPIRA Club Federation became a very powerful organization with very successful programs. The most notable ones were the summer leadership study trips to Puerto Rico, the annual conference to evaluate and plan the federation program, the Areyto Leadership Initiation Ceremony, the Annual Graduation Dance, and the Annual Colleges and Universities Fair. The important fact about the model of the work in clubs was that it was invented by the youth.

About two weeks after we opened the offices on West 72nd Street in Manhattan, a young woman came in and asked if she could meet with the director. I received her and she proceeded to tell me, "I am a high school student in Brooklyn. I read in the newspaper that ASPIRA is organizing Puerto Rican youths in high schools. I came to inform you that I already have organized my own club in our high school. We met and decided that I should come to find out how you will work with us We are ready."

"We think that in order to make a reality of the idea that Aspirantes have the strength to be a force in the fight for the rights of Puerto Rican students and adults, the clubs should be organized into a federation of clubs called the ASPIRA Club Federation (ACF). On the blackboard, they drew a scheme showing the relationship of each club to the federation and the relationship of the ACF to the ASPIRA board of directors. It was a delight to see the youths already becoming a force for change, seeing themselves as joining the strength of loose clubs to a body that could influence the board of ASPIRA. I presented their scheme to the board of directors, since it included the proposal that the ACF elect three members to the board of directors of ASPIRA! The proposal was accepted, and today in New York and in the ASPIRAs in other states, the ACF elects five members to the board of directors of the agency. The ACF in New York also proposed to the staff of ASPIRA that an association of parents of club members be organized.

The expectation was that the ASPIRA Club Federation could be an instrument of power for the Aspirantes, to be exercised against the power of the overall society when it used its strength to oppress the youth. This principle was tested in a demonstration staged in front of Gov. Nelson Rockefeller's house. The ACF was protesting the City University of New York [CUNY] raising its admission requirements. The governor had approved these "higher" standards. The CUNY tuition-free colleges were the institutions that most of the college-bound Puerto Rican high school graduates attended. Most Aspirantes planning to attend CUNY held jobs after school while in high school in order to contribute to their families' income and in order to buy clothing and books for themselves. The announcement of the higher required grade point so late in the school year gave them no opportunity to raise borderline averages. The ACF and the parents' association mounted a picket of a three-ring line consisting of a man, a woman, and a student, symbolizing a mother, a father, and their child. The picket was led by parents holding a casket they borrowed from one of the Puerto Rican funeral parlors. On the casket, they placed a very large sign that said, "Rockefeller, you killed the future of high school Puerto Rican youth who worked all year to attend CUNY and now cannot make it." The picket line circled the block where Gov. Rockefeller had his New York City home. The press and television covered the orderly picketing, chanting, and marching. The mounted police were there the whole time to keep order. We, the ASPIRA staff, were deployed at key spots across the street from the picketing to prevent provocateurs from causing trouble. A student and a parent were spokespersons to the press and television. Leaflets explaining the situation were distributed. It was a successful demonstration. The governor's office asked ASPIRA, the ACF, and the parents' association to meet and give them a list of the affected students. All students affected entered college the next autumn.

The reader will understand why ASPIRA became the most important work of my life. In terms of numbers, ASPIRA of New York alone, from 1963 to 1999, can easily be shown to have touched the lives of approximately 36,000 young people from Puerto Rican and other Latino groups. This is a conservative estimate, using the number of thirty clubs a year with twenty members each—and we know some years we had many more clubs, and some were larger. But numbers do not tell the complete story. So I must tell you about the principles, the values, the philosophy upon which we, the founders, built the model of service. The most important of these has been the grounding of ASPIRA in the knowledge and value that people are born, grow up, and develop fully and best in a community. We believe that the uprooting of our children from their community has been deadly to their ability to learn and to their sense of worth. The immigrant family did not have the supportive environment of an extended family, neighborhood, and friends. Human beings live in families and in communities because they need these for their survival and development of their full potential. I challenge this society to test these statements and to find out if these are the reasons why our youths have so many problems in the United States.

A second principle upon which ASPIRA was founded is that there is a continuous developmental chain that prompts the emergence and maintains the growth of leadership from one generation to another. In order to provide a community with those leaders, it needs to identify and solve its problems and to guide the group through good and difficult times. That leadership emerges in a continuum through the contact and education of potential leaders from one generation to another. The potential leaders must have the opportunity to challenge and take over the mantle of leadership from older, established leaders.

Potential leaders must engage in the educational process that affords them the opportunity to learn history, new technology, and skills that will help them to identify problems and learn how to solve them. Leaders, new and old, must engage in the development, nurturing, and demonstration of ethical commitment to their communities.

Another important pillar in the founding of ASPIRA was the need to establish an institution that would insure that the youth of our community would be educated to acquire the knowledge and skills available to grow fully to their maximum potential. We also hoped to insure that they could occupy positions at all levels of the institutions of the society and earn a living, but also contribute to the needs of their family, their community, and the total society.

The challenge we imposed on ourselves was to invent a model that would operate on those principles, values, and philosophical commitments. We succeeded in doing so. Today, there are Aspirantes who went through the process and are in leadership and professional positions throughout the city of New York and in many other cities across the country. They work in corporations; in city, state, and federal agencies as top leaders; in universities; in social and educational agencies at top-level positions as scientists, entrepreneurs, and artists. Some have returned to serve as staff or board members of ASPIRA in various states. They make real the commitment that they pledged while they were members of a club. Many of the Aspirantes are engaging in organizing new agencies to deal with community problems. Others have played central roles in organizing ASPIRAs in other states. Today, there are seven ASPIRAs: in Connecticut, New York, Pennsylvania, Illinois, Florida, and Puerto Rico. They are served by a national office in Washington, D.C.

I left ASPIRA of New York in 1966. For several weeks, I drove across the United States to see the rest of the country. The real and most important reason for my trip was to disconnect myself from the organization. I wanted very much for the board to select a new director without any input from me. I had been in the position since 1961, and I felt that it was time to leave. I was the only director that the board and staff had ever known. We had learned together and grown together as a family. I was leaving the agency to take a teaching position at the Columbia School of Social Work, my alma mater. I was leaving the agency in the hands of Yolanda Sánchez, the program director who had been my student, while a new director was being selected. Louis Nuñez was the assistant director of the institution. In these two persons, I believed that there was significant experience and sense of continuity to move forward. I also had decided to leave because my philosophy of leadership has always been that the top person must step down to open up opportunities for new people. In spite of my convictions that I was making the right decision for myself and the agency, I felt sad because I was leaving friends and an organization that had become a big part of my life, and its people had become family to me.

Since leaving ASPIRA, I have been fortunate to have visited all of the affiliates and to attend conferences, participate in the inauguration of new centers, and in graduations at their schools. I am most satisfied and feel a great sense of pride to know that the work that we began in 1961 continues and has made an impact on the lives of thousands of young people.

Whenever I travel to give speeches, receive awards, or attend conferences, I always meet Aspirantes who share their accomplishments with me and thank me for having made the resources of the institution available. I have heard their wonderful stories as I travel from one end of the country to the other. I hear these stories from faculty, elected officials, businessmen, artists, scientists, writers. Without a doubt, I feel enormously proud as I refer to all these people as "the children that I had."

When I hear of the problems of any affiliate, it pains me in a very personal way. Over the years, I have heard negative comments and criticism of ASPIRA. From time to time, I am told that individuals have used an affiliation with ASPIRA to advance their own careers. With regard to those who have claimed a relationship to the founding of the institution, I can only say that many persons supported our efforts, including Puerto Rican teachers, community leaders, and aspiring political figures. I wish to acknowledge the support of the community in our work. For those who have used positions on the board or staff for personal advancement, I have nothing to say.

Criticism is difficult to accept. ASPIRA has been accused of "creaming," by serving students who are already bound for college while not maintaining sufficient activities to reach and motivate the truly needy. I know that, over time, the ASPIRAs may have yielded to the obligations of funding sources and reshaped their original objectives. I have always directly criticized the pattern of fundraising that obligates an institution to one major source of funding or to a governmental funding base that too frequently controls and alters the original mission of an institution. Also, I have always been clear that it is vital to maintain the base of ASPIRA as a Puerto Rican entity, although other populations are served.

Over the years, I have been asked to meet with ASPIRA students.

While I lived in Puerto Rico, they would visit me yearly as part of their annual trips. I have always been asked questions regarding the origins, mission, and objectives of the institution and the relevance of maintaining an institution that is Puerto Rican. I have not always felt that my insistence on maintaining certain founding principles has been well received by new boards, but I have been consistent in my position that ASPIRA is not simply a service entity. It is supposed to be a movement with a national network that acts as an advocate for youths and their community. The ASPIRA bilingual education consent decree, won at court, was one of the major efforts that grew out of this tradition. Many Young Lords Party members and leaders in "the student revolts" developed or reinforced their sense of cultural identity and affiliation as members of ASPIRA clubs. Members of the first graduating clubs of ASPIRA entered college and formed the pivotal base of movements for Puerto Rican Studies programs at universities.

The charge that ASPIRA was founded as a conservative social service entity is simply not true. I challenge any critic to review the original documents to determine the true nature of our intent and our commitment to social change.

Source: Excerpt is reprinted with permission of the publisher of *Memoir of a Visionary: Antonia Pantoja*, by *Antonia Pantoja* (Houston: Arte Público Press—University of Houston © 2002), pp. 24–25, 93–109.

323. Excerpt from Bernard Weinraub, "War Hits Home in Death of Bronx Soldier," 1966

The Puerto Rican Nationalists as well as Puerto Rican youth were critical of the war in Vietnam, seeing the struggle of the Vietnamese people as a struggle for liberation. The Vietnamese had been a colony of France and when the French left, the United States assumed the role of occupier. Many of these nationalists drew parallels between the status of Vietnam and that of Puerto Rico. This discontent with the war was fanned by early casualties and the feeling that Puerto Ricans were dying in disproportionately high numbers. In 1966, the body of Ángel Rafael Luna, a young Puerto Rican soldier, was returned from Vietnam to New York and then to Puerto Rico. He was the first soldier to die from the South Bronx. He was 22 years old. The following excerpt is from an article that memorializes the event and the suffering of the Puerto Ricans, as well as their contributions.

Mrs. Luna began trembling. "Has my boy been killed?" she said.

"Yes," the major replied.

Mr. Luna ran into the apartment and phoned his son-in-law, José Rangel, a postman who lives two blocks away, "Angel esta muerto, Angel esta muerto," he gasped. "Ay, Dios, Ay, Dios."

By the time Mr. Rangel arrived, the major had gone—he apparently spoke no Spanish and the Lunas speak little English. A doctor was called for Mrs. Luna and neighbors began arriving....

Mrs. Luna said she wanted her son buried where he was born, in Barranquitas, P. R. She had saved several hundred dollars for his college education—he had graduated from Theodore Roosevelt High School—but the money will be used, instead, for the plane fare to the funeral....

Source: Bernard Weinraub, "War Hits Home in Death of Bronx Soldier," *New York Times*; December 23, 1966, p. 27.

324. Excerpt from "Badillo Scores Young Lords for Attack on Puerto Rican," 1970

Undoubtedly the most militant group in the Puerto Rican community during the Sixties was the Young Lords. Many members were former gang kids who found a cause. Indeed, in the Puerto Rican communities gang activities declined as youth became political. They had a purpose. They participated with groups such as the Students for a Democratic Society (SDS) (1962–1969), which was a national student organization that personified the New Left. SDS was popular on college campuses where they led opposition to the Vietnam War and called for the democratization of higher education. The Young Lords were also active in other leftist groups. They confronted many groups that attempted to party build and control their own agenda. The New York Young Lords lived and worked in El Barrio in East Harlem. The organization itself began in Chicago and then spread to other cities. Its aim was to unite Spanish-speaking people against oppression. They engaged in activities such as cleaning up the streets. In Harlem in 1970 they led an 11-day occupation of an East Harlem church. They were arrested singing, "Que Bonita

Bandera," a Puerto Rican folk song. Not everyone was enamored with the Lords. In the following excerpt, former Bronx Borough president Herman Badillo (1929–) criticized their tactics.

Former Bronx Borough president Herman Badillo scored members of the Young Lords yesterday for throwing eggs and tomatoes at Puerto Rico's Gov. Luis Ferre in Sunday's Puerto Rican Day parade here.

"We have the right to dissent in this country," Mr. Badillo said, "and I have fought hard all my life to protect that right. But the Young Lords, of all people, should realize that it is possible to sit down and solve problems without violence."

Source: "Badillo Scores Young Lords for Attack on Puerto Rican," *New York Times*, June 9, 1970, p. 83.

325. Excerpt from José Yglesias, "Right On with the Young Lords," 1970

The Young Lords emerged as the leading Puerto Rican youth organization of the late 1960s. Its direct action and defense of the barrio attracted idealistic Puerto Rican youth. The following excerpt describes an uprising against New York officials over the lack of sanitation services in East Harlem.

Suddenly in East Harlem last summer people began throwing garbage and wrecked furniture into the middle of the streets. Traffic was stopped frequently, midtown businessmen avoiding the clog of the East River Drive found themselves inside stifling cars in an area whose residents looked upon their discomfiture with little sympathy.... The Mayor's office got the message and a 24-hour pickup of garbage was begun. For a while, El Barrio, that part of Harlem where the first Puerto Rican migrants settled, was cleaner than anyone remembered. With this "garbage riot," the Young Lords first made their presence felt in New York....

The rush thereafter by young Puerto Ricans to join the Lords ... was so great that the organization had to close its rolls temporarily and take steps ... to prevent police and F.B.I. agents fiom infiltrating.... "We believe armed self-defense and armed struggle are the only ways to liberation.... We want a socialist society."

Source: "Right On with the Young Lords," *New York Times*, June 7, 1970, p. 215.

326. Excerpt from Linda Ocasio, "Portrait of an Organizer: Edgar deJesus," 1996

In the 1960s, the Young Lords was transformed from a street gang into a political organization in Chicago. In prison, José "Cha Cha" Jiménez, one of the seven founders of the Young Lords street gang, met Fred Hampton and other Black Panther Party members. The Black Panthers were organized to promote civil rights and to defend the African American community. They were militant, dressing in uniforms, and like the U.S. military, wore berets which in their instance were black. Jiménez found common ground with the Panthers. Upon his release from prison, Cha Cha transformed the Young Lords into a politically conscious organization committed to the liberation of the Puerto Rican people. They believed in political control of the community and the responsiveness of its institutions to it. Chapters spread to New York and elsewhere. The following is an excerpt of a portrait of Edgar deJesus, a Young Lord organizer.

When Edgar deJesus was growing up in East Harlem in the late 1960s, he was surrounded by the sights and sounds of a generation awakening to its own power. The Young Lords, a group of young Puerto Ricans committed to seizing the day on behalf of a community, commandeered a local church as the site for a children's breakfast program. It was the beginning of a community offensive that demanded respect and better services for the residents of the neighborhood known as El Barrio. "The offensive was happening in front of our faces," deJesus recalls. "It focused everyone on poverty."

Seared into his memory are the discussions that erupted over the dinner table or on the street about the causes of poverty. "It's illogical to have poverty in the richest country in the world," he remembers thinking. "It was the simple concept of why is there a division of rich and poor." DeJesus also recalls his father, a hotel waiter and shop steward, arguing vigorously in defense of the trade union movement as crucial to the economic stability of Latino families like his own.

DeJesus, now 40, is the assistant manager and director of organizing for the NY/NJ Regional Joint Board of the Union of Needle-trades, Industrial and Textile Employees (UNITE). The 350,000-member union was formed in July 1995 by a merger of the International Ladies' Garment Workers' Union (ILGWU) and the Amalgamated Clothing and Textile Workers Union (ACTWU). It is not only in his official UNITE capacity that deJesus is influencing the labor movement; he is also a member of the New York City Hispanic Labor Committee in East Harlem and the AFL-CIO Labor Council on Latin American Advancement.

Through his participation in these advisory bodies, deJesus has helped articulate a northeast Latino perspective on NAFTA and issues of trade that provided an important counterpoint to the pro-NAFTA drumbeat of the Clinton Administration and Latino business leaders. "Eddie managed to build a very solid roundtable of Latino unionism, including Puerto Ricans, Cubans, and Dominicans," says Hector Figueroa, an analyst with Service Employees International Union (SEIU). "He has made unions more sensitive to the needs of Latinos, especially in the Northeast, which tend to be overlooked."

Figueroa also credits deJesus with helping to reconnect the labor and civil rights movement, an alliance that has unravelled in the 33 years since Martin Luther King, Jr., marched on Washington D.C. with black and white union leaders at his side. "Eddie makes a contribution on a national agenda. He moves the labor movement, not just the Latino issues within the labor movement," says Figueroa. DeJesus also has ties with the Puerto Rican movement: he is a board member of the Institute for Puerto Rican Policy and a former vice president of the National Congress of Puerto Rican Rights.

For deJesus, his stint as a teenage Puerto Rican activist lit the fire for a lifelong commitment to social justice. "I wouldn't be here if it weren't for that experience," he says. His experience is significant for the U.S. labor movement, as it seeks to re-energize itself, in part by addressing the issues of minority communities that it had ignored in the past.

By the time Eddie joined with the Young Lords in 1973–1974, the group had splintered and evolved into the Puerto Rican Revolutionary Workers Organization, a Marxist-Leninist group. That group eventually crumbled, fueled by paranoia and mistrust, which deJesus and others now attribute to deliberate government subversion—a fate common to radical left political groups in the 1970s. "From 1975 to 1976 was the most demoralized period in my life," deJesus says. After dropping out of Brooklyn College, he took refuge in family, marrying his high school sweetheart, Yolanda. Together they went to work in a bookbinding factory on 10th Avenue in Manhattan.

In addition to what he observed on the streets of East Harlem, deJesus had another influence shaping his political and organizing principles: his father. "My father was my first teacher of trade unionism," deJesus says. "My father made it clear, that if it weren't for the union, we wouldn't have anything." The evidence was all around him: Puerto Rican families who had a least one parent in a union stayed together and were financially stable, whether they lived in East Harlem, the Bronx, or the Lower East Side.

However, deJesus' first experience with a union was not what he expected at all. At the bookbinding factory he joined with coworkers to decertify a Teamsters local that was not representing the Latino workers. "They were disgruntled with the union and the union reps," he recalls. The experience gave him a chance to put into practice his beliefs about what a union should do for its members. "I was seeing in reality what I had theorized about," he says. Later, he and his wife moved on to a metal factory; she did clerical work for a jewelry workers union and he became a metal spinner.

By 1980, much of the fury that had splintered the Puerto Rican movement began to fade for deJesus, and he started contacting activists that he had lost touch with in Chicago and Canada. He reconnected to the Puerto Rican movement through the National Congress of Puerto Rican Rights, where he established a labor task force. Through the task force, he published for two years a newspaper called *El Obrero Boricua* (The Puerto Rican Worker). "We became the more activist Latino voice of the labor movement," he says. At that time he was also working with the Workers Education Center in Manhattan, which melded radical politics with labor-rights awareness. In 1985, he completed a study of Puerto Rican workers in New York City.

DeJesus began to draw the attention of older Latino labor leaders, including Edward Gonzalez, a onetime organizer for the ILGWU who taught at Cornell University's School of Industrial and Labor Relations. "He looked at my work with the task force and put me into labor law courses at Cornell," deJesus recalls. Gonzalez also did something more. He introduced deJesus to trade union veterans. "They were not radicals, just basic trade unionists who spent all their lives building unions," deJesus recalls. "That was probably the beginning of my left politics merging with my trade unionism in practice." After two years at Cornell, deJesus headed the school's Puerto Rican Latino Studies program for trade unionists.

From there, he worked as an organizer, business agent, and eventually administrator for the Capmakers Union Local 2 of ACTWU. Today he oversees organizing for the New York/New Jersey region of UNITE from his office in Union City, NJ. And the Latino communities he works with are not just Puerto Ricans, Cubans, and Dominicans. In the textile mills of Passaic and Paterson, Colombian and Peruvian workers predominate, and with them comes a more militant legacy of activism, deJesus observes: "They're used to the state negotiating with unions and general strikes. There, negotiations are done region or statewide. Here, it's done factory by factory."

In addition to reaching out to the Latino community in all of its diversity, DeJesus says strengthening the link between labor and the civil rights movement is a continuing effort. Recalling the 1963 March on Washington, he has a tone of wistfulness as he lists some of the unions that linked arms with Rev. King: the UAW, AFSCME, and the Steelworkers. "I'm waiting for that to happen with the Latino labor movement," he says.

Source: Linda Ocasio, "Portrait of an Organizer: Edgar deJesus," NACLA *Report on the Americas*, Volume 30, Number 3 (November/December 1996), p. 27.

327. Young Lords, "Young Lords Party: 13 Point Program and Platform," 1969

The Young Lords, later Young Lords Organization, became the Young Lords Party. It was a Puerto Rican nationalist organization that became increasingly militant and formed a party to carry out the principles of the organization, which was the liberation of all oppressed people, especially the Puerto Rican people, called *Borinquen* in the Taíno language of the first inhabitants of the island. Evolving from a youth gang, it fought urban renewal that was evicting their families. They fought police abuses and led demonstrations for better public services. The following document is the Party's platform, the principles to which it adhered.

THE YOUNG LORDS PARTY IS A REVOLUTIONARY POLITICAL PARTY FIGHTING FOR THE LIBERATION OF ALL OPPRESSED PEOPLE.

1. WE WANT SELF-DETERMINATION FOR PUERTO RICANS, LIBERATION ON THE ISLAND AND INSIDE THE UNITED STATES.

For 500 years, first Spain and then United States have colonized our country. Billions of dollars in profits leave our country for the United States every year. In every way we are slaves of the gringo. We want liberation and the Power in the hands of the People, not Puerto Rican exploiters.

QUE VIVA PUERTO RICO LIBRE.

2. WE WANT SELF-DETERMINATION FOR ALL LATINOS.

Our Latin Brothers and Sisters, inside and outside the United States, are oppressed by amerikkkan [American] business. The Chicano people built the Southwest, and we support their right to control their lives and their land. The people of Santo Domingo continue to fight against gringo domination and its puppet generals. The armed liberation struggles in Latin America are part of the war of Latinos against imperialism.

QUE VIVA LA RAZA!

3. WE WANT LIBERATION OF ALL THIRD WORLD PEOPLE.

Just as Latins first slaved under Spain and the Vanquis, Black people, Indians, and Asians slaved to build the wealth of this country. For 400 years they have fought for freedom and dignity against racist Babylon (decadent empire). Third World people have led the fight for freedom. All the colored and oppressed peoples of the world are one nation under oppression.

NO PUERTO RICAN IS FREE UNTIL ALL PEOPLE ARE FREE!

4. WE ARE REVOLUTIONARY NATIONALISTS AND OPPOSE RACISM.

The Latin, Black, Indian, and Asian people inside the U.S. are colonies fighting for liberation. We knew that Washington, Wall Street, and City Hall will try to make our nationalism into racism; but Puerto Ricans are of all colors and we resist racism. Millions of poor white people are rising up to demand freedom and we support them. These are the ones in the U.S. that are stepped on by the rulers and the government. We each organize our people, but our fights are the same against opposition and we will defeat it together. POWER TO ALL OPPRESSED PEOPLE!

5. WE WANT COMMUNITY CONTROL OF OUR INSTITUTIONS AND LAND.

We want control of our communities by our people and [control of] programs, to guarantee that all institutions serve the needs of our people. People's control of police, health services, churches, schools, housing, transportation, and welfare are needed. We want an end to attacks on our land by urban removal, highway destruction, universities and corporations.

LAND BELONGS TO ALL THE PEOPLE!

6. WE WANT A TRUE EDUCATION OF OUR CREOLE CULTURE AND SPANISH LANGUAGE.

We must learn our history of fighting against cultural, as well as economic genocide by the yanqui [Yankee]. Revolutionary culture, culture of our people, is the only true teaching.

7. WE OPPOSE CAPITALISTS AND ALLIANCES WITH TRAITORS.

Puerto Rican rulers, or puppets of the oppressor do not help our people. They are paid by the system to lead our people down blind alleys, just like the thousands of poverty pimps who keep our communities peaceful for business, or the street workers, who keep gangs divided and blowing each other away. We want a society where the people socialistically control their labor.

VENCEREMOS! [We shall overcome]

8. WE OPPOSE THE AMERIKKKAN [AMERICAN] MILITARY

We demand immediate withdrawal of U.S. military forces and bases from Puerto Rico, Vietnam, and all oppressed communities inside and outside the U.S. No Puerto Rican should serve in the U.S. Army against his Brothers and Sisters, for the only true army of oppressed people is the people's army to fight all rulers.

U.S. OUT OF VIETNAM, FREE PUERTO RICO!

9. WE WANT FREEDOM FOR ALL POLITICAL PRISONERS.

We want all Puerto Ricans freed because they have been tried by the racist courts of the colonizers, and not by their own people and peers. We want all freedom fighters released from jail.

FREE ALL POLITICAL PRISONERS!

10. WE WANT EQUALITY FOR WOMEN, MACHISMO MUST BE REVOLUTIONARY ... NOT OPPRESSIVE.

Under capitalism, our women have been oppressed by both the society and our own men. The doctrine of machismo has been used by our men to take out their frustrations against their wives, sisters, mothers, and children. Our men must support their women in their fight for economic and social equality, and must recognized that our women are equals in every way within the revolutionary ranks.

FORWARD, SISTERS, IN THE STRUGGLE!

11. WE FIGHT ANTI-COMMUNISIM WITH INTERNATIONAL UNITY.

Anyone who resists injustice is called a Communist by "the man" and condemned. Our people are brainwashed by television, radio, newspapers, schools, and books to oppose people in other countries fighting for their freedom. No longer will our people believe attacks and slanders because they have learned who the real enemy is and who their real friends are. We will defend our Brothers and Sisters around the world who fight for justice against the rich rulers of this country.

VIVA CHE!

12. WE BELIEVE ARMED SELF-DEFENSE AND ARMED STRUGGLE ARE THE ONLY MEANS TO LIBERATION.

We are opposed to violence—the violence of hungry children, illiterate adults, diseased old people, and the violence of poverty and profit. We have asked, petitioned, gone to courts, demonstrated peacefully, and voted for politicians full of empty promises. But we still ain't free. The time has come to demand the lives of our people against repression and for revolutionary war against the businessman, politician, and police when a government oppresses our people, we have the right to abolish it and create a new one.

BORICUA IS AWAKE! ALL PIGS BEWARE!

13. WE WANT A SOCIALIST SOCIETY.

We want liberation, clothing, free food, education, health care, transportation, utilities, and employment for all. We want a society where the needs of our people come first, and where we give solidarity and aid to the peoples of the world, not oppression and racism.

HASTA LA VICTORIA SIEMPRE!

Source: The Young Lords Party, 13-Point Program and Platform, Palante, Young Lords, The Original Program and Platform of the Young Lords (October 1969), http://younglords.info/resources/platform_old.html.

328. Excerpts from Young Lords, "The Ideology of the Young Lords Party," 1969

The Young Lords was a Puerto Rican street gang that began in Chicago, then spread to New York and other U.S. cities. The Young Lords evolved into the Young Lords Party, a militant revolutionary organization in the late 1960s and 1970s. Although freedom from oppression was their main focus, the Young Lords also worked locally to create a better environment for people living in the barrios through efforts like a free-breakfast program for school-aged children. The Young Lords helped raise the consciousness of the barrios of New York, Chicago, and elsewhere by promoting a more proactive agenda to bring democracy to the people. Its *grito* or cry was

Power to the People
Panther Power to the Black Panther Party
Young Lord Power to the Young Lords

The following excerpts focus on the ideology of the organization.

INTRODUCTION

This is the beginning of the ideology of the Young Lords Party. What is ideology? It is a system of ideas, of principles, that a person or group uses to explain to them how things operate in the world. Our ideology was developed out of the experiences of almost two years of struggling everyday with our people against their oppression.

The systematic ideas and principles in this pamphlet are guiding us as to the best way to lead the liberation struggle of the Puerto Rican nation. These are not fixed, rigid ideas, but constantly developed as we constantly work to serve and protect the people.

There are certain principles that are fixed and unchangeable to us, through. First, is collective leadership, not individual leadership. One individual can never see the whole of a problem. Only collectives of people, working together, can solve problems correctly. Second, we can understand nothing unless we understand history. One of the problems of the Puerto Rican and amerikkkan [American] revolutionary movements is that they have not done systematic, scientific study of their history and so do not yet understand the countries that they wish to liberate. Third, a revolutionary must be one with the people, serving, protecting, and respecting the people at all times.

"Wherever a Puerto Rican is,
the duty of a Puerto Rican
is to make the revolution."
GLORIA GONZALEZ,
FIELD MARSHAL....

ON HISTORY & DIALECTICS

The Young Lords Party has always believed in the correct studying of our history, the history of the nation. Puerto Ricans are told we have no past, not as good as the oppressor's past. So finding out the truth is a good thing. See, the game that the amerikkkan enemy runs is to tell us that we ain't got no history, no roots, no tradition, no nothing. In this way, we are made to feel as though we have just popped up, and when we move against the enemy, we move blindly. If we had a knowledge of history, we could study the mistakes and successes of those who came before; instead of starting anew, we could begin where the last generation left off.

It is time that all Puerto Ricans get down to studying our history. This serves three purposes:

1. We'll be able to check out what our ancestors did and did not do. Also, we'll get a sense of our people's development. In a national liberation struggle like ours, a movement must be built that comes from the people, from our experiences, sorrows, joys. There is a certain way to organize the Puerto Rican nation, as opposed to say, the Polish nation.
2. Studying history allows us to see the enemy's master plan develop, such as the one being used to control Puerto Ricans.
3. Finding out about our roots gives us a certain pride in the knowledge that we have withstood oppression for so long. We must transmit this righteous pride to all of our people.

Let me run something down on history. In school, or in society in general, we are taught that events in history take place because of a few "great" individuals, like

Napoleon or George Washington (specifically, "great" white males). We are taught that history goes in cycles, that it repeats itself.

This is all jive. In the Young Lords Party, we are training ourselves in thinking scientifically, in looking at things from an orderly point of view to arrive at the right conclusion. All Puerto Ricans concerned with their people must begin to see things in a scientific way.

Scientific? Well, we learned in school that the way a scientist approaches a problem is by way of a thing called the scientific method. The scientist first say[s], "What do I want to get out of this thing after I understand it? Where do I want to go? Now what would be the best way of getting through this problem and to my goal?" And then the scientist lays out each step, one by one, until the goal is reached. This is the way we must lay out the revolution, using our passion, our feelings, to keep us going, step by step, until we are free. This means that we will become something called "dialectical materialists." What does this mean?

First, take the word dialectics. Dialectics is the study of contradictions.

What is a contradiction? We've heard about something being contradictory, right? Like say you're having a discussion with someone, and then they say one thing and you say the opposite. That's a contradiction, and it must be resolved one way or the other. The both of you could have an argument and walk away, or a unity of thing between you will arise. Contradictions are everywhere, even in nature. Say you have a herd of pigs, the last herd left. Then say there are some people who are starving, and they come across the pigs, a decision has to be made. The people or the pigs. That's a contradiction.

A Puerto Rican in, say, high school who hears their history teacher say "history repeats itself," will say, "No good, teacher. History flows, like a river, and the course that river takes depends on how contradictions are resolved. In other words, history is always moving ahead, teacher, going forward, once a contradiction is dealt with (resolved). Sometimes a contradiction is resolved in a way that it only looks as though history repeats itself." That sister or brother would say, "See, let's say you have a nation where most of the people are starving, and a few people in power are eating well. That's a contradiction. It could be resolved either by the people rising against those in power, like in Cuba in 1959, or by those in power taking the country into a war against another country, like the United States in 1941 against Japan (sometimes the rulers of a country go to war so that the people forget their internal problems, like their stomachs)." This Puerto Rican would say, "That's history, that's life: you have contradictions, they get resolved, which changes history's course, and since there are always contradictions, there will always be new changes."

Some contradictions are the ones between machismo and male-female liberation, or between capitalism and socialism.

The second word is materialism. This means that all of these contradiction[s] occur in the real world, the world we can see around us. Many times, for example, the economic facts of life cause other things to happen. Yet, we are taught in school that the United States went into World War I "to make the world safe for Democracy." This is a lie. The U.S.A. went into World War I for the same reason it went into the Mexican-American invasion, Spanish-Amerikkkan [American] invasion, Korean, and Indo-China Wars—economics. Wealth. As an imperialist country, amerikkka [American] resolves the contradiction of constantly needing more wealth to keep its machinery running by going to war to rip off land (Puerto Rico from Spain) and to put people to work at home. (Defense contracts=factories=employment=products= consumers). Scientific analysis show that it is materialism, real things, that exist in the world. Part of dialectics is that everything has its opposite, and the opposite of materialism is metaphysics, idealism. Idealism is ideas that have nothing to do with reality. It's like saying that the reason why flowers grow is because of magic, or why people are here is because man was made from dirt, and woman came from man's rib. The reason why flowers grow or why people are here is because of certain scientific laws of nature. That is real. That is materialism.

With this kind of thinking in mind we can now briefly cover Puerto Rican and Black history. Why? Well, there are contradictions between people and the enemy; these are natural contradictions since it is the enemy that enslaves us. Contradictions with the enemy are antagonistic, non-friendly. These differences are resolved ultimately through war. Then there are contradictions among the people. We have been divided and conquered by the enemy in hundreds of ways—housewives against prostitutes, young against old, men against women, Puerto Ricans against Afro-Americans, unionized workers against non-union workers, workers against drug addicts, families against other families, one ... against another. Theses contradictions should be kept non-antagonistic and settled among ourselves, as friends so we can unite against the enemy.

So, in studying Black and Puerto Rican history, we look at the history of the contradictions between Blacks and Puerto Ricans as differences among brothers and sisters oppressed by the Yankee.

Source: Pamphlet entitled "The Ideology of the Young Lords Party," Palante, Young Lords, The Original Program and Platform of the Young Lords (October 1969), pp. 5, 7–9 http://younglords. info/resources/platform_old.html.

329. Young Lords, "Position on Women's Liberation," May 1971

In the late 1960s, New York City's Young Lords developed a unique brand of radical politics that influenced later generations. They were ahead of their time in advocating a brand of nationalism and gender equality. The Young Lords demanded rights for legal abortion and contraception, but called for an end to sterilization abuse. There was intense debate between male and female Young Lords in the evolution of a feminist ideology. The Young Lords Party (YLP) attempted to integrate feminism into their unique nationalist perspective. The following is its stance on Women's Liberation.

Puerto Rican, Black, Asian, Native American, and other Third World Women (women of color) are becoming more aware of how we have been especially oppressed. Women have historically been at the bottom of the ladder; under capitalism, this has been intensified so that we are oppressed three ways. First, we are oppressed as Puerto Ricans, Blacks, Chicanas, Native Americans, or Asians (Third World People). Second, we are oppressed as women. Third, we are oppressed by our own men who have been brainwashed by this capitalist system into believing a whole set of false, empty standards of what manhood is supposed to be—machismo.

The Third World Woman thus becomes the most oppressed person in the world today.

Wherever there is oppression, a movement develops to end that oppression. Third World Women have been and are still being oppressed, and therefore, there is a movement for their liberation. Third World Women have always struggled in many different ways. This struggle, however, should not be confused with the Women's Liberation Movement. There are many differences—differences in the background of the women involved and differences about how best to end the oppression of women.

In the Young Lords Party we disagree with the analysis made by the right wing. We feel that the greatest conflict in the world today lies between capitalism (and capitalism's invasion of other countries, imperialism) and socialism, and people's drives to bring socialism to their countries, to their lives. We believe that the new society we are talking about will not come about by women separating themselves from men, but through sisters and brothers struggling with one another, working together, to deal with the negative things inside all of us. For sisters, this is feeling that we are supposed to be passive towards brothers, you know, let them run things; with brothers, this is feeling that we are supposed to be superior or better than sisters, you know, acting out those macho roles. The Party knows that Puerto Rican, Black, and other Third World Women make up over half of the Revolutionary Army; in the struggle for the liberation of Puerto Ricans, sisters and brothers must press for the equality of women—the women's struggle is part of the Revolution within the Revolution.

What is a man? What is a woman? Nonconsciously [subconsciously], we believe a man is strong, aggressive, hairy, decisive, hard, cold, firm, and intelligent. Nonconsciously [subconsciously], a women is weak, timid, smooth, soft-spoken, scatterbrained, soft, warm, dumb, and loving. Both of these sets of descriptions are a result of the way we have been trained nonconsciously [subconsciously]. From the time that we are born, we are taught by our parents and by the society to be a "man" or a "woman" and to live up to those false characteristics we are supposed to have. These personality traits are part of the way we are supposed to be.

See, originally in the Party, we didn't understand these concepts. We knew that brothers were messing over sisters and we said machismo and male chauvinism must be eliminated. We did not understand that brothers were acting out the roles that this society had assigned to them. Brothers had trouble understanding why some of the ways they related to sisters was wrong because they had been taught to be this way. We said, "But that's the way a man is supposed to be."

On the other hand, we would criticize our sisters for being passive and allowing men to mess them over. We did not understand that everything in a woman's experience in this society conditions and prepares us to be shy and timid. Everything in a woman's experience conditions us to accept leadership from men and to accept our roles as someone who cooks, sews, and takes care of children.

The right wing in the women's movement says men are evil and can't be changed. Babies are not born oppressors. Therefore, our major enemy is capitalism rather than men.

But there ain't no doubt about it, there are a few rich men who control this planet. They are our enemies. Not because they are men, but because they are capitalists. Some of the rulers are women (and some of them are in the right-wing women's movement). They are also our enemy, not because they are women, but because they are capitalists.

There is a center position in the women's movement. These are liberals, reformers, who merely demand "more rights for women." There is a left-wing, and the best of these women, are revolutionaries who understand who the real enemy is. But both the center and the left wing made no attempt at stopping the right, or exposing them for what they are—pigs, agents and supporters of the enemy. They must do so now.

The progressives must see that most of the right wing in the women's movement are white, and their racism is being reinforced heavily against Third World People, brothers and sisters.

We reject those women's groups that turn their backs on socialism because they say it was created by men, or they reject groups like the YLP [Young Lords Party] who have discipline because, they say, discipline and structure is a man's thing. We support those groups that are anti-capitalist, anti-imperialist, and see the fight for women's liberation as part of the fight for socialism.

All oppressed people together will make the Revolution within the Revolution and end all kind of oppression.

UNIDOS VENCEREMOS!
FORWARD SISTERS IN THE STRUGGLE!
Central Committee
YOUNG LORDS PARTY
Source: Position on Women's Liberation (May 1971), Palante, p. 17. http://younglords.info.

330. Excerpt from Peter Kihss, "'La Guardia School' Taking Hispanic Radical's Name," 1976

Puerto Rican nationalist Pedro Albizu Campos (1891–1965) was not the ordinary radical. He was a devout Catholic who loved his island, his identity, and his flag, which he wanted to fly over a sovereign Puerto Rican nation. For his insurgence he was jailed and spent much of his life in jail during the 1930s and 1950s—some say he was tortured and, like others, poisoned by radiation used in experiments on prisoners. By the 1970s, he was revered and considered a martyr to the cause of Puerto Rican independence. Under Albizu Campos, the Nationalist Party of Puerto Rico became a major force in the fight for independence. But it was also smashed by police infiltration and persecution. Some 10 years after his death, the Puerto Rican community fought to name a New York City elementary school in his memory. It was opposed by those that called him a terrorist, but in the end the community won out. They won the right to name its own heroes. The following excerpt memorializes this event.

The name of Mayor Fiorello H. La Guardia is to be removed from a Harlem public school in favor of the name of Pedro Albizu Campos, the Puerto Rican nationalist leader who turned to violence and terrorism in seeking Puerto Rico's independence....

Mr. Albizu Campos turned "anti-Yanqui" [anti-Yankee] after he encountered discrimination against him as an Army volunteer in World War I. He led the Nationalist Party, whose supporters staged a bloody revolt in 1950, sought to assassinate

President Harry S. Truman at that time, and shot five members of the House of Representatives in Washington in 1954.

Source: *New York Times,* April 19, 1976, p. 59.

331. Excerpt from Nicholas M. Horrock, "F.B.I. Releases Most Files on Its Programs to Disrupt Dissident Groups," 1977

COINTELPRO was a contraction for the names of a series of FBI counterintelligence programs formally employed between 1956–1971. Its purpose was to neutralize political dissidents. It came about in response to the reversal of a law that outlawed the Communist Party in the heat of the Cold War. When Congress reversed the policies developed in large part by the House Committee on Un-American Activities (HUAC) and Sen. Joseph McCarthy (1908–1957), the FBI responded by organizing COINTELPRO, a program designed to "neutralize" those who could no longer be prosecuted but were persons who FBI Director J. Edgar Hoover considered dangerous subversives. A "communist front organization" was defined as anyone Hoover called a Communist or a fellow traveler—a person who may not be a Communist but was sympathetic to its goals. The FBI used these programs to conduct surveillance on individuals and organizations, often disrupting the organizations by infiltrating them. Nationalists were discredited. The following excerpt memorializes the release and declassification of COINTELPRO documents—many are available on the Internet today.

The bureau [FBI] had Cointelpros against Yugoslavian groups, Cuban groups, and the Socialist Workers Party, as well as the Puerto Rican nationalists, left-leaning antiwar radicals, black extremist groups, and white militants. There was no clear formula that caused a particular group to become a target, though only one traditional criminal organization was ever involved.

Source: Nicholas M. Horrock, "F.B.I. Releases Most Files on Its Programs to Disrupt Dissident Groups," *New York Times,* November 22, 1977, p. 26.

332. Excerpt from Felix Cortés, Angel Falcón, and Juan Flores, "The Cultural Expression of Puerto Ricans in New York: A Theoretical Perspective and Critical Review," 1976

Music was and is extremely important to the Caribbean peoples of New York. In the following excerpt, Joe Falcón, a street musician in New York City from the 1950s to 1970s tells about the influence of Puerto Rican Studies on his music that was, as Falcón calls it, "political."

I am Puerto Rican. I came to this country in 1952 with my three brothers and one sister. My father and mother were here already working and saving money to send for us. My father, who is dead now, was a mechanic but had to do work in a plastic factory to earn a living. He earned extra money by fixing cars in his improvised shop right on the street. My mother was a seamstress in the garment district, and when she came home she would prepare dinner and afterwards do part-time work sewing women's hats in a shop that operated out of a small storefront across the street from where we lived.

In 1969, I was very much influenced by the takeover of City College by a Third World student coalition which was demanding Puerto Rican Studies and other relevant programs geared to their needs. Right then and there and with the direct contact of other musicians such as myself, I realized for the first time that I wanted to play a music that related to today's realities, not yesterday's. I was concerned in reaching an audience that related to these experiences. The music that grew out of this experience became hard, violent, and heavy with resistance.

It was rarely performed. It just got stored up—so when it came out, it sounded more like one big mass noise of incoherent sound. It was a dual process—on the one hand it served as a cleansing process and on the other it did away with antiquated patterns and built new ones to take its place. New musical ideas were forged, integrating itself with known popular forms. It renewed the process of music playing and made it vital and important again.

Music to me then is more than just performing. It's studying, organizing around young men and women musicians such as the Lexington Avenue Express Percussion Workshop whose concept is to help develop better learning procedures and healthy attitudes, to learn through the history of music what we, as Third World people, have in common and by nourishing from other musics, we enrich all. That is why the history of this process is the key to knowledge, education, and real proletarian culture.

Joe Falcón, Street Musician
New York City

Source: Felix Cortés, Angel Falcón, and Juan Flores, "The Cultural Expression of Puerto Ricans in New York: A Theoretical Perspective and Critical Review," *Latin American Perspectives*, Vol. 3, No. 3, Puerto Rico: Class Struggle and National Liberation (Summer 1976), p. 117.

333. Excerpt from Wayne King, "4 Nationalists Are Welcomed as Heroes in Puerto Rico," 1979

In 1950, Puerto Rican nationalist Oscar Callazo attempted to assassinate President Harry S. Truman (1884–1972) while the president was staying at Blair House, the vice president's residence in Washington, D.C. He was arrested, convicted, and served 28 years in prison. Meanwhile, on March 1, 1954, four members of the Puerto Rican Nationalist Party led what they considered a revolutionary attack on the U.S. Congress, Lolita Lebrón, age 34; Rafael C. Miranda, age 25; Andres Figueroa Cordero, age 29; and Irving Flores Rodríguez, age 29, opened fire in the House chamber in the hopes of sparking a rebellion for the liberation of Puerto Rico. They succeeded in wounding five representatives, were tried, imprisoned, and served time. In the context of the 1960s civil rights movement and the anti-colonial wars (most of the Third World had been occupied by European nations and these wars were fought to drive the occupation forces out), the struggle for Puerto Rican independence increased in significance. In 1979, President Jimmy Carter pardoned Puerto Rican nationalists, including Lebrón, who was released from prison after serving 25 years and remained unrepentant for her actions. When she returned to San Juan, 5,000 people turned out to greet her. Puerto Rican Gov. Carlos Romero Barceló (1932–) opposed the release of the nationalists because he considered them terrorists and was afraid of popular reaction when they returned to Puerto Rico and a resurgence of nationalism. The following excerpts document their release and provide comments from Lebrón and Callazo.

In an apparent reference to Gov. Carlos Romero Barceló, who opposed the release of the nationalists, she [Lebrón] added: "The puppets of the Americans who tried to force us to humble ourselves as a condition for our release have failed. We did not humble ourselves."

Mr. Collazo called for the unification of all the pro-independence organizations on the island. "This is not the time for personal quarrels but the time to unite to bring about a free Puerto Rico today, not a century from now."

Source: Wayne King, "4 Nationalists Are Welcomed as Heroes in Puerto Rico," *New York Times*, September 13, 1979, p. B23.

334. Excerpt from "Socialism" from "Pastoral Letter of the Nicaraguan Episcopate," November 17, 1979

Liberation Theology, a movement within the Catholic Church to give a political voice to the poor, took place in Latin America from the 1960s through the 1990s. It came about during a time of Church reform and was a reaction to developmentalism, which led to a greater dependence of Latin American countries on U.S. markets. The marketplace, rather than ameliorating the plight of the poor, had worsened it, hastening a decline of small farms. Popular sentiment turned to nationalism that encouraged populist leaders. Progressive priests and ministers encouraged lay participation in the church setting the stage for a movement for basic education and the first base ecclesial communities during the 1960s. The Second Vatican Council was convened by Pope John XXIII in 1962 and brought about sweeping reforms. By the time Pope Paul VI closed the Second Vatican Council in 1965, these changes gave a theoretical justification for activities developed under the auspices of a theology of progress, of authentic secularization, and human advancement. Christian groups were reformed to bring about social and political liberation (freedom). In the definition of liberation theology, religious salvation was not defined by prayer, the next world, or even faith but in the faithful's relationship to the material world. In Central America, orders such as the Jesuits, Maryknolls, and Franciscans actively formed *comunidades de base* (base communities) and organized study groups to raise the consciousness of believers. Jesus Christ was a liberator. According to the Theology of Liberation, the mission of Christianity was to bring justice to the poor and oppressed. Rather than discouraging political activism, it encouraged it. Liberation theology acknowledged that the church had been an ally of the ruling elite. Immediately, the new consciousness was at odds with the rich, who blamed the priests for the discontent and protests which led to the fall of Nicaraguan dictator Anastasio Somoza (1925–1980). The following article includes a pastoral letter from the Nicaraguan bishop that gives the Church's stance on socialism. It takes a sharp turn from previous Church policy.

It [is] expressed, at times even with anguish, the fear that the present Nicaraguan process is headed toward socialism. People have asked us, the bishops, what we think about that. If, as some think, socialism debilitates people by usurping their character of being free protagonists of history, if it aims to submit people blindly to the manipulations and dictates of people who arbitrarily exercise power, such a spurious or false socialism we could not accept. Neither could we accept a socialism which takes from man the right to have a religious motivation to his life or to express publicly those motivations and convictions, whatever be his religious faith.

Equally unacceptable would be to deny to parents the right to educate their children according to their convictions [and] other rights of the human person. If, on the other hand, socialism signifies, as it ought to signify, pre-eminence of the interests of the majority of Nicaraguans and a model of a nationally planned economy that is progressively participatory, then we have nothing to object to. A social plan that guarantees the common destiny of the wealth and resources of the country and permits the satisfaction of the fundamental necessities of everyone and an improvement of the human quality of life seems to us just. Socialism implies a growing diminution of injustices and the traditional inequalities between city and country, between the remuneration for intellectual and manual work; if it signifies participation of the worker in the control of the process, thereby overcoming economic alienation, there is nothing in Christianity which would contradict this process. Rather, Pope John Paul II just recalled to mind in the United Nations the problems caused by the radical separation between work and property.

If socialism supposes power [is] exercised from the perspective of the great majority and increasingly shared by the organized people in a manner which leads toward a true transferal of power to the popular classes. Again one will find in the faith only motivation and support. If socialism produces cultural processes that awaken the dignity of our masses and encourages them to assume responsibilities and to demand their rights, then we are dealing with a humanization which converges with the human dignity that our faith proclaims. With respect to the class struggle, we think that one [of the] things [is] the dynamic fact of the class struggle which ought to produce just transformation of societal structures, and another thing is class hatred which is directed against persons and contradicts radically the Christian obligation to conduct oneself by love.

Our faith assures us that it is a fundamental Christian obligation to master the world, transforming the land and the rest of the resources for production. In order to permit people to live and to make of this Nicaraguan land a land of justice, solidarity, peace, and liberty, in which everyone will acquire a sense of the Christian announcement of the reign of God.

What is more, we have confidence that the revolutionary process will be something original, creative, profoundly national, and in no manner a simple imitation of other processes. With the majority of Nicaraguans, what we aim for is a process that will lead finally toward a fully and authentically non-capitalist Nicaragua, neither dependent nor totalitarian.

Translated by James Russell

Source: Penny Lernoux, "The Church Revolutionary in Latin America," pp. 623–624. Reprinted with permission from the May 24, 1980 issue of *The Nation.* For subscription information, call 1-800-333-8536. Portions of each week's *Nation* magazine can be accessed at http://www.thenation.com.

335. Excerpts from "U.S. Formally Recognizes New Nicaragua Regime," 1979

From the 1930s until the end of 1979, the United States attempted to prop up the government of Nicaraguan dictator Anastasio Somoza (1925–1980).

Somoza was pro-United States and anti-Communist—he also promoted his economic interests and oppressed the poor. When Somoza was about to fall out of power, President Jimmy Carter's Secretary of State, Cyrus Vance (1917–2002), spoke about the dangers of "intervention" in the affairs of a country, intimating that Communists were behind the opposition to Somoza. Vance suggested that the Organization of American States (OAS) not intervene in the process of national reconciliation after the overthrow of Somoza. However, the OAS acted independently and condemned Somoza's "inhuman conduct" that included a 30-year military rule. Clearly, the United States wanted to prevent a takeover by the Sandinistas, as the leftist faction of the guerrillas were called. Somoza claimed that the Sandinistas were getting help from Cuba and Panama, both of whose governments were at odds with U.S. policy in the region. The following excerpts merely documents the fall of Somoza, which began a series of civil wars in the region.

Managua, Nicaragua (UPI)—The new revolutionary government in Nicaragua was formally recognized today by the United States, which said it would consider a request to extradite former dictator Anastasio Somoza....

A member of the five-man ruling Junta, Sergio Ramirez, said the new leaders of Nicaragua want to ask Somoza "many questions" because the former dictator "and his friends" drained the national treasury of funds when they left.

Source: "U.S. Formally Recognizes New Nicaragua Regime," *Los Angeles Times*, July 24, 1979, p. B2.

PART XIX
Chicanos, the 1960s, and Heritage

The decade of the sixties brought dramatic social change for Mexico. It officially had a population of 35 million—17 million lived in rural areas. The decade saw a further decline of ruralism; by the end of the decade the rural population numbered about 20 million and the urban at 30 million. This trend accelerated and in 1980 24 million lived in rural Mexico and 48 million in urban spaces. By the 70s the annual urban growth rate averaged 4.89 percent while the rural rate was 1.51 percent. The impact of the population shift was blurred by Mexico's postwar economic boom that brought temporary prosperity. As Mexico's economy slowed American and Mexican economist blamed Mexicans for having too many babies rather than the commercialization of agriculture and failed policies that expected the marketplace to industrialize the country. The decline of ruralism as Chicano historian Ernesto Galarza (1905–1984) called it had far reaching consequences. Texas bordered the heart of Mexico's population with four Mexican states that bordered it with six million people.

From 1946 to 1964, the United States also experienced an exceptionally high birth rate that has since come to be known as the "Baby Boom Generation"; when 76 million babies were born in the United States during this period. From 1950 and 1960 the Spanish-surnamed population in the Southwest increased by 51 percent. Immigration from Mexico accounted for some of the growth. However, Mexican American fertility ran ahead of its Euro-American counterparts. At this point the African American population of 18.9 million outnumbered the Mexican American population by almost five to one. U.S. Mexicans were bunched geographically in the Southwest and to a lesser extent in the Midwest. Texas and California accounted for housing 82 percent of the U.S. Mexican population. The 1960 U.S. census recorded 3,464,999 Spanish-surnamed persons in the Southwest (a dramatic undercount) who earned a per capita income of $968, compared with $2,047 for white Americans, and $1,044 for nonwhites. They lived in deteriorated and overcrowded houses and unemployment was higher among Chicanos than among whites. The median school grade for Spanish-surnamed persons in the Southwest that were 14 years of age and over was 8.1, versus 12.0 for Euro-Americans and 9.7 for other nonwhites. The median school grade attained by Spanish-surnamed in Texas was 4.8.

Older Mexican American organizations such as the League of United Latin American Citizens and the American G.I. Forum still protected the interests of the Mexican community. Newer more politically focused organizations such as the Mexican American Political Association in California (MAPA), the Viva Kennedy Clubs, and Political Association of Spanish-Speaking Organizations (PASO) in

Texas were more visible. Meanwhile, a younger generation of middle class Mexican Americans were becoming more active in these organizations and others—demanding better education for Mexican American children. Much of this activity and the focus on education were driven by Mexican American women and César Chávez's farm-work movement that was spearheaded by Chicana organizers such as Dolores Huerta.

The decade was dominated by youth and the Black Civil Rights Movement. Educational programs such as the Educational Opportunities Program (EOP) in California and like programs in other regions recruited Mexican American students to the university that gave impetus to the Chicano Youth Movement that lasted from 1968 to 1971. In Texas the youth movement was led by the Mexican American Youth Organization (MAYO). As with most progressives they embraced issues of Black Civil Rights and youth movements while taking up their own identity. By 1969 the word Chicano symbolized the new and more militant approach than that of previous decades. The Mexican American and Chicano movements left a legacy which was carried over into the 1970s. It also created memories such as the School Walkouts (1968) across the country, the Chicano Moratorium of 1970, and La Raza Unida Party victories in Texas.

By 1973, it was clear that the United States had lost the Vietnam War. The administration of Richard Nixon (1913–1994) was on the rocks, and he resigned the following year. The end of the war triggered an economic recession and then came the customary racist nativism that made scapegoats of Mexican immigrants who had historically done the work shunned by Euro-Americans. The 1965 amendments to the Immigration Act were not the cause of this migration but it did allow Asians and white Europeans to immigrate in larger numbers. In the decade of the fifties, 53 percent of immigrants were European, 25 percent Latin American, and 6 percent Asian. Economic factors—not the 1965 Immigration Act—drove Mexican migrations. Before the Act, Mexicans were not on a quota. Indeed, Mexicans were placed on a quota of 20,000 U.S. immigration visas by 1978—which it quickly exhausted.

During the 1970s, binational agreements such as the Border Industrial Program, which created a special trade zone along the border, attracted large numbers of Mexican workers to *maquila* factories in northern Mexico. These factories initiated economic and demographic growth along the border. But these factories were temporary and did little to build an industrial infrastructure in the country. Like the bracero (guest worker) program (1942–1964) it further magnetized the border. This along with the decline of ruralism uprooted millions of Mexicans. The entry of hundreds of thousands of hungry Mexicans into the United States triggered the 1972 California Legislature's Dixon/Arnett Immigration Bill that sought to punish undocumented immigrants by imposing employer sanctions and other punitive measures. That year CASA (Centros de Acción Social Autónomo, or Centers for Autonomous [Independent] Social Actions) led by Bert Corona and Soledad "Chole" Alatorre led a march of 10,000 in protest of Dixon/Arnett that set the template for the modern protection of the foreign-born movement among Chicanos.

The recessions generated so-called taxpayer revolts that helped shift the tax burden to the middle and working classes. In 1978, California's Proposition 13 limited taxation to 1 percent of the full value of the property. Eventually wealthy homeowners and business and commercial property owners purchasing property before that date were paying fewer taxes than the poor. It had a devastating impact on the schools where Latino students were becoming the majority.

The final blow was the Bakke case (1978). It ended the notion that American society should be socially and economically leveled through education. Affirmative action programs initiated by President Lyndon B. Johnson and Richard Nixon were scuttled. The notion that civil rights programs had discriminated against white males and was "reverse racism" was legitimated by the courts. This further limited access to education to Latinos and Blacks. The Mexican American voices that follow are heard within the context of this history, and they represent the struggle of that community to bring about entitlements under the U.S. constitution.

336. Excerpts from José Angel Gutiérrez, "Oral History Interview with Albert Peña, Jr.," July 2, 1996

In 1960 the percentage of the U.S. born population was at an all time high—standing at 85 percent. In 1970, of the 5.3 million Mexican origin people counted by the census 2.3 million were immigrants or first generation. This data suggests that at the start of the sixties the core of the Mexican American population had been around for a considerable length of time and its leadership was more settled than in previous generations. The median age of the Spanish surname population in the Southwest, mostly Mexican in 1960, was 20 years of age versus 30 for the white population that was supposedly a baby boom generation. Mexican American organizations were dominated by the over thirty crowd which sometimes caused generational conflicts during the decade. Albert Peña, Jr. (1917–present) came from this older established group of leaders. He cannot, however, be typed as a member of a particular generation—getting along with both groups. He attended St. Mary's University on San Antonio's west side and graduated from the South Texas School of Law in Houston. The first Mexican-American to be elected to the Bexar County Commission, encompassing San Antonio, Texas. He served there for sixteen years until he was defeated in 1972. Appointed Municipal Court he served as Presiding Judge from 1982. The following is an excerpt from an interview with one of Texas' leading politicos.

My father was from Laredo. He came [when I] ... was five years old ... from Laredo to San Antonio.... My dad went to the fifth grade.... And I was with the first wave at St. Mary's. St. Mary's, under the G. I. Bill of Rights, ... the war was over on the fifteenth, 1945, and I enrolled in that same year at St. Mary's....

The first thing [he was involved in after law school] was the Hondo discrimination case, school segregation case, you know, that was my first case. I was just out of law school in 1951.... I had joined the American G. I. Forum. Dr. Hector Garcia asked me to investigate segregation complaints in Hondo. Up until that time, there was only one, one case, one federal case in, of record. That was the Gus Garcia case and it was written by Gus García and his law partner, I forget who it was. It was before Judge Ben Rice here in San Antonio. And they held that segregation of Mexicanos was unconstitutional, but you could hold them in the first grade until they learned how to speak English. And what happened was that some of these children were being held in the first grade up until, for six years, and so they were, they were segregated. The ideal case was Hondo because there they had two schools. One they called the West Ward School, and if you were Mexicano, you went to the West Ward School up until the seventh grade; the other one was called the Main Plant.

So, I went down there and I was supposed to talk to a fellow by the name of Max Orta. I arrived in Hondo and knocked on the door and it was one of those typical Mexicano where they had ... the window on the front porch and ... they wouldn't let me in. They said, "What do you want?" So I had to talk to them through the door. I told them that I was a lawyer and that I had been asked by the Mexican-American G. I. Forum to investigate school segregation. They said, "You are probably like the rest of them that come down here and investigate and never do anything. You take our money and never investigate us." I said, "first of all, I am not going to charge you anything and if there is segregation, I will follow through with it." So, finally they let me in and they told me what the situation was. Just poured it out to you. And I did check. They did have two schools. So, the first thing I did, I went and talked to the superintendent and I told him this is what I found and I said, this is unconstitutional and he said, "Well, I can't do anything about it. You are going to have to talk to the school board." We didn't have any money, we didn't have no MALDEF or we didn't have any money to go to federal court or probably didn't know how to get into federal court, but anyway, so I asked for a hearing before the school board and they granted me a hearing. And within a couple of weeks, I would have a hearing, so I did. I had a hearing. I took my client, Max Orta and I sat him down. He was the only Mexicano there and they had brought in a law firm, big law firm in from Houston, to represent the school board. They had about four or five lawyers there, and I was there. I made my pitch and I said, "I have only one, I have only one witness." I had already told them what I had found. They had two schools. Clearly unconstitutional. And of course, their excuse was that they were teaching them how to speak English. I said, "the person who made the complaint speaks fluent English, but I have one, only one witness," and they thought I was going to call Max Orta. I called the superintendent. The superintendent came and I said, "You remember when I visited in your office and I gave you the statistics about what was happening in Hondo and you told me that that was true? You had two schools. One for white and one for Mexicans." He said, "yeah, that is correct." "And you told me you couldn't do anything about it?" "That is correct." And I said, "well, that is all. You may sit down. I have one witness." "You don't have anymore witnesses?" The law firms, they wanted to jump on somebody and they didn't have the, they didn't have the, they could have asked for a witness, you know. They could have called my Max Orta. Max Orta was pretty smart. I think he could have held his own, but ... the superintendent was a good enough witness. He proved my case. "That is it. This is my case. I have proven my case," and so they say, "we will let you know and we will let you know what our decision is." So ... we waited for a decision, and finally they said that they believed that what they were doing was constitutional and they cited the Garcia case. They said that these people ... had not learned how to speak English.... They never had any tests whether they could speak English, Spanish, or German, or anything.... I appealed it then to the State Board [of Education]. The State Board sat on it. We couldn't get any decision from them and the people in Hondo are getting, they were getting pissed off at me because I was like the rest of them; I wasn't doing anything. So, I called a meeting of the, a special meeting in Hondo and invited all the Mexicano families and bring all the Mexicano families and we met at the Guadalupe Church and I told them, "... This is my first case and I am not the best lawyer in the country but, we are going to integrate these schools." This was just before the fall semester. "And we are going to go and we are going to enroll our kids in the Main Plant, and we are going to stay there if it takes all day or it takes a week or it takes a month. But we are going to stay there until they enroll our children in the school." And that is what we did.... "And what is your name?" "My name is, my name is Mr. Albert Fuentes and I want to enroll my daughter here in this school." They say, "well, you have to go to the West Ward School." So they would get back in line and that is all there is. We stayed there all day and we were singing. I advised them not to be violent, just sing and have a good time and just stay there, just, and right after, this was in the morning, about eight o'clock and about one o'clock, they got the, they received a telegram from Austin, from the State Board saying, integrate. So, we had won our case and what had happened was that some newspaper picked it up and the State School Board called a hurried meeting and decided that, they were told by their lawyers the best thing to do is integrate, because they are going stay there, because this Albert Peña, he is a radical, and I don't know what else they called me. But he is going to stay there until you integrate them, so that is what they did was that they integrated both schools. They didn't have enough room for them to all go to West Ward so they went to the West Bay. They integrated the West Ward School and both schools were integrated....

[Through the 1950s Peña was active, elected County Commissioner in 1960. He belonged to the liberal faction of the Mexican American community. That year he got involved with the Viva Kennedy Clubs.]

José Angel Gutiérrez: ... where did the idea come to form these Viva Kennedy clubs?

[After] the [1960 Democratic Party] convention, a fellow by the name of, of Carlos McCormick [head of la Alianza Hispano Americana], where he got the McCormick, I don't know, from Phoenix, had just been named the, the, the national chairman of the to-be organized the Viva Kennedy clubs.... It was the Kennedy's idea. But this, Carlos McCormick talked them into it.... So, Carlos McCormick came down to Bexar County and said that he had contacted people throughout South Texas for a chairman of the Viva Kennedy Clubs to be organized. And the majority wanted me to do it.... we organized. We didn't take any money because we decided that we were not going to accept any money from anybody. We were going to do it on our own. We sold one dollar memberships. You wanted to belong to the Viva Kennedy, you gave us a dollar if you had it. It you didn't have a dollar, you became a member anyway. I went and I traveled, I traveled throughout South Texas organizing Viva Kennedy clubs. The only group we didn't organize was El Paso which was too far and they wanted to have their own group there, but we organized every other, every other county in South Texas, including Houston, Austin, and so forth.... he carried Texas by about the, by a small majority, maybe about two thousand, four thousand votes and we received a telegram and I lost it ... congratulating Viva Kennedy. And that had it not been for Viva Kennedy, he would not have carried Texas, and if he had not carried Texas, he would not now be president of the United States. So, we got the recognition we want. We did it. We did it without the state group or money or anything, we did it on our own.... I don't remember exactly, but I know that after, after the Viva Kennedy, ... we decided to continue with PASO, Political Association of Spanish Speaking Organizations in Texas, and as a result of that, we met with people from, well, before that we met with people from MAPA, we met some people from New Mexico, all, four or five states.... we came to a Spanish Speaking Organization, but the idea was to, you know, you had the G. I. Forum, you had all these groups and they were all non-political, so we wanted a group where they could all become part of a political group. They all agreed on that; and MAPA never changed its name and neither did the people in, I don't think anybody changed their name....

[Peña remained a force in Texas and San Antonio politics throughout the 1960s, instrumental in the forming the Southwest Council of La Raza and the Mexican American Legal and Education Foundation.]

Source: Oral History Interview with Albert Peña, Jr., by José Angel Gutiérrez, CMAS 15, Special Collections, University of Texas at Arlington Library, Arlington, Texas.

337. Excerpts from *Time* Magazine, "Revolt of the Mexicans," April 12, 1963

Crystal City, Texas, a small town of 10,000, in the Winter Garden region of Southwest Texas, where the majority was Mexican people. It was chosen by PASO (Political Association of Spanish-Speaking Organizations), a get-out-the-Mexican-vote drive. For it also ran a slate of candidates for the city council. PASO had been born out of the Viva Kennedy Clubs of 1960 that helped elect John F. Kennedy to the U.S. presidency. PASO's slate of candidates for the city council was successful electing Juan Cornejo, a local Teamsters Union business agent, along with four other Mexican Americans. The electoral coup only lasted two years, but it lit a spark for later successes: In 1969 La Raza Unida Party began its takeover of the city. In 1963, it spawned leaders such are José Angel Gutiérrez (1944–) who founded the Mexican American Youth Organization (MAYO) in 1967, and La Raza Unida Party in 1969. When the *Time* article was published, it caused a stir among Mexican Americans nationally. The feeling was that the group had finally made it on the national scene. The sleeping giant had awakened and it was going to become a national power group. For them, *Time* magazine was the big time.

[In] Crystal City stands a statue of Popeye, a symbol of the town's claim that it is "the spinach capital of the world." Otherwise, Crystal City (pop. 10,000) is like a lot of other farm towns in South Texas. Mexican Americans outnumber Anglo Americans four to one, but the Anglos run the place....

The revolt in Crystal City was managed by a three-year-old Texas organization called Viva Kennedy during the presidential campaign, now named PASO (short for Political Association of Spanish-Speaking Organizations). Dedicated to the advancement of Mexican Americans. PASO chose Crystal City as a test site for a get-out-the-Mexican-vote drive.... Says Albert Fuentes, the PASO official who led the campaign: "We have done the impossible. If we can do it in Crystal City, we can do it all over Texas. We can awake the sleeping giant." On Election Day, the Mexicans have learned, all South Texans are equal.

Source: Excerpt from *Time Magazine*, April 12, 1963. http://www.time.com/time/magazine/article/0,9171,828075,00.html.

338. Excerpts from the Voting Rights Act, 1965

Blacks and Mexicans had systematically been disenfranchised by poll taxes in Texas which charged people a fee to vote. Moreover, the state administered literacy tests which purposely excluded Mexicans and African Americans. Further it was impossible to get minorities elected because of gerrymandering that mapped secure white majority districts. Mexican American organizations such as the League of United Latin American Citizens and the American G.I. Forum had sued to no avail. The Black Civil Rights Movement led by Martin Luther King brought new urgency to the issue pressuring Congress to pass the 1965 Voting Rights Act and giving President Lyndon B. Johnson the opportunity to sign it. The poll tax was abolished and the legal mechanism set in place for voting rights.

An Act to enforce the Fifteenth Amendment to the Constitution of the United States, and for other purposes.

Be it enacted by the Senate and House of Representatives of the United States of America in Congress assembled, That this Act shall be known as the "Voting Rights Act of 1965."

...

SEC. 2

No voting qualification or prerequisite to voting, or standard, practice, or procedure shall be imposed or applied by any State or political subdivision to deny or abridge the right of any citizen of the United States to vote on account of race or color.

SEC. 3

(a) Whenever the Attorney General institutes a proceeding under any statute to enforce the guarantees of the Fifteenth Amendment in any State or political subdivision, the court shall authorize the appointment of Federal examiners by the United States Civil Service Commission in accordance with Section 6 to serve for such period of time and for such political subdivisions as the court shall determine is appropriate to enforce the guarantees of the Fifteenth Amendment (1) as part of any interlocutory order if the court determines that the appointment of such examiners is necessary to enforce such guarantees or (2) as part of any final judgment if the court finds that violations of the Fifteenth Amendment justifying equitable relief have occurred in such State or subdivision: Provided, That the court need not authorize the appointment of examiners if any incidents of denial or abridgement of the right to vote on account of race or color (1) have been few in number and have been promptly and effectively corrected by State or local action, (2) the continuing effect of such incidents has been eliminated, and (3) there is no reasonable probability of their recurrence in the future.

(b) If in a proceeding instituted by the Attorney General under any statute to enforce the guarantees of the Fifteenth Amendment in any State or political subdivision the court finds that a test or device has been used for the purpose or with the effect of denying or abridging the right of any citizen of the United States to vote on account of race or color, it shall suspend the use of tests and devices in such State or political subdivisions as the court shall determine is appropriate and for such period as it deems necessary.

(c) If in any proceeding instituted by the Attorney General under any statute to enforce the guarantees of the Fifteenth Amendment in any State or political subdivision the court finds that violations of the Fifteenth Amendment justifying equitable relief have occurred within the territory of such State or political subdivision, the court, in addition to such relief as it may grant, shall retain jurisdiction for such period as it may deem appropriate and during such period no voting qualification or prerequisite to voting, or standard, practice, or procedure with respect to voting different from that in force or effect at the time the proceeding was commenced shall be enforced unless and until the court finds that such qualification, prerequisite, standard, practice, or procedure does not have the purpose and will not have the effect of denying or abridging the right to vote on account of race or color: Provided, That such qualification, prerequisite, standard, practice, or procedure may be enforced if the qualification, prerequisite, standard, practice, or procedure has been submitted by the chief legal officer or other appropriate official of such State or subdivision to the Attorney General and the Attorney General has not interposed an objection within sixty days after such submission, except that neither the court's finding nor the Attorney General's failure to object shall bar a subsequent action to enjoin enforcement of such qualification, prerequisite, standard, practice, or procedure.

SEC. 4

(a) To assure that the right of citizens of the United States to vote is not denied or abridged on account of race or color, no citizen shall be denied the right to vote in any Federal, State, or local election because of his failure to comply with any test or device in any State with respect to which the determinations have been made under Subsection (b) or in any political subdivision with respect to which such determinations have been made as a separate unit, unless the United States District Court for the District of Columbia in an action for a declaratory judgment brought by such State or subdivision against the United States has determined that no such test or device has been used during the five years preceding the filing of the action for the purpose or with the effect of denying or abridging the right to vote on account of race or color: Provided, That no such declaratory judgment shall issue with respect to any plaintiff for a period of five years after the entry of a final judgment of any court of the United States, other than the denial of a declaratory judgment under this section, whether entered prior to or after the enactment of this Act, determining that denials or abridgments of the right to vote on account of race or color through the use of such tests or devices have occurred anywhere in the territory of such plaintiff. An action pursuant to this subsection shall be heard and determined by a court of three judges in accordance with the provisions of Section 2284 of Title 28 of the United States Code and any appeal shall lie to the Supreme Court. The court shall retain jurisdiction of any action pursuant to this subsection for five years after judgment and shall reopen the action upon motion of the Attorney General alleging that a test or device has been used for the purpose or with the effect of denying or abridging the right to vote on account of race or color.

If the Attorney General determines that he has no reason to believe that any such test or device has been used during the five years preceding the filing of the action for the purpose or with the effect of denying or abridging the right to vote on account of race or color, he shall consent to the entry of such judgment.

(b) The provisions of Subsection (a) shall apply in any State or in any political subdivision of a state which (1) the Attorney General determines maintained on

November 1, 1964, any test or device, and with respect to which (2) the Director of the Census determines that less than 50 percentum of the persons of voting age residing therein were registered on November 1, 1964, or that less than 50 percentum of such persons voted in the presidential election of November 1964.

A determination or certification of the Attorney General or of the Director of the Census under this section or under Section 6 or Section 13 shall not be reviewable in any court and shall be effective upon publication in the *Federal Register*.

(c) The phrase "test or device" shall mean any requirement that a person as a prerequisite for voting or registration for voting (1) demonstrate the ability to read, write, understand, or interpret any matter, (2) demonstrate any educational achievement or his knowledge of any particular subject, (3) possess good moral character, or (4) prove his qualifications by the voucher of registered voters or members of any other class.

(d) For purposes of this section no State or political subdivision shall be determined to have engaged in the use of tests or devices for the purpose or with the effect of denying or abridging the right to vote on account of race or color if (1) incidents of such use have been few in number and have been promptly and effectively corrected by State or local action, (2) the continuing effect of such incidents has been eliminated, and (3) there is no reasonable probability of their recurrence in the future.

(e)(1) Congress hereby declares that to secure the rights under the Fourteenth Amendment of persons educated in American-flag schools in which the predominant classroom language was other than English, it is necessary to prohibit the States from conditioning the right to vote of such persons on ability to read, write, understand, or interpret any matter in the English language. (2) No person who demonstrates that he has successfully completed the sixth primary grade in a public school in, or a private school accredited by, any State or territory, the District of Columbia, or the Commonwealth of Puerto Rico in which the predominant classroom language was other than English, shall be denied the right to vote in any Federal, State, or local election because of his inability to read, write, understand, or interpret any matter in the English language, except that, in States in which State law provides that a different level of education is presumptive of literacy, he shall demonstrate that he has successfully completed an equivalent level of education in a public school in, or a private school accredited by, any State or territory, the District of Columbia, or the Commonwealth of Puerto Rico in which the predominant classroom language was other than English.

SEC. 5

Whenever a State or political subdivision with respect to which the prohibitions set forth in Section 4(a) are in effect shall enact or seek to administer any voting qualification or prerequisite to voting, or standard, practice, or procedure with respect to voting different from that in force or effect on November 1, 1964, such State or subdivision may institute an action in the United States District Court for the District of Columbia for a declaratory judgment that such qualification, prerequisite, standard, practice, or procedure does not have the purpose and will not have the effect of denying or abridging the right to vote on account of race or color, and unless and until the court enters such judgment no person shall be denied the right to vote for failure to comply with such qualification, prerequisite, standard, practice, or procedure: Provided, That such qualification, prerequisite, standard, practice, or procedure may be enforced without such proceeding if the qualification, prerequisite, standard, practice, or procedure has been submitted by the chief legal officer or other appropriate official of such State or subdivision to the Attorney General and the Attorney General has not interposed an objection within sixty days after such submission, except that neither the Attorney General's failure to object nor a declaratory judgment entered under this section shall bar a subsequent action to enjoin enforcement of such qualification, prerequisite, standard, practice, or procedure. Any action under this section shall be heard and determined by a court of three judges in accordance with the provisions of Section 2284 of Title 28 of the United States Code and any appeal shall lie to the Supreme Court.

SEC. 6

Whenever (a) a court has authorized the appointment of examiners pursuant to the provisions of Section 3(a), or (b) unless a declaratory judgment has been rendered under Section 4(a), the Attorney General certifies with respect to any political subdivision named in, or included within the scope of, determinations made under Section 4(b) that (1) he has received complaints in writing from twenty or more residents of such political subdivision alleging that they have been denied the right to vote under color of law on account of race or color, and that he believes such complaints to be meritorious, or (2) that, in his judgment (considering, among other factors, whether the ratio of nonwhite persons to white persons registered to vote within such subdivision appears to him to be reasonably attributable to violations of the Fifteenth Amendment or whether substantial evidence exists that bona fide efforts are being made within such subdivision to comply with the Fifteenth Amendment), the appointment of examiners is otherwise necessary to enforce the guarantees of the Fifteenth Amendment, the Civil Service Commission shall appoint as many examiners for such subdivision as it may deem appropriate to prepare and maintain lists of persons eligible to vote in Federal, State, and local elections. Such examiners, hearing officers provided for in Section 9(a), and other persons deemed necessary by the Commission to carry out the provisions and purposes of this Act shall be appointed, compensated, and separated without regard to the provisions of any statute administered by the Civil Service Commission, and service under this Act shall not be considered employment for the purposes of any statute administered by the Civil Service Commission, except the provisions of Section 9 of the Act of August 2, 1939, as amended (5 U.S.C. 118i), prohibiting partisan political activity: Provided, That the Commission is authorized, after consulting the head of the appropriate department or agency, to designate suitable persons in the official service of the United States, with their consent, to serve in these positions. Examiners and hearing officers shall have the power to administer oaths.

SEC. 7

(a) The examiners for each political subdivision shall, at such places as the Civil Service Commission shall by regulation designate, examine applicants concerning their qualifications for voting. An application to an examiner shall be in such form as the Commission may require and shall contain allegations that the applicant is not otherwise registered to vote.

(b) Any person whom the examiner finds, in accordance with instructions received under Section 9(b), to have the qualifications prescribed by State law not inconsistent with the Constitution and laws of the United States shall promptly be placed on a list of eligible voters. A challenge to such listing may be made in accordance with Section 9(a) and shall not be the basis for a prosecution under Section 12 of this Act. The examiner shall certify and transmit such list, and any supplements as appropriate, at least once a month, to the offices of the appropriate election officials, with copies to the Attorney General and the attorney general of the State, and any such lists and supplements thereto transmitted during the month shall be available for public inspection on the last business day of the month and, in any event, not later than the forty-fifth day prior to any election. The appropriate State or local election official shall place such names on the official voting list. Any person whose name appears on the examiner's list shall be entitled and allowed to vote in the election district of his residence unless and until the appropriate election officials shall have been notified that such person has been removed from such list in accordance with Subsection (d): Provided, That no person shall be entitled to vote in any election by virtue of this Act unless his name shall have been certified and transmitted on such a list to the offices of the appropriate election officials at least forty-five days prior to such election.

(c) The examiner shall issue to each person whose name appears on such a list a certificate evidencing his eligibility to vote.

(d) A person whose name appears on such a list shall be removed therefrom by an examiner if (1) such person has been successfully challenged in accordance with the procedure prescribed in Section 9, or (2) he has been determined by an examiner to have lost his eligibility to vote under State law not inconsistent with the Constitution and the laws of the United States.

SEC. 8

Whenever an examiner is serving under this Act in any political subdivision, the Civil Service Commission may assign, at the request of the Attorney General, one or more persons, who may be officers of the United States, (1) to enter and attend at any place for holding an election in such subdivision for the purpose of observing whether persons who are entitled to vote are being permitted to vote, and (2) to enter and attend at any place for tabulating the votes cast at any election held in such subdivision for the purpose of observing whether votes cast by persons entitled to vote are being properly tabulated. Such persons so assigned shall report to an examiner appointed for such political subdivision, to the Attorney General, and if the appointment of examiners has been authorized pursuant to Section 3(a), to the court.

SEC. 9

(a) Any challenge to a listing on an eligibility list prepared by an examiner shall be heard and determined by a hearing officer appointed by and responsible to the Civil Service Commission and under such rules as the Commission shall by regulation prescribe. Such challenge shall be entertained only if filed at such office within the State as the Civil Service Commission shall by regulation designate, and within ten days after the listing of the challenged person is made available for public inspection, and if supported by (1) the affidavits of at least two persons having personal knowledge of the facts constituting grounds for the challenge, and (2) a certification that a copy of the challenge and affidavits have been served by mail or in person upon the person challenged at his place of residence set out in the application. Such challenge shall be determined within fifteen days after it has been filed. A petition for review of the decision of the hearing officer may be filed in the United States court of appeals for the circuit in which the person challenged resides within fifteen days after service of such decision by mail on the person petitioning for review but no decision of a hearing officer shall be reversed unless clearly erroneous. Any person listed shall be entitled and allowed to vote pending final determination by the hearing officer and by the court.

(b) The times, places, procedures, and form for application and listing pursuant to this Act and removals from the eligibility lists shall be prescribed by regulations promulgated by the Civil Service Commission and the Commission shall, after consultation with the Attorney General, instruct examiners concerning applicable State law not inconsistent with the Constitution and laws of the United States with respect to (1) the qualifications required for listing, and (2) loss of eligibility to vote.

(c) Upon the request of the applicant or the challenger or on its own motion the Civil Service Commission shall have the power to require by subpoena the attendance and testimony of witnesses and the production of documentary evidence relating to any matter pending before it under the authority of this section. In case of contumacy or refusal to obey a subpoena, any district court of the United States or the United States court of any territory or possession, or the District Court of the United States for the District of Columbia, within the jurisdiction of which said person guilty of contumacy or refusal to obey is found or resides or is domiciled or transacts business, or has appointed an agent for receipt of service of process, upon application by the Attorney General of the United States shall have jurisdiction to issue to such person an order requiring such person to appear before the Commission or a hearing officer, there to produce pertinent, relevant, and nonprivileged documentary evidence if so ordered, or there to give testimony touching the matter under investigation, and any failure to obey such order of the court may be punished by said court as a contempt thereof.

SEC. 10

(a) The Congress finds that the requirement of the payment of a poll tax as a precondition to voting (i) precludes persons of limited means from voting or imposes unreasonable financial hardship upon such persons as a precondition to their exercise of the franchise, (ii) does not bear a reasonable relationship to any legitimate State interest in the conduct of elections, and (iii) in some areas has the purpose or effect of denying persons the right to vote because of race or color. Upon the basis of these findings, Congress declares that the constitutional right of citizens to vote is denied or abridged in some areas by the requirement of the payment of a poll tax as a precondition to voting.

(b) In the exercise of the powers of Congress under Section 5 of the Fourteenth Amendment and Section 2 of the Fifteenth Amendment, the Attorney General is authorized and directed to institute forthwith in the name of the United States such actions, including actions against States or political subdivisions, for declaratory judgment or injunctive relief against the enforcement of any requirement of the payment of a poll tax as a precondition to voting, or substitute therefor enacted after November 1, 1964, as will be necessary to implement the declaration of Subsection (a) and the purposes of this section.

(c) The district courts of the United States shall have jurisdiction of such actions which shall be heard and determined by a court of three judges in accordance with the provisions of Section 2284 of Title 28 of the United States Code and any appeal shall lie to the Supreme Court. It shall be the duty of the judges designated to hear the case to assign the case for hearing at the earliest practicable date, to participate in the hearing and determination thereof, and to cause the case to be in every way expedited.

(d) During the pendency of such actions, and thereafter if the courts, notwithstanding this action by the Congress, should declare the requirement of the payment of a poll tax to be constitutional, no citizen of the United States who is a resident of a State or political subdivision with respect to which determinations have been made under Subsection 4(b) and a declaratory judgment has not been entered under Subsection 4(a), during the first year he becomes otherwise entitled to vote by reason of registration by State or local officials or listing by an examiner, shall be denied the right to vote for failure to pay a poll tax if he tenders payment of such tax for the current year to an examiner or to the appropriate State or local official at least forty-five days prior to election, whether or not such tender would be timely or adequate under State law. An examiner shall have authority to accept such payment from any person authorized by this Act to make an application for listing, and shall issue a receipt for such payment. The examiner shall transmit promptly any such poll tax payment to the office of the State or local official authorized to receive such payment under State law, together with the name and address of the applicant.

SEC. 11

(a) No person acting under color of law shall fail or refuse to permit any person to vote who is entitled to vote under any provision of this Act or is otherwise qualified to vote, or willfully fail or refuse to tabulate, count, and report such person's vote.

(b) No person, whether acting under color of law or otherwise, shall intimidate, threaten, or coerce, or attempt to intimidate, threaten, or coerce any person for voting or attempting to vote, or intimidate, threaten, or coerce, or attempt to intimidate, threaten, or coerce any person for urging or aiding any person to vote or attempt to vote, or intimidate, threaten, or coerce any person for exercising any powers or duties under Section 3(a), 6, 8, 9, 10, or 12(e).

(c) Whoever knowingly or willfully gives false information as to his name, address, or period of residence in the voting district for the purpose of establishing his eligibility to register or vote, or conspires with another individual for the purpose of encouraging his false registration to vote or illegal voting, or pays or offers to pay or accepts payment either for registration to vote or for voting shall be fined not more than $10,000 or imprisoned not more than five years, or both: Provided, however, That this provision shall be applicable only to general, special, or primary elections held solely or in part for the purpose of selecting or electing any candidate for the office of President, Vice President, presidential elector, Member of the United States Senate, Member of the United States House of Representatives, or Delegates or Commissioners from the territories or possessions, or Resident Commissioner of the Commonwealth of Puerto Rico.

(d) Whoever, in any matter within the jurisdiction of an examiner or hearing officer knowingly and willfully falsifies or conceals a material fact, or makes any false, fictitious, or fraudulent statements or representations, or makes or uses any false writing or document knowing the same to contain any false, fictitious, or fraudulent statement or entry, shall be fined not more than $10,000 or imprisoned not more than five years, or both.

SEC. 12

(a) Whoever shall deprive or attempt to deprive any person of any right secured by Section 2, 3, 4, 5, 7, or 10 or shall violate Section 11(a) or (b), shall be fined not more than $5,000, or imprisoned not more than five years, or both.

(b) Whoever, within a year following an election in a political subdivision in which an examiner has been appointed (1) destroys, defaces, mutilates, or otherwise alters the marking of a paper ballot which has been cast in such election, or (2) alters any official record of voting in such election tabulated from a voting machine or otherwise, shall be fined not more than $5,000, or imprisoned not more than five years, or both.

(c) Whoever conspires to violate the provisions of Subsection (a) or (b) of this section, or interferes with any right secured by Section 2, 3 4, 5, 7, 10, or 11(a) or (b) shall be fined not more than $5,000, or imprisoned not more than five years, or both.

(d) Whenever any person has engaged or there are reasonable grounds to believe that any person is about to engage in any act or practice prohibited by Section 2, 3, 4, 5, 7, 10, 11, or Subsection (b) of this section, the Attorney General may institute for the United States, or in the name of the United States, an action for preventive relief, including an application for a temporary or permanent injunction, restraining order, or other order, and including an order directed to the State and State or local election officials to require them (1) to permit persons listed under this Act to vote and (2) to count such votes.

(e) Whenever in any political subdivision in which there are examiners appointed pursuant to this Act any persons allege to such an examiner within forty-eight hours after the closing of the polls that notwithstanding (1) their listing under this Act or registration by an appropriate election official and (2) their eligibility to vote, they have not been permitted to vote in such election, the examiner shall forthwith notify the Attorney General if such allegations in his opinion appear to be well founded. Upon receipt of such notification, the Attorney General may forthwith file with the district court an application for an order providing for the marking, casting, and counting of the ballots of such persons and requiring the inclusion of their votes in the total vote before the results of such election shall be deemed final and any force or effect given thereto. The district court shall hear and determine such matters immediately after the filing of such application. The remedy provided in this subsection shall not preclude any remedy available under State or Federal law.

(f) The district courts of the United States shall have jurisdiction of proceedings instituted pursuant to this section and shall exercise the same without regard to whether a person asserting rights under the provisions of this Act shall have exhausted any administrative or other remedies that may be provided by law.

SEC. 13

Listing procedures shall be terminated in any political subdivision of any State (a) with respect to examiners appointed pursuant to Clause (b) of Section 6 whenever the Attorney General notifies the Civil Service Commission, or whenever the District Court for the District of Columbia determines in an action for declaratory judgment brought by any political subdivision with respect to which the Director of the Census has determined that more than 50 percentum of the nonwhite persons of voting age residing therein are registered to vote, (1) that all persons listed by an examiner for such subdivision have been placed on the appropriate voting registration roll, and (2) that there is no longer reasonable cause to believe that persons will be deprived of or denied the right to vote on account of race or color in such subdivision, and (b), with respect to examiners appointed pursuant to Section 3(a), upon order of the authorizing court. A political subdivision may petition the Attorney General for the termination of listing procedures under Clause (a) of this section, and may petition the Attorney General to request the Director of the Census to take such survey or census as may be appropriate for the making of the determination provided for in this section. The District Court for the District of Columbia shall have jurisdiction to require such survey or census to be made by the Director of the Census and it shall require him to do so if it deems the Attorney General's refusal to request such survey or census to be arbitrary or unreasonable.

SEC. 14

(a) All cases of criminal contempt arising under the provisions of this Act shall be governed by Section 151 of the Civil Rights Act of 1957 (42 U.S.C.1995).

(b) No court other than the District Court for the District of Columbia or a court of appeals in any proceeding under Section 9 shall have jurisdiction to issue any declaratory judgment pursuant to Section 4 or Section 5 or any restraining order or temporary or permanent injunction against the execution or enforcement of any provision of this Act or any action of any Federal officer or employee pursuant hereto.

(c)(1) The terms "vote" or "voting" shall include all action necessary to make a vote effective in any primary, special, or general election, including, but not limited to, registration, listing pursuant to this Act, or other action required by law prerequisite to voting, casting a ballot, and having such ballot counted properly and included in the appropriate totals of votes cast with respect to candidates for public or party office and propositions for which votes are received in an election. (2) The term "political subdivision" shall mean any county or parish, except that, where registration for voting is not conducted under the supervision of a county or parish, the term shall include any other subdivision of a State which conducts registration for voting. (d) In any action for a declaratory judgment brought pursuant to Section 4 or Section 5 of this Act, subpoenas for witnesses who are required to attend the District Court for the District of Columbia may be served in any judicial district of the United States: Provided, That no writ of subpoena shall issue for witnesses without the District of Columbia at a greater distance than one hundred miles from the place of holding court without the permission of the District Court for the District of Columbia being first had upon proper application and cause shown.

SEC. 15

Section 2004 of the Revised Statutes (42 U.S.C.1971), as amended by Section 131 of the Civil Rights Act of 1957 (71 Stat. 637), and amended by Section 601 of the Civil Rights Act of 1960 (74 Stat. 90), and as further amended by Section 101 of the Civil Rights Act of 1964 (78 Stat. 241), is further amended as follows:

(a) Delete the word "Federal" wherever it appears in Subsections (a) and (c); (b) Repeal Subsection (f) and designate the present Subsections (g) and (h) as (f) and (g), respectively.

SEC. 16

The Attorney General and the Secretary of Defense, jointly, shall make a full and complete study to determine whether, under the laws or practices of any State or States, there are preconditions to voting, which might tend to result in discrimination against citizens serving in the Armed Forces of the United States seeking to vote. Such officials shall, jointly, make a report to the Congress not later than June 30, 1966, containing the results of such study, together with a list of any States in which such preconditions exist, and shall include in such report such recommendations for legislation as they deem advisable to prevent discrimination in voting against citizens serving in the Armed Forces of the United States.

SEC. 17

Nothing in this Act shall be construed to deny, impair, or otherwise adversely affect the right to vote of any person registered to vote under the law of any State or political subdivision.

SEC. 18

There are hereby authorized to be appropriated such sums as are necessary to carry out the provisions of this Act

SEC 19

If any provision of this Act or the application thereof to any person or circumstances is held invalid, the remainder of the Act and the application of the provision to other persons not similarly situated or to other circumstances shall not be affected thereby.

Approved: August 6, 1965

Source: United States Department of Justice, Civil Rights Division, http://www.usdoj.gov/crt/voting/intro/intro_b.htm.

339. Marcos de León, "Statements of Philosophy and Policy as They Pertain to the Acculturation and Education of the Mexican-American," 1964

By the end of the 1950s, there was considerable political activity among those that some have called the Mexican American GI Generation—veterans of World War II and the Korean War. Angry because the Democratic Party had failed to support Mexican Americans for statewide office in 1958, the next year Mexican American Democrats met at Fresno, California and founded the Mexican American Political Association (MAPA). In 1960, when John F. Kennedy ran for president many MAPA chapters were incorporated into the Viva Kennedy Clubs. After the 1960 presidential campaign, there was an effort to form a nationwide Mexican American political group. However, Texans were not able to agree to join MAPA because of the word Mexican, which they believed would offend Euro-American Democrats. They formed the Political Association of Spanish-Speaking Organizations (PASO). However, the biggest issue for Mexican American activists during the 1960s was the failure of the education system, which many believed could be improved through the political process. According to the 1960 Census, the median [grade completed] in the Southwest for Latinos was 7.1 years; for whites 12.1; in California 8.6 and 12.2 respectively; and Texas 4.8 years and 11.5 respectively. Mexican Americans underscored how whites had benefited from post–World War II programs whereas Mexican Americans were falling further behind. Much of the gap was caused by the stubborn and nativist insistence to teach only in English. The League of United Latin American Citizens (LULAC), which had been formed in 1929, proposed a pre-school program that would teach students 400 words in English. These 400 words would help the transition of Spanish-speaking students, giving them a head start. One of the innovators of the time was Los Angeles school teacher Marcos de León who said that the Mexican was the marginal person who had a hamburger in one hand and a taco in the other. The following piece was not published, but de León handed out thousands to educators in the 1960s as he appeared on countless panels. It was one of the few works on the Mexican American child and addressed the differences between assimilation and acculturation.

I. PRINCIPLES

1. The purposes of education in American Democracy, as defined by the Educational Policies Commission specifying the function of the school are to be implemented as basic principles.

II. CONCEPTS

1. To strengthen the underpinnings of these principles and make the acculturative process a smoother and more stable process, the following concepts are offered as imperatives.
    (a) Accept the reality of the Anglo Saxon and Hispanic ethic as they exist in the Western Hemisphere, meeting and throwing circles of influence over one another in the Southwest, creating a permanent and perpetual historical cultural continuum through the movement of peoples.

(b) This cultural buffer area forms the framework for the process of acculturation affecting both groups, from which emanates two subconcepts; the culture within a culture concept and the function of the school having to become twofold, i.e., perpetuating the core of values of the cultures of which the school is a functional part.

(c) Within this framework any "long- or short-term goal" educational program to be effected has to be based on the values, cultural potential, and educational needs of both communities, together with the needs of all individuals, including ages, abilities, interests, cultural differences, and socioeconomic status. This is the motivation, the "glue" that will hold it together.

(d) Embrace a functional theory of culture and its relation to the growth of human personality and how such a person adjusts to a maximum [of] the demands of the two cultures: bilingual in the true sense, and the proud inheritor of both the Anglo Saxon and Hispanic traditions, thus permitting greater social mobility, participation, and acceptance as a useful citizen to his community and the nation. This entails a broader acceptance of the acculturation process as an educational precept.

III. RECOMMENDATIONS

1. The school-community idea be given greater depth in meaning, better purpose in implementation. These two entities have long been geometrical parallel lines: Never meeting to explore and exploit their potential.

(a) The creation of a core of counselors to serve as liaison workers between school and community, establish and supervise programs in which the leadership of both school personnel and community are to be utilized to a maximum. Wherever possible, these counselors should be bilingual, especially, where the demand for Spanish exists as the spoken vernacular.

2. To Strengthen Cultural Awareness and Self-Image:

(a) Spanish should be taught as early as possible on the Elementary level and coordinated with the English Program and made a "must" or a strong elective for non-academic students in the Junior and Senior High Schools;

(b) Units on History, Literature, Art, Music, regional dress, and foods concerning Spain, Mexico, and other Latin American Countries be developed in the present courses in Social Studies, Home Economics, and Art, not only for the purpose expressed above, but also to create a more informed general citizenry.

3. Establish a definite and specific program for compensatory education with the objective of supplementing the normal education effort and preparing the Mexican American child to compete and achieve within the existing education program:

(a) Such programs whether in the Elementary, Junior High, or Senior High School should have continuity as determined by (1) "e" under Concepts; (2) stipulations made by Federal and State Authorities.

(b) These programs can be extensive and costly as the "Higher Horizon Program" in New York City, or smaller target areas can be selected involving the community, curriculum, guidance, counseling, attendance, and tutorial areas as specific projects.

(c) While it is recommendable that such programs be made available for the Elementary, Junior High, and Senior High Schools, it is strongly recommended that a great deal of concentrated effort be placed within pre-school, the Elementary, and Junior High Schools.

4. The total concept of education as to philosophy and program can certainly be extended and implemented in the area of Adult Education.

5. It is strongly recommended that the potential leadership in the various schools as well as the community be utilized to affect any program within the District.

   (a) In-service training for teachers and community leaders is recommended, preferably in small groups with the technique of the workshop at its best.

   (b) Utilize panels, speakers, and seminars for this purpose, correlating any effort with compiled materials in a kit containing historical, sociological, and sta-tistical materials, and recommendations as to philosophy and programs.

6. Develop continuing flexible programs of testing, guidance, and counseling which will permit the discovery as early as possible of the potential and creativeness of each child, the identification and development of the academically able student, the so-called "slow gifted" and the culturally different child, motivating him to-ward definite educational goals, thus preventing him from becoming misplaced within the school as to ability and interest and thus becoming a drop-out.

7. Expanding and modernizing the vocational program of the comprehensive high school so as to give adequate adaptability to a technological[ly] changing community.

8. In reference to community relations and communications it is urged that bulle-tins be developed which are more meaningful to the general public and more interesting in format especially when they are intended to be sent home, and that Spanish be used in the appropriate areas.

9. Recruit, hire, and place bilingual teachers, counselors, and administrators *who have understanding of the Mexican American child and his community*.

10. Consultants should be utilized to the fullest extent to (1) aid school personnel set-up projects; (2) act as consultant for such, for teachers' in-service training, and in-service training for community leaders.

Source: Unpublished manuscript, 1964.

340. Excerpts from National Education Association, *Invisible Minority*: *Report of the NEA-Tucson Survey on the Teaching of Spanish to the Spanish Speaking*, 1966

In the 1960s, Mexican Americans continued to live mostly in the five southwest states, with pockets or enclaves in the Midwest and Northwest. By the mid-1960s, it was obvious that Mexican children were not receiving educations equal to those of their Anglo peers. In 1966, the National Education Associa-tion (NEA) released an important document entitled, *Invisible Minority*: *Report of the NEA-Tucson Survey on the Teaching of Spanish to the Spanish Speak-ing*, that investigated teaching in the five Southwest states. It discussed the problems of the Mexican American, and identified some of the more promising programs. The report advocated the teaching of identity and pride of heritage as a way to motivate students. The significance of the report is that it set the stage for bilingual education programs, validating what Mexican American educators had been claiming for years—that teaching Spanish-speaking chil-dren only in English would never work.

While a majority of the Spanish-speaking people in the Southwest were born in this country and are citizens of the United States, they tend to be regarded both by themselves and others as Mexicans. The term Mexican American would be more nearly accurate. More important than technicalities, however, is how they feel ... how they regard themselves.

Me. To begin with, I am a Mexican. That sentence has a scent of bitterness as it is written. I feel that if it weren't for my nationality I would accomplish more. My being a Mexican has brought about my lack of initiative. No matter what I attempt to do, my dark skin always makes me feel that I will fail.

Another thing that "gripes" me is that I am such a coward. I absolutely will not fight for something even if I know I'm right. I do not have the vocabulary that it would take to express myself strongly enough.

Many people, including most of my teachers, have tried to tell me I'm a leader. Well, I know better! Just because I may get better grades than most of my fellow Mexicans doesn't mean a thing. I could no more get an original idea in my head than be President of the United States. I don't know how to think for myself.

I want to go to college, sure, but what do I want to be? Even worse, where do I want to go? These questions are only a few that trouble me. I'd like to prove to my parents that I can do something. Just because I don't have the gumption to go out and get a job doesn't mean that I can't become something they'll be proud of. But if I find that I can't bring myself to go to college, I'll get married and they'll still get rid of me.

After reading this, you'll probably be surprised. This is the way I feel about myself, and nobody can change me. Believe me, many have tried and failed. If God wants me to reach all my goals, I will. No parents, teachers, or priest will change the course that my life is to follow. Don't try.

This was a paper turned in by a 13-year old girl for an English assignment in the eighth grade of a school in one of the Southwestern states. The assignment was to write about "Me." The melancholy tone of the essay would suggest that the youngster was a "loner"—obscure, unattractive, not very popular. But no. She was attractive, articulate, an honor student, member of the band, outstanding in girls' athletics, popular among her fellow students, admired by her teachers. "She never *seemed* to be a child with a problem," remarked one of the teachers, in some puzzlement, after reading "Me."

The problem can be stated plainly and simply: The young girl who wrote that essay was Mexican American. If she, with all her advantages, felt that her lot inevitably would be failure, how must thousands of other Mexican American children—many of them less endowed physically and intellectually—view their own prospects?

357 YEARS OF HISTORY

To understand the problem fully, we must understand how it came about. The first white people to migrate into what is now the American Southwest were Spanish-speaking. They came by way of Mexico during the period of Spain's colonial expansion and settled portions of the Southwest even before the founding of the Plymouth Colony. Plymouth was established in 1620, but the first Spaniards settled at Santa Fe, New Mexico, a full 11 years before that—in 1609. By 1680, there were some 2,500 Spanish-speaking settlers in what we now call New Mexico. By 1790, there were an estimated 23,000 Spanish-speaking people in the five Southwestern states covered by this study area. Indeed, the white population of the Southwest—what there was of it—was practically all Spanish. New Mexico had the largest concentration.

But soon after the 13 colonies gained their independence from England, the migration of English-speaking Americans into the Southwest began. Mexico, its own independence newly won from Spain, encouraged such migration. This vast Southwestern area, stretching from the western border of Louisiana to the Pacific, belonged to Mexico. She was anxious to see it settled and developed, and few Mexican colonists were moving there. So the government of Mexico granted large blocks of land to contractors who would bring in colonists. The response was large and prompt. By 1835, there were 25,000 to 35,000 American farmers, planters, and traders in Texas, and more were on the way.

WHAT IS BEING DONE: SOME SPECIFICS

Encouraging and exciting programs directed specifically to a more appropriate educational accommodation of children in bi-cultural communities have been developed in some places. The following reports are illustrative of the wide variety of innovative practice the NEA-Tucson Survey Committee observed in the schools selected for visitation.

Laredo, Texas

Laredo is a Texas border community of some 65,000 population, located on the Rio Grande, just opposite its Mexican counterpart, Nuevo Laredo. Its economic sustenance derives in good part from the pursuits of agriculture and a busy Air Force base.

Two school districts serve the metropolitan area of Laredo. The larger of the two in population is the Laredo Independent School District, serving the city of Laredo proper. Far larger in area is the United Consolidated Independent School District. It is larger, in fact, than Rhode Island, taking in no less than 2440 square miles and entirely surrounding the Laredo Independent School District on three sides, with the Rio Grande constituting the fourth side. Located within the far-flung boundaries of the United Consolidated Independent School District are the suburban homes of some of Laredo's Air Force families and ranches and farms where many Mexican American families live.

The district operates three elementary schools and a unique high school, much of which has been built underground. This school was built underground to provide fallout protection in case of a nuclear attack on Laredo Air Force Base, to shut out the disrupting screams of jet planes, and for economy's sake. An underground school uses less land, is more economical to air condition, requires no shades or blinds or window cleaning and offers no tempting midnight target for vandals with air rifles.

The educational program of United Consolidated Independent School District has one strong common denominator: bilingualism. Students, Anglo American as well as Mexican American, are encouraged to become truly bilingual—speaking, reading, and writing fluently in both English and Spanish. English instruction and Spanish instruction go side by side.

One Year at a Time

Federal funds had not yet become available for the Laredo "biliteracy" program (as they were subsequently to become available under the Elementary-Secondary Education Act of 1965). The United Consolidated Independent School District had to finance the program itself. And so it started the first year with only the first grade. The next year it expanded to the second grade. It was bilingualism not merely for the Mexican American child but for both Mexican American and Anglo American—for all children.

Eventually bilingualism will extend through all the grades, including high school. Yet even now the high school reflects the beneficial effects of the bilingual-bicultural revolution taking place. Picturesquely displayed at the high school's main entrance, on equal terms, are the proud symbols of the two neighbor nations—the American eagle and the Mexican eagle. They are vividly colored, stylized cutouts made by students and suspended from wire supports. Student artwork is displayed all through the school, and there is stress throughout on the worthiness of each of the two cultures. An unmistakable *esprit de corps* prevails among the students. They walk proudly. They dress neatly—all of them.

Bilingualism: A Valid Objective

The Laredo program and other similar programs that we observed in our Survey—plus our own experiences and independent studies—have persuaded us beyond any doubt of the validity of bilingualism. Unhappily, a large majority of Southwestern school districts have no bilingual programs. In a few instances, such programs exist but they are conducted inadequately. Most school districts have yet to discover that bilingualism can be a tool. It can be a tool—indeed the most important tool—with which to educate and motivate the Mexican American child. It can be the means by which he achieves an affirmative self-concept—by which he comes to know who and what he is, takes pride in his heritage and culture, and develops a sense of his own worth. It can be an invaluable asset to him as an adult, economically, intellectually, and socially. One of the proofs of the validity of this approach, it seems to us, is the fact that children born and receiving their early schooling in Mexico or some other Spanish-speaking country generally do better in our schools than Mexican Americans born here.

RECOMMENDATIONS FOR DESIRABLE PROGRAMS

This, then, might be the time to make some recommendations that the NEA-Tucson Survey Committee believes to be basic in the education of native speakers of Spanish:

1. Instruction in pre-school and throughout the early grades should be in both Spanish and English.
2. English should be taught as a second language.
3. Contemporaneously there should be emphasis on the reading, writing, and speaking of good Spanish, since Mexican American children are so often illiterate in it.
4. A well-articulated program of instruction in the mother tongue should be continued from pre-school through the high school years.
5. All possible measures should be taken to help Mexican American children gain a pride in their ancestral culture and language.
6. Schools should recruit Spanish-speaking teachers and teachers' aides. Beyond that, a special effort should be made to encourage promising young Mexican Americans in high school and college to consider education as a career.

7. Schools, colleges, and universities should conduct research in bilingual education, train or retrain bilingual teachers, create appropriate materials and, in general, establish a strong tradition of bilingual education.

Source: The Invisible Minority. Report of the NEA-Tucson Survey on the Teaching of Spanish to the Spanish Speaking; Department of Rural Education, National Education Association, 1201 Sixteenth Street, N.W., Washington, D.C., 20036, 1966.

341. Ernesto Galarza, "La Mula No Nacio Arisca," 1966

Every ethnic or racial group in the United States takes pride in the pioneers who made it in the United States despite overwhelming odds. Ernesto Galarza (1905–1984) was such a pioneer. He received a doctorate from Columbia University. Galarza quit a well-paying job the Pan American Union—a group that had organized to promote unity, peace, and economic trade among American nations—to organize farmworkers in the Southwest in the late 1940s. Galarza soon found that this was impossible because of the collusion of the federal officials, local authorities, and large growers. He wrote a series of books exposing their abuse of the use of *braceros* to break strikes. His career included a crusade for bilingual programs and other policy considerations. He gave the following speech before the Center for the Study of Democratic Institutions in Santa Barbara, California—an institute formed by Robert Maynard Hutchinson to bring about democratic reforms. The title in English is "The mule was not born stubborn ... it was made this way." The theme was that Mexicans and blacks were not sullen or resentful because they were born that way but because society made them that way.

When I am asked to take part in conferences or meetings in which the topic is the Mexican American in California, I ask myself: "Why the Mexican Americans?"

It may be that our liberal conscience demands that we talk publicly about this sick spot in our society. Nevertheless, we should not think that the presumed Mexican American problem can be reduced, by public discussion, to the dimensions of one state, abstracting it from those of the nation and of the world. Nor should we think that it can be understood by using an intellectual tool that is comfortable and disarming but untenable: the concept of the subculture.

My working definition of culture runs like this: A culture is characterized by: a) the uses it makes of its material environment; b) the accepted or tolerated relations between the individuals that compose it; c) the symbols, conventional signs, and utilities of everyday behavior; and d) the values by which the society measures its moral performance.

By this rule-of-thumb I see only one culture in the United States: it is the culture of the American people—all of them.

Thus, I do not think we can legitimately presume that there is a subculture of Mexican Americans which explains their depressed conditions of life, or that there is a subculture of Negroes which explains their economic deprivation these past three hundred years.

What the concept of subculture implies, but does not say in so many words, is that alien cultures of a lower grade somehow intruded themselves into the American super-culture. If the Negro family today, for instance, is too often damaged by the absentee father, the working mother, and the delinquent youth, it is said to be a characteristic of their subculture. The concept shines most brightly when we talk about the discomforts of American society—dilapidated housing, crime, and unemployment. It is upon minorities that these discomforts fall most heavily. It is they, to be sure, who populate the ghettos, but it is our entire society, the American society, that spawns slums and breeds poverty.

I am not attempting to lay blame. I am trying to discover connections and relationships. What I see is that, among Negro and Mexican American minorities, what shows up vividly as local color and dramatic contrast are, in truth, cracks and tears in the seamless fabric of American society.

It is not the subcultures that are in trouble. It is the American culture itself.

And what have been some of the major strikes against Mexican Americans and Negroes?

One is the pattern of land ownership, control, and use that has developed in America during the past half century. Out of this pattern came the tractoring-out of the southern sharecropper, the withering of the family farm, and the massive importation of foreign agricultural laborers.

The resulting flight from the soil took millions to the cities, which were already suffering from urban cramps. We have begun to call these cities "ports of entry." The term has happy connotations: it suggests the migrant minority is on its way to better things—that is has *made* connections, not *broken* them.

But, in fact, the minority man finds the port congested with people like himself. They, like him, are becoming obsolete as a result of mechanization, automation, and cybernation—American cultural products that are radically altering job requirements, opportunities, and tenure. He finds that those sections of the big city where he has found transient refuge are also becoming obsolete. Here, another American culture concept, acted out with bulldozers, awaits him: urban redevelopment. As soon as a section shows speculative promise, it attracts speculative capital and entire neighborhoods go under. The Mexican American poor move with their anxieties to another place.

These and other massive social decisions are not for the Mexican American poor to make, or even take part in. These choices, and the complicated devices by which they are applied, are not even understood by the poor. To understand them, they would need an educational system that would deal factually and critically with them. But the Mexican American, on the average, barely gets through eight or nine years of school, so that even if the high schools and colleges were undertaking the task, which by and large they are not, they would not be reaching the minority man.

Mexican Americans in California *have* made progress since the Forties. They are subject to less ethnic discrimination. They have also begun to climb the lower rungs of the economic ladder. Ninety percent of the people I knew as a boy were farmworkers; now, far more than 10 per cent of us work as professors, journalists, bureaucrats, and so on. This change is only recent, but the process is increasing in scope and pace. With new jobs has come an ability to articulate. Today perhaps we even have too many spokesmen. In any event, the time is past when the Mexican American was not heard from. Now he says what he wants.

So far, we have been testing the mechanics of American democracy.

Those of us who have climbed two or three rungs up the ladder have had opportunities to learn how Anglo Americans do things—how they run political parties;

how they caucus; how they lobby; how they manipulate all of those niceties of political contrivance, some clean and some unclean; how they use them, sometimes for personal benefit and sometimes for the good of the commonwealth. And two general kinds of Mexican American leaders have emerged: those who conclude that the American political system doesn't have to be tested with values—it works for 195,000,000 people and what more could anyone ask; and those of us who are trying to see whether it really works in terms of human values.

At the same time, the Mexican American community has lost ground—important ground. Our leadership has been dispersed. Political appointments have sent men of distinction to Sacramento, Washington, and abroad. Distance does something to these men: their values and ideas change; politically and ideologically, not just residentially, they are separated from the community. Individuals are entitled to personal satisfaction in life, but, for the community, political dispersal has meant and means political decapitation.

Strains have also occurred within the community. Mechanization and automation, in industry, agriculture, and trade services, have thrown many thousands of Mexican Americans out of work. In farming, machines now pick tomatoes, grapes, oranges, and so on. Where the packing houses and canneries used to employ 85,000 people at the peak of production, they now employ around 45,000. Large groups of Mexican American families have had a steady income cut away, and have been forced to disperse and be mobile. These nuclei of community have broken down as a result.

Marginal workers have not been helped by the trade union movement. Indeed, the trade union leadership helped destroy the farm labor union we organized in the Forties. We had posed the twin issues of power and exploitation in agriculture, but the union leaders shrank from their responsibility to help farmworkers, leaving thousands to a cruel fate. However, they taught the Mexican American community a lesson: the trade unions cannot be a taproot of our salvation. They are interested only in workers who are continuously employed, even though vast numbers of people are now unemployed and probably always will be. Lose your job, or stop paying union dues, and you are no longer "sir" or "brother."

The disintegration of the Mexican American community is apparent in the numerous "shoestring" and "doughnut" communities in which thousands of Mexican Americans live. The "shoestrings" grow along the banks of irrigation ditches, where water is available and land is cheap; here, displaced migrants have pitched their trailers and shacks, and the profile of their settlements is, a shoestring; the classical example is South Dos Palos. The "doughnut" type is found in the city, in places like *La Rana* (The Frog) in Torrance. There, as in many other places, Mexican American families settled as farmworkers, but now they are surrounded by progress, and they can only wait to be pushed out by urban redevelopment. This community, one might say, is a hole where poor people live surrounded by people with dough.

Among Mexican Americans, the proportion of wasted, discarded, obsolete, or unneeded workers is growing higher. Personal and family anchorage to work they can do and to people they know is becoming more precarious. For these men and women the closest thing to an economic taproot is seasonal hiring in the fields and cyclical employment in the cities. The prevailing mood in the poverty pockets is thus one of puzzlement, insecurity, and resentment. And as insecurity deepens, puzzlement is giving way to the conviction that there is no way out, and resentment is heightening to the point where life is fulfilled not by making progress toward a goal but by shooting at a target.

The welfare services designed for the Mexican Americans and other minorities, diverse and ingenious as they are, are no answer or substitute, for around them no sense of community can arise, no organization of interests can emerge, and from them no effective action can result. Each social service, gigantic like everything else in America, is institutionalized; and each institution asserts its jurisdiction over a slice of the individual or the family. In the battle of jurisdictions, the human meaning of integration, of integrity, is lost.

Vertical integration no longer means a man standing securely upon and belonging to the earth—free of mind and responsible of spirit. It has come to mean the putting together of economic components into smooth-running financial and technical mechanisms.

The demands of the economy and the palliatives of social welfare are manifestations of the American culture as a whole, not of any supposed subculture within it. They originate in the centers of real power and of effective decision. No program for action with regard to the Mexican American minority, or any other minority, therefore, can be more than a provisional tactic to gain time (if there is much left).

What is this provisional tactic? It is the grouping of the poor through organization, around the resources provided by the federal government in various Acts, notably the Economic Opportunity Act of 1964.

As a result of this Act, the Mexican American minority, to take it as an illustration, has the legal opportunity to participate in the initiation, planning, and administration of social services that have heretofore been of the hand-me-down type. Local residents are now able to create a cluster of activities around which democratic organization can take form, and within which they will be able to maintain responsible relationships. The politics of power, inescapable in any event, can be reduced to more manageable proportions.

But if the federal resources are to be subordinated to local community action, local residents must be provided with organizers responsible to them. I am not talking of organizers who are deft with the gimmickry of community organization, but of those who are skilled in recognizing what the vital interests of poor people really are. These interests will in many respects coincide with the services that the federal government stands ready to finance. When they do, the objective of the local community becomes the preparation of action programs and the organization of the neighborhood around them. Into these programs the Mexican Americans themselves must move. Their training must begin from the moment they take on a role, however modest, in a program.

What is the ultimate goal of such action programs? It is simply the re-creation of a human web of relations that will serve to produce a genuine community. Community is all that man has been able to invent to give him at least an approximation to security in his transit through life. I say re-creation deliberately, for there have been times and places in the American past when such relations did exist and did function. But the web of community, these last fifty years, has been strained and rent. If it is to be patched now and perhaps rewoven later, men must do it by their own efforts. I realize that it is only a patching that I am suggesting. It is only the choice of a road, not the end of a journey. But it may be the only road not beset by anger, despair, and violence.

The war on poverty is, at this stage, a mere skirmish. It cannot become a war until Congress appropriates the money to mount a massive attack on unemployment. The problem is not simply to create jobs but to influence the basic decisions, like the allocation of resources, that society makes. Decisions about where the money is to be invested, for instance, are what creates jobs. And to these decisions, the poor are not a party.

Discrimination must be ended, in employment and in every other phase of social relations.

We must also battle for "anthropomorphic education." This is a terrible phrase, but what I mean is that schools have to teach children, not systems. Experiments in Los Angeles have proven that one teacher with fifteen pupils and one expert assistant can do a much better job than one teacher with forty pupils and no assistant. Remarkable discovery! We have to press to make that teacher-student ratio universal because it will mean that the status and authority of the upper strata of administrators will be downgraded and the greatest prestige and largest salaries will go to kindergarten teachers. We cannot give an inch in this battle.

Private wealth can provide a cutting edge in the reconstruction of communities. It could start projects at those points where the government says "no"—and the government can do this without ever really saying "no." There are a lot of experiments the Congress is not going to finance, and there are areas in which federal funds and services either are a handicap or are useless, anyway. Some indispensable things will never happen if we wait for federal funds.

Does the Mexican American community merely want to catch up with the Anglo American culture? The question is important, and we had better be careful before we say "Yes." My experience—in farm labor, in academic work, in politics—has taught me a lot of things about the Anglo American culture that I do not like. Its economic system, for instance, produces certain values and behavior that I don't want to catch up with! Mexican Americans have an opportunity to discriminate between the different values, behavior, and institutions in the pervading culture, and we had better choose wisely.

All my life I have heard that the trouble with the Mexican American is that he is too apathetic. As a boy, in Mexico, I lived among people who, viewed from the outside, were extremely apathetic. Nobody was interested in knowing who was going to be the next president of Mexico, or who the military commander of our zone was. Nobody cared about the location of the nearest college or high school. They were interested in tomorrow's ration of corn.

When we came to California, Anglo Americans preached to us about our apathy and scolded us. And I thought: Are we really so? Of course we are not. What is mistaken for apathy is simply a system of self-defense inherited by people with a long history of being kicked around. And if they don't inherit it, they learn quickly. They learn that they are surrounded by hostile men and forces that will do them in at every turn. They naturally become indifferent and unresponsive. But it is not apathy: it is self-protection. *La mula no nació arisca*—the mule isn't born stubborn, he's made stubborn.

In the village where I was born, men carried a money belt tied around their waists, and in it they kept all the money they possessed. They worked with the belt on, and they slept with it; they trusted nobody. As they progressed a little further, they put their money in a sock, which was purchased specially for the purpose; since nobody wore socks. Their circle of confidence had increased, but still they hid the sock under the corn crib in their cottage and left their women to protect it. Still a little further along came the piggy bank, which they usually placed on a shelf. Their circle of confidence had expanded further: all the family was trusted, friends too, even strangers who would drop by. Finally there came the sign of maturity: the bank account. Now, not only men were trusted but also a system, run by men who were not seen or even known.

These four stages of social evolution illustrate the so-called apathy of Mexican Americans. How can anybody accuse that villager who kept his money in a belt tied around his body of being apathetic? Considering the circumstances, he was a pretty smart Mexican.

It is often assumed that Mexican Americans need to be "emancipated"; after all, a lot of us used to live in a different culture in Mexico, and survived a feudal economy and society. The mayor of San Francisco remarked once that his city was going to build such a wonderful cultural center that it would make Los Angeles look "like a little Mexican village." Well, what's so wrong with that village? I have some good memories of Janco, my birthplace. There were no electric lights there, but in the evening, as the sun went down, people would sit in front of their cottages and talk by the twilight. And when it was dark the kids were sent to bed, and later the young men and women. Then the men would talk, not about small things but important ones. Some nights we heard a rumble of voices, lasting far into the morning. When I would awaken I would go to the yard and count the number of slits made by machetes in the hard-baked earth, and I would know how many men had gathered. It was these men who sparked the revolution in my village. And it was villages like these that started one of the most portentous events in the history of the Americas: the Mexican Revolution. In my yard.

I have not really been talking of fundamentals here. Not until the economy provides all men with sufficient incomes; not until mothers can stay home and take care of their children; not until massive investments of money are made in places like Watts; not until urban development becomes a weapon for something other than transferring doughnut communities from one part of the landscape to another, will the job of reconstructing communities have begun.

Are Mexican Americans ready? That I don't know, but some of us intend to find out.

Source: Ernesto Galarza, "La Mula No Nació Arisca," *Center Diary*, September–October 1966, pp. 26–32.

342. Excerpts from Previously Classified, Sanitized U.S. Department of State Telegram on the Tlatelolco Massacre, Mexico City, 1968

From 1933 and 1980, Mexico quadrupled its population. The fertility rate among Mexican women was 4.6 percent in 1950, and rose to 7.2 percent in 1970. World War II accelerated the modernization and industrialization of the country, displacing peasant farmers who fled to the cities—especially, to Mexico City, which would grow to 15 million by the late 1970s. The growing gap between rich and poor caused unrest among the peasants and workers. As with youth worldwide, more students attended the universities and preparatory schools where they conceptualized poverty. In Mexico City, students were incensed by a government crackdown on street vendors and efforts of government officials to hide the City's poverty in preparation of Mexico's hosting of the 1968 Olympic Games. This touched off a series of demonstrations during the summer of 1968 with sporadic confrontations between the Mexican police and military and the protestors. On October 2, 1968, 10,000 to 15,000 university and high school students gathered in La Plaza de las Tres Culturas at Tlatelolco (in Mexico City) in the rain to listen to student leaders condemn the army occupation of the National Autonomous University of Mexico (UNAM)— the largest and most prestigious university in Mexico. An army of at least 5,000 soldiers, and more than 300 tanks and other vehicles, surrounded the plaza and fired without warning at the demonstrators. When the shooting stopped, hundreds of people lay dead or wounded; 2,000 demonstrators were beaten and jailed. Most critics agree that Mexican President Gustavo Díaz Ordaz (1911–1979) orchestrated the violence to justify a broad crackdown on demonstrations that he considered embarrassing on the eve of the 1968 Olympic Games. Tales of the massacre outraged Chicano students in the United States. The following previously classified document shows CIA involvement with the Mexican Government before October 2.

FM AMEMBASSY MEXICO
TO SECSTATE WASHDC 7106

MEXICO 6234
PASS TO WHITE HOUSE

SANITIZED
E.O. 12356, Sec. 3.4
NLJ 95–120
By *isp*. NARA, Date 10-4-95

1. Mexican govt has solid evidence corroborating public charges of mexico city police chief that communist party engineered july 26 student fracas. Govt evidence also includes indications of soviet embassy complicity (including taunt by a PCM official that security police would find no important documents since they were all in soviet embassy).

2. Mexicans often blame foreign elements for such incidents and PCM lately has stressed its desire to pursue legal means but embassy considers that strong possibility exists moscow has ordered PCM to adopt more militant tactics. One motive may be soviet desire to counter impact on PCM of czech events. PCM paper, La voz De Mexico, after initially carrying favorable articles on czechoslovakia, completely silent on events in last few weeks, linked to this may be desire to strengthen internation discipline of PCM as also suggested by refurbishing and more prompt publication by PCM of international communist journal revista internacional.

3. Moscow and PCM may be seeking to take play away from pro-cuban extremists though elements of complicity also seem present. Pro-soviet and pro-cuban student elements joined in july 26 celebration of cuban anniversary. Revista internacional april issue containing article taking more friendly attitude to cuban tactics has just been issued here and may have been interpreted as signal for stronger tactics by PCM. Fact that cuban ambassador went to merida instead of staying in capital for july 26 fiesta suggests he may have known what was coming though he wanted to avoid any suggestion of cuban involvement.

4. While seeking to avoid direct involvement, soviets may believe that mexican anxiety to avoid any diplomatic contretemps with communist world as olympics

near gives soviet embassy more room for subversive maneuver. However, they know they risk strong government crackdown on PCM. Statement by mexican police chief who linked recent riots with olympics bound to recall to PCM and moscow president's warning on may 7 in talk with PCM politburo that government will crack down hard if PCM foments disorder in next few months. But PCM used to crackdowns and moscow may be proceeding by lenin's old injunction "better fewer but better."

5. Dept may wish to pass moscow.

Freeman

Source: Kate Doyle, "The Tlatelolco Massacre U.S. Documents on Mexico and the Events of 1968," Document 5, July 30, 1968 [Communist Role in Student Protest] U.S. Embassy in Mexico, secret telegram http://www.gwu.edu/~nsarchiv/NSAEBB/NSAEBB99/Doc5.pdf.

343. Excerpts from Eugene Nelson, Jr., "Huelga: New Goals for Labor," 1967

If the Chicano Movement did not start with César Chávez (1927–1993), he certainly made the cause known throughout the United States. Until the 1960s, few white Americans outside the Southwest knew who Mexican Americans were. It was Chávez who gave them a national forum. He was born into a farmworker family. After a stint in the Navy, he returned to the San Jose barrio of Sal Si Puedes (Get out If You Can) and became involved with the Community Service Organization (CSO) that was formed in 1947. The CSO was an offshoot of Saul Alinksy's Industrial Areas Foundation (IAF), which trained community organizers. He rose through the ranks and became the CSO president in the late 1950s. In 1962, he left a well-paying job, and along with fellow CSO organizer Dolores Huerta, began organizing farmworkers. In Delano, California, they founded the National Farm Workers Association (NFWA). On September 8, 1965, Filipino farmworkers initiated the Delano grape strike for higher wages. The NFWA supported the strike. Chávez combined trade union tactics with civil rights tactics such as the nonviolent strategies of Martin Luther King, Jr., and India's Mahatma Gandhi. Chávez went on hunger strikes and launched secondary boycotts of grapes to bring attention to *la causa*, the cause. The following excerpts are from an article by one of the early organizers of the farmworkers' union.

If the word *huelga* has not yet appeared in an English language dictionary, along with other Spanish words which have come into common usage in English, it surely will soon. As many Americans must know by now, "huelga" means "strike." As fewer know, it refers to a certain type of agricultural strike which is also a social movement, interpreted by different people in different ways, and capable at any time of shooting off in new directions which may significantly affect the lives of all Americans. The potentiality is there, despite the fact that at present only a tiny percentage of the American workforce is involved, that these workers are among the most poorly educated of all, and that eventually their number must decline. Even on the surface, the strike and the movement in California, later in Texas, have been exciting and significant.

The *huelga* began in September of 1965 as just another agricultural strike. When about 1,000 Filipino American members of the Agricultural Workers Organizing Committee of the AFL-CIO left their jobs in the vineyards of Delano, California, demanding to be paid the $1.40 an hour that was guaranteed to the last of the Mexican *braceros* who had been allowed to work in the United States. Delano was also the headquarters of the independent National Farm Workers Association [NFWA], a unique union which was a combination of labor and social service organization, administering to all the major needs of its 2,000 Mexican American members. The NFWA, headed by César Chávez, joined the strike against thirty-six grape growers, presenting the uncommon spectacle of an alliance of two unions and two ethnic groups, plus a smattering of Anglos, Negroes, and Puerto Ricans.

In corrupt and poverty-stricken Starr County, Texas, where farmworkers earn as little as 40¢ an hour, the movement also exploded last June when 700 melon pickers went out on strike. A subsequent farmworkers' march to Austin united Mexican American groups throughout the state in the demand for a state minimum wage of $1.25 an hour and union contracts for the striking workers. Gov. John Connally and Atty. Gen. Waggoner Carr refused to meet the marchers at the capitol on Labor Day, and many observers say the rebuff was responsible for Carr's defeat in the United States Senate race against Republican John Tower.

On May 15, the United Farm Workers signed their first recognition agreement with a Texas grower—Virgilio Guerra, who will be employing about sixty men in the cantaloupe harvest. Meanwhile, the strike and boycott, launched with the same nationwide machinery that forced Schenley to negotiate, is gaining momentum as the harvest peak nears.

There has been new organizing activity among farmworkers in Oregon, Washington, Wisconsin, New Mexico, Arizona, and Florida. About one-tenth of America's farmworkers were included for the first time this year under the national minimum wage law, starting at $1 an hour. And it is predicted that this year or next farmworkers will be included by Congress in the collective bargaining rights guaranteed other workers under the National Labor Relations Act, thus eliminating the grave injustice largely responsible for their depressed situation in the first place.

Source: Eugene Nelson, Jr. "Huelga: New Goals for Labor," pp. 724–725. Reprinted with permission from the June 5, 1967 issue of *The Nation*. For subscription information, call 1-800-333-8536. Portions of each week's *Nation* magazine can be accessed at http://www.thenation.com.

344. Excerpts from Rubén Salazar, "State Calls for Probe of Judge in Latin Slurs," 1969

Rubén Salazar was a muckraking reporter for the Los Angeles Times who later became the news director for KMEX-TV. He was killed by Los Angeles a sheriff deputy during the August 29, 1970 anti-Viet Nam War demonstration. His voice was heard throughout the 1960s exposing discrimination toward Mexican Americans. The following is part of a blistering attack on San Jose (California) Superior Court Judge Gerald S. Chargin who during the sentencing of a seventeen year old Mexican American youth who allegedly had sex with his 15 year old mentally retarded sister generalized an attack on all Mexicans. Chargin was censured but allowed him to remain on the bench.

"You are lower than animals and haven't the right to live in organized society— just miserable, lousy rotten people.... Maybe Hitler was right. The animals in our society probably ought to be destroyed because the have no right to live among human beings....

The judge then went on to say that the girl who is pregnant, "probably will have a half dozen and three or four marriages before she is 18." ...

Source: Rubén Salazar, "State Calls for Probe of Judge in Latin Slurs," *Los Angeles Times*, October 3, 1969, p. 3.

345. Remarks of Hon. James G. O'Hara of Michigan about the Proclamation of the Delano Grape Workers for International Boycott Day, House of Representatives, May 10, 1969

Charismatic labor activist Dolores Huerta (1930–) was born in New Mexico and grew up in Stockton at the northwest end of California's San Joaquín Valley. Huerta had been an organizer with the Community Service Organization (CSO) and worked as a teacher. She left these secure jobs to join labor activist César Chávez (1927–1993) to organize farmworkers. Huerta became the most prominent Chicana labor leader in the United States. Huerta was a seasoned organizer who lobbied in Sacramento, California, traveled the country organizing boycott committees, and spoke to workers. Speaking for the farmworkers' union, Huerta called for an international grape boycott which eventually became an international cause with supporters refusing to eat grapes until the growers signed contracts with the union. The following is a resolution by the Hon. James G. O'Hara of Michigan, which includes the call for the Delano Grape Boycott.

Mr. Speaker, last Saturday, May 10, was proclaimed International Boycott Day by the Delano grape workers. Consumers everywhere were called upon to withhold their patronage from stores selling table grapes. When the Congress enacted the National Labor Relations Act over 30 years ago, agriculture workers were excluded from the provisions [of] this act. In effect, the Congress made second-class citizens of farmworkers by refusing to protect their right to form unions and to bargain collectively with their employers. For the past 7 years, efforts on the part of the grape workers to bargain collectively have been largely ignored by the growers. Without the protection of the law, the workers had nowhere to go but to the public.

Two years ago, the farmworkers of California called upon consumers to boycott grapes in an effort to force the growers to recognize the rights of the workers and to bargain collectively with them. The boycott has been more and more effective as the public has become more and more aware of the plight of the farmworkers. By boycotting grapes, consumers tell growers that they will not purchase their product until they know that the workers who harvest it are assured of a just wage, humane working conditions, job security, and other employee benefits taken for granted by most working men and women in America.

Mr. Speaker, I insert the proclamation of the Delano grape workers for International Boycott Day at this point in the Record:

Proclamation of the Delano Grape Workers for International Boycott Day, May 10, 1969. We, the striking grape workers of California, join on this International Boycott Day with the consumers across the continent in planning the steps that lie ahead on the road to our liberation. As we plan, we recall the footsteps that brought us to this day and the events of this day. The historic road of our pilgrimage to Sacramento later branched out, spreading like the unpruned vines in struck fields, until it led us to willing exile in cities across this land. There, far from the earth we tilled for generations, we have cultivated the strange soil of public understanding, sowing the seed of our truth and our cause in the minds and hearts of men.

We have been farmworkers for hundreds of years and pioneers for seven. Mexicans, Filipinos, Africans, and others, our ancestors were among those who founded this land and tamed its natural wilderness. But we are still pilgrims on this land, and we are pioneers who blaze a trail out of the wilderness of hunger and deprivation that we have suffered even as our ancestors did. We are conscious today of the significance of our present quest. If this road we chart leads to the rights and reforms we demand, if it leads to just wages, humane working conditions, protection from the misuse of pesticides, and to the fundamental right of collective bargaining, if it changes the social order that relegates us to the bottom reaches of society, then in our wake will follow thousands of American farmworkers. Our example will make them free. But if our road does not bring us to victory and social change, it will not be because our direction is mistaken or our resolve too weak, but only because our bodies are mortal and our journey hard. For we are in the midst of a great social movement, and we will not stop struggling 'til we die, or win!

We have been farmworkers for hundreds of years and strikers for four. It was four years ago that we threw down our plowshares and pruning hooks. These Biblical symbols of peace and tranquility to us represent too many lifetimes of unprotesting submission to a degrading social system that allows us no dignity, no comfort, no peace. We mean to have our peace, and to win it without violence, for it is violence we would overcome—the subtle spiritual and mental violence of oppression, the violence subhuman toil does to the human body. So we went and stood tall outside the vineyards where we had stooped for years. But the tailors of national labor legislation had left us naked. Thus exposed, our picket lines were crippled by injunctions and harassed by growers; our strike was broken by imported scabs; our overtures to our employers were ignored. Yet we knew the day must come when they would talk to us, as equals.

We have been farmworkers for hundreds of years and boycotters for two. We did not choose the grape boycott, but we had chosen to leave our peonage, poverty, and despair behind. Though our first bid for freedom, the strike, was weakened, we would not turn back. The boycott was the only way forward the growers left to us. We called upon our fellow men and were answered by consumers who said—as all men of conscience must—that they would no longer allow their tables to be subsidized by our sweat and our sorrow: They shunned the grapes, fruit of our affliction.

We marched alone at the beginning, but today we count men of all creeds, nationalities, and occupations in our number. Between us and the justice we seek now stand the large and powerful grocers who, in continuing to buy table grapes, betray the boycott their own customers have built. These stores treat their patrons' demands to remove the grapes the same way the growers treat our demands for union recognition—by ignoring them. The consumers who rally behind our cause are responding as we do to such treatment—with a boycott! They pledge to withhold their patronage from stores that handle grapes during the boycott, just as we withhold our labor from the growers until our dispute is resolved.

Grapes must remain an unenjoyed luxury for all as long as the barest human needs and basic human rights are still luxuries for farmworkers. The grapes grow sweet and heavy on the vines, but they will have to wait while we reach out first for our freedom. The time is ripe for our liberation.

Source: May 17, 1969, *Congressional Record*, 91st Cong., 1st sess.

346. Excerpts from *Salvador B. Castro et al., Petitioners v. the Superior Court of Los Angeles County*

Salvador B. Castro (1933–), a Korean War (1950–1953) veteran, was a Los Angeles school teacher. When his students walked out of classes in five Los Angeles high schools in 1968, he walked out with them. Castro knew that his students' grievances and demands were justified, so he felt morally obligated to work with them and walk out in solidarity. According to Castro, a teacher's job did not stop at the edge of the school yard. Even before the 1968 Blowouts, Castro had been involved in the Viva Kennedy campaign to elect President John F. Kennedy (1917–1963) in 1960, and helped found the Mexican American Education Committee (1964) in Los Angeles, California, to unite Mexican American educators to improve education. Castro was forcefully transferred from Belmont High to Lincoln High after he encouraged Mexican American students to run a slate for student government. At Lincoln, he developed ties with high school and college students from Eastside schools. They met and discussed the inequalities within the Los Angeles schools and the need for bilingual courses and courses that taught them about Mexican culture. Castro helped students formulate demands presented to the school board. District officials ignored the students' demands. In March 1968, five public schools in East Los Angeles (Roosevelt, Wilson, Lincoln, Garfield, and Belmont), with the help of local Chicano college students, walked out. Castro was arrested and charged with 15 counts of conspiracy to disrupt public schools and 15 counts of conspiracy to disturb the peace. Twelve others, many of whom were Brown Berets (youths who organized as a para-military group to defend the barrios) were also arrested and charged with conspiracy. The charges were dropped in 1972. The following is an excerpt from the court case.

SUMMARY: Defendants, indicted on charges arising out of high school disturbances, petitioned the Court of Appeal for a writ of prohibition to restrain the Superior Court from further prosecution of the charges. At the time of application for the writ, the indictment consisted of three charges. Four of the defendants were charged with the misdemeanor of disturbing the peace and all of them were charged with felonies of conspiracy to violate Ed. Code, § 16701, making it a misdemeanor to willfully disturb any public school or any public school meeting, and conspiracy to disturb the peace and quiet of the neighborhood and persons in the proximity thereof. The court granted the writ as to the two felony charges and denied it as to the misdemeanor charge. Presiding Justice Kaus, who wrote the lead opinion, took the view that the circumstantial evidence relied upon by the prosecution to support the charge of conspiracy to disturb the peace was sufficient under conventional methods of evaluating proof in conspiracy cases, but that, inasmuch as defendants were engaged in the exercise of fundamental First Amendment rights, stricter standards of proof were called for. Justice Stephens, concurring, did not agree that the position of the prosecution was supported under conventional methods of evaluating proof. He was of the opinion that the evidence relied upon to support the charge was inadequate to be of ponderable legal significance, reasonable in nature, credible, and of solid value. Justice Reppy dissented as to this count.

Presiding Justice Kaus, with Justice Reppy concurring, held that prosecution of the charge of conspiracy to willfully disturb a public school or public school meeting should be prohibited on the ground that Ed. Code, § 16701, making such activity a misdemeanor, was overbroad, in that the statutory language encompassed conduct that was protected by the First Amendment. Justice Stephens concurred in the result as to this count but did not agree that the statute was overboard. He took the view that it was unconscionable to create a felony (by charging conspiracy) from the cooperative commission of a misdemeanor which was of such nature that the Legislature had provided that no jail term could be countenanced.

The three justices concurred in denying prohibition as to the misdemeanor charge of disturbing the peace, holding that a factual issue was presented as to whether prosecution was barred by a prior dismissal of a similar charge in municipal court. (Opinion by Kaus, P. J. Concurring opinion by Stephens, J. Concurring and dissenting opinion by Reppy, J.) ...

Petitioners, Salvatore B. Castro, Moctezuma Esparza, Henry Gomez, Frederic Bernard Lopez, Carlos Michael Montez, Carlos Munoz, Gilberto Cruz Olmeda, Ralph Luna Ramirez, Joe Angel Razo, Eliezer Lozado Risco, David John Sanchez, J. Patricio Sanchez, Richard Vigil....

The evidence before the grand jury showed that between March 5 and March 8, 1968, there occurred certain disturbances at four high schools in Los Angeles. Essentially these took the form of a large number of Mexican American students attempting to leave or actually leaving the school grounds and attending protest meetings. The alleged reason for these so-called "walkouts" was a protest against conditions in the schools which were claimed to provide the students with inferior education....

1. On March 5, at Garfield High School threats and "obscenities" were hurled at police officers and school officials;

2. At Roosevelt High School on March 6, several petitioners caused a chain by which a gate to the school was closed to snap open, permitting about two hundred students to leave the school premises;

3. At Belmont High School ... on March 7, garbage cans were tossed down the steps by students and fire alarms were broken. Fires were set in trash cans and fights broke out. Rocks and bottles were thrown. None of petitioners were shown to be directly involved;

4. The next day, again at Belmont, a few rocks were thrown by students and cherry bombs were ignited. Again, no involvement by any petitioner was shown.

Apart from the charge contained in Count VIII, these violations are not before us, except to the extent that their commission and the aiding and abetting of their commission by some petitioners is circumstantial evidence of the felonies charged in Counts XV and XVI. The thrust of those counts is simply that petitioners, none of whom was a student at any of the schools affected, planned the walkouts and took certain steps—"overt acts"—toward the accomplishment of their objective....

"In January or February, petitioner Castro had informed the UCLA Chapter of UMAS that high school students were talking about walking out. UMAS passed a motion assuming responsibility as monitors to protect the high school students. Then there were several meetings with petitioner Castro about proposals to be submitted to the Board of Education and the walkouts.... Petitioners Risco, Razo, and Esparza, and possibly Munoz, attended some of these meetings. Signs were made sometime in February for use during the walkouts...."

In addition there was offered, against petitioner Castro only, a radio broadcast he made on May 14, 1968. The People's summary of the broadcasts as follows: "... Castro outlined the history of the walkouts and indicated that he had asked college students to assist by making signs and monitoring the walkouts. Petitioner Castro received help from California State, UCLA and Valley State. East L.A. College would not endorse the program. An unexpected walkout at Wilson prematurely triggered one at Garfield. Petitioner Castro then advised that the other two schools would have to have a walkout in order to show unity to the Board of Education. He explained that the Lincoln walkout was called for 10:00 and 12:00 was set for Roosevelt. He explained how well the walkout which led to Hazard Park was supervised by the college and high school monitors.

"Petitioner Castro indicated that the kids were angry because the first wave of walkouts had some defects. So the planning for further walkouts began. Intelligence reports about Thursday's walkouts, availability of signs, and the weather were considered. It was planned that all four schools would walk out about 9:00 A.M. and the students would meet in Hazard Park. He described the plans for Garfield, Roosevelt, and Lincoln High Schools and analyzed what happened at Belmont."

It is thus apparent that the People do not even claim direct proof that the walkouts, as planned, were to involve criminal disturbances of the peace. Further, it is evident that there is no direct proof that any of petitioners, except Castro, Risco, Razo, Esparza, and possibly Munoz, were directly proved to have been parties to the planning of the walkouts. What the People do claim, in essence, is:

1. That other petitioners were circumstantially proved to have been participants in the planning of the walkouts by their presence and actions at the walkout sites, whether or not they behaved illegally; and

2. That the illegal nature of the plan may be inferred from the readiness with which some of those who were directly or circumstantially proved to have been planners violated the law....

Just how insensitive a tool the conventional conspiracy approach can be in a case such as the one at bar is illustrated by one of the People's own arguments in this case. Answering [the] petitioners' point that any disturbances during the walkouts were spontaneous and unanticipated, which, petitioners urge, is proved by the fact that they recruited monitors from various sympathetic groups at local colleges, the People argue: "12,300 students were enrolled at the four high schools. Even discounting students who would be normally absent on any given day, monitoring the students would be a tremendous job. Inherent in such a large-scale operation was the certainty of school disruption since total success would leave the schools without students and a partial walkout would result in agitating the non-participants in order to achieve total unity...."

Thus, if the student walkout was a violation of law or regulations made pursuant to law, and if the "chill" ran only toward discouraging that, and there was very small likelihood that it would discourage adult group demonstrations not intended to bring about student walkouts, no sufficient interference with rights of free speech is brought about by the circumstantial evidence rule available in the conspiracy prosecution.

Source: *Salvador B. Castro et al., Petitioners, v. The Superior Court of Los Angeles County, Respondent; The People, Real Party in Interest* Civ. No. 34178 Court of Appeal of California, Second Appellate District, Division Five *9 Cal. App. 3d 675;* 88 Cal. Rptr. 500; 1970 Cal. App. LEXIS 1985, July 17, 1970.

347. Excerpts from Rodolfo "Corky" Gonzales, "I Am Joaquín," 1967

One of the national Chicano leaders was Rodolfo "Corky" Gonzales (1928–2005) who was a boxer, a poet, and an activist. In the mid-sixties, Corky founded the Crusade for Justice, a community organization. In 1968, he led the Chicano delegation to Washington, D.C. for the Poor People's March, a march on Washington organized by civil rights leaders. In March 1969, under his auspices, the National Chicano Youth Liberation Conference was held in Denver, Colorado. The conference produced El Plan Espiritual de Aztlán (the Spiritual Plan of Aztlán) that demanded self-determination for Chicanos. Aztlán was the legendary birthplace of the Aztec tribe and a symbol that Mexican Americans were an original part of the Southwest. Corky believed in direct action and he expressed the aspirations of urban youth. His poem, "I am Joaquín," expresses the confusion in the Chicanos' search for identity and hopes of Chicano youth. The following excerpts from this poem were written during the height of youth activism in 1968. At the time, there was a schism between the new and the old generations with the newer generation refusing to compromise. The Chicano Movement, 1968–1973, attempted to resolve the identity crisis by self-identifying and calling themselves Chicano, a pejorative term that had been used by the older generation to refer to low-class Mexicans. Youth took up the term Chicano because it precisely identified those at the bottom strata of society—the very people whose conditions they were trying to improve.

Yo soy Joaquín,
perdido en un mundo de confusión:
I am Joaquín, lost in a world of confusion,
caught up in the whirl of a gringo society,
confused by the rules, scorned by attitudes,
suppressed by manipulation, and destroyed by modern society.
My fathers have lost the economic battle
and won the struggle of cultural survival.
And now! I must choose between the paradox of
victory of the spirit, despite physical hunger,
or to exist in the grasp of American social neurosis,
sterilization of the soul and a full stomach.
Yes, I have come a long way to nowhere,
unwillingly dragged by that monstrous, technical,
industrial giant called Progress and Anglo success....

I look at myself.
I watch my brothers.
I shed tears of sorrow. I sow seeds of hate.
I withdraw to the safety within the circle of life—
MY OWN PEOPLE
I am Cuauhtémoc, proud and noble,
leader of men, king of an empire civilized
beyond the dreams of the gachupín Cortés,
who also is the blood, the image of myself.
I am the Maya prince.
I am Nezahualcóyotl, great leader of the Chichimecas.
I am the sword and flame of Cortés the despot
And I am the eagle and serpent of the Aztec civilization.
I owned the land as far as the eye
could see under the Crown of Spain,
and I toiled on my Earth and gave my Indian sweat and blood
for the Spanish master who ruled with tyranny over man and
beast and all that he could trample
But ... THE GROUND WAS MINE.
I was both tyrant and slave.
As the Christian church took its place in God's name,
to take and use my virgin strength and trusting faith,
the priests, both good and bad, took—
but gave a lasting truth that Spaniard Indian Mestizo
we're all God's children.
And from these words grew men who prayed and fought
for their own worth as human beings, for that
GOLDEN MOMENT of FREEDOM.
I was part in blood and spirit of that courageous village priest
Hidalgo who in the year eighteen hundred and ten
rang the bell of independence and gave out that lasting cry—
El Grito de Dolores
"Que mueran los gachupines y que viva la Virgen de Guadalupe...."
I sentenced him who was me I excommunicated him, my blood.
I drove him from the pulpit to lead a bloody revolution for him and me....
I killed him.
His head, which is mine and of all those
who have come this way,
I placed on that fortress wall
to wait for independence. Morelos! Matamoros! Guerrero!
all compañeros in the act, STOOD AGAINST THAT WALL OF INFAMY
to feel the hot gouge of lead which my hands made.
I died with them ... I lived with them.... I lived to see our country free.
Free from Spanish rule in eighteen-hundred-twenty-one.
Mexico was free??
The crown was gone but all its parasites remained,
and ruled, and taught, with gun and flame and mystic power.
I worked, I sweated, I bled, I prayed,
and waited silently for life to begin again.
I fought and died for Don Benito Juárez, guardian of the Constitution.

I was he on dusty roads on barren land as he protected his archives
as Moses did his sacraments.
He held his Mexico in his hand on
the most desolate and remote ground which was his country.
And this giant little Zapotec gave not one palm's breadth
of his country's land to kings or monarchs or presidents of foreign powers.
I am Joaquín.
I rode with Pancho Villa,
crude and warm, a tornado at full strength,
nourished and inspired by the passion and the fire of all his earthy people.
I am Emiliano Zapata.
"This land, this earth is OURS."
The villages, the mountains, the streams
belong to Zapatistas.
Our life or yours is the only trade for soft brown earth and maize.
All of which is our reward,
a creed that formed a constitution
for all who dare live free!
"This land is ours....
Father, I give it back to you.
Mexico must be free...."
I ride with revolutionists
against myself.
I am the Rurales,
coarse and brutal,
I am the mountain Indian,
superior over all.
The thundering hoof beats are my horses. The chattering machine guns
are death to all of me:
Yaqui
Tarahumara
Chamala
Zapotec
Mestizo
Español.
I have been the bloody revolution,
The victor,
The vanquished.
I have killed
And been killed.
I am the despots Díaz
And Huerta
And the apostle of democracy,
Francisco Madero.
I am
The black-shawled
Faithful women
Who die with me
Or live
Depending on the time and place.

I am faithful, humble Juan Diego,
The Virgin of Guadalupe,
Tonantzín, Aztec goddess, too.
I rode the mountains of San Joaquín.
I rode east and north
As far as the Rocky Mountains,
And
All men feared the guns of
Joaquín Murrieta.
I killed those men who dared
To steal my mine,
Who raped and killed my love
My wife.
Then I killed to stay alive.
I was Elfego Baca,
living my nine lives fully.
I was the Espinoza brothers
of the Valle de San Luis.
All were added to the number of heads that in the name of civilization
were placed on the wall of independence, heads of brave men
who died for cause or principle, good or bad.
Hidalgo! Zapata!
Murrieta! Espinozas!
Are but a few.
They dared to face
The force of tyranny
Of men who rule by deception and hypocrisy.
I stand here looking back,
And now I see the present,
And still I am a campesino,
I am the fat political coyote—

I am the masses of my people and
I refuse to be absorbed.
I am Joaquín.
The odds are great
But my spirit is strong,
My faith unbreakable,
My blood is pure.
I am Aztec prince and Christian Christ.
I SHALL ENDURE!
I WILL ENDURE.

Source: Rodolfo "Corky" Gonzales, "I am Joaquín," http://www.escuelatlatelolco.org.

348. Excerpts from El Plan Espiritual de Aztlán, 1969

El Plan de Aztlán (1969) was adopted at the first National Chicano Youth Liberation Conference in Denver, Colorado, March 1969. It was collectively written but its main contributor was Chicano poet Baltazar Urista who went by the name Alurista. The plan expressed the growing nationalist consciousness of the Chicano generation. It represented the reaction of youth to generations of discrimination against people of Mexican extraction. Racist nativists have criticized the plan for the use of the word Aztlán, the place of origin of the Aztecas, which is a historical fact. Aztlán existed in the territory taken from Mexico through war. Right wing critics say that the plan calls for Chicano control of the Chicano community—their barrios (neighborhoods). Black Americans want to control their neighborhoods and Native Americans wish to remain in control of the few lands that have been left to them. This is why there are ethnic políticos. Critics also call the phrase, *La Raza* [The Race] racist because it singles out people of Mexican origin as being special. However, speakers such as President Theodore Roosevelt have expressed the belief that Americans are a special people. No similar charge is leveled at Jewish Americans for supporting Israel or claiming to be the chosen people; Armenian Americans for going to Armenian churches; or Italian Americans for joining Italian organizations.

In the spirit of a new people that is conscious not only of its proud historical heritage but also of the brutal "gringo" invasion of our territories, *we*, the Chicano inhabitants and civilizers of the northern land of Aztlán from whence came our forefathers, reclaiming the land of their birth and consecrating the determination of our people of the sun, *declare* that the call of our blood is our power, our responsibility, and our inevitable destiny.

We are free and sovereign to determine those tasks which are justly called for by our house, our land, the sweat of our brows, and by our hearts. Aztlán belongs to those who plant the seeds, water the fields, and gather the crops, and not to the foreign Europeans. We do not recognize capricious frontiers on the bronze continent.

Brotherhood unites us, and love for our brothers makes us a people whose time has come and who struggles against the foreigner "gabacho" who exploits our riches and destroys our culture. With our heart in our hands and our hands in the soil, we declare the independence of our mestizo nation. We are a bronze people with a bronze culture. Before the world, before all of North America, before all our brothers in the bronze continent, we are a nation, we are a union of free pueblos, we are *Aztlán*.

FOR *LA RAZA* TO DO. *FUERA DE LA RAZA NADA* [OUTSIDE THE RACE NOTHING]

Program

El Plan Espiritual de Aztlán sets the theme that the Chicanos (La Raza de Bronze) must use their nationalism as the key or common denominator for mass mobilization and organization. Once we are committed to the idea and philosophy of El Plan de Aztlán, we can only conclude that social, economic, cultural, and political independence is the only road to total liberation from oppression, exploitation, and racism. Our struggle then must be for the control of our barrios, campos, pueblos, lands, our economy, our culture, and our political life. El Plan commits all levels of Chicano society—the barrio, the campo, the ranchero, the writer, the teacher, the worker, the professional—to La Causa.

Nationalism

Nationalism as the key to organization transcends all religious, political, class, and economic factions or boundaries. Nationalism is the common denominator that all members of La Raza can agree upon.

Organizational Goals

1. UNITY in the thinking of our people concerning the barrios, the pueblo, the campo, the land, the poor, the middle class, the professional—all committed to the liberation of La Raza.

2. ECONOMY: economic control of our lives and our communities can only come about by driving the exploiter out of our communities, our pueblos, and our lands and by controlling and developing our own talents, sweat, and resources. Cultural background and values which ignore materialism and embrace humanism will contribute to the act of cooperative buying and the distribution of resources and production to sustain an economic base for healthy growth and development. Lands rightfully ours will be fought for and defended. Land and realty ownership will be acquired by the community for the people's welfare. Economic ties of responsibility must be secured by nationalism and the Chicano defense units.

3. EDUCATION must be relative [relevant] to our people, i.e., history, culture, bilingual education, contributions, etc. Community control of our schools, our teachers, our administrators, our counselors, and our programs.

4. INSTITUTIONS shall serve our people by providing the service necessary for a full life and their welfare on the basis of restitution, not handouts or beggar's crumbs. Restitution for past economic slavery, political exploitation, ethnic and cultural psychological destruction and denial of civil and human rights. Institutions in our community which do not serve the people have no place in the community. The institutions belong to the people.

5. SELF-DEFENSE of the community must rely on the combined strength of the people. The front line defense will come from the barrios, the campos, the pueblos, and the ranchitos. Their involvement as protectors of their people will be given respect and dignity. They, in turn, offer their responsibility and their lives for their people. Those who place themselves in the front ranks for their people do so out of love and carnalismo. Those institutions which are fattened by our brothers to provide employment and political pork barrels for the gringo will do so only as acts of liberation and for La Causa. For the very young there will no longer be acts of juvenile delinquency, but revolutionary acts.

6. CULTURAL values of our people strengthen our identity and the moral backbone of the movement. Our culture unites and educates the family of La Raza towards liberation with one heart and one mind. We must insure that our writers, poets, musicians, and artists produce literature and art that is appealing to our people and relates to our revolutionary culture. Our cultural values of life, family, and home will serve as a powerful weapon to defeat the gringo dollar value system and encourage the process of love and brotherhood.

7. POLITICAL LIBERATION can only come through independent action on our part, since the two-party system is the same animal with two heads that feed from the same trough. Where we are a majority, we will control; where we are a

minority, we will represent a pressure group; nationally, we will represent one party: La Familia de La Raza!

Action

1. Awareness and distribution of El Plan Espiritual de Aztlán. Presented at every meeting, demonstration, confrontation, courthouse, institution, administration, church, school, tree, building, car, and every place of human existence.

2. September 16, on the birthdate of Mexican Independence, a national walk-out by all Chicanos of all colleges and schools to be sustained until the complete revision of the educational system: its policy makers, administration, its curriculum, and its personnel to meet the needs of our community.

3. Self-defense against the occupying forces of the oppressors at every school, every available man, woman, and child.

4. Community nationalization and organization of all Chicanos: El Plan Espiritual de Aztlán.

5. Economic program to drive the exploiter out of our community and a welding together of our people's combined resources to control their own production through cooperative effort.

6. Creation of an independent local, regional, and national political party.

A nation autonomous and free—culturally, socially, economically, and politically—will make its own decisions on the usage of our lands, the taxation of our goods, the utilization of our bodies for war, the determination of justice (reward and punishment), and the profit of our sweat.

El Plan de Aztlán is the plan of liberation!

Source: El Plan Espiritual de Aztlán.

349. Excerpts from Chicano Coordinating Council on Higher Education, *El Plan de Santa Barbara: A Chicano Plan for Higher Education*, 1969

El Plan de Santa Barbara: A Chicano Plan for Higher Education was written by the Chicano Coordinating Council on Higher Education (CHE) that was formed in about 1969 to coordinate the establishment of Chicano Studies programs. The plan represents the synthesis of a three-day conference of educators, students, and community activists on the campus of the University of California at Santa Barbara. It was a 155-page document of proposals for a curriculum in Chicano Studies, the role of community control in Chicano education, and the necessity of Chicano political independence. Written in the form of a manifesto, it called for the implementation of Chicano Studies educational programs throughout California and caused the founding of M.E.Ch.A. (Movimiento Estudiantil Chicano de Aztlán), a Chicano student group. *El Plan de Santa Barbara* was adopted in 1969.

MANIFESTO

For all peoples, as with individuals, the time comes when they must reckon with their history. For the Chicano the present is a time of renaissance, of *renacimiento*. Our people and our community, *el barrio* and *la colonia*, are expressing a new consciousness and a new resolve. Recognizing the historical tasks confronting our people and fully aware of the cost of human progress, we pledge our will to move. We will move forward toward our destiny as a people. We will move against those forces which have denied us freedom of expression and human dignity. Throughout history, the quest for cultural expression and freedom has taken the form of a struggle. Our struggle, tempered by the lessons of the American past, is an historical reality.

For decades, Mexican people in the United States struggle to realize the "American Dream". And some, a few, have. But the cost, the ultimate cost of assimilation, required turning away from el barrio and la colonia. In the meantime, due to the racist structure of this society, to our essentially different life style, and to the socio-economic functions assigned to our community by Anglo American society—as suppliers of cheap labor and dumping ground for the small-time capitalist entrepreneur—the barrio and colonia remained exploited, impoverished, and marginal.

As a result, the self-determination of our community is now the only acceptable mandate for social and political action; it is the essence of Chicano commitment. Culturally, the word *Chicano*, in the past a pejorative and class-bound adjective, has now become the root idea of a new cultural identity for our people. It also reveals a growing solidarity and the development of a common social praxis. The widespread use of the term Chicano today signals a rebirth of pride and confidence. Chicanismo simply embodies and ancient truth: that a person is never closer to his/her true self as when he/she is close to his/her community.

Chicanismo draws its faith and strength from two main sources: from the just struggle of our people and from an objective analysis of our community's strategic needs. We recognize that without a strategic use of education, an education that places value on what we value, we will not realize our destiny. Chicanos recognize the central importance of institutions of higher learning to modern progress, in this case, to the development of our community. But we go further: we believe that higher education must contribute to the information of a complete person who truly values life and freedom.

The destiny of our people will be fulfilled. To that end, we pledge our efforts and take as our credo what José Vasconcelos [Mexican philosopher] once said at a time of crisis and hope: "At this moment we do not come to work for the university, but to demand that the university work for our people."

POLITICAL ACTION

Introduction

For the Movement, political action essentially means influencing the decision-making process of those institutions which affect Chicanos, the university, community organizations, and non-community institutions. Political action encompasses the elements which function in a progression: political consciousness, political mobilization, and tactics. Each part breaks down into further subdivisions. Before continuing with specific discussions of these three categories, a brief historical analysis must be formulated.

Historical Perspective

The political activity of the Chicano Movement at colleges and universities to date has been specifically directed toward establishing Chicano student organizations

(UMAS, MAYA, MASC, M.E.Ch.A., etc.) and institutionalizing Chicano Studies programs. A variety of organizational forms and tactics have characterized these student organizations.

One of the major factors which led to political awareness in the '60s was the clash between Anglo American educational institutions and Chicanos who maintained their cultural identity. Another factor was the increasing number of Chicano students who became aware of the extent to which colonial conditions characterized their communities. The result of this domestic colonialism is that the barrios and colonias are dependent communities with no institutional power base and significantly influencing decision making. Within the last decade, a limited degree of progress has taken place in securing a base of power within educational institutions.

Other factors which affected the political awareness of the Chicano youth were: the heritage of the Chicano youth movements of the '30s and '40s; the failure of the Chicano political efforts of the '40s and '50s; the bankruptcy of the Mexican American pseudo-political associations; and the disillusionment of Chicano participants in the Kennedy campaigns. Among the strongest influences of Chicano youth today have been the National Farm Workers Association, the Crusades for Justice, and the Alianza Federal de Pueblos Libres, the civil rights, the Black Power, and the anti-war movements were other influences.

As political consciousness increased, there occurred a simultaneously a renewed cultural awareness which, along with social and economical factors, led to the proliferation of Chicano youth organizations. By the mid 1960s, MASC, MAYA, UMAS, La Vida Nueva, and M.E.Ch.A. appeared on campus, while the Brown Berets, Black Berets, ALMA, and la Junta organized the barrios and colonias. These groups differed from one another depending on local conditions and their varying state of political development. Despite differences in name and organizational experience, a basic unity evolved.

These groups have had a significant impact on the awareness of large numbers of people, both Chicano and non-Chicano. Within the communities, some public agencies have been sensitized, and others have been exposed. On campuses, articulation of demands and related political efforts have dramatized NUESTRA CAUSA. Concrete results are visible in the establishment of corresponding supportive services. The institutionalization of Chicano Studies marks the present stage of activity; the next stage will involve the strategic application of university and college resources to the community. One immediate result will be the elimination of the artificial distinction which exists between the students and the community. Rather than being its victims, the community will benefit from the resources of the institutions of higher learning.

POLITICAL CONSCIOUSNESS

Commitment to the struggle for Chicano liberation is the operative definition of the ideology used here. Chicanismo involves a crucial distinction in political consciousness between a Mexican American (or Hispanic) and a Chicano mentality. The Mexican American or Hispanic is a person who lacks self-respect and pride in one's ethnic and cultural background. Thus, the Chicano acts with confidence and with a range of alternatives in the political world. He is capable of developing an effective ideology through action.

Mexican Americans (or Hispanics) must be viewed as potential Chicanos. Chicanismo is flexible enough to relate to the varying levels of consciousness within La Raza. Regional variations must always be kept in mind as well as the different levels of development, composition, maturity, achievement, and experience in political action. Cultural nationalism is a means of total Chicano liberation.

There are definite advantages to cultural nationalism, but no inherent limitations. A Chicano ideology, especially as it involves cultural nationalism, should be positively phrased in the form of propositions to the Movement. Chicanismo is a concept that integrates self-awareness with cultural identity, a necessary step in developing political consciousness. As such, it serves as a basis for political action, flexible enough to include the possibility of coalitions. The related concept of La Raza provides an internationalist scope of Chicanismo, and La Raza Cosmica furnishes a philosophical precedent. Within this framework, the Third World concept merits consideration.

POLITICAL MOBILIZATION

Political mobilization is directly dependent on political consciousness. As political consciousness develops, the potential for political action increases.

The Chicano student organization in institutions of higher learning is central to all effective political mobilization. Effective mobilization presupposes precise definition of political goals and of the tactical interrelationships of roles. Political goals in any given situations must encompass the totality of Chicano interests in higher education. The differentiations of roles required by a given situation must be defined on the basis of mutual accountability and equal sharing of responsibility. Furthermore, the mobilization of community support not only legitimizes the activities of Chicano student solidarity [but is] axiomatic in all aspects of political action.

Since the movement is definitely of national significance and scope, all student organizations should adopt one identical name throughout the state and eventually the nation to characterize the common struggle of La Raza de Aztlán. The net gain is a step toward greater national unity which enhances the power in mobilizing local campus organizations.

When advantageous, political coalitions and alliances with non-Chicano groups may be considered. A careful analysis must precede the decision to enter into a coalition. One significant factor is the community's attitude toward coalitions. Another factor is the formulation of a mechanism for the distribution of power that ensures maximum participation in decision making: i.e., formulation of demands and planning of tactics. When no longer politically advantageous, Chicano participation in the coalition ends.

CAMPUS ORGANIZING: NOTES ON M.E.Ch.A.

Introduction

M.E.Ch.A. is a first step to tying the student groups throughout the Southwest into a vibrant and responsive network of activists who will respond as a unit to oppression and racism and will work in harmony when initiating and carrying out campaigns of liberation for our people.

As of present, wherever one travels throughout the Southwest, one finds that there are different levels of awareness of different campuses. The student movement is, to a large degree, a political movement and as such must not elicit from our people the negative reason. To this end, then we must re-define politics for our people to be a means of liberation. The political sophistication of our Raza must be raised so that they do not fall prey to apologists and *vendidos* [sellouts] whose whole interest is their personal career of fortune. In addition, the student movement is more than a political movement, it is cultural and social as well. The spirit of M.E.Ch.A. must be one of *hermandad* [brotherhood] and cultural awareness. The ethic of profit and competition, of greed and intolerance, which the Anglo society offers, must be replaced by our ancestral communalism and love for beauty and justice. M.E.Ch.A. must bring to the mind of every young Chicano that the liberations of this people from prejudice and oppression is in his hands and this responsibility is greater than personal achievement and more meaningful than degrees, especially if they are earned at the expense of his identity and cultural integrity.

M.E.Ch.A., then, is more than a name; it is a spirit of unity, of brotherhood, and a resolve to undertake a struggle for liberation in society where justice is but a word. M.E.Ch.A. is a means to an end.

Function of M.E.Ch.A.—To the Student

To socialize and politicize Chicano students of their particular campus to the ideals of the movement. It is important that every Chicano student on campus be made to feel that he has a place on the campus and that he/she has a feeling of familia with his/her Chicano brothers, and sisters. Therefore, the organization in its flurry of activities and projects must not forget or overlook the human factor of friendship, understanding, trust, etc. As well as stimulating hermandad, this approach can also be looked at in more pragmatic terms. If enough trust, friendship, and understanding are generated, then the loyalty and support can be relied upon when a crisis faces the group or community. This attitude must not merely provide a social club atmosphere but the strengths, weaknesses, and talents of each member should be known so that they may be utilized to the greatest advantage. Know one another. Part of the reason that students will come to the organization is in search of self-fulfillment. Give that individual the opportunity to show what he/she can do. Although the Movement stresses collective behavior, it is important that the individual be recognized and given credit for his/her efforts. When people who work in close association know one another well, it is more conductive to self-criticism and reevaluation, and this every M.E.Ch.A. person must be willing to submit to. Periodic self-criticism often eliminates static cycles of unproductive behavior. It is an opportunity for fresh approaches to old problems to be surfaced and aired; it gives new leadership a chance to emerge; and must be recognized as a vital part of M.E.Ch.A. M.E.Ch.A. can be considered a training ground for leadership, and as such no one member or group of members should dominate the leadership positions for long periods of time. This tends to take care of itself considering the transitory nature of students.

Recruitment and Education

Action is the best organizer. During and immediately following direct action of any type—demonstrations, marches, rallies, or even symposiums and speeches—new faces will often surface and this is where much of the recruiting should be done. New members should be made to feel that they are part of the group immediately and not that they have to go through a period of warming up to the old membership. Each new member should be given a responsibility as soon as possible and fitted into the scheme of things according to his or her talents and interests.

Since the college student is constantly faced with the responsibility of raising funds for the movements, whether it be for legal defense, the grape boycott, or whatever reason, this is an excellent opportunity for internal education. Fundraising events should always be educational. If the event is a symposium or speech or debate, [it] is usually an excellent opportunity to spread the Chicano Liberation Movement philosophy. If the event is a *pachanga* [party] or *tardeada* [festival] or *baile* [dance], this provides an excellent opportunity to practice and teach the culture in all its facets. In addition, each M.E.Ch.A. chapter should establish and maintain an extensive library of Chicano materials so that the membership has ready access to material which will help them understand their people and their problems. General meetings should be educational. The last segment of each regular meeting can be used to discuss ideological or philosophical differences, or some event in the Chicanos' history. It should be kept in mind that there will always be different levels of awareness within the group due to the individual's background or exposure of the movement. This must be taken into consideration so as not to alienate members before they have had a chance to listen to the argument for liberation.

The best educational device is being in the barrio as often as possible. More often than not, the members of M.E.Ch.A. will be products of the barrio; but many have lost contact with their former surroundings, and this tie must be reestablished if M.E.Ch.A. is to organize and work for La Raza.

The following things should be kept in mind in order to develop group cohesiveness: 1) know the talents and abilities of each member; 2) every semester, [individuals] must be given a responsibility, and recognition should be given for their efforts; 3) if mistakes are made, they should become learning experiences for the whole group and not merely excuses for ostracizing individual members; 4) since many people come to M.E.Ch.A. seeking self-fulfillment, they must be seized to educate the student to the Chicano philosophy, culture, and history; 5) of great importance is that a personal and human interaction exist between members of the organization so that such things as personality clashes, competition, ego-trips, subterfuge, infiltration, provocateurs, cliques, and mistrust do not impede the cohesion and effectiveness of the group. Above all, the feeling of hermandad must prevail so that the organization is more to the members than just a club or a clique. M.E.Ch.A. must be a learning and fulfilling experience that develops dedication and commitment.

A delicate but essential question is discipline. Discipline is important to an organization such as M.E.Ch.A. because many may suffer form the indiscretion of a few. Because of the reaction of the general population to the demands of the Chicano, one can always expect some retribution or retaliation for gains made by the Chicano, be it in the form of legal actions or merely economic sanction on the campus. Therefore, it becomes essential that each member pull his load and that no one be allowed to be dead weight. *Carga floja* is dangerous, and if not brought up to par, it must be cut loose. The best discipline comes from mutual respect, and therefore, the leaders of the group must enjoy and give this respect. The manner of enforcing discipline, however, should be left up to the group and the particular situation.

Planning and Strategy

Actions of the group must be coordinated in such a way that everyone knows exactly what he is supposed to do. This requires that at least rudimentary organizational methods and strategy be taught to the group. Confusion should be avoided, with the different plans and strategies clearly stated to all. The objective must be clear to the group at all times, especially during confrontations and negotiations. There should be alternate plans for reaching the objectives, and these should be explained to the group so that it is not felt that a reversal of position or capitulation has been carried out without their approval. The short- as well as the long-range values and effects of all actions should be considered before actions are taken. This assumes that there is sufficient time to plan and carefully map out actions, which brings up another point: don't be caught off guard, don't be forced to act out of haste; choose your own battleground and your own time schedule when possible. Know your power base and develop it. A student group is more effective if it can claim the support of the community and support on the campus itself from other sectors than the student population.

The Function of M.E.Ch.A.—To the Campus Community

Other students can be important to M.E.Ch.A. in supportive roles; hence, the question of coalitions. Although it is understood and quite obvious that the viability and amenability of coalition varies from campus to campus, some guidelines might be kept in mind. These questions should be asked before entering into any binding agreement. Is it beneficial to tie oneself to another group in coalition, which will carry one into conflicts for which one is ill-prepared or involve one with issues on which one is ill-advised? Can one sagely go into a coalition where one group is markedly stronger than another? Does M.E.Ch.A. have an equal voice in leadership and planning in the coalition group? Is it perhaps better to enter into a loose alliance for a given issue? How does leadership of each group view coalitions? How does the membership? Can M.E.Ch.A. hold up its end of the bargain? Will M.E.Ch.A. carry dead weight in a coalition? All of these and many more questions must be asked and answered before one can safely say that he/she will benefit from and contribute to a strong coalition effort.

Supportive groups. When moving on campus it is often well-advised to have groups who are willing to act in supportive roles. For example, there are usually any number of faculty members who are sympathetic, but limited as to the numbers of activities they will engage in. These faculty members often serve on academic councils and senates and can be instrumental in academic policy. They also provide another channel to the academic power structure and can be used as leverage in negotiation. However, these groups are only as responsive as the ties with them are nurtured. This does not mean, compromise M.E.Ch.A.'s integrity; it merely means laying good groundwork before an issue is brought up, touching bases with your allies before hand.

Sympathetic administrators. This a delicate area, since administrators are most interested in not jeopardizing their positions and often will try to act as buffers or liaison between the administration and the student group. In the case of Chicano administrators, it should not be assumed, he/she must be given the chance to prove his/her allegiance to La Causa. As such, he/she should be the Chicano's person in the power structure instead of the administration's Mexican American. It is from the administrator that information can be obtained as to the actual feasibility of demands or programs to go beyond the platitudes and pleas of unreasonableness with which the administration usually answers proposals and demands. The words of the administrator should never be the deciding factor in students' actions. The student must, at all times, make their own decisions. It is very human for people to establish self-interest. Therefore, students must constantly remind the Chicano administrators and faculty where their loyalty and allegiance lie. It is very easy for administrators to begin looking for promotions just as it is very natural for faculty members to seek positions of academic prominence.

In short, it is the students who must keep after Chicano and non-Chicano administrators and faculty to see that they do not compromise the position of the student and the community. By the same token, it is the student who must come to the support of these individuals if they are threatened for their support of the student. Students must be careful not to become a political lever for others.

Function of M.E.Ch.A.—Education

It is a fact that the Chicano has not often enough written his/her own history, his/her own anthropology, his/her own sociology, his/her own literature. He/she must do this if he is to survive as a cultural entity in this melting pot society, which seeks to dilute varied cultures into a gray upon gray pseudo-culture of technology and materialism. The Chicano student is doing most of the work in the establishment of study programs, centers, curriculum development, entrance programs to get more Chicanos into college. This is good and must continue, but students must be careful not to be co-opted in their fervor for establishing relevance on the campus. Much of what is being offered by college systems and administrators is too little too late. M.E.Ch.A. must not compromise programs and curriculum which are essential for the total education of the Chicano for the sake of expediency. The students must not become so engrossed in programs and centers created along established academic guidelines that they forget the needs of the people which these institutions are meant to serve. To this end, barrio input must always be given full and open hearing when designing these programs, when creating them, and in running them. The jobs created by these projects must be filled by competent Chicanos, not only the Chicano who has the traditional credentials required for the position, but one who has the credentials of the Raza. Too often in the past, the dedicated pushed for a program only to have a vendido sharp-talker come in and take over and start working for his Anglo administrator. Therefore, students must demand a say in the recruitment and selection of all directors and assistant directors of student-initiated programs. To further insure strong if not complete control of the direction and running of programs, all advisory and steering committees should have both student and community components as well as sympathetic Chicano faculty as member.

Tying the campus to the barrio. The colleges and universities in the past have existed in an aura of omnipotence and infallibility. It is time that they be made responsible and responsive to the communities in which they are located or whose members they serve. As has already been mentioned, community members should serve on all programs related to Chicano interests. In addition to this, all attempts must be made to take the college and university to the barrio, whether it be in form of classes giving college credit or community centers financed by the school for the use of community organizations and groups. Also, the barrio must be brought to the campus, whether it be for special programs or ongoing services which the school provides for the people of the barrio. The idea must be made clear to the people of the barrio that they own the schools and the schools and all their resources are at their disposal. The student group must utilize the resources open to the school for the benefit of the barrio at every opportunity. This can be done by hiring more Chicanos to work as academic and non-academic personnel on the campus; this often requires exposure of racist hiring practices now in operation in many colleges and universities. When functions, social or otherwise, are held in the barrio under the sponsorship of the college and university, monies should be spent in the barrio. This applies to hiring Chicano contractors to build on campus, etc. Many colleges and universities have publishing operations which could be forced to accept barrio works for publication. Many other things could be considered in using the resources of the school to the barrio. There are possibilities for using the physical plant and facilities not mentioned here, but this is an area which has great potential.

M.E.Ch.A. in the Barrio

Most colleges in the Southwest are located near or in the same town as a barrio. Therefore, it is the responsibility of M.E.Ch.A. members to establish close working relationships with organizations in the barrio. The M.E.Ch.A. people must be able to take the pulse of the barrio and be able to respond to it. However, M.E.Ch.A. must be careful not to overstep its authority or duplicate the efforts of another organization already in the barrio. M.E.Ch.A. must be able to relate to all segments of the barrio, from the middle-class assimilationists to the *vatos locos*.

Obviously, every barrio has its particular needs, and M.E.Ch.A. people must determine, with the help of those in the barrio, where they can be most effective. There are, however, some general areas which M.E.Ch.A. can involve itself. Some of them are: 1) policing social and governmental agencies to make them more responsive in a humane and dignified way to the people of the barrio; 2) carrying out research on the economic and credit policies of merchants in the barrio and exposing fraudulent and exorbitant establishments; 3) speaking and communicating with junior high and high school students, helping with their projects, teaching them organizational techniques, supporting their actions; 4) spreading the message of the movement by any media available—this means speaking, radio, television, local newspaper, underground paper, poster, art, theaters; in short, spreading propaganda of the Movement; 5) exposing discrimination in hiring and renting practices and many other areas which the student because of his/her mobility, his/her articulation, and his/her vigor should take as his/her responsibility. It may mean at times having to work in conjunction with other organizations. If this is the case and the project is one begun by the other organization, realize that M.E.Ch.A. is there as a supporter and should accept the direction of the group involved. Do not let loyalty to an organization cloud responsibility to a greater force—la Causa.

Working in the barrio is an honor, but is also a right because we come from these people, and as such, mutual respect between the barrio and the college group should be the rule. Understand at the same time, however, that there will initially be mistrust and often envy on the part of some in the barrio for the college student. This mistrust must be broken down by a demonstration of affection for the barrio and La Raza through hard work and dedication. If the approach is one of a dilettante or of a Peace Corps volunteer, the people will know it and act accordingly. If it is merely a cathartic experience to work among the unfortunate in the barrio— stay out.

Of the community, for the community. *Por la Raza habla el espiritu*.

Source: M.E.Ch.A., Pan American University, http://www.panam.edu/orgs/MEChA/st_barbara.html.

350. Excerpts from José Angel Gutiérrez, "Mexicanos Need to Control Their Own Destinies," 1970

The following are excerpts from a speech made on May 4, 1970, in San Antonio, Texas, by José Angel Gutiérrez, (1944–), a founder of the Texas La Raza Unida Party (1970). At the time of the speech he was the newly elected president of the Crystal City school board. Gutiérrez was a student of politics. A 1962 graduate of Crystal City High School in Crystal City, Texas, he worked on the takeover of the Crystal City Council in 1963. He earned a bachelor's, master's, PhD, and JD from Texas A&M University at Kingsville; St. Mary's University in San Antonio, Texas; the University of Texas at Austin; and the University of Houston, Law School, respectively. He co-founded the Mexican American Youth Organization (MAYO) in 1967, Mexican American Unity Council (MAUC) in 1968, and La Raza Unida Party in 1970—just to name a few. Gutiérrez is a respected scholar, having written numerous books and conducted nearly 100 oral interviews with Tejanos (Mexican Texans) during the 1960s and 1970s. The following speech is important because it explains why Chicanos believed they should have their own political party.

As you know, there is a new political party in Southwest Texas. It's called La Raza Unida Party. The history of this party is rather interesting.

For years the Chicano farmworker has made up the majority of the population in the South Texas counties. But he goes trucking across this country on his summer vacation (laughter), and so he's never there to vote. Yet this is precisely the time the primaries are held—in May. And he is already vacationing in his resort area by the time the runoffs are held in June. So, you see, we are in fact not even able to vote.

We have had other problems which we have known about for a long time. For instance, the fact that the Mexicano can't cope with the culture of the monolingual creatures that abound in South Texas. You see, we're literate in Spanish, so we can't recognize the name of John Waltberger on the ballot, but we sure as hell recognize Juan García. (Laughter.)

Supposedly in this kind of a democratic society the citizenry is encouraged to participate in the political process—but not so in South Texas.

Someone asked me recently whether I thought any type of system other than the American political system could work in South Texas. I thought about it for a minute and suggested that the question be reworded because we ought to try the American system first. (Applause.)

They accuse me and Mexicanos in Cristal [Crystal City], in Cotulla and Carrizo Springs, of being unfair. One gringo lady put it very well. She was being interviewed around April 6, right after the school board elections and before the city council elections. The guy from *Newsweek* asked her to explain the strange phenomena that were occurring in these counties: a tremendous voter turnout and a tremendous amount of bloc voting. She said, "Well, this is just terrible! Horrible! A few days ago we elected a bunch of bum Mexicans to the city council." And the reporter said, "Well, they are 85 percent of this county." And she replied, "That's what I mean! They think they ought to run this place!"

By all these little things you can begin to understand how to define the word "gringo," which seems to be such a problem all the time. It's funny, because the Mexicano knows what a gringo is. It's the gringos themselves that are worried about what the hell it is. (Laughter.) Let me elaborate on it.

I'm not going to give you a one-sentence thing on them; I feel they deserve at least two sentences. (Laughter.) The basic idea in using the word "gringo" is that it means "foreigner." The gringos themselves say, "It's Greek to me." So the Mexicano says, "It's griego [Greek] to me." That is one explanation of its origins, according to Professor Americo Paredes of the University of Texas. Another is, of course, the traditional one about the United States troops coming into Mexico with "green coats." The Mexicanos would say, with our own pronunciation, "Here come the 'green coats.'" And there are other explanations.

The word itself describes an attitude of supremacy, of xenophobia—that means you're afraid of strangers. I pick up a fancy word here and there. This attitude is also found in institutions, such as the Democratic Party. It's in policies like the one that says you can't speak Spanish in school because it's un-American. It's in the values of people who feel that unless Mexican music is played by the Tijuana Brass or the Baja Marimba Band it's no good. You can't eat tacos de chorizo [sausage tacos] around the corner for 20 cents. You've got to go up there to La Fonda [fancy Anglo-owned Mexican restaurant] and eat a $3.50 Mexican plate that gives you indigestion. (Applause and laughter.)

The formation of this party came about because of the critical need for the people to experience justice. It's just like being hungry. You've got to get food in there immediately, otherwise you get nauseous, you get headaches and pains in your stomach.

We were Chicanos who were starved for any kind of meaningful participation in decision making, policy making, and leadership positions. For a long time we have not been satisfied with the type of leadership that has been picked for us. And this is what a political party does, particularly the ones we have here. I shouldn't use the plural because we only have one, and that's the gringo party. It doesn't matter what name it goes by. It can be Kellogg's, All-Bran, or Shredded Wheat, but it's still the same crap.

These parties, or party, have traditionally picked our leadership. They have transformed this leadership into a kind of broker, a real estate guy who deals in the number of votes or precincts he can deliver or the geographical areas he can control. And he is a tape recorder—he puts out what the party says.

A beautiful example of this is Ralph Yarborough [Democratic senator from Texas]. The only thing he does for Chicanos is hire one every six years. He's perfectly content with the bigoted sheriff and Captain Allee [Texas Rangers] and the guys that break the strikes in El Rio Grande City and with (Wayne) Connally [brother of former Texas governor John Connally] and all these other people. Well, he gets beaten, and he knows why. The Republicans, the Birchers, the Wallace-ites and all these people went over to support Bentsen in the primaries. Yet I just read in the paper this afternoon that he said, "As always, I will vote a straight Democratic ticket in November."

There is only one other kind of individual who does that kind of work and that's a prostitute....

Four years ago, when the guy who is now running for commissioner in La Salle County in La Raza Unida Party ran in the Democratic primaries, it cost him one-third of his annual income! That's how much it costs a Chicano with a median income of $1,574 per family per year. With the third party, it didn't cost him a cent.

On top of the excessive filing fees, they have set fixed dates for political activity, knowing that we have to migrate to make a living. We are simply not here for the May primaries. Did you know that in Cotulla, Erasmo Andrade [running in the Democratic primary for state senator in opposition to Wayne Connally] lost by over 300 votes because the migrants weren't there? In the Democratic primaries you're not going to cut it. In May there are only 16 more Chicano votes than gringo votes in La Salle County. But in November the margin is two-and-one-half to one in favor of Chicanos.

So you see that what's happening is not any big miracle. It's just common sense. The trouble is that everybody was always bothered and said, "We can't get out of the Democratic Party. Why bite the hand that feeds you?" Well, you bite it because it feeds you slop. (Laughter and applause.) Others say, "Well, why don't you switch over and join the Republican Party?" Well, let's not even touch on that one.

Why can't you begin to think very selfishly as a Chicano? I still haven't found a good argument from anyone as to why we should not have a Chicano party. Particularly when you are the majority. If you want to implement and see democracy in action—the will of the majority—you are not going to do it in the Democratic Party. You can only do it through a Chicano party. (Applause.)

But you see there is another, more important, reason, and that is that Mexicanos need to be in control of their destiny. They need to make their own decisions. We need to make the decisions that are going to affect our brothers and maybe our children. We have been complacent for too long.

Did you know that not one of our candidates in La Salle County had a job the whole time they were running, and that they still can't get jobs? The same thing happened in Dimmit County. In Uvalde this is one of the reasons there's a walkout. They refused to renew the teaching contract of José García, who ran for county judge. That's a hell of a price to pay. But that's the kind of treatment that you've gotten.

You've got a median educational level among Mexicanos in Zavala County of 2.3 grades. In La Salle it's just a little worse—about 1.5 grades.

The median family income in La Salle is $1,574 a year. In Zavala it's about $1,754. The ratio of doctors, the number of newspapers, the health, housing, hunger, malnutrition, illiteracy, poverty, lack of political representation—all these things put together spell one word: colonialism. You've got a handful of gringos controlling the lives of muchos Mexicanos. And it's been that way for a long time.

Do you think things are going to get better by putting faith in the Democratic Party and Bentsen? Or that things are going to get better because you've got a few more Chicanos elected to office now within the traditional parties? Do you think that things are going to get better now that the U.S. Commission on Civil Rights has officially claimed that there is discrimination against Mexicanos? They've finally found out it's for real—we're discriminated against! (Laughter.) Do you think that things are going to get better simply because kids are walking out of schools—kids who can't vote, who in many cases can't convince the community to stand behind them?

No, it's not going to get better. We are going to have to devise some pretty ingenious ways of eliminating these gringos. Yet they don't really have to be too ingenious. All you have to do is go out there and look around and have a little common sense.

It stands to reason that if there are two grocery stores in town and we are the ones who buy from them, then if we stop buying from them they are going to go down. If you talk about transferring the wealth, that's how you do it....

In 1960, there were 26 Texas counties in which Chicanos were a majority, yet not one of those counties was in the control of Chicanos. If you want to stand there and take that you can. You can be perfectly content just like your father and your grandfather were, *con el sombrero en la mano* [with hat in hand].

That's why most of our traditional organizations will sit there and pass resolutions and mouth off at conventions, but they'll never take on the gringo. They'll never stand up to him and say, "Hey, man, things have got to change from now on. *Que pase lo que pase* [Let whatever happens happen]. We've had it long enough!"

This is what we've got to start doing. If you don't go third party, then you've got to go the independent route, because there is no other way you are going to get on the November ballot. And don't try to put in a write-in candidate. That never works....

The recent elections here in April for school board and city council demonstrated something that many people knew was a fact. It was almost like predicting that the sun is going to come up in the morning; if you can count, you know what the results are going to be. But an interesting factor is going to enter in now. We won in an off year in the nonpartisan races, which means that we were able to elect a minority to these positions. So now the establishment has all summer long to figure out how to stop the Maxicano. This is where we get back to the old tricks and lies of the gringo.

They tried the "outside agitator" bit on me but it didn't work because I was born in Crystal City. So they changed gears. Then they tried the "Communist" one for a while-until they found out I was in the U.S. Army Reserves. (Laughter and applause.) Then somewhere they dug up my "kill a gringo" thing of about a year ago when I said that I would kill a gringo in self-defense if I were attacked....

Another lie is the white liberal approach. "I like Mexican food. Oh, I just love it!" And this is the kind of guy who's got the *molcajete* [Aztec mortar and pestle for cooking] sitting as an ash tray in his living room. (Applause and laughter)

This kind of character is the one that cautions you, be careful. Don't be racist in reverse. It's bad enough that gringos don't like 'Meskins' and 'Meskins' don't like gringos. You have to talk things over. You have to turn the other cheek. You've got to be nice. You've got to be polite. You can't use foul language in public. You have to have a constructive program.

They ask us, "What are you going to do for the schools in Crystal City?" And when we answer, "Bring education," they don't know what the hell we're talking about.

You see, that's another thing about the liberal. They always love to make you feel bad. And oh, my God, we hate to hurt the feelings of a good Anglo liberal, don't we? Well, hell, tell them the truth!

We've been hurting for a long time. They think we've got education, but we know different. How come we have 71 percent dropouts in Crystal City? It's miseducation. We ain't got teachers down there, we've got Neanderthals. These are the kinds of problems we are going to be faced with by the time November comes along. But a lot of people ain't going to buy it. The kids in the schools aren't going to stand for it. They see what this whole gringo thing has done to their parents, what it's done to our community, what it's done to our organizations. And nothing is going to prevent them from getting what is due them.

There's no generation gap in Crystal City. To the old people who are experienced this is nothing new. The older people in Crystal City, who have experienced years and years of humiliation and blows to their dignity, know what's going on. There was a problem for a while with the 25- to 45-year-olds who were trying to be gringos. But that's no longer true. You see, those are the parents of these kids, and these kids got their parents straight very early in the game. (Applause.) ...

You know, civil rights are not just for those under 21. They're for everybody—for grandma, for daddy and mama, and *los chamaquitos* [children] and *primos* [cousins] and sisters, and so on. We've all got to work together. That means that all of us have to pitch in. And this is why in Crystal City you no longer hear "Viva La Raza" and "Chicano Power" and "La Raza Unida" all over the place. We don't talk about it anymore because it's a reality. You see, there la familia Mexicana esta organizada [the Mexican family is organized]. Aztlán has begun in the southwest part of Texas. (Prolonged applause.)

Our actions have made "La Raza Unida" more than just a slogan. Beginning with the walkout, we began organizing and moving in to counter-attack every time the gringo tried to put pressure on the Mexicano. Boycott his store. Point the finger at him. Expose him for the animal that he is. Bring in the newspapers and photographers and the tape recorders. Let the world see it....

So don't let anybody kid you. We are the consumers, we are the majority. We can stop anything and we can make anything in South Texas if we stick together and begin using common sense.

This third party is a very viable kind of alternative. It's a solution. For once you can sit in your own courthouse and you don't have to talk about community control because you are the community. And we are not talking about trying to run for Congress because you are sitting on the school board and then four years from now you're going to run for county judge. That's not the name of the game either.

We are talking about bringing some very basic elements into the lives of Mexicanos—like education and like making urban renewal work for Mexicanos instead of being the new way of stealing land. We got screwed once with the Treaty of Guadalupe-Hidalgo and now we're getting it under "Model Cities" and urban renewal. (Applause.)

You can be as imaginative as you want and do almost anything you want once you run units of government. I'll give you an example. Everyone publicizes the fact that the Panthers are feeding kids all over the country. And everybody pours out money at cocktail parties and gets very concerned about little kids eating in the morning.

Well, the gringos in Cristal pulled out another one of their gimmicks and just a few days before the elections they decided to experiment with a pilot program of feeding kids in the morning. It was going to last for six weeks and feed 30 kids. They were going to watch them. They were going to experiment, study, conduct a survey to see if they grew an inch. (Laughter.)

Well, right now in Crystal City any kid who wants to eat can eat. Free breakfast in all the schools. You can do that, you see. You can also be very, very friendly to your opposition. You can rule them out of order when they get out of hand. You can slap them on the hand: "That's a no no!

They can't hold an illegal' meeting like they tried yesterday with the school board while I was out of town. They tried to take advantage of the fact that I was out of town to hold a special meeting. But the law says you must give three days' notice. So the gringos failed in their attempt to hire a principal to their liking. We don't need to be experts in parliamentary procedure. All we have to do is follow the book and tell them, "No, no! You can't do that!" (Laughter and applause.)

Let me be serious for a few minutes, because I think we have laughed enough. Mario was talking about having a third party in Bexar County by 1972. Good luck, Mario. (Applause.)

It doesn't matter if you don't agree with MAYO because this thing is no longer just MAYO. The response that we've had to this third party in all sections of our communities has been overwhelming. You saw the results. You can count votes just as I did.

The third party is not going to get smaller. It's going to get bigger.

You have three choices. First, you can be very active in this thing. For once we are not talking about being anti-Democrat or pro-Republican or pro-Democrat and anti-Republican. We are talking about being for La Raza, the majority of the people in South Texas. So there are a lot of things you can do and be very actively involved in.

If you don't choose that route, you can stay home and watch baseball and just come out and vote. But otherwise stay home. Don't get in the way.

The third thing you can do is lend your support, your general agreement. Often we are too critical of ourselves, and the gringo misunderstands that. He says, "You're disorganized, there's no unity among you." Hell, he can't understand an honest discussion when he hears one.

So, you've got these three roles that you can play. Or you can get very, very defensive and say, "This is wrong, this is un-American because you're bloc voting." But don't forget that the Democrats do it too. You can say that this is racism in reverse, but don't forget that we are the majority. And you can say that this is going to upset the whole situation in the state of Texas because we will never be able to elect a senator, because we're segregating ourselves and cutting ourselves apart and that this is not what we should be trying to do, that we should be trying to integrate, etc., etc. Well, before you go on your warpath or campaign, come down and tell that to my sheriff. Tell him how much you like him. Or, better yet, move on down the road a bit and tell it to Ranger Allee himself.

Build your constituency; build your community—that's how we will be electing three and possibly four congressmen in the very near future. There's going to be another congressman in Bexar County, and there's not room for all of them on the North side [Anglo section of San Antonio]. (Laughter and applause.) So we have some very interesting developments coming up.

To the gringos in the audience, I have one final message to convey: Up yours, baby. You've had it, from now on. (Standing ovation.)

Source: José Angel Gutiérrez at UCLA, clnet.ucla.edu/research/docs/razaunida/control.htm.

351. Excerpt from Ernesto B. Vigil, *The Crusade for Justice: Chicano Militancy and the Government's War on Dissent*, 1999

Ernesto Vigil refused induction into the military forces in 1968 during the Vietnam War. Other Chicanos like Sijisfredo Avilés (1968) from Chicago who served three years in jail; Rosalio Muñoz (1969) from Los Angeles, California; and Sal Baldenegro (1968) from Tucson, Arizona; refused induction. Ernesto had joined the Crusade for Justice (Denver, Colorado) as a teenager in 1968, and was heavily involved in civil rights causes. The following excerpt from his book *The Crusade for Justice: Chicano Militancy and the Government's War on Dissent*, gives his side of the story. Vigil helped redefine the words *patriotism* and *valor*.

RESISTING THE DRAFT: "COURTS OF LAW, NOT OF JUSTICE"

In November 1967, the author dropped out of Vermont's Goddard College and moved to Philadelphia for a short time. One consequence of leaving college was losing the deferment from military service that college students then enjoyed. I read of the indictment of Dr. Benjamin Spock, a renowned pediatrician, for urging youths to resist the draft, and in January 1968, I mailed my draft card to the Denver office of the Selective Service System. The draft card was accompanied by a poem composed for me by a hippie friend, and a letter I myself wrote on my twentieth birthday. It stated: I hereby submit my draft card as a gesture of my dissatisfaction and disaffection for the social, governmental, and political system of this nation. This is the gesture of a free person with a free will and should be understood as such for it is also a token of my determination to remain so. My country is not my god; I will—and must—first serve the dictates of my mind, heart, and conscience. There are laws and values that are higher than those of this nation's government, and sometimes these come from the conscience of one lone individual: they cannot be legislated by politicians, nor enforced by policemen and soldiers. In this belief I now state that I will not fight the war of a power and system that I feel is unjust, hypocritical, deceitful, inadequate, and detrimental to the happiness and best interests of its own people and the people of the other nations of the world....

Source: Ernesto B. Vigil, *The Crusade for Justice*. © 1999. Reprinted by permission of The University of Wisconsin Press. p. 73.

352. Excerpts from Herman Baca, "The Day the Police Rioted! Remembering 32 Years Ago," August 15, 2002

Herman Baca (1943–) has been at the forefront of organizing efforts in the barrio (neighborhood) in National City, San Diego County. He has worked closely with many of the leading figures of the Chicano movement, including

César Chávez, Dolores Huerta, Reies López Tijerina, Rodolfo Corky Gonzales, and others. He was a prime mover of the Mexican American Political Association (MAPA), established in 1959 to politically organize Mexican Americans, and later an organizer with La Raza Unida political party during the early 1970s. He was the founder and president of the San Diego-based Committee on Chicano Rights, which focuses on abuses toward undocumented Mexican immigrants. Baca had been at the forefront of the protection of the foreign born. The following passage talks about what he saw on August 29, 1970, during the largest Chicano anti-war protest to that date.

In 1970, I was 27 years of age, married, had two children, and was a printer. I had been politically involved in the Chicano movement for 2 years and was president of the National City chapter of MAPA. My involvement up to that point had been in organizing protests for the boycott of grapes in support of the United Farm Workers [UFW], working on local issues (police brutality, immigration, zoning, youth) and electoral politics....

Chicanos, at that time comprised but 6% of this nation's population, but made up 20% of the causalities in Vietnam! Young whites started to receive college deferments, and white controlled draft boards begin to draft (in record numbers) poor people, blacks, and especially Chicanos for Vietnam.

After five years of war, reality finally hit home. Young Chicanos were dying in obscene numbers, and numerous "body bags" carrying young dead Chicanos were being returned to the homes of grieving families throughout the U.S....

August 29, 1970, finally arrived, we (three other individuals and myself) arrived in Los Angeles on Saturday morning around 7:00 A.M. The first thing I witnessed, was something that I had never seen before. Thousands upon thousands of Chicanos from all over the U.S., some from New Mexico, Texas, Colorado, Arizona, and the Midwest, who had all gathered for a political event. Five hundred to one thousand persons from San Diego attended the demonstration.

The demonstration turned out to be the largest protest to be organized by Chicanos in their 130 years' history as a conquered people in the U.S.

I remember that the march started late (around 10:00 or 11:00 A.M.), and that it was a very hot day. As we walked, some people were behind the banner of the Virgin de Guadalupe; others carried MAPA, brown berets, M.E.Ch.A., Crusade for Justice, UFW, etc., banners. We all walked in unity, and I felt that most of us were marching to end a war that was destroying our most precious heritage—our youth....

While waiting, I asked a friend if he wanted to go and get something to drink. We journeyed to a liquor store by the park and while there we noticed that some individuals were leaving the store without paying for their merchandise. As we traveled back, I remember pointing out to my friend that hundreds of sheriffs and police officers were stationed across the street on Whittier Blvd. Being naive, both of us though it odd, but not threatening [so we] continued into the park.

As we sat down we heard and then saw a commotion coming from the direction where we had just left. We could see that the sheriff and police were starting to line up. Suddenly, without any provocation, the sheriff and police began to advance on the peaceful crowd. At the time, most of the crowd, which was in front of the park, had absolutely no idea or knowledge of what was happening.

At one point, security (the Brown Berets) rushed forward and attempted to explain to the police that everything was under control. But it was no use; a full-fledged instigated police riot was now under way. The Brown Berets were attacked and beaten.

As the police advanced, I witnessed scenes that I will never forget. Before my eyes, hundreds of our people, children, woman, young and old persons were being beaten, tear gassed, maimed, and arrested.

The police and sheriff's deputies appeared to be totally out of control and crazed with a desire to hurt, maim, and kill Chicanos.

Many of us remembered the Zoot Suit riots, and it was 1940 all over again!

In self-defense Chicanos, witnessing what was happening, and suffering from 130 years of oppression, racism, and discrimination stood up, and fought back.

I remember at one point the bright sky suddenly turning black because of the number of objects that were being thrown back at the police. People were throwing bottles, cans, dirt, sticks, and anything they could get their hands on to protect themselves.

People were mad and there was fierce hand-to-hand fighting. Young Chicanos were going up to the police, landing one good body blow knowing that the police would immediately club them down. a lot of people were being maced, beaten, and arrested.

Source: "The Day the Police Rioted! Remembering 32 Years Ago!" Herman Baca Committee on Chicano Rights. National City, California August 15, 2002. Courtesy Herman Baca Archives, Mandeville Special Collections Library, University of California, San Diego, http://orpheus.ucsd.edu/speccoll/esting/htm;/mss0649a.html.

353. Excerpts from Congressman Henry B. González's Congressional Speech of April 22, 1969

In the following excerpts, Texas Congressman Henry B. González expresses doubts about the tactics of Chicano youth. Up to this point, González had been considered a liberal and a maverick of sorts. Elected to Congress in the late 1950s, he had sponsored and supported civil rights legislation. However, González disagreed with the confrontational tactics of the Mexican American Youth Organization (MAYO) and labeled them chauvinistic and accused the organization of bigotry. Many Chicano youth responded by labeling González's statement "red baiting," pointing out that he had congressional immunity to misrepresent.

I, and many other residents of my part of Texas and other Southwestern States—happen to be what is commonly referred to as a Mexican American.... What is he to be? Mexican? American? Both? How can he choose? Should he have pride and joy in his heritage, or bear it as a shame and sorrow? Should he live in one world or another, or attempt to bridge them both?

There is comfort in remaining in the closed walls of a minority society, but this means making certain sacrifices; but it sometimes seems disloyal to abandon old ideas and old friends; you never know whether you will be accepted or rejected in the larger world, or whether your old friends will despise you for making a wrong choice. For a member of this minority, like any other, life begins with making hard choices about personal identity. These lonely conflicts are magnified in the social crises so clearly evident all over the Southwest today. There are some groups who demand brown power, some who display a curious chauvinism, and some who affect the other extreme. There is furious debate about what one should be and what one should do.... I understand all this, but I am profoundly distressed by what I see happening today.... Mr. Speaker, the issue at hand in this minority group today is hate, and my purpose in addressing the House is to state where I stand: I am against hate and against the spreaders of hate; I am for justice, and for honest tactics in obtaining justice.

The question facing the Mexican American people today is what do we want, and how do we get it?

What I want is justice. By justice I mean decent work at decent wages for all who want work; decent support for those who cannot support themselves; full and equal opportunity in employment, in education, in schools; I mean by justice the full, fair, and impartial protection of the law for every man; I mean by justice decent homes, adequate streets, and public services....

I do not believe that justice comes only to those who want it; I am not so foolish as to believe that good will alone achieves good works. I believe that justice requires work and vigilance, and I am willing to do that work and maintain that vigilance....

It may well be that I agree with the goals stated by militants; but whether I agree or disagree, I do not now, nor have I ever believed that the end justifies the means, and I condemn those who do. I cannot accept the belief that racism in reverse is the answer for racism and discrimination; I cannot accept the belief that simple, blind, and stupid hatred is an adequate response to simple, blind, and stupid hatred; I cannot accept the belief that playing at revolution produces anything beyond an excited imagination; and I cannot accept the belief that imitation leadership is a substitute for the real thing. Developments over the past few months indicate that there are those who believe that the best answer for hate is hate in reverse, and that the best leadership is that which is loudest and most arrogant; but my observation is that arrogance is no cure for emptiness.

All over the Southwest, new organizations are springing up; some promote pride in heritage, which is good, but others promote chauvinism, which is not; some promote community organization, which is good, but some promote race tension and hatred, which is not good; some seek redress of just grievances, which is good, but others seek only opportunities for self aggrandizement, which is not good....

Unfortunately, it seems that in the face of rising hopes and expectations among Mexican Americans there are more leaders with political ambitions at heart than there are with the interests of the poor at heart; they do not care what is accomplished in fact, as long as they can create and ride the winds of protest as far as possible. Thus, we have those who play at revolution, those who make speeches but do not work, and those who imitate what they have seen others do, but lack the initiative and imagination to set forth actual programs for progress....

Not long after the Southwest Council of La Raza opened for business, it gave $110,000 to the Mexican American Unity Council of San Antonio; this group was apparently invented for the purpose of receiving the grant. Whatever the purposes of this group may be, thus far it has not given any assistance that I know of to bring anybody together; rather it has freely dispensed funds to people who promote the rather odd and I might say generally unaccepted and unpopular views of its directors. The Mexican American Unity Council appears to specialize in creating still other organizations and equipping them with quarters, mimeograph machines, and other essentials of life. Thus, the "unity council" has created a parents' association in a poor school district, a neighborhood council, a group known as the Barrios Unidos—or roughly, united neighborhoods—a committee on voter registration and has given funds to the militant Mexican American Youth Organization (MAYO); it has also created a vague entity known as the "Universidad de los Barrios" which is a local gang operation. Now, assuredly all these efforts may be well intended; however it is questionable to my mind that a very young and inexperienced man can prescribe the social and political organizations of a complex and troubled community; there is no reason whatever to believe that for all the money this group has spent, there is any understanding of what it is actually being spent for, except to employ friends of the director and advance his preconceived notions. The people who are to be united apparently don't get much say in what the "unity council" is up to....

Militant groups like MAYO regularly distribute literature that I can only describe as hate sheets, designed to inflame passions and reinforce old wounds or open new ones; these sheets spew forth racism and hatred designed to do no man good. The practice is defended as one that will build race pride, but I never heard of pride being built on spleen.

Source: Congressional Record, 91st Cong., 1st Sess., April 22, 1969, in *Mexican American Voices*, http://www.digitalhistory.uh.edu.

354. Excerpts from MAYO document on Student Walkouts, Crystal City, Texas, 1973

MAYO, the Mexican American Youth Organization, was formed in 1967 as an organization to fight for the civil rights of Mexican Americans. Founded by José Angel Gutiérrez (1944–), Willie C. Velásquez (1944–1988), Mario Compeán, and others in San Antonio, Texas, the organization was dedicated to the planned transformation of the situation Mexicans faced in Texas. MAYO members were key to the formation of La Raza Unida Party, which was organized because neither the Democrats nor Republicans were addressing Chicano issues or running Chicano candidates. Willie Velásquez later founded the Southwest Voters Registration and Education Project (1972), which led national registration drives—literally registering hundreds of thousands of Latinos. MAYO led at least 18 school walkouts throughout Texas. The major walkouts were in Crystal City, Kingsville, Edgewood, and Lanier High Schools in San Antonio. Gutiérrez and his wife Luz moved back to Crystal City specifically to plan a political takeover of the city. The following excerpts are from Gutiérrez on the walkouts.

The Crystal City, Texas, school walkouts organized by MAYO in 1969–1970 precipitated other Chicano Movement activity in the Winter Garden District, such as the rise of La Raza Unida Party. Below are the demands that MAYO organizers and their local supporters, known as the Ciudadanos Unidos, wanted school administrators to concede before they would call off the strike and return to classes. The detailed set of demands required that the school board allow greater input from the Chicano community in order to insure, among other things, that students would be less subject to discrimination and that course content would reflect the needs of the Mexican American majority in Crystal City.

WALKOUT DEMANDS

Walkout demands were that all elections concerning the school be conducted by the student body. Concerning class representatives, the petition asked that the qualifications such as personality, leadership, and grades be abolished. These factors do not determine whether the student is capable of representing the student body. The students are capable of voting for their own representatives. The representatives are representing the students, not the faculty. All nominating must be done by the student body, and the election should be decided by a majority vote.

The present method of electing the most handsome, beautiful, most popular, and most representative is elected [sic] by the faculty. The method of cumulative voting is unfair.

National Honor Society—the grades of the students eligible must be posted on the bulletin board well in advance of selection. The teachers should not have anything to do with electing the students.

An advisory board of Mexican American citizens should be a part of the school administration in order to advise on the needs and problems of the Mexican American.

No other favorites should be authorized by school administrators or board members unless submitted to the student body in a referendum.

Teachers, administrators, and staff should be educated; they should know our language—Spanish—and understand the history, traditions, and contributions of Mexican culture. How can they expect to teach us if they do not know us? We want more Mexican American teachers for the above reason.

We want immediate steps taken to implement bilingual and bicultural education for Mexican Americans. We also want the schoolbooks revised to reflect the contributions of Mexicans and Mexican Americans to the U.S. society, and to make us aware of the injustices that we, Mexican Americans, as a people have suffered in an "Anglo" dominant society. We want a Mexican American course with the value of one credit.

We want any member of the school system who displays prejudice or fails to recognize, understand, and appreciate us, Mexican Americans, our culture, or our heritage removed from Crystal City's schools. Teachers shall not call students any names.

Our classes should be smaller in size, say about twenty students to one teacher, to insure more effectiveness. We want parents from the community to be trained as teachers' aides. We want assurances that a teacher who may disagree politically or philosophically with administrators will not be dismissed or transferred because of it. Teachers should encourage students to study and should make class more interesting, so that students will look forward to going to class....

There should be a manager in charge of janitorial work and maintenance details, and the performance of such duties should be restricted to employees hired for that purpose. In other words, no more students doing janitorial work.

We want a free speech area plus the right to have speakers of our own.

We would like September 16 as a holiday, but if it is not possible, we would like an assembly with speakers of our own. We feel it is a great day in the history of the world because it is when Mexico had been under the Spanish rule for about three hundred years. The Mexicans were liberated from the harsh rule of Spain. Our ancestors fought in this war, and we owe them tribute because we are Mexicans, too.

Being civic-minded citizens, we want to know what the happenings are in our community. So, we request the right to have access to all types of literature and to be able to bring it on campus. The newspaper in our school does not carry sufficient information. It carries things like the gossip column, which is unnecessary.

The dress code should be abolished. We are entitled to wear what we want. We request the buildings open to students at all times.

We want Mr. Harbin to resign as principal of Fly Jr. High.

We want a Mexican American counselor fully qualified in college opportunities. We need more showers in the boys' and girls' dressing rooms.

Source: "MAYO document, José Angel Gutiérrez files, Crystal City, Texas, 1973" is reprinted with permission of the publisher of *Testimonio: A Documentary History of the Mexican American Struggle for Civil Rights*, F. Arturo Rosales, ed. (Houston: Arte Público Press—University of Houston © 2000), pp. 387–388.

355. José Angel Gutiérrez, "Oral History Interview with Viviana Santiago Cavada," 1998

Vivian Santiago was one of dozens of young volunteers that migrated to Crystal City, Texas, in the late 1960s/early 1970s. She had been active in the Mexican American Youth Organization (MAYO), an organization mostly of Chicano college and high school students; La Raza Unida Party, organized to represent Chicano issues and elect Chicano candidates; and other activist groups. In Crystal City she headed the *Voluntarios de Aztlán* (Volunteers of Aztlán) and was elected to the school board. The following are excerpts from an interview taken by José Angel Gutiérrez telling about how Santiago became an activist and got involved in Chicano politics. Viviana is today an attorney.

Ms. Cavada: Father, Jorge Antolin Santiago, … born and raised in Santa Isabel, Puerto Rico … My mother was born and raised in Gonzalez, Texas. My, grandfather on my mother's side was from the Candelaria clan in New Mexico and Spain, and on her mother's side it's Indian, Maya, Plata, Mexico.…

I was a school teacher … during the Kingsville … walkout. And what I … [signed] a petition supporting the walkout in Kingsville while I was a teacher … I had a bunch of teachers from, the Eagle Pass Independent School District sign the petition. There were about twenty three teachers … I didn't think anything of it … we participated in that march [the twenty three teachers] … in Del Rio. We took a whole delegation. But [there was] … an uproar.… I got in trouble with the administration … and they told me that they were not renewing my contract because … this petition I had circulated and sent to Kingsville. I guess they made a big deal about teachers supporting … the walkout.… I got harassed. The … assistant principal called me in, a guy named Masters, a gringo, he says, "What do you people want anyway?" "And I said, '"You people?"'" So, we got into it and it was not a very nice thing … they did not renew my contract.… It was before the MAYO convention of

December of '69. I kept on looking for another job everywhere, but it wasn't until I went to Premont, Premont ISD [Independent School District]. They were interested in hiring me.

[She is called back and the superintendent says] "I'm sorry we can't hire you." ... you know, the thing in Del Rio, all the people, and also the petition, you know, that everybody had signed, all the teachers had signed. And he said, he looked at me and he says, "Look, I really like you. I really would like to hire you. But," he says, "Don't even try to apply in any school district in Texas ... You will not get hired...."

[Santiago went work with Project SER.] It was a really good program, A jobs ... program, but half the board was G.I. Forum, half the board was LULAC.... Willie Bonilla ... was on the board ... [he] said, "Don't go to that MAYO convention or you won't have a job." So we went anyway. The three of us. And when we came back they got rid of, they got rid of me at this board meeting. And they said, "Well, the reason that we have to let Viviana go is because she was never really hired." Wait. Back then I was Vivian, OK, Santiago. I did not become Viviana until I went to Crystal City, Texas, and José Angel named me Viviana. Even though my mother, my grandmother always called me Viviana, my grandparents, my aunts, and uncles, I was Viviana to them.... I went and visited [Bonilla] ... in his law office and I said, "Why are you doing this? Why are you, why are you so against us having gone to the ... the MAYO convention?" ... I had no place else to go. But I really wanted to go to Crystal City and they were asking for Voluntarios de Aztlán (Volunteers of Aztlán) [a project run by La Raza Unida]. And I said, "That's fine. I can live with...." My car payments back then were thirty five to fifty dollars a month, so I figured I can go do that. I can be teaching at their walkout, you know. I can, you know, I can do anything and, and, and as a *Voluntaria* (Volunteer) and a minimum of a hundred a month. So, I called you and I said, "I need at least a hundred a month." And you said, "Don't worry about it. We'll find you a place to stay. You don't have to pay for your room and board, you know. We're going to help you out." And so, I went. And it was great.

Didn't get a hundred a month but I did get a place to stay. And the credit union was very lax on my payments, you know. So what I did was I tried to generate my own, my own work, my own income. So, I started writing proposals and finally did get some money in for me. And, and of course, for the community. And that was with the Presbyterian Church, the Women of the Church United came in with a grant. They called it, we called it, the Border Project....

Source: Oral History Interview with Viviana Cavada, 1998 by José Angel Gutiérrez. CMAS No. 66, University of Texas Arlington.

356. Excerpts from H. Joaquín Jackson and David Marion Wilkinson, *One Ranger: A Memoir*, 2005

Joaquín Jackson's career as a Texas Ranger, which was controlling Mexicans, stretched from 1966 to 1993. He has been called the icon of the modern Texas Rangers, heralded by white Texans and hated and feared by Mexicans. He followed the legendary and cruel Ranger Capt. Alfred Y. Allee, Sr., who is remembered by many Mexicans as a Gestapo captain. The following excerpts from Jackson's book give insights into La Raza Unida Party and the reaction to its taking power. It puts a human face on the Rangers.

I spent a few days piecing together all the information I could about the crime. When I knew who I wanted and where they'd fled I drove down to inform my captain, who was probably hosing off the latest coat of Chicano militant José Angel Gutiérrez's urine from the Ranger Company D sign. (These two political adversaries were locked into a dance of mutual scorn and confrontation that included Gutiérrez's pissing on the sign to provoke Captain Allee. It usually worked.)

By then I was already mighty fond of Capt. Allee. He'd lived long enough to see the world of South Texas that had spawned him reinvent itself. Toward the end of his career, he couldn't understand the changes swirling around him. Capt. Allee was sixty-two in 1967 (although no one knew for sure); however, he was still all man and in firm command of his company. After I'd spent twenty-four hours with that man, I would have followed him into hell with a hotdog. I don't know a single Ranger who served under Capt. Allee and didn't respect and admire him. But me? I came to love him like the father I lost to the Depression and to the great drought of the 1950s.

THE RECONQUEST OF AZTLÁN: AN ANGEL ON MY ASS

What I remember most about that warm November evening is the shouting. I hear angry voices threatening me and every other law enforcement and voting official ensconced in the Zavala County courthouse. A mass of Mexican Americans—most on foot, but a few idling in battered Chevrolet Impalas and Ford Falcons and a '50s-vintage Dodge pickup-swirls around us. People who used to be migrant workers have turned into militants. White-haired women, the wind tugging at the scarves around their heads, offer fresh *frijoles* wrapped in homemade tortillas to their friends to stave off the chill. A few cowboy hats dot the heads of *viejos*, but I see far more bandanas and baseball caps in that mass of T-shirts and unbuttoned flannels. Beneath their Mexican wedding shirts, some of the young, hard-eyed men have pistols stuffed into their jeans waistbands. If things don't go right tonight, lots of folks are going to get hurt.

Inside the courthouse, Anglos thump their #2 pencil erasers against tally pages as they stare at padlocked precinct boxes. Camel cigarettes burn down. Smoke hangs heavy in the air and black coffee cools in untouched Styrofoam cups. The election officials, along with the entire Mexican American community of Zavala County, know those boxes are crammed full with ballots marked in favor of La Raza Unida Party candidates.

I watch the anguished expressions of the Anglo election judges, county commissioners, sheriff, police chiefs, and politicos as they deliberate the dilemma before them in silence. They're wondering if they can do what they've always done. Maybe the storm outside will blow over. Or maybe this is the moment when nearly 150 years of unchallenged Anglo rule of South Texas crumbles. None of us in authority knows how we got here. We all understand very well, however, that we have just stepped into unknown territory, the cusp of change. Staring at those ballot boxes and all those troubled expressions, I understand that we have to make the right decision or many innocent and not-so-innocent people could die together on the segregated streets of Crystal City. We need to do the right thing. I'm not sure that we're capable of doing that.

Now I hear the amplified voice of one handsome, gifted, resourceful, intensely motivated, and very angry man—José Angel Gutiérrez. I don't know him. We met for the first time this morning soon after the precincts opened. But he's fairly certain he knows me. To him, I am *el Rinche,* Mexican slang for a Texas Ranger ever since the war of 1848, the embodiment of Anglo oppression, a man authorized to crack his head wide open if he doesn't obey the law. In fact, Gutiérrez not only knows that I'm mentally and physically able and thoroughly trained to gain compliance by whatever means necessary, he expects me to shove the law aside whenever it suits me and enforce the status quo.

For this young Chicano militant, obeying Anglo law lies at the root of his people's problems. The law is the means by which the American system has excluded an entire ethnic group of citizens. He and his organizers have gone to some trouble to qualify Mexican American candidates for this fall's ballot and then register thousands of Mexican Americans to vote for them. In other words, they are using the democratic system to gain a voice in how they are governed.

But should that effort fail tonight and yet another election be stolen from them, I know their frustration will escalate into outrage, and then violence. The pistols tucked into their pants are just the beginning. There are shotguns and rifles stowed in their vehicles. They are ready to confront violence with violence. This demonstration is not the end of a contested, highly emotional election. It is a gathering of kindling awaiting the first spark of civil war—the Texas outbreak of the racial bloodshed we've seen in Chicago, Watts, and Montgomery, and throughout the Deep South after Martin Luther King's assassination. Tonight the battle for civil rights in America has clawed its way to my home.

The protestors wave banners that read *No hay nada que Dios no pueda realizar* ("There is nothing that God can't make happen") and *Viva La Raza.* They march and shout slogans as they idle in their cars, waiting for us to announce the election's outcome. And so there I stand, the man who's always said that politics and law enforcement don't mix, between the Mexican American people of my jurisdiction, whom I've sworn to protect, and their Anglo authorities, whom I've sworn to support but who are, the sheriff included, likely about to be voted out of office. Tonight they're at each other's throats.

The city police officers, who have no riot training, are so outnumbered that it wouldn't matter if they had mastered crowd control. The sheriff's deputies suffer from the same limitations, only their situation is further complicated because they are loyal to a boss who's going to need a new job. Due to numerous escalating confrontations between city and county authorities and the Chicano population of Crystal City, much bad blood flows between them. Many of the Mexican American police officers and sheriff's deputies are more loyal to their families and their neighbors than to the badge. There is only one neutral law enforcement official—only one Ranger.

Before this protest escalates into a violent confrontation, I'm going to surprise Gutiérrez and every disenfranchised Mexican American Texan he represents. I'm going to expect him and everyone else in this county to abide by the law. Gutiérrez didn't see that coming. No one else did, either. It's a simple issue, really. And it will change life in this brushy part of the world forever.

As with most of the broader events that occurred when I was a Ranger, the cause of this clamor reaches back into history. To understand what was happening in 1972, you have to consider the social structure of South Texas that evolved after San Jacinto.

It's no secret that the settlement of Texas involved cultures in perpetual conflict. It seems that neither the Anglos nor Mexican (Tejano) people were blessed with a tolerance of the other's traits and reputations. Even their table manners appalled one another. Furthermore, open-mindedness was a worthless virtue when it came to survival on the northern Mexican frontier. Resourcefulness and blind determination offered more utility in an era when the daily struggle for survival granted little time for reflecting on the cultural assimilation already in progress around them. Hard lives; tough, aggressive people. Narrow minds.

The Anglo pioneers were notorious for setting aside their Protestant teachings when it came to their relationships with people of darker skin. They saw no reason to alter their convictions and prejudices as they crossed the Sabine River into the Mexican state of Coahuila y Tejas. Ignoring the mixed nature of their own ancestry, they quietly subordinated the mestizos upon first encounter. The thousands of Anglos who entered Mexico during the Empresario era without the proper documentation, by the way, were known derisively as "wetbacks."

If nothing else, however, the land ultimately bound these reluctant neighbors to one another. Although there were conflicts and misunderstandings, the first Anglo settlers in Texas lived amicably with the Mexican *norteños, 108 Tejanos.* Until the Texas Revolt of 1836, the social scheme was working peacefully, especially as Anglos discovered that they had little choice but to adopt time-proven Mexican methods of land use and animal husbandry, and their aggressive self-protection against the Plains Indian tribes.

Anglo and Tejano fought and died together in the joint revolt against the dictator Santa Anna, who had usurped the Mexican Constitution of 1824. On the other hand, many Texas Anglos (especially those who had lived in Texas the longest and had the most to lose) supported Santa Anna's regime during the Texas revolution. The Texas War for Independence was a complex, multicultural, regional struggle against an oppressive regime, a remote theater of the civil war already raging between the centralist and federalist factions in Mexico.

After San Jacinto, the infant Republic of Texas lured thousands of Anglo settlers in search of cheap land and unbounded opportunity. These people, who had no idea about the value of Mexican culture and no inclination whatsoever to experience it, viewed Tejanos—and all Mexicans—as a vanquished and inferior race, a shiftless breed entirely capable of what they considered to be the massacres at the Alamo and Goliad. The hard lines thus drawn, Tejanos who had lived in this country for a century or more found themselves excluded from the nation that they had helped to build.

This tragic occurrence was compounded after the Mexican War of 1848, when thousands of Mexicans were stranded behind the borders of a new nation that wanted little to do with them. The Mexican Americans of Texas were never slaves, but the social structure forced upon them by the Anglo majority rendered them little more than serfs—the condition that had first propelled millions of the Americas' European immigrants to the New World. Tejanos were politically, socially, and economically sterilized because Anglo Texas society believed they deserved it. Even more arrogant was the prevailing notion that Mexican Americans were better off in segregated Texas than in Mexico.

This wound festered for decades. Anglo and Mexican American alike were born into such a system and generally accepted it. Anglo landowners, farmers, ranchers, professionals, and businessmen who created unchallenged feudal estates in the fertile farm and lush ranch country of South Texas were keen to maintain the status quo.

But the Mexican Americans were reduced to poverty, humiliation, institutional-ized ignorance, and government-sanctioned apathy. Today, we recognize this as rac-ism. A decade ago, it was known as apartheid. For generations of South Texans, however, it was just the way it was. Lots of folks probably didn't think twice about it. Those of us with a conscience knew it wasn't right. But none of us knew what to do about it.

In the early 1960s, José Angel Gutiérrez emerged from the barrios of Crystal City with a vision for his people. He told them that the American Southwest had once been *Aztlán,* originally homeland of Mesheeca—the warrior nation misnamed by the Spanish as the Aztecs. Today geographers and cartographers believe the heart of the Mesheeca's earliest empire ranged from beyond Texas to somewhere in Utah. Gutierrez's general concept however, reminded Mexican Americans that their ancestors had been the masters of their domain. He looked around and realized that they didn't need guns or armies to win this inevitable battle. The secret to recon-quering Aztlán lay in the democratic power to vote.

I've never come close to agreeing with Gutiérrez's controversial politics, but I can tell you that he's one of the most interesting men I've ever met. I'll probably argue with him until my last breath, but I'll always admire him.

José Angel Gutiérrez's father rode with Pancho Villa. The story goes that José Gutiérrez was a young medical student at the outbreak of the Mexican Revolution. Villa basically impressed into service an entire class of reluctant medical students as physicians for his troops.

While I couldn't speculate on medical student José Gutiérrez's political convic-tions, it appears that he gradually fell under Villa's spell and fought against the Mex-ican Government for close to twenty years. He lived through several battles and several wives, rose in the military and political arenas, and was appointed *coman-dante* of Torreon, Coahuila. He earned the trust of Torreon's citizens, who ultimately elected him as their mayor. At last Villa was murdered, and in 1929, young Dr. Gutiérrez was exiled north of the Rio Bravo for the rest of his life.

Dr. Gutiérrez took his fifth wife, Concepcíon Fuentes, and opened a medical practice in Crystal City. A gifted and passionate speaker, he traveled the Rio Grande valley cities lecturing on such topics as "The Price of Honor" and "The Art of Love." Among the Mexican American community he so often inspired, Dr. Gutiérrez was depicted in the flyers that advertised his appearances as *"el pico de oro,"* the mouth of gold.

Dr. Gutiérrez's interests, passions, and loyalty lay across the river in Mexico. Well advanced in age when his fifth wife gave birth to her first and only son, he passed away before the boy reached his thirteenth birthday. "Make sure they bury me in Mexico," would be among his last words to his child.

José Angel Gutiérrez had enjoyed a privileged life as long as his father lived. The community Dr. Gutiérrez cared for showed their appreciation in daily gestures—few pesos here, fresh tamales there, *gracias a su padre* heard everywhere. The boy was welcomed in Anglo-owned stores and restaurants where no other Mexican American dared set foot. He could even bill his purchases to his father's account.

Young José Angel was sent, as a learning experience, to wash dishes for twenty cents an hour in the bleak *bracero* camp operated by the California Packing Corp., which later evolved into Del Monte. He rode the truck to the fields with the migrant workers at four in the morning, seven days a week, observing the bare conditions of the laborers' clapboard barracks and outdoor privies, the American diet forced on people who detested it, the dismally low wages, and the transience of their mean employment. The workers were not even welcome at the local Catholic mass. After his father passed on, José Angel Gutiérrez was not simply exposed to this life of segregation, he was sentenced, along with all of his kind, to live it.

The Jim Crow social structure of Crystal City was typical of its time.

The Mexican American community faced three basic employment options: the Del Monte cannery, local ranches, or seasonal work on farms up north. All paid a low hourly wage. Close to a thousand households earned less than $3,000 annually, the poverty level for a family of four at the time. More than half the Chicano families did not have a toilet, and a third had no indoor plumbing. One section of town had no access to city water or sewage. The streets of Anglo neighborhoods were meticulously maintained while the barrio roads were left unpaved. There were Anglo-only days at the public swimming pool—when the water was freshest.

Those of Gutiérrez's community who wanted to vote for candidates promising change, up until 1966, first had to pay a $1.75 poll tax. For most, the privilege to vote for Anglo Democrats was hardly worth the effort or the expense. This was the "separate but equal" world that bred José Angel Gutiérrez.

The Texas public school system would not allow him to speak his parents' native language. The history and social studies curriculum ignored his ancestors' contributions. Mexican American kids were excluded from sports teams and cheerleading squads and "most beautiful" elections. José Angel Gutiérrez, son of a revolutionary, had his nose rubbed in all of this. When he came of age, it became his turn to rebel.

Gutiérrez possessed a number of attributes that served him well when came time to confront Anglo authority. He radiated cunning, resourcefulness, intelligence, and charisma. A tireless worker and a gifted, passionate speaker, he was further armed with the conviction that he was right.

José Angel quickly established himself among Mexican Americans and Anglos alike as a leader *con huevos*, a force to be reckoned with—and, for some, to be feared. Among whites he was considered a militant and even a Communist; for Mexican Americans he was a hero....

Everyone sensed the tension. Before daylight, I was cruising between my home in Uvalde and Crystal City, the epicenter of the burgeoning La Raza Unida Party and the most likely scene of violence in the 1972 county elections. Upon arrival, I idled around each of the six or so voting precincts in Zavala County to make sure everything was in order and that there was no improper electioneering in progress.

Things seemed quiet as I made small talk with the chain-smoking election judges and their clerks. They were anxious about how the day would go. It was rumored that some La Raza Unida activists were prepared to shoot it out, but officials remained hopeful that the voting process would run smoothly. As day broke, I felt there was a good chance things would. I left for Sheriff Lewis Sweeten's office to share a cup of coffee and get his impression of the situation.

I'd had a sip or two of coffee when the call came in from the election judge of Precinct 5 informing us that he had encountered serious problems. Precinct 5 was the Zavala County road administrator's office, which sat on the west side of Crystal City on Highway 83.

Texas bestows election judges with the same powers held by district justices on Election Day only. Generally speaking, when one of these daylong despots cries foul, droves of law enforcement officers come running. On this day, they summoned me.

Once I'd connected Gutiérrez's agenda with the incident location, I pretty much got the picture before I ever set foot on the scene. That particular precinct's election judge's distinguished appearance would soon prove illusory. I knew this bird, and in my opinion he was an arrogant, loud-mouthed, obnoxious all-service carpet lawyer, businessman, rancher, and renowned redneck. If Gutiérrez's people were worried about election corruption, they had probably stormed the right precinct. I knew enough about both Gutiérrez and this jackass election judge to assume that we had the makings of a full-blown riot on our hands.

My suspicions weren't far off base. Across the highway were hundreds of banner-waving protestors, most of whom were shouting *Viva La Raza!* At the front door of the precinct, a bilingual brawl was spilling onto the front porch. The Anglo judge was directing his clerks and sheriff's deputies to carry the still-seated Chicano poll watchers out the door. Gutiérrez and his group, including the wellhead-sized body-guards who were always with him in those days, were shoving them back inside. The poll watchers, knuckles white and faces damned determined, clung to their chairs like bare-bronc riders.

No place but South Texas could a county election get as rowdy as this. I love everything about my home state, but politics almost always disintegrates into an ugly, mud-slinging shouting match. Pour racism into the pot and contested elections take on all the characteristics of a blood feud.

I don't remember exactly how I did it—probably set off a bomb or something—but the first step was to get the brawlers' attention and shut down all that clawing and caterwauling. This was more or less accomplished, except for the hundreds of folks across the street. They kept on protesting, but they weren't the immediate problem.

The acrimony gave way to an eerie moment as quiet as a mouse pissing on a piece of cotton. As soon as Sheriff Sweeten and I restored order, the election judge began to throw his weight around. He said the poll watchers—Richard Diaz, Richard Gatica, Rebecca Perez (whose husband Rey was a fine police officer and would one day be elected district judge), and Luz Gutiérrez (wife of José Angel)—would have to go. He claimed that Precinct 5 was too damn small to accommodate *any* poll watchers of any inclination and still allow people room to vote, which was sort of true.

These four La Raza Unida activists would rather nail their feet to the floor than break eye contact with the ballot box. The framers of Texas election law probably envisioned a fair and impartial election judge overseeing the process. Whoever nominated this *Hee-Haw* henchman hadn't come close to the ideal. He didn't just resent Mexican American poll watchers at his precinct; he wanted them hauled off in chains.

I could see that the election official was distraught that the word "arrest" didn't come out of my mouth. The expressions of the Mexican American activists darkened also, mainly because I think the presence of a Texas Ranger signaled foreboding and doom. (Especially here, in Zavala County, where in 1963 a Chicano political movement was violently oppressed old-school-style by the Rangers. Things were different now, but local residents didn't understand that yet.) I didn't give that crowd the confrontation they wanted either. I'd disappointed everyone right off the bat. Not a good start. When the poll watchers didn't twitch the first muscle fiber toward getting out of those seats, I began sorting through my options. None of them was any good.

I was thinking about ordering everybody to give me enough peace to sort through this mess when out of the pack came José Angel Gutiérrez waving a book, which in his hands is a far more deadly weapon than any other.

"Ranger, can I just show you something?" he asked with the book already open to the appropriate passage.

"Sure," I said, and soon my eyes were following a few sentences in the *Texas Election Code*. Basically, the law provided for two poll watchers to be present at any precinct for each candidate on the ballot. I think close to thirty offices were up for election that year.

I looked at the election judge. "Are you aware of this?" I asked him.

"According to the law, they're entitled to have maybe sixty people sit over the poll, which would be ridiculous here. But they're only asking for four."

José Angel said nothing while I pursued this line of questioning. It was a rare occasion when the modern, Americanized version of the "Mouth of Gold" would let others talk.

"I'm aware of the law," the judge snapped. I sensed a haughty tone, but I can be more definite when describing the man himself. He was an asshole. "I'm the election judge. This is my precinct. I don't want 'em in here and that's the end of it."

South Texas has long been notorious for its dubious elections, especially when Lyndon Johnson and Coke Stevenson squared off for the Senate seat back in 1948. Many historians agree that the election was stolen from Stevenson in Duval County, where dead people not only took a surprising interest in politics, they also voted in alphabetical order.

I'd like to think that this sort of thing didn't go on in Zavala County, but the election judge's behavior did little to support my hopes. Years later when Gutiérrez and I sat together with a couple of college professors and discussed these events, he stated that when La Raza Unida Party members posted poll watchers at the precincts, La Raza candidates won their elections. When they didn't, La Raza candidates lost. Readers can draw their own conclusions.

"These four people have a right to be here," I said to the judge. "Are you gonna let them sit over that box or not?"

More stubborn than he was thick, the election judge shook his head. His refusal was a complete abuse of his ephemeral powers, but what are you going to do? I felt like the next move was an end run around him.

I looked at José Angel and said, "I tell you what. Let's go talk to a real judge and see what he's got to say about all this." I hoped that District Judge Jack Woodley could override the election judge, or at least talk some sense into him.

Gutiérrez seemed shocked by my suggestion, but he quickly climbed on board, with one caveat. "We've gotta go in my car," he said. He pointed to the mob. "If I go with you, they'll think that you arrested me and all hell will break loose."

I told the election judge to sit tight and suspend voting long enough for us to return with a final determination. Confident that things would go his way, he seemed happy with that plan.

Before much else happened, José Angel stuck a La Raza Unida pin on my shirt. You don't ever want to put your hands on a uniformed officer, and I've never let anyone touch me without serious repercussions. But this was an act of political symbolism rather than a threat, and I had to admire the man's gumption. The crowd erupted in victory as I crawled into the passenger seat of his car. *El Rinche* has been subdued by *la Raza*. Okay.

About then Gutiérrez looked at my Ranger badge, noticed my name, and then, as his expression clouded, took in all six foot five of my hopelessly Scotch-Irish features. "How did you ever get a name like *Joaquín*" he asked me. They always ask. I always tell them.

At Sheriff Sweeten's office we placed a call to District Judge Woodley in Sabinal, whom I quickly aprised of the delicate situation at Precinct 5. Judge Woodley informed me (and later Gutiérrez) that he had no authority to override the election judge's decision—determination I question to this day. He nevertheless informed us both that there were civil remedies available to La Raza Unida *after* the election, an expensive proposition for a grassroots workers' movement and a long time to wait for a prize legally won. His best advice was to work out some sort of compromise with the election judge. Gutiérrez and I climbed back into his car with the unspoken intention to do just that.

When we returned to Precinct 5, the mob reignited. Sheriff Sweeten was visiting with the election judge and that party ended, too. I advised the election official that the district judge strongly suggested that we avoid a lot of hassle (not to mention media scrutiny) by allowing the La Raza Unida Party to post just four of the sixty watchers they were entitled to inside his absurd shack. He refused.

Two of the four poll watchers were women, and there were a number of students and young children with the mob across the street. I'd have to sit tight on this situation or somebody was going to get hurt. But I could at least try and bluff the son of a bitch.

"Okay," I said. I pointed across the street at six hundred armed and angry protestors. "You're on your own." I waved for Sheriff Sweeten and his deputies to follow me, and we all started for the door.

"Wait a minute, Ranger," the election judge said. I took a deep breath and spun on my heel. "You can tell *them* they can put two poll watchers in here," he said. "Can't have four."

"Are you sure about that?" I asked him. "Can't have four but they can have two?" He nodded. Good enough.

I went outside and informed Gutiérrez that the election judge had relented, sort of, and I suggested to the activist that he learn in a hurry to like it. José Angel seemed happy enough and immediately sent in Luz and Rebecca, who were still clamped into their chairs. They dragged themselves inside the precinct for the long vigil.

We all knew that the main event would unfold later, when the local officials tallied the election results. But La Raza Unida had won the first, and most important, round. It seemed to me like a minor episode, yet its repercussions have lasted to this day.

For Anglo office holders, the writing was on the wall.

Later that same night, results were phoned in to the district clerk at the Zavala County courthouse, where absentee votes had been counted during the day. Outside stood a big chalkboard with both candidates' names along with a changing tally of votes.

After the election judges count their ballots, the boxes are sealed and padlocked. If there's a court order in place, a Ranger arrives to pick up the box. I don't recall if this was the case in 1972. The precinct ballot boxes began to arrive at the courthouse for a second tally and the final figure.

La Raza Unida activists hung around. Gutiérrez and others, megaphones in hand, blared angry speeches in Spanish. They wanted to see the numbers go up on the board, and I remember thinking God help us if they aren't what they ought to be.

Inside the courthouse all was quiet. Somber-faced election judges and their clerks started to drift in. I knew that Sheriff Sweeten had poked around about the opening for a feedlot manager for Chapparosa Ranch. Other officials would be checking the employment listings in the Uvalde and San Antonio newspapers next Sunday. José Angel Gutiérrez had just orchestrated the conquest of Aztlán—the part of it that he was born in anyway. Politically speaking, Zavala County belonged to La Raza Unida. The last thing the party members demanded was to have the Anglo authorities come out and tell them so to their faces.

They hadn't done that and the crowd was growing increasingly agitated.

That's when I wondered if these officials were thinking about fudging the numbers. I didn't hear a single person in the courthouse suggest that they do anything of the sort, but they weren't in a hurry to report the election results either. Every now and then one of them would stare at me as if to evaluate my expression. I hope it sent the right message. I hope I urged them to tell the truth.

All the election officials needed to do was take a good look at my badge and consider what that silver cinco peso stands for. Every day of my Ranger career that badge compelled me to reach for the ideal. I expected the same of them. Regardless of their personal opinions and prejudices they didn't disappoint me. They rose to the occasion and reported the true tally of the votes, knowing that the results would cost them their jobs. I was as proud of them as I was of the underdog Mexican Americans who had just won back their county.

After midnight, morose clerks posted the final numbers, and angry demonstrations soon gave way to jubilation. Conservative Texas Democrats were buried alive in a Raza Unida landslide. Chalking the tally on that green board seemed like a small thing, a perfunctory duty. For the Mexican American community of Zavala County, however, it was like the Berlin Wall crashing down.

On his way home, José Angel Gutiérrez sauntered up with a grin that I would come to know all too well and invited me over for a drink. I declined, but I don't think he was disappointed.

I would have liked to have had that drink with him. He probably noticed that I was on duty that night. The invitation stands.

La Raza Unida's reign in Zavala County and throughout South Texas proved short-lived. The reasons are complex and maybe beyond a Ranger's grasp. I suspect that differences arose within the party, fracturing what in 1972 was a solid, unified movement as La Raza Unida battled a common foe. Things dramatically changed. Alliances unraveled the Democrats regrouped. Anglo candidates, however, did not recover their hold on South Texas. Mexican American candidates began to run as Democrats and ultimately, strange as it may seem, as Republicans.

More Mexican Americans became educated. With education, many moved into the large Texas cities, which funneled them directly into the American middle class and beyond. They changed America and America changed them.

There's an old racist statement in Texas that went something like this:

You rarely find a rich Mexican in Texas. As soon as a Mexican makes lots of money, he becomes *Spanish*. That's not true anymore. There are many powerful, wealthy, and influential Mexican Americans throughout Texas. An affluent Laredo banker and businessman was the Democratic candidate for governor in 2002, while a schoolteacher named Victor Morales ran in 1996 and 2002 for the U.S. Senate. It was inconceivable that any Mexican American could launch viable campaigns for such high offices when I became a Ranger in 1966.

We now celebrate Cinco de Mayo and Diez y Seis. Our children are taught in school about the Mexican contribution to our state. South Texas politicians, authorities, business owners, and law enforcement officials are overwhelmingly Hispanic. Year by year the playing field in Texas becomes more level. But Aztlán belongs again to La Raza.

Mexicans served with the Texas Rangers back in frontier days. The first Mexican American inducted into the modern Ranger service, however, was a friend of mine from Uvalde, named Arturo Rodriguez. Many more would walk in Arturo's boots. In 2002, almost a quarter of the Rangers are Hispanic. That's a long way to travel in thirty years, my friends.

I can't wait to see where we are in another three decades. Even José Angel Gutiérrez will be surprised. It's beyond me to speculate, too. But I can guarantee you two things: we're all going there together, and it's going to be something to see.

Source: From *One Ranger: A Memoir* by H. Joaquín Jackson and David Marion Wilkinson, Copyright © 2005. By permission of the University of Texas Press. pp. 46, 63–75.

357. Excerpts from Reies López Tijerina, "A Letter from the Santa Fe Jail," 1969

The activities of Chicano activist Reies López Tijerina (1926–) have to be read in the context of New Mexican history where the question of land still burns, and where many northern villagers say that the United States violated the Treaty of Guadalupe (1848), which set the terms for the incorporation of New Mexico into the United States. The treaty had guaranteed property rights and the legal precedents of Mexican and Spanish laws. At the time of the conquest, the northern part of New Mexico was settled by Pueblo Indians and Mexican villagers who lived on communal lands. Not only did the small farms belong to the villagers, but so did the use of communal lands that included forests and grazing lands. The U.S. occupation changed the land tenure system. Communal villages were privatized and the use of grazing lands and forests was taken from the villagers. Tijerina wrote "A Letter from the Santa Fe Jail" while imprisoned there in 1969. This letter was modeled after Martin Luther King, Jr.'s, famous "Letter from the Birmingham Jail." Tijerina was one of the more militant Chicano activists of the sixties, leading the struggle to restore Spanish and Mexican land grants to Hispanos and Chicanos guaranteed by the Treaty of Guadalupe Hidalgo. Tijerina founded the Alianza of Pueblos and Pobladores (Alliance of Towns and Settlers) in 1963. A charismatic preacher, he traveled through the land telling how Tío Samuel (Uncle Sam) had dispossessed New Mexicans by nationalizing the forests and privatizing their communal lands. Tío Samuel had reduced a once self-sufficient people to beggars forced to take food stamps. In October 1966, Alianza members occupied part of the "Echo Amphitheater Park" in the Carson National Forest that belonged to the San Joaquín del Río de Chama grant. The next year Tijerina led a raid on the Tierra Amarilla Courthouse. In March 1968, he led the Chicano contingent of the Poor People's March in Washington, D.C., one of the final initiatives of black civil rights leader, Martin Luther King, who was involved in the planning of the march but assassinated before it was held. Tijerina was sentenced to two years in a federal prison in 1970 for charges related to the 1967 Tierra Amarilla Courthouse raid. In 1974, he began serving another sentence. The following letter explains his grievances and why he was in jail.

From my cell block in this jail I am writing these reflections. I write them to my people, the Indo-Hispanos, to my friends among the Anglos, to the agents of the Federal government, the state of New Mexico, the Southwest, and the entire Indo-Hispano world—"Latin America."

I write to you as one of the dearest victims of the madness and racism in the hearts of our present-day politicians and rulers.

At this time, August 17, I have been in jail for 65 days—since June 11, 1969, when my appeal bond from another case was revoked by a federal judge. I am here today because I resisted an assassination attempt led by an agent of the federal government—an agent of all those who do not want anybody to speak out for the poor, all those who do not want Reies López Tijerina to stand in their way as they continue to rob the poor people, all those many rich people from outside the state with their summer homes and ranches here whose pursuit of happiness depends on thievery, all those who have robbed the people of their land and culture for 120 years....

What is my real crime? As I and the poor people see it, especially the Indo-Hispanos, my only crime is UPHOLDING OUR RIGHTS AS PROTECTED BY THE TREATY OF GUADALUPE HIDALGO, which ended the so-called Mexican-American War of 1846–1848. My only crime is demanding the respect and protection of our property, which has been confiscated illegally by the federal government. Ever since the treaty was signed in 1848, our people have been asking every elected president of the United States for a redress of grievances. Like the Black people, we too have been criminally ignored. Our right to the Spanish land grant pueblos is the real reason why I am in prison at this moment.

Our cause and our claim and our methods are legitimate. Yet even after a jury in a court of law acquitted me last December, they still call me a violent man. But the right to make a citizen's arrest, as I attempted to make that day on Evans, is not a violent right. On the contrary, it is law and order—unless the arrested son resists or flees to avoid prosecution. No honest citizen should avoid a citizen's arrest.

This truth is denied by the conspirators against the poor and by the press, which they control. There are also the Silent Contributors. The Jewish people accused the Pope of Rome for keeping silent while Hitler and his machine persecuted the Jews in Germany and other countries. I support the Jews in their right to accuse those who contributed to Hitler's acts by their Silence. By the same token, I denounce those in New Mexico who have never opened their mouths at any time to defend or support the thousands who have been killed, robbed, raped of their culture. I don't know of any church or Establishment organization or group of elite intellectuals that has stood up for the Treaty of Guadalupe Hidalgo. We condemn the silence of these groups and individuals and I am sure that, like the Jewish people, the poor of New Mexico are keeping a record of the Silence which contributes to the criminal conspiracy against the Indo-Hispano in New Mexico.

As I sit in my jail cell in Santa Fe, capitol of New Mexico, I pray that all the poor people will unite to bring justice to New Mexico. My cell block has no day light, no ventilation of any kind, no light of any kind. After 9 P.M., we are left in a dungeon of total darkness. Visiting rules allow only 15 minutes per week on Thursdays from 1 to 4 P.M. so that parents who work cannot visit their sons in jail. Yesterday, a 22-year-old boy cut his throat. Today, Aug. 17, two young boys cut their wrists with razor blades and were taken unconscious to the hospital. My cell is dirty and there is nothing to clean it with. The whole cell block is hot and suffocating. All my prison mates complain and show a daily state of anger. But these uncomfortable conditions do not bother me, for I have a divine dream to give me strength: the happiness of my people.

I pray to God that all the Indo-Hispano people will awake to the need for unity, and to our heavenly and constitutional responsibility for fighting peacefully to win our rights. Already the rest of the Indo-Hispano world—Latin America—knows of our struggle. It is too late to keep the story of our land struggle from reaching the ears of the Indo-Hispano world. All the universities of Latin America knew about our problems when Rockefeller went there last summer. Will Latin America ignore our cry from here in New Mexico and the Southwest? Times have changed and the spirit of the blood is no longer limited by national or continental boundaries.

The Indo-Hispano world will never trust the United States as long as this government occupies our land illegally. The honest policy of the United States will have to begin at home, before Rockefeller can go to Latin America again to sell good relations and friendship. Our property, freedom, and culture must be respected in New Mexico, in the whole Southwest, before the Anglo can expect to be trusted in South America, Mexico, and Canada.

This government must show its good faith to the Indo-Hispano in respect to the Treaty of Guadalupe Hidalgo and the land question by forming a presidential committee to investigate and hold open hearings on the land question in the northern part of New Mexico. We challenge our own government to bring forth and put all the facts on the conference table. We have the evidence to prove our claims to property as well as to the cultural rights of which we have been deprived. We are Right—and therefore ready and willing to discuss our problems and rights under the Treaty with the Anglo federal government in New Mexico or Washington, D.C., directly or through agents.

This government must also reform the whole educational structure in the Southwest before it is too late. It should begin in the northern part of New Mexico, where 80% of the population is [sic] Indo-Hispanos, as a pilot center. If it works here, then a plan can be developed based on that experience in the rest of the state and wherever the Indo-Hispano population requires it.

Because I know We Are Right, I have no regrets as I sit in my jail cell. I feel very, very proud and happy, to be in jail for the reason that I am. June 8 in Coyote could have been my last day on earth. My life was spared by God, and to be honored by that miracle at Coyote will keep me happy for many years to come. I am sure that not one of my prison days is lost. Not one day has been in vain. While others are free, building their personal empires, I am in jail for defending and fighting for the rights of my people. Only my Indo-Hispano people have influenced me to be what I am. I am what I am, for my brothers.

Source: Reies López Tijerina Collection, University of New Mexico, Albuquerque.

358. Excerpts from *Carlos Montez [sic] et al., Petitioners v. the Superior Court of Los Angeles County, Respondent;* The People, August 7, 1970

Carlos Montes, a co-founder of the Brown Berets, a Chicano power movement organization, was one of the leaders of the East Los Angeles school Blowouts, in which students walked out at five high schools in predominately Chicano East Los Angeles in 1968. Montes was active in cases of police brutality and led protests at the East L.A. sheriffs' station. The Brown Berets were a nationalist organization that was an outgrowth of the Young Chicanos for Community Action that met at the Piranya Coffee House in 1967. Under the leadership of David Sánchez, a young Chicano activist, some of the members of the group evolved into the Brown Berets. They wore the berets as a sign of resistance and their intent to defend the barrio, the Chicano community or neighborhood. The Brown Berets established about 14 chapters throughout the Southwest; their national headquarters was in East L.A. The Los Angeles Police Department and sheriffs targeted the Brown Berets—harassing, infiltrating the group, and arresting members. Montes was framed by these officers and indicted for setting fires at the Biltmore Hotel in downtown Los Angeles on April 24, 1969. A California Department of Education conference was taking place there at the time, and Gov. Ronald Reagan was the keynote speaker. Chicano demonstrators disrupted Reagan's speech and were removed by the police. Meanwhile, during Reagan's speech, a fire broke out in a linen closet on the tenth floor. The Los Angeles grand jury indicted 10 Chicanos, 6 for arson, burning personal property, burglary, malicious destruction of electrical lines, and conspiracy to commit felonies. The defendants became known as the Biltmore Six. Later testimony revealed that Los Angeles Police Officer Fernando Sumaya had infiltrated the berets and probably provoked many of the incidents. (Sumaya had attempted to infiltrate the student group at San Fernando Valley State and was expelled because of provocations.) Montes fled before prosecution and did not return until 10 years later when he gave himself up. He was tried and acquitted. The defendants sought to quash the original indictment.

Defendants, charged with various felonies, moved to quash the indictment on the ground that eligible persons of their class, namely, Spanish-surnamed Mexican American citizens had been systematically excluded from consideration for nomination to the grand jury. It was stipulated that the trial court could consider the record in another case in which a similar claim was made with respect to the grand jury for the county for the previous year. Thirty-four superior court judges had been called as witnesses by the defendants in that case and 70 were subpoenaed in the instant case. Under the rules of court for the county, each superior court judge was entitled to nominate two persons to the grand jury annually. Six witnesses were actually called, one of whom was the judge presiding over the hearing. Based on the number of Spanish-surnamed Mexican American citizens selected as grand jurors for the current year, the court found that statistically, a prima facie case of discrimination had not been made. It ruled that the judges subpoenaed could not be interrogated.

The Court of Appeal granted defendants' petition for a writ of prohibition restraining the trial court from further proceeding in the case without first reopening the hearing on the motion to quash or, alternatively, in its discretion, proceeding to hear the motion de novo.

In holding that the trial court erred in refusing to permit interrogation of the judges, the court took the view that failure to make a prima facie case of discrimination statistically did not preclude defendants from attempting to show, as they proposed to do, that, with very few exceptions, the judges of the superior court were by reason of birth, education, residence, wealth, social and professional associations, and similar factors, not acquainted with the qualifications of eligible potential grand jurors of defendants' class and that they did not make an adequate effort to overcome this alleged deficiency. The prosecution's contention that defendants failed to make an adequate offer of proof was rejected. Opinion by Kaus, P. J., with Stephens and Reppy, JJ., concurring.)

> COUNSEL: Oscar Zeta Acosta, Neil M. Herring, Margolis, McTernan, Smith, Scope & Herring and Hugh R. Manes for Petitioners.
> No appearance for Respondent.
> Evelle J. Younger, District Attorney, Harry Wood and Arnold T. Guminski, Deputy District Attorneys, for Real Party in Interest....

In May 1969, the Los Angeles County Grand Jury handed down a six-count indictment charging petitioners with a variety of serious felonies. Each petitioner was named in at least one count. Eventually petitioners moved to quash the indictment on the ground that the grand jury had been illegally constituted in that eligible grand jurors of a class to which petitioners belong, namely, "Spanish-surnamed Mexican American citizens" had been systematically excluded from consideration for nomination to the grand jury. At the hearing it was stipulated that the court could consider the record made before another judge in another case, *People v. Castro et al.*, in which a similar claim with respect to the 1968 grand jury had been made by the defendants in that case, some of whom are also petitioners in this proceeding. There is also some overlapping of legal representation. In *People v. Castro* the defendants had called 34 Los Angeles County Superior Court judges as witnesses to support their contention. Significantly, at the time the motion in the case at bar was heard, the People had already argued in the prohibition proceeding in *Castro* that the defendants there had not called an adequate number of judges. The reason for calling judges as witnesses on motions such as these is that each judge in Los Angeles County is annually entitled to nominate two persons to the grand jury. (Rule 29 § 2, Rules of Superior Court, Los Angeles County.) ...

Before the proceedings in the case at bar started on October 7, 1969, the defense had subpoenaed 70 superior court judges as witnesses. They were placed "on call" by the judge who heard the motion. During the ensuing hearing petitioners called six other witnesses, one of whom was the judge presiding over the hearing. One of the purposes of calling the judge was to illustrate, as part of an offer of proof on which the court insisted, what questions petitioners intended to propound to the 70 judges under subpoena....

"The Court finds that for the 1969 Grand Jury, ten persons of Spanish surname have been nominated, of which I believe six or seven were considered as Mexican-Americans. Therefore, it cannot be said that Mexican-Americans or persons with Spanish surnames were excluded from the 1969 Grand Jury. In view of that fact, I will hold that it is immaterial what has preceded the 1969 Grand Jury, as long as the 1969 Grand Jury that indicted these defendants were [*sic*] properly chosen, and in my opinion they were. The rest becomes immaterial. So the motion to quash will be denied...." The People concede that this finding is based on implied findings that petitioners had established that they were members of a legally cognizable class (*Hernandez v. Texas*, 347 U.S. 475, 477–478 [98 L.Ed. 866, 869–870, 74 S.Ct. 667]) and that seven members of that class were among the one hundred and eighty-plus nominees for the 1969 grand jury. There is some argument in the record concerning the percentage of the population comprised by the class and some more argument concerning the percentage of members of the class eligible for grand jury service. We have no need to settle these controversies. While it does appear that even if we give the People the benefit of every doubt, petitioners' class was still underrepresented in 1969, for the purpose of this opinion we readily accept the proposition that the 1969 underrepresentation was insufficient to make out a prima facie case of discrimination. Nor need we decide the extent to which petitioners, in order to make out such a prima facie case from statistics alone, were entitled to rely on the 1959–1968 figures as well as on the 1969 comparison....

We believe that petitioners justly complain that the court's ruling, in effect, permitted them to call their judicial witnesses only if the statistical evidence made it unnecessary for them to do so....

"The Court: Well, I will repeat what I said at the start, Mr. Acosta. If I come to the decision that there was discrimination in the nominations for the 1969 Grand Jury, which is the Grand Jury that indicted these defendants, it will then become pertinent as to whether it is an intentional, arbitrary, and systematic exclusion or discrimination over a period of time.

Mr. Acosta: Now, is your Honor going to make this decision prior to the calling of any judge witnesses?

The Court: Yes.... So far as I am concerned, if there is nondiscrimination of the 1969 Grand Jury, then these defendants were indicted by a validly constituted Grand Jury.

Mr. Manes: Well, excuse me a moment, your Honor. How can you reach that decision, your Honor, without having afforded us the opportunity of completing our case? Now, we have yesterday at great length tried to show your Honor that the evidence in its present posture insofar as we are concerned is incomplete because we wanted to rely, in addition to statistical evidence, we wanted to rely upon standards which were used by the selectors selecting and nominating the Grand Jury for 1969.

The Court: I think it is a simple proposition. Were there Mexican-Americans or Spanish people with Spanish surnames on the Grand Jury that indicted these people?" ...

Petitioners want us to hold on the basis of the *Castro* record and the additional evidence which they did produce in this case that the 1969 Grand Jury was illegally constituted. Obviously, this we cannot do. Had the basic error not been committed, the 70 judges would have testified. Then, depending on the nature of their testimony, the People would have had an opportunity to rebut whatever prima facie case petitioners had made out. If we held now that on the evidence so far adduced the grand jury had been illegally selected and ordered the indictment quashed, we would be depriving the People of a chance to prove their case.

The alternative writ is discharged. Let a peremptory writ of prohibition issue prohibiting the respondent court from any further proceedings in the case entitled *People of the State of California v. Carlos Montez et al.*, being its number A-244906, without first reopening the hearing on the petitioners' motion to quash the indictment and proceeding in accordance with the views expressed in this opinion or, alternatively, in its discretion, proceeding to hear said motion de novo.

Source: Court of Appeal of California, Second Appellate District, Division Five *10 Cal. App. 3d 343;* 88 Cal. Rptr. 736; 1970 Cal. App. LEXIS 1845, August 7, 1970.

359. Enrique Hank López, "Overkill at the Silver Dollar," 1970

The level of Los Angeles Police Department and Sheriff's Department deputies violence at the Chicano Moratorium on August 29, 1970, shocked many Chicanos and other progressives. The murder of journalist Rubén Salazar enraged Angelinos. Around 30,000 peaceful demonstrators against the war in Vietnam marched through East Los Angeles, gathering for festivities at Laguna Park. There were men, women, children, young, and old gathered as police with little or no provocation attacked, clubbing and tear-gassing the demonstrators. Hundreds were arrested and police killed three Chicanos—among them, respected journalist Rubén Salazar (1928–1970) at the Silver Dollar Café in East Los Angeles. Salazar had been covering the moratorium. The Chicano community called the death of Salazar, the director of news at KMEX, the Spanish language television station, and a reporter for the *Los Angeles Times*, an assassination. They thought that Salazar had been targeted by the sheriff's deputies because of a series of articles and news reports critical of police abuse. It was too much of a coincidence that Salazar had been ordered to stay in the Silver Dollar while a missile projectile was fired into the establishment, hitting Salazar in the head. Hank López, a well-known attorney and writer who unsuccessfully ran for California's lieutenant governor in 1958, penned the following piece on the death of Salazar. It was one of the more eloquent tributes.

It was nearly midnight, and the barrio strangely quiet, quiet with fear. I had just left the Carioca restaurant with a dozen *tortillas de maíz* in a paper bag. I was spending the night before the funeral at my mother's house, and she'd promised to cook my favorite breakfast of *menudo con chile*. The tortillas, naturally, were essential.

Suddenly, a police car screeched to a stop at the curb. Two cops jumped out and pushed me against the wall, frisking me from top to bottom with rough insolent hands. They said not a word, and neither did I. I was simply not *macho* enough to protest. A cop like these had blasted the skull of my friend Rubén Salazar, the Chicano columnist for the *Los Angeles Times*, in the Silver Dollar Café, and I was frankly afraid to cross them.

They have also arrested about 300 Chicanos since the police riot that erupted during the East Los Angeles peace rally that Rubén was covering on the afternoon he was killed. I didn't want to be "prisoner 301"—and, having flown all the way from New York, I certainly didn't want to miss Rubén's funeral. So I accepted the indignity of their frisk with a gut-souring meekness. This is all familiar stuff to anyone who has lived in a Chicano barrio. And when they yanked off my shoes and shook them upside-down, I clamped my mouth to hold back the sour saliva that I'd like to spit in their faces.

"What do you do?" one of them asked.

"I'm a lawyer and a writer."

"Oh—one of those guys," in a tone suggesting one of those smart-ass spicks.

Suddenly noticing the brown paper bag in my hand, one of these guardians of the peace grabbed it and quickly shuffled through the tortillas in an apparent search for marijuana or heroin. Finding none, he gave them back.

Later on I threw the tortillas into a trash can—they must have had a hundred cop fingerprints on them.

They let me go finally—a tribute to my meekness, to what I would rather call my old barrio wisdom. The pragmatism of fear. And in my confusion and resentment (or was it again a sense of prudent resignation?), I had not noticed their badge numbers. Nor would I be able to recognize their faces again. I'm afraid all cops' faces have begun to look alike to me. And that's tragic, in a way, because two years ago I wrote to Mayor Lindsay and the New York Police Commissioner, commending a police officer who had been extremely kind (fatherly kind) to my 10-year-old daughter when she was injured near our apartment while we were away, the baby sitter having gone astray. He had taken her to a hospital and stayed by her side for five hours. So it's not in me to be a cop hater.

Just below Soto and Brooklyn Avenue, while searching vainly for a cab on those deserted streets, I saw a police helicopter swishing over me like a giant insect, its bright, harsh searchlights probing the dark alleys and back yards of the barrio.

I wondered then if the police regard us Mexican-Americans as a community of barricaded criminals. The phrase came easily at that moment because that very afternoon the *Times* had quoted an expert as saying that the kind of missile that killed Rubén "should be used only against a barricaded criminal." Gene Pember, a consultant for the Peace Officers Standards and Training Commission, had told newsmen that the high-velocity tear-gas projectile that pierced Rubén's skull should never be used for crowd control, that "the thing is like a young cannon, really." Such missiles, he said, could go through a thick stucco wall. "That's what they are for—to penetrate a house or an object behind which a dangerous suspect has barricaded himself. But even then they should never be fired at a person."

The 10-inch missile that killed Salazar was fired by a sheriff's deputy *through an open doorway* at a point-blank range of 15 feet. The deputy who fired that missile may not have known it was Rubén Salazar he was shooting, but he certainly knew it was a Chicano.

Yet, not once during the entire week following this obvious example of heedless slaughter would Sheriff Pitchess admit that his men might have been even slightly negligent. Sam Houston Johnson once told me that his brother LBJ suffered from a profound inability to say "I'm sorry"—to admit any error, however inconsequential. Certainly, a tragic flaw in a human being, and I wonder if the Los Angeles sheriff shares that affliction. Far from blaming any of his men, he keeps talking about "outside agitators."

Small wonder that my fellow Chicanos are willing to believe almost any accusation against the police. When the *Times* subsequently devoted its entire front page to blown-up photos from a community newspaper called *La Raza*, quoting at length from an article titled "The Murder of Rubén Salazar"—they may have begun to entertain even that suspicion.

Earlier that evening (several hours before the cops frisked me), I had attended a rally of Chicanos at the All Nations Auditorium, where I heard their collective rage and frustration—my own as well—burst from the throats of one speaker after another, the packed listeners periodically stamping their feet and raising clenched fists as a symbol of "Chicano Power." The speeches were mostly in English, but occasionally resorted to a schizolingual amalgam of English and Spanish to stress a vital point. ("Let's show *los Pinches placas* that we're men—*que* no bastard cop *nos puede chingar!*") Tough barrio language, most of it spoken with the bitterness of long years of resentment, some of it with a hushed, melancholy sense of bitter resignation.

When Corky Gonzalez was introduced, a thunder of shoes stomped the floor and a chorus of "viva Chicano power" echoed from the walls, throbbing in my head, sending an expectant chill up my spine. But there was no flaming rhetoric from the much loved leader of the Crusade for Justice—no call to arms, no threat of violence. There was instead an urgent plea for Chicano unity, for a grass-roots drive for political power, for a reclaiming of "the occupied territory of Aztlán," that portion of the United States that once belonged to Mexico. It sounded more like a psychic take-back than a real one. The muted anger in his voice was spiced with humorous irony when he told the crowd, "I was busted at the peace rally and charged with suspicion of robbery because I had $325 in my billfold. To the *gabacho* cops, I guess it's awful damned suspicious for a Chicano to have that much bread."

Clearly moved by Corky's mesmeric hold on the audience, Rene Anselmo (an Anglo millionaire who owns three TV stations) instantly donated $100 to the bail-bond fund for the 300 Chicanos who had been arrested since the riot. By coincidence, Captain Ernest Medina—defendant in the My Lai massacre case—was in Los Angeles during that same period, seeking donations for his defense from fellow Mexican-Americans. I doubt that he could have raised 2¢; from the people who heard Corky, though I'm told that American Legionnaires in his hometown think him a hero.

After the rally, I went to the Carioca bar-restaurant to eat Mexican food. It was also a sentimental gesture. The last time I had seen Rubén Salazar we had come to this restaurant, mostly to hear the mariachi trio that entertains here. They had played our favorite *Adelita* and *Siete Leguas*, songs of the Mexican Revolution that led us into a pleasant nostalgic mood. I had once written that my father was the only private in Pancho Villa's army, and he was now claiming that *his* father was the only private, smiling in that gentle way he had, his eyes shining with impish enjoyment. What better basis for a deep and abiding friendship than our mutual conviction that *each* of our fathers was the only private in that famous rebel *División del norte?*

Our conversation became serious after a while. Rubén was deeply concerned about the laggard pace of bilingual education programs for Chicano children in the early grades. Most educators know that everyone's greatest, most intense period of learning is from birth to the age of 5. For a Chicano, that fast-paced, crucial learning is acquired in Spanish or in a "pocho" combination of Spanish and English. But the day he enters kindergarten—a day of intense anxiety even for a child from the most secure Anglo environment—that learning tool is snatched away. He's not permitted to speak the only language he knows. So he sits in frustration, confusion, and fright as the teacher and the "more advantaged" kids talk in alien sounds, making him feel dumb and lost. The experience is repeated hour after hour, day after day, until he's ultimately defeated. There is no one more fragile than a 5-year-old child on alien turf.

The Chicano brings failure to school with him; he has no chance of success, no possibility of the "reward and reinforcement" that child educators feel is indispensable. The high school dropout rate for Mexican-Americans (58 percent in some Chicano ghettos—higher than the rate for black students) is a belated symptom of the dropping out that begins on the first day of kindergarten.

"Why can't they teach our Chicano kids in both Spanish and English?" asked Rubén, fingering an empty glass. "If they could have genuine bilingual classes—Spanish in the morning and English in the afternoon—there would be some trace of comforting familiarity between school and their home. They could feel successful in Spanish, capable of learning. They wouldn't feel dumb, they wouldn't quit trying as they do now. With a gradual transition in kindergarten and the first two grades, English would be easier."

His convictions were an echo of educational theories developed by Dr. Jerome Bruner, director of Harvard's Center for Cognitive Studies, who has said that ghetto youngsters often face insuperable linguistic and environmental obstacles.

Ordering another round of margaritas that evening, we talked of other problems that bedevil Chicano kids. Thinking of the kid-glove treatment used on the Kennedy-Shriver cousins when they were arrested for possession of marijuana, we were both sure that a Chicano or black teenager would have been summarily convicted and sent to a reformatory for at least six months.

I told Rubén of my first encounter with the juvenile court system as a lawyer (I'd had several as a child). A Mexican-American woman had called my office in a state verging on hysteria. Her 13-year-old son—let's call him Ramón Gómez—had been picked up by the police and whisked off in a squad car, but no one at the local precinct station would tell her where he was. Within half an hour we were at the Hollenbeck Station in East Los Angeles, and were informed that Ramón wasn't there. No record of his arrest. Then we hurried to the Juvenile Detention Home, where the desk captain said there was no booking on a Ramón Gómez. But as we were leaving, a young Chicano trustee told us that a boy answering Ramon's description had been taken from the detention home to the Los Angeles General Hospital. "He had a bloody bandage on his face." Checking the prison ward at the hospital, we learned two hours later that he'd received treatment for a fractured nose and then been returned to the detention home.

When we tried to see him at the so-called home, we were told he couldn't have visitors—nor could I see him in my capacity as his attorney. Angered by this refusal (any adult prisoner can see a lawyer), I went to a bail bondsman, who told me that kids weren't entitled to release on bail. Then I called several judges, who told me that they couldn't order his release on a writ of *habeas corpus* because children weren't entitled to that constitutional right.

When I finally saw the boy, he told me that he'd been accused of trying to break into a bubble-gum machine. "I put a penny in there and the gum didn't come out, so I was shaking it when the police came by. And when I tried to explain what happened, one of them slapped me. Then when I protested, they got me in the car, and one of them started punching my face with his closed fist, calling me a smart-aleck spick. That's how my nose got busted."

The Kafkaesque nightmare continued the next day at Ramón's hearing in juvenile court. The judge immediately informed me that I couldn't act as his lawyer "because this is not a criminal proceeding."

"Then why are you treating him like a criminal?" I asked. "Why has he been detained in that jail?"

"That's not a jail," he said rather testily, "It's only a detention home."

Paraphrasing Gertrude Stein, I said: "It has barred cells like a jail and barred gates to keep those kids inside, and a jail is a jail is a jail—no matter what name you give it."

But he still wouldn't let me appear as Ramon's lawyer, so his mother and I just sat there watching the nightmare proceedings of that quick-justice cafeteria called a "court." Not only were the juvenile defendants (almost all of them black or Chicano) denied lawyers; they couldn't face their accusers, they couldn't cross-examine witnesses against them, they couldn't object to rank hearsay testimony, they weren't protected by any of the normal rules of evidence. They were, in fact, unable to invoke any of the constitutional safeguards that are available to known gangsters.

And when I asked the judge for a transcript of the hearing after he had sentenced Ramon to six months in a reformatory, his mother pleaded with me not to appeal the case. "If we raise a big fuss," she said, "they'll only make it tougher on Ramón when he gets out. He'll be a marked man. We Chicanos don't have a chance."

Rubén had a film of tears in his eyes when I told him about Ramón. "*Como son pinches,*" he said. "How can they be such bastards with little kids? And think of all the other Ramons who've been in the same bag."

Ramón Gómez must be 20 years old by now. He may have been one of the tight-mouthed militants in the angry crowd at the All Nations Auditorium on the night before Rubén's funeral, listening to one speaker comment on the tear-gassing of children at the peace rally, listening to the bitter irony in Corky Gonzalez's [sic] voice. He's heard, as most Chicanos have, that Corky is a marked man, that the FBI probably shadows him from one state to another as he goes from campus to campus, from barrio to barrio, asking his brown brothers to join in common cause. Ramón knows from personal experience (as do too many Chicanos who have been brutalized by certain cops, by the juvenile court system, by those crime-breeding reformatories), knows with a sickening fear that the police may some day crowd in on Corky, and that tragic violence may result.

But quite aside from his own not likely to be forgotten experience with the law, Ramón knows about inferior ghetto schools with indifferent teachers, about poor substandard housing, about high unemployment in the barrio, about radio and television shows that demean and insult his fellow *paisanos*. And he must be aware that local and federal government agencies largely ignore the plight of 8 million invisible Mexican-Americans. And he certainly knows that the television networks, national magazines, and news syndicates are generally deaf to the despairing voices of the barrio, although the more strident voices from black ghettos get ample notice.

Those same news media have been outraged by the alarming increase of cop killers—and it is well they should be, for any killing is abhorrent. But they should also know that the phrase is sometimes reversed in the ghetto—that Chicanos and blacks and poor whites often talk about killer cops with equal abhorrence.

Ramón and the rest of us Chicanos have been urged to turn a deaf ear to the dangerous cry of the militant, to listen instead to the voices of reason, to the voices of the people like Rubén Salazar. And though I myself felt slightly less than reasonable when those two cops shoved me against the wall on a dark lonely street, I would certainly agree that our only hope is reason and good will.

One must also hope that the police and other authorities will come to realize that reason flows both ways, that this fragile society can ill afford the frightening consequences of the kind of overkill that silenced the most reasonable voice of Rubén Salazar.

Source: Enrique Hank López, "Overkill at 'The Silver Dollar,'" pp. 365–368. Reprinted with permission from the October 19, 1970 issue of *The Nation*. For subscription information, call 1-800-333-8536. Portions of each week's *Nation* magazine can be accessed at http://www.thenation.com.

360. Excerpt from a Statement by Elma Barrera, 1970

There was considerable debate in the Chicano movement on the gender question in the 1970s. The Chicano Movement was nationalist and often held distorted notions of culture. As the movement progressed, many began to question assumptions made by Chicano leaders and themselves. The dialogue was opened by Chicanas but also by the Communist press. The struggle to level gender relations dated back to the influence of Socialist and anarchist theory in the 1860s. Many Mexican women did not accept the traditional role assigned to them. The Women's Question was raised even within the Partido Liberal Mexicano (PLM) that led the resistance against Mexican dictator Porfirio Díaz (1830–1915). The issue of gender equality also was raised during the Mexican women's suffrage movement of the 1930s. In the 1960s, there was a confluence of more educated women and civil rights. Mexican American women began to question their position within the Mexican American and Chicano movements. Influenced by the civil rights and feminist movements, they began to conceptualize the question of equality vis-a-vis Chicanas. With the emergence of Chicanas, gender equality became an overriding demand. These voices were clearest in leftist forums, and soon spread to mainstream organizations. In 1970, MAPA (Mexican American Political Association) formed a women's caucus at their annual convention. With varying degrees of success, women's workshops were formed at most major Chicano conferences. The Chicano Youth Liberation Conferences of 1969, 1970, and 1971 in Denver, Colorado, held women's workshops. The Comisión Feminil Mexicana (Mexican Feminine Commission) was formed at the Mexican American National Issues Conference in Sacramento, California. Meanwhile Texano Chicanas played a major role in the formation of La Raza Unida Party. Elma Barrera, an organizer of a national Chicana conference held in May 1971, in Houston, Texas, made the following statement at a national abortion conference attended by over 1,000 women held in July 1971.

I have been told that the Chicana's struggle is not the same as the white woman's struggle. I've been told that the problems are different and that ... the Chicana's energies are needed in the barrio and that being a feminist and fighting for our rights as women and as human beings is anti-Chicano and anti-male.

But let me tell you what being a Chicana means in Houston, Texas. It means learning how to best please the men in the Church and the men at home, not in that order.

You know, it's really funny the way that the Church has ... grasped onto this "sinful" thing about abortion and birth control. It's really funny how the laws only apply to the woman and not to the man.... Chicano men ... fool around, have mistresses, and yet, when it comes to abortion or birth control with their wives, it's a sin....

I will take just one minute to read the two resolutions which came out of the Sex and the Chicana Workshop: "Free, legal abortions and birth control for the Chicano community, controlled by the Chicanas. As Chicanas, we have the right to control our own bodies."

And then out of the workshop on Marriage—Chicana Style: "We as mujeres de La Raza recognize the Catholic Church as an oppressive institution and do hereby resolve to break away and not to go to them to bless our union. So be it resolved that the national Chicana conference go on record as supporting free and legal abortions for all women who want or need them."

SEX AND THE CHICANA

We feel that in order to provide an effective measure to correct the many sexual hangups facing the Chicano community the following resolutions should be implemented:

I. Sex is good and healthy for both Chicanos and Chicanas and we must develop this attitude.

II. We should destroy the myth that religion and culture control our sexual lives.

III. We recognize that we have been oppressed by religion and that the religious writing was done by men and interpreted by men. Therefore, for those who desire religion, they should interpret their Bible, or Catholic rulings according to their own feelings, what they think is right, without any guilt complexes.

IV. Mothers should teach their sons to respect women as human beings who are equal in every respect. No double standard.

V. Women should go back to the communities and form discussion and action groups concerning sex education.

VI. Free, legal abortions and birth control for the Chicano community, controlled by Chicanas. As Chicanas we have the right to control our own bodies.

VII. Make use of church centers, neighborhood centers, and any other place available.

"Liberate your mind and the body will follow."

"A quitarnos todos nuestros complejos sexuales para tener una vida mejor y feliz" (Let's cast off all our sexual complexes to have a better and happier life).

MARRIAGE—CHICANA STYLE

Reaffirmation that Chicano marriages are the beginnings of Chicano families which perpetuate our culture and are the foundation of the movement.

Points brought up in the workshop:

1. Chicano marriages are individual and intimate and solutions to problems must be primarily handled on an individual basis.
2. A woman must educate and acquaint herself with outside issues and personal problem sexual hangups, etc.).
3. It is the responsibility of Chicanas with families to educate their sons and thus change the attitudes of future generations.
4. Chicanas should understand that Chicanos face oppression and discrimination, but this does not mean that the Chicana should be a scapegoat for the man's frustrations.
5. With involvement in the movement, marriages must change. Traditional roles for Chicanas are not acceptable or applicable.

RESOLUTIONS

I. We, as mujeres de La Raza, recognize the Catholic Church as an oppressive Institution and do hereby resolve to break away and not go to it to bless our unions.

II. Whereas: Unwanted pregnancies are the basis of many social problems, and

Whereas: The role of Mexican-American women has traditionally been limited to the home, and

Whereas: The need for self-determination and the right to govern their own bodies is a necessity for the freedom of all people, therefore,

BE IT RESOLVED: That the National Chicana Conference go on record as supporting free family planning and free and legal abortions for all women who want or need them.

III. Whereas: Due to socio-economic and cultural conditions, Chicanas are often heads of households, i.e., widows, divorcees, unwed mothers, or deserted mothers, or must work to supplement family income, and

Whereas: Chicana motherhood should not preclude educational, political, social, and economic advancement, and

Whereas: There is a critical need for a 24-hour childcare center in Chicano communities, therefore,

BE IT RESOLVED: That the National Chicana Conference go on record as recommending that every Chicano community promote and set up 24-hour day care facilities, and that it be further resolved that these facilities will reflect the concept of La Raza as the united family, and on the basis of brotherhood (La Raza), so that men, women, young, and old assume the responsibility for the love, care, education, and orientation of all the children of Aztlán.

IV. Whereas: Dr. Goldzieher of SWRF has conducted an experiment on Chicana women of westside San Antonio, Texas, using a new birth control drug, and

Whereas: No human being should be used for experimental purposes, therefore,

BE IT RESOLVED: That this Conference send telegrams to the American Medical Association condemning this act. Let it also be resolved that each Chicana women's group and each Chicana present at the conference begin a letter writing campaign to:

Dr. Joseph Goldzleher, Director

c/o SW Foundation for Research & Education

San Antonio, Texas

RELIGION

I. Recognize the Plan de Aztlán

II. Take over already existing Church resources for community use, i.e., health, Chicano awareness, public information of its resources, etc.

III. Oppose any institutionalized religion.

IV. Revolutionary change of Catholic Church or for it to get out of the way.

V. Establish communication with the barrio and implement programs of awareness to the Chicano movement.

Source: Mirta Vidal, *Chicanas Speak Out! Women: New Voice of La Raza.* Copyright © 1971 by Pathfinder Press. Reprinted by permission. http://latino.sscnet.ucla.edu/research/docs/chicanas/vidal.htm.

361. Excerpts from Marjorie Heins, *Strictly Ghetto Property: The Story of Los Siete de La Raza*, 1972

The Mission District of San Francisco has almost always been a multi-Latino barrio where Mexicans have shared the streets with Central, South, and Caribbean Americans. Consequently, the culture of the area has often differed from that of the rest of California. Caribbean musical sounds were usual and its ideas were more what many Chicanos at the time called Third World. In 1969, two plainclothes policemen approached seven young men while they were moving furniture. An altercation followed and an officer died from a gunshot wound. Swarms of officers went to the building, fired automatic rifles, and flooded the building with tear gas. In Santa Cruz, seven youths were later arrested for murder and attempted murder. All were Central American—four Salvadorans, one Nicaraguan, and one Honduran. They had been involved in the Mission Rebels, a youth group, but had been politicized by the times. At trial, the defendants insisted the police had drawn their guns. Since the police officers were in plain clothes, the young Central Americans did not know these men were police officers. The trial lasted a year and a half, and the seven were acquitted. "Los Siete" Defense Committee helped raise the consciousness of youth while it helped the defendants in their defense. The following is from a book about Los Siete, the seven. It shows the influence of the Chicano Movement in politicizing the Mission District and vice versa.

A little after 10:20 A.M. on May 1, 1969, a police officer was shot to death in San Francisco's Latin barrio, the Mission District. Newspapers said that the dead cop and his partner had been attacked by members of a "burglary ring" they had staked out; police were seeking an undetermined number of "Latin hippie-types" as suspects. After a week of what the papers called "the largest manhunt in the history of Northern California," six young Latin Americans were arrested for the murder.

About a month later, I got involved in a short-lived underground newspaper called *Dock of the Bay.* Somebody on the staff mentioned that a new and probably newsworthy radical organization called *Los Siete de la Raza* had been formed in the Mission District. So on a hot June day I went to a small storefront in the heart of the Mission and spoke to a young man named Ralph Ruiz who was in charge of press relations for the organization.

Los Siete de la Raza, Ralph told me, meant "the seven of the race," or of the Latin American people, and it referred to the seven suspects in the recent cop killing, six of whom had been arrested. The new organization had been formed by friends of the seven, to help in their legal defense.

I asked Ralph what the seven now under arrest were like. He said they were all "bad brothers," a compliment in ghetto or barrio language, meaning they were tough. But, he added, they weren't hoodlums, as the papers had said: several of them had been involved in recruiting other young Latinos for a special Readiness Program.... All six were politically radical.

Ralph told me the media had already condemned the six with sensationalist headlines and strict adherence to the police version of the incident. In fact, he said, the two cops involved were a notorious plainclothes ... One played the good guy and the other played the motherfucker." It was the "good guy" who had been killed. Ralph said the six were considered heroes in the barrio for having stood up to these two "pigs."

My next stop was the office of the *San Francisco Chronicle*, the larger of the city's two dailies, where I bought copies of all the back issues containing articles about the incident. After studying these articles, I understood what Ralph meant: the *Chronicle* had taken its stories from police announcements and the stories all played on racial stereotypes, leaving little room for doubt that all six Latinos charged with murder were guilty.

From the articles and from my talk with Ralph I wrote my first story on Los Siete for *Dock of the Bay*. I began to follow the pre-trial hearings in the case, and to get to know other people in the Los Siete organization. One of them, Donna James, had attended San Francisco State College, been active in the recent strike there, and finally quit school to work with Los Siete full time. Like Ralph, Donna had known several of the "brothers," as the six who were arrested came to be called. When, almost a year after the incident, Ramparts Press suggested I write a book on Los Siete, Donna agreed to give me help and advice.

The need for such a book was obvious. The police hoped to convict all six in jail and with the help of the dead policeman's widow had begun a vigorous pro–capital punishment campaign. Mayor Joseph Alioto, conscious of the law-and-order reaction which followed the college strikes of 1968 and '69, had called the suspects "punks" and offered a $5,000 reward for information leading to the capture of each. Responding to these pressures, the city's mass media steered clear of any in-depth reportage about the lives of the six young men, the conditions in the Mission District which produced their confrontation with the two cops, or the political consciousness which led to the formation of the Los Siete defense organization....

Some of the changes Pinky noticed when he got out of jail had to do with rising political consciousness among La Raza people. A brown movement was beginning, which would replace feelings of hopelessness and inferiority among La Raza with pride and determination to change the conditions of their lives. This movement got its start in 1965 with the struggle of Chicano farmworkers in California's San Joaquin Valley. César Chávez, Dolores Huerta, and other organizers had founded the National Farm Workers Association (later the United Farmworkers Organizing Committee) in Delano, California, and in October 1965 joined with a largely Filipino union to strike against Delano grape growers for higher wages and union recognition. The growers refused to recognize the union and pretended there was no strike. They sprayed pesticides near the strikers, got injunctions against bullhorns and rallies, and imported scabs from skid rows, depressed rural areas, and Mexico.

The workers turned to boycotting Delano's second largest grape grower, the Schenley Corporation.

The strike and boycott captured the imaginations of Chicanos and other sympathetic people across the country. In San Francisco, protesters succeeded in stopping grape shipments when longshoremen refused to cross their picket line. The farmworkers' symbol, a stylized eagle derived from an Aztec migration myth, appeared on buttons and, as graffiti, on the walls of Mission High.

In March 1966, the farmworkers held a pilgrimage through three hundred miles of California's San Joaquin Valley, from Delano to Sacramento. They marched behind an image of the Virgin of Guadalupe, Mexico's patron saint, the same saint whose image was carried by Miguel Hidalgo and the Indians of his parish when they began the war for Mexican independence in 1810.

"We are conscious of the historical significance of our pilgrimage," the NFWA (National Farm Workers Association) wrote in its Plan of Delano.

It is clearly evident that our paths travel through a valley well known to all Mexican farmworkers ... because along this very same road, in this very same valley, the Mexican race has sacrificed itself for the last hundred years....

We are sons of the Mexican Revolution, a revolution of the poor seeking bread and justice.... Across the San Joaquin Valley, across California, across the entire Southwest of the United States, wherever there are Mexican people, wherever there are farmworkers, our movement is spreading like flames across a dry plain.

When the farmworkers arrived in Sacramento they learned that Schenley had finally agreed to come to the bargaining table. Eventually, all the wine growers accepted the union. A few years later, the huge table-grape-growing corporations began to give in. The struggle spread to other parts of the country, and to other crops.

Among those who marched to Sacramento was a young Chicano from south Texas, Aaron Manganiello. Manganiello was already a veteran of civil rights sit-ins, jazz tours with John Handy's Freedom Band, and Berkeley's Vietnam Day Committee. He would eventually have a strong influence on three of Los Siete—Mario and Tony Martínez and Nelson Rodríguez—and on the political direction of the organization that grew up around their case. (Manganiello was one of the first to emphasize the need for brown radicals to study Marxist literature.) With the growth of the farmworkers' struggle, Manganiello, like many other politically minded brown people, saw the need for some kind of organized movement in the urban barrios.

The Brown Berets were one response to this need. Founded by David Sánchez, who was once elected Los Angeles's "outstanding high school student," the Berets combined paramilitary-type training with a desire to establish cultural and political self-determination for La Raza in the Southwest, the area which the Chicano movement calls *Aztlán*. In March 1968, the Berets led a massive walkout of Chicano high school students in Los Angeles. They were demanding courses in their cultural history, teachers who lived in their communities, bilingual instruction, an end to corporal punishment, and an end to students doing janitorial work. The walkout spread the name of the Brown Berets across the Southwest, and many young Chicanos began, unofficially, to call themselves Berets.

Aaron Manganiello and a friend, Manuel Gómez, convinced the Los Angeles Berets to let them set up an official Northern California branch in Oakland. Chapters soon spread to barrios in dozens of cities throughout the country. The chapters varied in their political outlook. Many were strongly "cultural nationalist," believing that Raza cultural unity was the best basis for organizing; others disagreed, feeling that this perspective was too narrow and could become damaging if an attachment to cultural traditions were to stand in the way of change....

Los Siete de la Raza began as a group of students and ex-students attempting to organize street youth around issues like police brutality. By the time the clinic and legal defense office were established in the spring of 1970, Los Siete was beginning to represent the interests of working families, the basic social unit in the Mission District. Coming out of a movement which consisted of students, radicals, and some street people, this was an essential transition.

People within Los Siete were trying to develop the historical understanding and self-discipline they considered necessary attributes of true revolutionaries. In developing this understanding and discipline they had to struggle with anti-intellectualism. As with the Young Lords in New York, members of Los Siete were supposed to read each day; the books were then discussed in political education classes. This reading, in addition to work at the clinic or legal defense, writing for and selling *Basta Ya!*, raising money, leafleting, public speaking, and, for some, school, jobs, or children to care for, imposed a heavy schedule. As a result, Los Siete remained small, with an increasing number of friends who worked with Los Siete projects but weren't actually members of the organization.

One of the most impressive aspects of Los Siete was the personal changes in many of its members. Although some people left to form new groups, or just to give up politics for a while, those who remained grew more responsible, articulate, dedicated, and mellow. Almost everyone in the group learned to speak convincingly in public, to read carefully and think analytically, and to shoulder responsibility.

The women in Los Siete grew stronger and more independent.

Like the Young Lords, Los Siete fought *machismo* in political work as well as in personal relations. This was no easy fight, since some young men who were fairly sophisticated radicals and good workers still wanted their wives or girlfriends to stay home and keep out of political work. Stronger women in the organization made a conscious effort to step aside and let other women take the lead.

People in Los Siete were trying to become revolutionaries, which necessarily required defining what "revolutionary" meant for brown people in the United States. Clearly it meant solidarity with wars of liberation such as the war in Indochina; and Los Siete, through *Basta Ya!*, tried to show people in the Mission that they, the Indochinese, and many guerrillas in Latin America had a common enemy: Yankee imperialism.

"Revolutionary" also meant devoted to changing the entire social and economic system. Los Siete members believed—partly because of their experience in poverty programs—that in the long run reforms were not going to improve conditions for the masses of Latin people. But they realized they were at the beginning of a long revolutionary process. Their immediate goal was not to "start the revolution then and there," as Bebe Melendez once put it, but to organize, educate, and learn from the people.

"Revolutionary" for Los Siete also meant "internationalist"; that is, rejecting cultural nationalism in favor of a class struggle which crossed racial and even national boundaries. But despite this opposition to cultural nationalism, Los Siete remained a brown organization. Its precise appeal was its concern for the needs of Latin people in a predominantly Latin area. Its members felt there was no use combining with other groups to form a multiracial organization until a significant number of brown people had been united around revolutionary demands. It was also important to Los Siete to remain within the brown movement which, despite its fragmented nature and the diversity of its political ideologies, held a tremendous appeal for Chicano and Latin youth—an appeal stemming from its proud, assertive new spirit, a spirit so important to people who have been discriminated against and taught they are inferior.

It's hard to say what success Los Siete has had after its first two years. The hostility of the powerful mass media has made its message difficult to spread; Los Siete's available avenues of communication with its people aren't nearly so powerful: a small, street-vended newspaper and day-to-day contacts at the clinic or legal defense office with people who often have little time to get involved in politics. But a few events toward the middle of 1971 indicated that people were beginning to make time.

Meetings, leafleting, and picketing around a threatened eviction of the clinic in the early summer of 1971 mobilized neighborhood people and developed a strong core of Los Siete partisans. The landlord, who owned a pharmacy on the ground floor of the building, wanted to get rid of the clinic and rent to some "real doctors with real patients and real money," as he put it, who would send people downstairs to buy at his store. (El Centro de Salud dispensed free drugs whenever possible and so didn't provide any clients for the drug store.)

When the landlord said he wouldn't renew the lease, Los Siete called meetings with people who had used the clinic, asking them to pass the word and boycott the pharmacy. In the week that followed, the pharmacy lost fifty percent of its business. When the landlord still didn't give in, picketing was begun. Insisting that community people must fight for the clinic or it wasn't worth saving, Los Siete resisted the temptation to use outside pressure from friendly doctors or other, mostly white, health professionals. Enough community people responded—a number of them housewives—to convince the landlord to reconsider after only one day of picketing. The women who had come to the clinic's defense would hopefully remain organized as a pressure group on health care issues in the Mission.

It would seem that after two years, Los Siete was at least moving in the right direction; that more genuine contacts had been made, more trust established, than by radical organizations in the past—especially in the Mission District, where political activity has been dominated either by the Democratic Party and its Mexican American friends, or by Office of Economic Opportunity-funded groups which are often full of opportunists. Los Siete is indigenous; it is not being paid by anyone to exist, and its members work mainly from idealistic motives—as Tony Herrera put it, "dedicated heart and soul to serving the people."

Source: Marjorie Heins, *Strictly Ghetto Property: The Story of Los Siete de La Raza* (Berkeley, CA: Ramparts Press, 1972), pp. 11–12, 49–51, 203–206.

362. Excerpts from Robert Kistler, "Women 'Pushed' into Sterilization, Doctor Charges," 1974

Sterilization has its roots in the Social Darwinist Eugenics Movement of the early 20th century when American eugenicists believed that people could be categorized according to intelligence and that the United States could genetically engineer its racial composition. The extreme position called for sterilization—a notion that was popular through the 1960s. There is evidence that even that individuals in President John F. Kennedy's Peace Corp, established in 1961, promoted sterilization programs. Domestically sterilizations were a major problem in the Puerto Rican, Chicano, and Native American communities. The following article documents the existence of sterilizations at one of the nations major doctor training hospitals—the County/University of Southern California facility at Los Angeles. It was a prestigious facility where interns practiced on low-income patients. A large percentage of these patients were minorities, especially Chicanos and Latinos. Physician Bernard Rosenfeld blew the whistle as the hospital used Latin patients for performing sterilizations without their consent. Often the women were given forms in English at the moment they were in labor. The women filed a $6 million law suit against the hospital. Rosenfeld who had no objection to abortion was horrified at the attitudes of fellow doctors who performed the sterilizations for racial and other reasons that included the fact that sterilization allowed the physicians to perform more complex surgical procedures. The only doctor who supported Rosenfeld and testified that these procedures were taking place was Juan Nieto. Thousands of women, mostly poor and minority were pushed into "voluntary" sterilization, according to Rosenfeld.

Thousands of women—most of them from low-income, minority groups—have been victimized by unregulated "voluntary" sterilization programs in some of the nation's most prestigious hospitals, according to evidence compiled by a Los Angeles physician-researcher.

Such abuses, the physician charges, historically have found fertile climates in the nation's giant, core-city teaching complexes such as the Los Angeles County-USC Medical Center, where medicine is high-volume, often impersonal—and practiced on patients who are generally poor, frightened and uneducated.

It is within the halls of these massive, loosely regulated institutions, according to Dr. Bernard Rosenfeld, that women—some while in the throes of childbirth—have been cajoled, pressured and sometimes coerced into consenting to surgical sterilization.

The operation is permanent and that chances of surgically reversing the procedure at some later date are relatively slight (between 20% and 30%, depending upon which study you believe).

[The only physician who would corroborate Resenfeld was Dr. Juan Nieto, 25.]

Source: Robert Kistler, "Women 'Pushed' into Sterilization, Doctor Charges," *Los Angeles Times*, December 2, 1974, p. A1.

363. Excerpts from the Seattle Civil Rights and Labor History Project, c. 1971

Chicano activism was not confined to California or Texas but prevalent throughout the Midwest and the Pacific Northwest, that included the states of Oregon and Washington. Although not in the Northwest, Utah was part of this grouping. Many of the Chicano activists were children of migrant workers who had come to work in productive agricultural farmlands like those of the Yakima Valley. As students they were inspired by United Farm Workers (UFW) volunteers who drifted into the valleys and college campuses asking students to support the grape boycott. This activism on the campuses in the Northwest began in the late 1960s with Chicano students making demands similar to their counterparts in the Southwest. University of Washington historian Professor Erasmos Gamboa, a student activist, has documented this history and broken the stereotype that Chicano history was a Texas-California affair. As with Southwest colleges and universities, the University of Washington became known in the late 1960s for student mobilizations against the war in Vietnam, against militarism on campus, and in favor of civil rights. Activism followed a familiar pattern: Chicano students were recruited by the Special Education Program in the fall of 1968, and soon afterward formed the United Mexican American Students (UMAS). The farmworkers were always a model. UMAS built links to the Yakima Valley and the local community. In the Seattle community, they helped found El Centro de la Raza, a clearinghouse for community organizations. All along, they pressed for the recruitment of more Mexican American students and the offering of Mexican American Studies classes.

The following are personal testimonies of student leaders at the University of Washington. They represent the experiences of most Chicano and Latino students who made the transformation from first-generation workers to students. They had to endure the racism and alienation of college life and looked to each other for a support network.

PEDRO ACEVEZ

Pedro Acevez was born in Wapato, Washington, and grew up in the nearby town of Toppenish. He grew up working on his father's farm, as well as doing farm labor in Oregon and Washington, before attending Yakima Valley College and Central Washington University. He transferred to the University of Washington in 1969, a move partly made possible by combining scholarships for both groups.

Acevez was active in MEChA de UW [Movimiento Estudiantil Chicano de Aztlán at University of Washington], and served as its President for one year. During his first school year, he worked with a number of MEChA students to help channel a spontaneous farmworker walkout in Yakima Valley into a United Farm Workers (UFW) organizing drive. During the 1970–71 school year, he served as a resident advisor on the "Chicano Floor," or 5th floor, of Lander Hall—though fired for returning home during an illness, student protests successfully pushed the UW to reinstate him.

Since graduating from the UW in 1975, Acevez has worked as a high school and community college math and science teacher, and currently works for the UW's Health Sciences Center.

RICARDO S. MARTÍNEZ, MECHA DE UW; JUDGE: SUPERIOR COURT; U.S. DISTRICT COURT

Judge Ricardo Martínez was born in the small town of Mercedes in Southern Texas. While in Texas, his family worked in the fields picking cotton, tomatoes, and other crops. When he was six, Martinez's family moved to Lynden, Washington, another small farming town. His family was one of the first Latino families that decided to stay in this area of Washington instead of living there seasonally as migrant workers.

Ricardo Martínez earned a BA from the University of Washington in 1975, and his JD in 1980. While attending the University of Washington, he was a member of Movimiento Estudiantil Chicano/a de Aztlán (MEChA).

After earning his law degree, Martínez worked for the King County Prosecutor's office. In 1989, Martinez began his career as a judge, serving on the King County Superior Court until 1998, and as a U.S. Magistrate Judge for the Western District of Washington until 2004. He currently serves as a United States District Judge for the Western District of Washington—having been nominated by President Bush in 2003 and confirmed by the Senate in 2004.

Quotes on staying in Washington: "Why not? Let's stay here." His parents decided to stay in Washington because they thought moving between migrant farming camps was not good for the children.

On MEChA: "The central theme was the ongoing struggle." All the Chicano groups on campus shared the same goal.

On the Chicano Floor: "Living on the floor in Lander Hall that was designated for Chicano students."

"All students of color come together for the betterment of everyone." The need for all people of color to work together.

JUAN JOSÉ BOCANEGRA MECHA; EL CENTRO DE LA RAZA, LA RAZA UNIDA PARTY; AMERICAN INDIAN MOVEMENT

Juan José Bocanegra was born in Reynosa, Tamaulipas, Mexico and grew up in Corpus Chisti, Texas. While he was in school in the 1950s and 1960s, Corpus Christi's public school system was being desegregated—"it was like a big war between Mexicanos and Anglos in that part of the country," he recalled.

After attending Texas A&I University [which has since changed its name to Texas A&M University] in Kingsville, TX from 1967–71, Bocanegra moved to Seattle to get a graduate degree in social work from the University of Washington. He has been a prominent Seattle-based activist ever since. During the 1970s, he played an active role in the Chicano movement and broader Third World Peoples' movements. He helped lead a successful campaign to diversify the UW School of Social Work and create its multi-ethnic practice program. He was active with the group that occupied the Beacon Hill School and founded El Centro de la Raza in 1972.

In 1973, Bocanegra moved to Brownsville, Texas for six months to run for City Council for the La Raza Unida Party—but was disqualified because he had not established legal residence there. After returning to Seattle, he assumed leadership over the South Seattle Community College Chicano English as a Second Language (ESL) Program after Roberto Maestas left that position to lead El Centro de la Raza. He was also active in the American Friends Service Committee's Third World Coalition. During the early to mid-1970s, Bocanegra became involved in solidarity work with local American Indian struggles—including the American Indian Movement (AIM), Frank's Landing demonstrations with the Nisqually Tribe, the Puyallup Tribe's takeover of the Cascadia Center in 1976, and the 1976 Trail of Self-Determination.

REBECCA SALDAÑA PCUN; UFW; SEIU LOCAL 6; STITCH

Rebecca Saldaña's father was a Mexican immigrant, and she was born and raised in Seattle. While attending Seattle University, Saldaña became active in farmworker solidarity campaigns, and after graduating became an organizer with Pineros y Campesinos Unidos del Noroeste (PCUN), a farmworker's union in Oregon. At PCUN, she coordinated its boycott of NORPAC Foods. Afterward, she was hired to be a Community Mobilizer for the Fair Trade Apple Campaign for the United Farmworkers of America (UFW)—a campaign that applied lessons learned in fair trade coffee campaigns to the domestic agricultural sector. She currently organizes janitors for SEIU Local 6, and is a Board Member of STITCH—"a network of women unionists, organizers, and activists that builds connections between Central American and U.S. women organizing for economic justice."

Her father's family immigrated from Mexico to the U.S. where he became a migrant farmworker. He eventually settled in Seattle, where he found a union job.

"I am a product of my parents." Rebecca describes the influence of her father's labor union and her mother's religion on her own political development.

"The Farm Workers of the Urban Area: From organizing farmworkers to organizing janitors."

Source: The Seattle Civil Rights and Labor History Project, http://www.civilrights.washington. edu. Courtesy of Pedro Acevez.

364. Excerpts from *Lau v. Nichols*, 1974

The demand for bilingual education has been part of the immigrant experience from the beginning. When the Germans arrived en mass they set up German-speaking schools, as did Jews and other immigrants. Throughout the early-twentieth century, Mexicans and other Latinos set up Spanish-speaking classes. It was a proven pedagogical method. In the mid 1960s, President Lyndon B. Johnson (1908–1973) told California Congressman Edward Roybal that when he was a school teacher in an all–Mexican American school, he found the students to be intelligent and that the only thing that held them back was the knowledge of English. The schools held them back until they learned English. Johnson considered it a waste of time and resources—why not teach them courses such as mathematics and history in Spanish and transition them into English instead of keeping them in the same class dooming them to failure? By the 1970s there were many Chinese American students and other immigrant children who were falling through the cracks and they demanded teachers who would address linguistic problems. They built on the Chicano experience and the movement toward bilingual education that came to a head in the mid 1960s. In the 1970s, bilingual education suffered setbacks when a federal judge in Denver decided in *Keyes v. School District Number One*, 413 U.S. 189 (1973), litigated by the Mexican American Legal Defense and Education Fund (MALDEF), the premier Mexican American legal defense organization, that placing children in bilingual classes violated anti-segregation laws. In 1974, the Supreme Court in *Lau v. Nichols* ordered federally funded school districts to "take affirmative steps" to give special help to students who did not know English and to open special programs for them. The ruling addressed language-based discrimination. The ruling was made in response to an Asian American suit in San Francisco but it had far-reaching implications for the Latino community.

LAU ET AL v. NICHOLS ET AL.
CERTIORARI TO THE UNITED STATES COURT OF APPEALS FOR THE NINTH CIRCUIT

No. 72-6520. Argued December 10, 1973—Decided January 21, 1974.

The failure of the San Francisco school system to provide English language instruction to approximately 1,800 students of Chinese ancestry who do not speak English, or to provide them with other adequate instructional procedures, denies them a meaningful opportunity to participate in the public educational program and thus violates § 601 of the Civil Rights Act of 1964, which bans discrimination based "on the ground of race, color, or national origin," in "any program or activity receiving Federal financial assistance," and the implementing regulations of the Department of Health, Education, and Welfare. Pp. 565–569. 483 F. 2d 791, reversed and remanded.

Douglas, 1., delivered the opinion of the Court, in which Brennan, Marshall, Powell, and Rehnquist, J.J., joined. Stewart, 1., filed an opinion concurring in the result, in which Burger, C. J., and Blackmun, J., joined, post, p. 569. White, 1., concurred in the result. Blackmun, 1., filed an opinion concurring in the result, in which Burger, C. 1., joined, post, p. 571.

Edward H. Steinman argued the cause for petitioners. With him on the briefs were Kenneth Hecht and David C. Moon.

Thomas M. O'Connor argued the cause for respondents. With him on the brief were George E. Krueger and Burk E. Delventhal.

Assistant Attorney General Pottinger argued the cause for the United States as amicus curiae urging reversal. With him on the brief were Solicitor General Bork, Deputy Solicitor General Wallace, Mark L. Evans, and Brian K. Landsberg.

Mr. Justice Douglas delivered the opinion of the Court.

The San Francisco, California, school system was integrated in 1971 as a result of a federal court decree, 339 F. Supp. 1315. See *Lee v. Johnson,* 404 U.S. 1215. The District Court found that there are 2,856 students of Chinese ancestry in the school system, 400 who do not speak English. Of those who have that language deficiency, about 1,000 are given supplemental courses in the English language. About 1,800, however, do not receive that instruction.

This class suit brought by non-English-speaking Chinese students against officials responsible for the operation of the San Francisco Unified School District seeks relief against the unequal educational opportunities, which are alleged to violate, inter alia, the Fourteenth Amendment. No specific remedy is urged upon us. Teaching English to the students of Chinese ancestry who do not speak the language is one choice. Giving instructions to this group in Chinese is another. There may be others. Petitioners ask only that the Board of Education be directed to apply its expertise to the problem and rectify the situation.

The District Court denied relief. The Court of Appeals affirmed, holding that there was no violation of the Equal Protection Clause of the Fourteenth Amendment or of § 601 of the Civil Rights Act of 1964, 78 Stat. 252, 42 U.S.C. § 2000d, which exclude from participation in federal financial assistance, recipients of aid which discriminate against racial groups. 483 F. 2d 791. One judge dissented....

We granted the petition for certiorari because of the public importance of the question presented, 412 U.S. 938.

The Court of Appeals reasoned that "Every student brings to the starting line of his educational career different advantages and disadvantages caused in part by social, economic, and cultural background, created and continued completely apart from any contribution by the school system," 483 F. 2d, at 797. Yet in our view the case may not be so easily decided. This is a public school system of California and

§ 71 of the California Education Code states that "English shall be the basic language of instruction in all schools." That section permits a school district to determine "when and under what circumstances instruction may be given bilingually." That section also states as "the policy of the state" to insure "the mastery of English by all pupils in the schools," and bilingual instruction is authorized "to the extent that it does not interfere with the systematic, sequential, and regular instruction of all pupils in the English language."

Moreover, § 8573 of the Education Code provides that no pupil shall receive a diploma of graduation from grade 12 who has not met the standards of proficiency in "English," as well as other prescribed subjects. Moreover, by § 12101 of the Education Code (Supp. 1973) children between the ages of six and 16 years are (with exceptions not material here) "subject to compulsory full-time education."

Under these state-imposed standards there is no equality of treatment merely by providing students with the same facilities, textbooks, teachers, and curriculum, for students who do not understand English are effectively foreclosed from any meaningful education.

Basic English skills are at the very core of what these public schools teach. Imposition of a requirement that, before a child can effectively participate in the educational program, he must already have acquired those basic skills is to make a mockery of public education. We know that those who do not understand English are certain to find their classroom experiences wholly incomprehensible and in no way meaningful.

We do not reach the Equal Protection Clause argument which has been advanced but rely solely on § 601 of the Civil Rights Act of 1964, 42 U.S.C. § 2000d, to reverse the Court of Appeals.

That section bans discrimination based "on the ground of race, color, or national origin," in "any program or activity receiving Federal financial assistance." The school district involved in this litigation receives large amounts of federal financial assistance. The Department of Health, Education, and Welfare (HEW), which has authority to promulgate regulations prohibiting discrimination in federally assisted school systems, 42 U.S.C. § 2000d-1, in 1968 issued one guideline that "School systems are responsible for assuring that students of a particular race, color, or national origin are not denied the opportunity to obtain the education generally obtained by other students in the system." 33 Fed. Reg. 4956. In 1970, HEW made the guidelines more specific, requiring school districts that were federally funded "to rectify the language deficiency in order to open" the instruction to students who had "linguistic deficiencies." 35 Fed. Reg. 11595.

By § 602 of the Act, HEW is authorized to issue rules, regulations, and orders to make sure that recipients of federal aid under its jurisdiction conduct any federally financed projects consistently with § 601. HEW's regulations, 45 CPR § 80.3 (b) (1), specify that the recipients may not....

"(ii) Provide any service, financial aid, or other benefit to an individual which is different, or is provided in a different manner, from that provided to others under the program;

"(iv) Restrict an individual in any way in the enjoyment of any advantage or privilege enjoyed by others receiving any service, financial aid, or other benefit under the program."

Discrimination among students on account of race or national origin that is prohibited includes "discrimination ... in the availability or use of any academic ... or other facilities of the grantee or other recipient." Id., § 80.5 (b).

Discrimination is barred which has that effect even though no purposeful design is present: a recipient "may not ... utilize criteria or methods of administration which have the effect of subjecting individuals to discrimination" or have "the effect of defeating or substantially impairing accomplishment of the objectives of the program as respect individuals of a particular race, color, or national origin." Id., § 80.3 (b) (2).

It seems obvious that the Chinese-speaking minority receive fewer benefits than the English-speaking majority from respondents' school system which denies them a meaningful opportunity to participate in the educational program—all earmarks of the discrimination banned by the regulations. In 1970, HEW issued clarifying guidelines, 35 Fed. Reg. 11595, which include the following:

"Where inability to speak and understand the English language excludes national origin-minority group children from effective participation in the educational program offered by a school district, the district must take affirmative steps to rectify the language deficiency in order to open its instructional program to these students."

"Any ability grouping or tracking system employed by the school system to deal with the special language skill needs of national origin-minority group children must be designed to meet such language skill needs as soon as possible and must not operate as an educational deadend or permanent track."

Respondent school district contractually agreed to "comply with title VI of the Civil Rights Act of 1964 ... and all requirements imposed by or pursuant to the Regulation" of HEW (45 CPR pt. 80) which are "issued pursuant to that title ..." and also immediately to "take any measures necessary to effectuate this agreement." The Federal Government has power to fix the terms on which its money allotments to the States shall be disbursed. *Oklahoma v. CSc,* 330 U.S. 127, 142–143. Whatever may be the limits of that power, *Steward Machine Co. v. Davis,* 301 U.S. 548, 590 et seq., they have not been reached here. Sen. Humphrey, during the floor debates on the Civil Rights Act of 1964, said: "Simple justice requires that public funds, to which all taxpayers of all races contribute, not be spent in any fashion which encourages, entrenches, subsidizes, or results in racial discrimination."

We accordingly reverse the judgment of the Court of Appeals and remand the case for the fashioning of appropriate relief. Reversed and remanded.

Source: 414 U.S. 563 (1974).

365. Excerpt from Manuel A. Machado, Jr., *Listen Chicano!*, 1978

During the 1960s and 1970s there was a break between old-time Mexican American historians and a newer generation of Chicano scholars who challenged what they considered the myths of history. One of the older scholars was Manuel Antonio Machado, Jr., a history professor at the University of Montana who had grown up in a different generation. A native of Nogales, Arizona, his book *Listen Chicano!* was meant to be provocative and a slap at the emerging field of Chicano history. The title was a parody on C. Wright Mills, *Listen, Yankee* (1960). Machado reduced the history of racism toward people of Mexican origin in the United States to cultural misunderstandings. Machado was of the school that Mexicans should pull themselves up by their bootstraps. He based his chapter on César Chávez on conservative author Ralph de Toledano's *Little Cesar*.

The Anglo has oppressed you, the Anglo has robbed you, the Anglo has stolen your dignity as a man and as a Mexican. Therefore, rally against the continuation of a system that negates your culture and oppresses your body and overthrow the shackles of Anglo imperialism. Lord save us from the propagandists!

Such calls to battle become more and more strident throughout the Southwest and California. The Mexican American is an awakening minority, becoming aware of its potential as a political and economic force, and the imperative of organization makes necessary a resort to demagoguery of the basest sort. The demagoguery of the Mexican American militant attempts to polarize all Mexican Americans into a single ethnic unit and subsequently organize this group into a viable political force. Such a maneuver bases itself upon a series of assumptions that convert the Mexican American into a homogeneous unit in which all members respond in similar if not identical fashion to a given set of stimuli.

The first of these assumptions, unfortunately, is that of ethnic homogeneity. It is assumed that the Mexican American comprises a single socio-economic unit. This belief, often held sacrosanct by both Anglos and militant Chicanos, fails to take into account the historical complexity of Mexican American evolution. There exists a patent failure to recognize the vast cultural and economic differences extant within the Mexican American community today.

Moreover, the homogeneity myth is fed by the lack of scholarly investigation about the Mexican American. With the exception of some industrious anthropologists who studied family life in Mexican American communities, very little work has been done to analyze the role of the Mexican American in the life of the United States. No generally accepted historical periods exist, and as a result, difficulties arise in an attempt to place this group in perspective. Scholarly investigators instead bare their bleeding hearts and join the hue and cry for Chicano solidarity and Brown Power while at the same time flagellating themselves with mea culpas.

Divisions within the Mexican American community further destroy ethnic cohesiveness. Mexican Americans often do not like the term *Mexican American*. If they are descended from the old stock that participated in the initial settlement of the Southwest and California, Mexican denotes a lower class status. Waves of immigration from Mexico since 1848 exacerbated further the divisions between old families and new arrivals.

In addition, as some Mexican Americans progressed up the socio-economic ladder, they blended more and more with the ultimately dominant Anglo culture. Mexican Americans are represented in all levels of society, and their socio-economic positions condition their responses more than any sort of amorphous appeal to ethnicity.

As if ethnic solidarity were not enough, the new Chicano militancy declares a racial solidity. Such a declaration negates absolutely the hybridized racial stock that is in fact Mexican. The Mexican American is told that his primary racial stock is Indian and not Spanish. His heroes are Mexico's Indian heroes. Spanish glory and achievement become, for the Mexican American, an ugly story of oppression and subjugation of Mexico's Indian people. Nonsense!

In the last ten years the Mexican American emerged as a power to be reckoned with in the Southwest and in California. In New Mexico, the Mexican American, who comprises approximately 40 percent of the population, received political sops. Dennis Chávez for years served as United States Senator from that state. Upon his death, Joseph Montoya went to Washington. In Texas, Congressman Henry González represents San Antonio. Yet, the last decade has seen the Mexican American organize and become a force at the local level. Mexican Americans now sit on school boards in Los Angeles, in Texas towns, and in communities throughout the Southwest. City councilmen in many areas now have Spanish surnames. All of this adds up to an imperative for consideration.

Into the breach steps the academician and the bleeding heart liberal, terms that occasionally might interchange without loss of meaning. Awareness by liberal spirits of restlessness in the barrios means that programs and agencies must be organized to compensate for the centuries of wrongdoing by the Anglos. An orgy of self-mortification begins. Suddenly the Mexican American becomes a "problem" to be studied but not necessarily understood. We must, proclaim the suddenly interested academics and liberals, care for our little brown brethren of barrio and field. We must give to them the benefits of the American way of life. We must eliminate those things in their existence that keep them from becoming full and active participants in the American way. In short, we must have "gringoized" Mexicans, fitting into some sort of arbitrary cultural mold.

Such ego flagellation becomes, at best, disgusting, for there is no attempt to understand the diverse cultural backgrounds that comprise the somewhat inchoate group called the Mexican American. Instead, the Anglo reformer, like the Chicano militant, grasps at the idea of cultural and racial homogeneity and attempts to force the Mexican American into an arbitrary slot.

Admittedly, the vast majority of the evidence on the Mexican American remains to be unearthed. Yet, it shall stay subsumed in archives and statistical tables until a modicum of rationality is restored and visceral, conditioned responses become aberrations instead of accepted hypotheses.

In all probability, the best approach to the study of the Mexican American lies in the area of comparative history. The vast majority of the Mexican American population inhabits a strip of land approximately two hundred miles north of the Mexican border in the Southwest and California. This political boundary, however, does not divide sharply the cultures that have fused in that region. As a result, the blending of cultures in the Southwest and in California necessitates analyses of those cultural components that have blended as well as conflicted when diverse cultural groups came into contact with each other.

This personalized essay will attempt to suggest some of those elements that need study before the Mexican American can be viewed with any sort of perspective. As a Mexican American, it offends me to receive condescension from Anglo colleagues and associates. Yet, their attitudes are, in a sense, predictable because they have no perspective in which to view the Mexican American. A broadened mind would certainly be more liberal than one that operated on a given set of assumptions.

Source: Manuel A. Machado, Jr. *Listen, Chicano!* (Chicago: Nelson-Hall Inc., 1978), pp. xiii–xvi.

366. Excerpt from the *University of California Regents v. Bakke*, 1978

In 1973, Allan Bakke, a 33-year-old Caucasian man, was denied admission to the University of California Medical School at Davis because of his age and a bad interview. His test scores were higher than the specially admitted minority students. Two years later he applied again. He was again rejected even though his test scores were considerably higher than most of the minorities admitted under a special program that reserved 16 out of 100 possible spaces for minorities on the basis that there were not enough black, brown, or Native American medical doctors. Bakke sued, claiming that his rights under the Equal Protection Clause of the 14th Amendment had been violated. The court ruled in his favor holding that race could not be a factor in admissions. It said nothing about legacy admissions (i.e., the children of alumni or wealthy donors). The following is an excerpt of the ruling of the U.S. Supreme Court.

The Medical School of the University of California at Davis (hereinafter Davis) had two admissions programs for the entering class of 100 students—the regular admissions program and the special admissions program. Under the regular procedure, candidates whose overall undergraduate grade point averages fell below 2.5 on a scale of 4.0 were summarily rejected. About one out of six applicants was then given an interview, following which he was rated on a scale of 1 to 100 by each of the committee members (five in 1973 and six in 1974), his rating being based on the interviewers' summaries, his overall grade point average, his science courses' grade point average, his Medical College Admissions Test (MCAT) scores, letters of recommendation, extracurricular activities, and other biographical data, all of which resulted in a total "benchmark score." The full admissions committee then made offers of admission on the basis of their review of the applicant's file and his score, considering and acting upon applications as they were received. The committee chairman was responsible for placing names on the waiting list and had discretion to include persons with "special skills." A separate committee, a majority of whom were members of minority groups, operated the special admissions program. The 1973 and 1974 application forms, respectively, asked candidates whether they wished to be considered as "economically and/or educationally disadvantaged" applicants and members of a "minority group" (blacks, Chicanos, Asians, American Indians). If an applicant of a minority group was found to be "disadvantaged," he would be rated in a manner similar to the one employed by the general admissions committee. Special candidates, however, did not have to meet the 2.5 grade point cut-off and were not ranked against candidates in the general admissions process. About one-fifth of the special applicants were invited for interviews in 1973 and 1974, following which they were given benchmark scores, and the top choices were then given to the general admissions committee, which could reject special candidates for failure to meet course requirements or other specific deficiencies. The special committee continued to recommend candidates until 16 special admission selections had been made. During a four-year period, 63 minority [438 U.S. 265, 266] students were admitted to Davis under the special program and 44 under the general program. No disadvantaged whites were admitted under the special program, though many applied. Respondent, a white male, applied to Davis in 1973 and 1974, in both years being considered only under the general admissions program. Though he had a 468 out of 500 score in 1973, he was rejected since no general applicants with scores less than 470 were being accepted after respondent's application, which was filed late in the year, had been processed and completed. At that time, four special admission slots were still unfilled. In 1974, respondent applied early, and though he had a total score of 549 out of 600, he was again rejected. In neither year was his name placed on the discretionary waiting list. In both years, special applicants were admitted with significantly lower scores than respondent's. After his second rejection, respondent filed this action in state court for mandatory, injunctive, and declaratory relief to compel his admission to Davis, alleging that the special admissions program operated to exclude him on the basis of his race in violation of the Equal Protection Clause of the Fourteenth Amendment, a provision of the California Constitution, and 601 of Title VI of the Civil Rights Act of 1964, which provides, inter alia, that no person shall on the ground of race or color be excluded from participating in any program receiving federal financial assistance. Petitioner cross-claimed for a declaration that its special admissions program was lawful. The trial court found that the special program operated as a racial quota, because minority applicants in that program were rated only against one another, and 16 places in the class of 100 were reserved for them. Declaring that petitioner could not take race into account in making admissions decisions, the program was held to violate the Federal and State Constitutions and Title VI. Respondent's admission was not ordered, however, for lack of proof that he would have been admitted but for the special program. The California Supreme Court, applying a strict-scrutiny standard, concluded that the special admissions program was not the least intrusive means of achieving the goals of the admittedly compelling state interests of integrating the medical profession and increasing the number of doctors willing to serve minority patients. Without passing on the state constitutional or federal statutory grounds, the court held that petitioner's special admissions program violated the Equal Protection Clause. Since petitioner could not satisfy its burden of demonstrating that respondent, absent the special program, would not have been admitted, the court ordered his admission to Davis.

Held: The judgment below is affirmed insofar as it orders respondent's admission to Davis and invalidates petitioner's special admissions program [438 U.S. 265, 267], but is reversed insofar as it prohibits petitioner from taking race into account as a factor in its future admissions decisions.

[Dissenting Opinion]

Opinion of Mr. Justice Brennan, Mr. Justice White, Mr. Justice Marshall, and Mr. Justice Blackmun, concurring in the judgment in part and dissenting in part.

The Court today, in reversing in part the judgment of the Supreme Court of California, affirms the constitutional power of Federal and State Governments to act affirmatively to achieve equal opportunity for all. The difficulty of the issue presented—whether government may use race-conscious programs to redress the continuing effects of past discrimination—[438 U.S. 265, 325] and the mature consideration which each of our Brethren has brought to it have resulted in many opinions, no single one speaking for the Court. But this should not and must not mask the central meaning of today's opinions: Government may take race into account when it acts not to demean or insult any racial group, but to remedy disadvantages cast on minorities by past racial prejudice, at least when appropriate findings have been made by judicial, legislative, or administrative bodies with competence to act in this area.

The Chief Justice and our Brothers Stewart, Rehnquist, and Stevens, have concluded that Title VI of the Civil Rights Act of 1964, 78 Stat. 252, as amended, 42 U.S.C. 2000d et seq., prohibits programs such as that at the Davis Medical School. On this statutory theory alone, they would hold that respondent Allan Bakke's rights have been violated and that he must, therefore, be admitted to the [Davis] Medical School. Our Brother Powell, reaching the Constitution, concludes that, although race may be taken into account in university admissions, the particular special admissions program used by petitioner, which resulted in the exclusion of respondent Bakke, was not shown to be necessary to achieve petitioner's stated goals. Accordingly, these Members of the Court form a majority of five affirming the judgment of the Supreme Court of California insofar as it holds that respondent Bakke "is entitled to an order that he be admitted to the University." 18 Cal. 3d 34, 64, 553 P.2d 1152, 1172 (1976).

Our Nation was founded on the principle that "all Men are created equal." Yet candor requires acknowledgment that the Framers of our Constitution, to forge the 13 Colonies into one Nation, openly compromised this principle of equality with its antithesis: slavery. The consequences of this compromise are well known and have aptly been called our "American Dilemma." Still, it is well to recount how recent the time has been, if it has yet come, when the promise of our principles has flowered into the actuality of equal opportunity for all regardless of race or color.

The Fourteenth Amendment, the embodiment in the Constitution of our abiding belief in human equality, has been the law of our land for only slightly more than half its 200 years. And for half of that half, the Equal Protection Clause of the Amendment was largely moribund so that, as late as 1927, Mr. Justice Holmes could sum up the importance of that Clause by remarking that it was the "last resort of constitutional arguments." *Buck v. Bell*, 274 U.S. 200, 208 (1927). Worse than desuetude, the Clause was early turned against those whom it was intended to set free, condemning them to a "separate but equal" status before the law, a status [438 U.S. 265, 327] always separate but seldom equal. Not until 1954—only 24 years ago—was this odious doctrine interred by our decision in *Brown v. Board of Education*, 347 U.S. 483 (Brown I), and its progeny, which proclaimed that separate schools and public facilities of all sorts were inherently unequal and forbidden under our Constitution. Even then inequality was not eliminated with "all deliberate speed." *Brown v. Board of Education*, 349 U.S. 294, 301 (1955). In 1968, and again in 1971, for example, we were forced to remind school boards of their obligation to eliminate racial discrimination root and branch. And a glance at our docket and at dockets of lower courts will show that even today officially sanctioned discrimination is not a thing of the past.

Against this background, claims that law must be "color-blind" or that the datum of race is no longer relevant to public policy must be seen as aspiration rather than as description of reality. This is not to denigrate aspiration; for reality rebukes us that race has too often been used by those who would stigmatize and oppress minorities. Yet we cannot—and, as we shall demonstrate, need not under our

Constitution or Title VI, which merely extends the constraints of the Fourteenth Amendment to private parties who receive federal funds—let color blindness become myopia which masks the reality that many "created equal" have been treated within our lifetimes as inferior both by the law and by their fellow citizens. [438 U.S. 265, 328] ...

The threshold question we must decide is whether Title VI of the Civil Rights Act of 1964 bars recipients of federal funds from giving preferential consideration to disadvantaged members of racial minorities as part of a program designed to enable such individuals to surmount the obstacles imposed by racial discrimination. We join Parts I and V-C of our Brother Powell's opinion and three of us agree with his conclusion in Part II that this case does not require us to resolve the question whether there is a private right of action under Title VI.

In our view, Title VI prohibits only those uses of racial criteria that would violate the Fourteenth Amendment if employed by a State or its agencies; it does not bar the preferential treatment of racial minorities as a means of remedying past societal discrimination to the extent that such action is consistent with the Fourteenth Amendment. The legislative history of Title VI, administrative regulations interpreting the statute, subsequent congressional and executive action, and the prior decisions of this Court compel this conclusion. None of these sources lends support to the proposition that Congress intended to bar all race-conscious efforts to extend the benefits of federally financed programs to minorities who have been historically excluded from the full benefits of American life....

The history of Title VI—from President Kennedy's request that Congress grant executive departments and agencies authority [438 U.S. 265, 329] to cut off federal funds to programs that discriminate against Negroes through final enactment of legislation incorporating his proposals—reveals one fixed purpose: to give the Executive Branch of Government clear authority to terminate federal funding of private programs that use race as a means of disadvantaging minorities in a manner that would be prohibited by the Constitution if engaged in by government.

This purpose was first expressed in President Kennedy's June 19, 1963, message to Congress proposing the legislation that subsequently became the Civil Rights Act of 1964. [438 U.S. 265, 330] Rep. Celler, the Chairman of the House Judiciary Committee, and the floor manager of the legislation in the House, introduced Title VI in words unequivocally expressing the intent to provide the Federal Government with the means of assuring that its funds were not used to subsidize racial discrimination inconsistent with the standards imposed by the Fourteenth and Fifth Amendments upon state and federal action.

"The bill would offer assurance that hospitals financed by Federal money would not deny adequate care to Negroes. It would prevent abuse of food distribution programs whereby Negroes have been known to be denied food surplus supplies when white persons were given such food. It would assure Negroes the benefits now accorded only white students in programs of high[er] education financed by Federal funds. It would, in short, assure the existing right to equal treatment in the enjoyment of Federal funds. It would not destroy any rights of private property or freedom of association." 110 Cong. Rec. 1519 (1964).

It was clear to Rep. Celler that Title VI, apart from the fact that it reached all federally funded activities even in the absence of sufficient state or federal control to invoke the Fourteenth or Fifth Amendments, was not placing new substantive limitations upon the use of racial criteria, but rather was designed to extend to such activities "the existing right to equal treatment" enjoyed by Negroes under those Amendments, and he later specifically defined the purpose of Title VI in this way:

"In general, it seems rather anomalous that the Federal Government should aid and abet discrimination on the basis of race, color, or national origin by granting money [438 U.S. 265, 331] and other kinds of financial aid. It seems rather shocking, moreover, that while we have on the one hand the 14th Amendment, which is supposed to do away with discrimination since it provides for equal protection of the laws, on the other hand, we have the Federal Government aiding and abetting those who persist in practicing racial discrimination.

"It is for these reasons that we bring forth Title VI. The enactment of Title VI will serve to override specific provisions of law which contemplate Federal assistance to racially segregated institutions." Id., at 2467.

Rep. Celler also filed a memorandum setting forth the legal basis for the enactment of Title VI which reiterated the theme of his oral remarks: "In exercising its authority to fix the terms on which Federal funds will be disbursed ... Congress clearly has power to legislate so as to insure that the Federal Government does not become involved in a violation of the Constitution." Id., at 1528.

Other sponsors of the legislation agreed with Rep. Celler that the function of Title VI was to end the Federal Government's complicity in conduct, particularly the segregation or exclusion of Negroes, inconsistent with the standards to be found in the antidiscrimination provisions of the Constitution. Rep. Lindsay, also a member of the Judiciary Committee, candidly acknowledged, in the course of explaining why Title VI was necessary, that it did not create any new standard of equal treatment beyond that contained in the Constitution:

"Both the Federal Government and the States are under constitutional mandates not to discriminate. Many have raised the question as to whether legislation is required at all. Does not the Executive already have the power in the distribution of Federal funds to apply those conditions which will enable the Federal Government itself to live up to the mandate of the Constitution and to require [438 U.S. 265, 332] States and local government entities to live up to the Constitution, most especially the 5th and 14th amendments?" Id., at 2467.

He then explained that legislation was needed to authorize the termination of funding by the Executive Branch because existing legislation seemed to contemplate the expenditure of funds to support racially segregated institutions. Ibid. The views of Reps. Celler and Lindsay concerning the purpose and function of Title VI were shared by other sponsors and proponents of the legislation in the House. Nowhere is there any suggestion that Title VI was intended to terminate federal funding for any reason other than consideration of race or national origin by the recipient institution in a manner inconsistent with the standards incorporated in the Constitution. The Senate's consideration of Title VI reveals an identical understanding concerning the purpose and scope of the legislation. Sen. Humphrey, the Senate floor manager, opened the Senate debate with a section-by-section analysis of the Civil Rights Act in which he succinctly stated the purpose of Title VI:

"The purpose of title VI is to make sure that funds of the United States are not used to support racial discrimination. In many instances the practices of segregation or discrimination, which title VI seeks to end, are unconstitutional. This is clearly so wherever Federal funds go to a State agency which engages in racial discrimination. It may also be so where Federal funds go to support private, segregated institutions, under the decision in *Simkins v. Moses H. Cone Memorial Hospital*, 323 F.2d 959 (C. A. 4, 1963) [cert. denied, 376 U.S. 938 (1964)]. In all cases, such discrimination is contrary to national policy, and to the moral sense of the Nation. Thus, Title VI is simply [438 U.S. 265, 333] designed to insure that Federal funds are spent in accordance with the Constitution and the moral sense of the Nation." Id., at 6544.

Sen. Humphrey, in words echoing statements in the House, explained that legislation was needed to accomplish this objective because it was necessary to eliminate uncertainty concerning the power of federal agencies to terminate financial assistance to programs engaging in racial discrimination in the face of various federal statutes which appeared to authorize grants to racially segregated institutions. Ibid. Although Senator Humphrey realized that Title VI reached conduct which, because of insufficient governmental action, might be beyond the reach of the Constitution, it was clear to him that the substantive standard imposed by the statute was that of the Fifth and Fourteenth Amendments.

Senate supporters of Title VI repeatedly expressed agreement with Sen. Humphrey's description of the legislation as providing the explicit authority and obligation to apply the standards of the Constitution to all recipients of federal funds. Sen. Ribicoff described the limited function of Title VI:

"Basically, there is a constitutional restriction against discrimination in the use of Federal funds; and Title VI simply spells out the procedure to be used in enforcing that restriction." Id., at 13333.

Other strong proponents of the legislation in the Senate repeatedly expressed their intent to assure that federal funds would only be spent in accordance with constitutional standards. See remarks of Sen. Pastore, Id., at 7057, 7062; Sen. Clark, Id., at 5243; Sen. Allott, Id., at 12675, 12677 [438 U.S. 265, 334].

Respondent's contention that Congress intended Title VI to bar affirmative-action programs designed to enable minorities disadvantaged by the effects of discrimination to participate in federally financed programs is also refuted by an examination of the type of conduct which Congress thought it was prohibiting by means of Title VI. The debates reveal that the legislation was motivated primarily by a desire to eradicate a very specific evil: federal financial support of programs which disadvantaged Negroes by excluding them from participation or providing them with separate facilities. Again and again supporters of Title VI emphasized that the purpose of the statute was to end segregation in federally funded activities and to end other discriminatory uses of race disadvantaging Negroes....

The conclusion to be drawn from the foregoing is clear. Congress recognized that Negroes, in some cases with congressional acquiescence, were being discriminated against in the administration of programs and denied the full benefits of activities receiving federal financial support. It was aware that there were many federally funded programs and institutions which discriminated against minorities in a manner inconsistent with the standards of the Fifth and Fourteenth Amendments but whose activities might not involve sufficient state or federal action so as to be in violation of these Amendments. Moreover, Congress believed that it was questionable whether the Executive Branch possessed legal authority to terminate the funding of activities on the ground that they discriminated racially against Negroes in a manner violative of the standards contained in the Fourteenth and Fifth [438 U.S.

265, 336] Amendments. Congress' solution was to end the Government's complicity in constitutionally forbidden racial discrimination by providing the Executive Branch with the authority and the obligation to terminate its financial support of any activity which employed racial criteria in a manner condemned by the Constitution.

Of course, it might be argued that the Congress which enacted Title VI understood the Constitution to require strict racial neutrality or color blindness, and then enshrined that concept as a rule of statutory law. Later interpretation and clarification of the Constitution to permit remedial use of race would then not dislodge Title VI's prohibition of race-conscious action. But there are three compelling reasons to reject such a hypothesis.

First, no decision of this Court has ever adopted the proposition that the Constitution must be color blind. See infra, at 355–356.

Second, even if it could be argued in 1964 that the Constitution might conceivably require color blindness, Congress surely would not have chosen to codify such a view unless the Constitution clearly required it.... It is inconceivable that Congress intended to encourage voluntary efforts to eliminate the evil of racial discrimination while at the same time forbidding the voluntary use of race-conscious remedies to cure acknowledged or obvious statutory violations. Yet a reading of Title VI as prohibiting all action predicated upon race which adversely [438 U.S. 265, 337] affects any individual would require recipients guilty of discrimination to await the imposition of such remedies by the Executive Branch. Indeed, such an interpretation of Title VI would prevent recipients of federal funds from taking race into account even when necessary to bring their programs into compliance with federal constitutional requirements. This would be a remarkable reading of a statute designed to eliminate constitutional violations, especially in light of judicial decisions holding that under certain circumstances the remedial use of racial criteria is not only permissible but is constitutionally required to eradicate constitutional violations. For example, in *Board of Education v. Swann*, 402 U.S. 43 (1971), the Court held that a statute forbidding the assignment of students on the basis of race was unconstitutional because it would hinder the implementation of remedies necessary to accomplish the desegregation of a school system: "Just as the race of students must be considered in determining whether a constitutional violation has occurred, so also must race be considered in formulating a remedy." Id., at 46. Surely Congress did not intend to prohibit the use of racial criteria when constitutionally required or to terminate the funding of any entity which implemented such a remedy. It clearly desired to encourage all remedies, including the use of race, necessary to eliminate racial discrimination in violation of the Constitution rather than requiring the recipient to await a judicial adjudication of unconstitutionality and the judicial imposition of a racially oriented remedy.

Third, the legislative history shows that Congress specifically eschewed any static definition of discrimination in favor of broad language that could be shaped by experience, administrative necessity, and evolving judicial doctrine. Although it is clear from the debates that the supporters of Title VI intended to ban uses of race prohibited by the Constitution and, more specifically, the maintenance of segregated [438 U.S. 265, 338] facilities, they never precisely defined the term "discrimination," or what constituted an exclusion from participation or a denial of benefits on the ground of race. This failure was not lost upon its opponents. Sen. Ervin complained:

"The word 'discrimination,' as used in this reference, has no contextual explanation whatever, other than the provision that the discrimination 'is to be against' individuals participating in or benefiting from federally assisted programs and activities on the ground specified. With this context, the discrimination condemned by this reference occurs only when an individual is treated unequally or unfairly because of his race, color, religion, or national origin. What constitutes unequal or unfair treatment? Section 601 and Section 602 of Title VI do not say. They leave the determination of that question to the executive department or agencies administering each program, without any guideline whatever to point out what is the congressional intent." 110 Cong. Rec. 5612 (1964).

See also remarks of Rep. Abernethy (Id., at 1619); Rep. Dowdy (Id., at 1632); Sen. Talmadge (Id., at 5251); Sen. Sparkman (Id., at 6052). Despite these criticisms, the legislation's supporters refused to include in the statute or even provide in debate a more explicit definition of what Title VI prohibited.

The explanation for this failure is clear. Specific definitions were undesirable, in the views of the legislation's principal backers, because Title VI's standard was that of the Constitution and one that could and should be administratively and judicially applied. See remarks of Sen. Humphrey (Id., at 5253, 6553); Sen. Ribicoff (Id., at 7057, 13333); Sen. Pastore (Id., at 7057); Sen. Javits (Id., at 5606–5607, 6050). Indeed, there was a strong emphasis throughout [438 U.S. 265, 339] Congress' consideration of Title VI on providing the Executive Branch with considerable flexibility in interpreting and applying the prohibition against racial discrimination. Attorney General Robert Kennedy testified that regulations had not been written into the legislation itself because the rules and regulations defining discrimination might differ from one program to another so that the term would assume different meanings in different contexts. This determination to preserve flexibility in the administration of Title VI was shared by the legislation's supporters. When Sen. Johnston offered an amendment that would have expressly authorized federal grantees to take race into account in placing children in adoptive and foster homes, Sen. Pastore opposed the amendment, which was ultimately defeated by a 56–29 vote, on the ground that federal administrators could be trusted to act reasonably and that there was no danger that they would prohibit the use of racial criteria under such circumstances. Id., at 13695.

Congress' resolve not to incorporate a static definition of discrimination into Title VI is not surprising. In 1963 and 1964, when Title VI was drafted and debated, the courts had only recently applied the Equal Protection Clause to strike down public racial discrimination in America, and the scope of that Clause's nondiscrimination principle was in a state of flux and rapid evolution. Many questions, such as whether the Fourteenth Amendment barred only de jure discrimination or in at least some circumstances reached de facto discrimination, had not yet received an authoritative judicial resolution. The congressional debate reflects an awareness of the evolutionary [438 U.S. 265, 340] change that constitutional law in the area of racial discrimination was undergoing in 1964.

In sum, Congress' equating of Title VI's prohibition with the commands of the Fifth and Fourteenth Amendments, its refusal precisely to define that racial discrimination which it intended to prohibit, and its expectation that the statute would be administered in a flexible manner, compel the conclusion that Congress intended the meaning of the statute's prohibition to evolve with the interpretation of the commands of the Constitution. Thus, any claim that the use of racial criteria is barred by the plain language of the statute must fail in light of the remedial purpose of Title VI and its legislative history. The cryptic nature of the language employed in Title VI merely reflects Congress' concern with the then-prevalent use of racial standards as a means of excluding or disadvantaging Negroes and its determination to prohibit absolutely such discrimination. We have recently held that "When aid to construction of the meaning of words, as used in the statute, is available, there certainly can be no 'rule of law' which forbids its use, however clear the words may appear on 'superficial examination.'" *Train v. Colorado Public Interest Research Group*, 426 U.S. 1, 10 (1976), quoting *United States v. American Trucking Assns.*, 310 U.S. 534, 543–544 (1940). This is especially so when, as is the case here, the literal application of what is believed to be the plain language of the statute, assuming that it is so plain, would lead to results in direct conflict with Congress' unequivocally expressed legislative purpose. [438 U.S. 265, 341] …

Properly construed, therefore, our prior cases unequivocally show that a state government may adopt race-conscious programs if the purpose of such programs is to remove the disparate racial impact its actions might otherwise have and if there is reason to believe that the disparate impact is itself the product of past discrimination, whether its own or that of society at large. There is no question that Davis' program is valid under this test. Certainly, on the basis of the undisputed factual submissions before this Court, Davis had a sound basis for believing that the problem of under representation of minorities was substantial and chronic and that the problem was attributable to handicaps imposed on minority applicants by past and present racial discrimination. Until at least 1973, the practice of medicine in this country was, in fact, if not in law, largely the prerogative of whites. In 1950, for example, while Negroes [438 U.S. 265, 370] constituted 10% of the total population, Negro physicians constituted only 2.2% of the total number of physicians. The overwhelming majority of these, moreover, were educated in two predominantly Negro medical schools, Howard and Meharry. By 1970, the gap between the proportion of Negroes in medicine and their proportion in the population had widened: The number of Negroes employed in medicine remained frozen at 2.2% while the Negro population had increased to 11.1%. The number of Negro admittees to predominantly white medical schools, moreover, had declined in absolute numbers during the years 1955 to 1964. Odegaard 19.

Moreover, Davis had very good reason to believe that the national pattern of underrepresentation of minorities in medicine would be perpetuated if it retained a single admissions standard. For example, the entering classes in 1968 and 1969, the years in which such a standard was used, included only 1 Chicano and 2 Negroes out of the 50 admittees for each year. Nor is there any relief from this pattern of underrepresentation in the statistics for the regular admissions program in later years.

Davis clearly could conclude that the serious and persistent underrepresentation of minorities in medicine depicted by these statistics is the result of handicaps under which minority applicants labor as a consequence of a background of deliberate, purposeful discrimination against minorities in education [438 U.S. 265, 371] and in society generally, as well as in the medical profession. From the inception of our national life, Negroes have been subjected to unique legal disabilities impairing access to equal educational opportunity. Under slavery, penal sanctions were imposed upon anyone attempting to educate Negroes. After enactment of the Fourteenth Amendment, the States continued to deny Negroes equal educational opportunity, enforcing a strict policy of segregation that itself stamped Negroes as inferior, Brown I, 347 U.S. 483 (1954), that relegated minorities to inferior educational institutions, and that denied them intercourse in the mainstream of professional life necessary to advancement. See Sweatt v. Painter, 339 U.S. 629 (1950). Segregation was not limited to public facilities, moreover, but was enforced by criminal penalties against private action as well. Thus, as late as 1908, this Court enforced a state criminal conviction against a private college for teaching Negroes together with whites. Berea College v. Kentucky, 211 U.S. 45. See also Plessy v. Ferguson, 163 U.S. 537 (1896).

Green v. County School Board, 391 U.S. 430 (1968), gave explicit recognition to the fact that the habit of discrimination and the cultural tradition of race prejudice cultivated by centuries of legal slavery and segregation were not immediately dissipated when Brown I, supra, announced the constitutional principle that equal educational opportunity and participation in all aspects of American life could not be denied on the basis of race. Rather, massive official and private resistance prevented, and to a lesser extent still prevents, attainment of equal opportunity in education at all levels and in the professions. The generation of minority students applying to Davis Medical School since it opened in 1968—most of whom [438 U.S. 265, 372] were born before or about the time Brown I was decided—clearly have been victims of this discrimination. Judicial decrees recognizing discrimination in public education in California testify to the fact of widespread discrimination suffered by California-born minority applicants; many minority group members living in California, moreover, were born and reared in school districts in Southern States segregated by law. Since separation of schoolchildren by race "generates a feeling of inferiority as to their status in the community that may affect their hearts and minds in a way unlikely ever to be undone," Brown I, supra, at 494, the conclusion is inescapable that applicants to medical school must be few indeed who endured the effects of de jure segregation, the resistance to Brown I, or the equally debilitating pervasive private discrimination fostered by our long history of official discrimination, cf. Reitman v. Mulkey, 387 U.S. 369 (1967), and yet come to the starting line with an education equal to whites.

Moreover, we need not rest solely on our own conclusion that Davis had sound reason to believe that the effects of past discrimination were handicapping minority applicants to the Medical School, because the Department of Health, Education, and Welfare, the expert agency charged by Congress with promulgating regulations enforcing Title VI of the Civil Rights Act of 1964, see supra, at 341–343, has also reached the conclusion that race may be taken into account in situations [438 U.S. 265, 373] where a failure to do so would limit participation by minorities in federally funded programs, and regulations promulgated by the Department expressly contemplate that appropriate race-conscious programs may be adopted by universities to remedy unequal access to university programs caused by their own or by past societal discrimination. See supra, at 344–345, discussing 45 CFR 80.3 (b) (6) (ii) and 80.5 (j) (1977). It cannot be questioned that, in the absence of the special admissions program, access of minority students to the Medical School would be severely limited and, accordingly, race-conscious admissions would be deemed an appropriate response under these federal regulations. Moreover, the

Department's regulatory policy is not one that has gone unnoticed by Congress. See supra, at 346–347. Indeed, although an amendment to an appropriations bill was introduced just last year that would have prevented the secretary of Health, Education, and Welfare from mandating race-conscious programs in university admissions, proponents of this measure, significantly, did not question the validity of voluntary implementation of race-conscious admissions criteria. See ibid. In these circumstances, the conclusion implicit in the regulations—that the lingering effects of past discrimination continue to make race-conscious remedial programs appropriate means for ensuring equal educational opportunity in universities—deserves considerable judicial deference. See, e. g., *Katzenbach v. Morgan*, 384 U.S. 641 (1966); UJO, 430 U.S., at 175–178 (opinion concurring in part)....

We disagree with the lower courts' conclusion that the Davis program's use of race was unreasonable in light of its objectives. First, as petitioner argues, there are no practical means by which it could achieve its ends in the foreseeable future without the use of race-conscious measures. With respect to any factor (such as poverty or family educational background) that may be used as a substitute for race as an indicator of past discrimination, whites greatly outnumber racial minorities simply because whites make up a far larger percentage of the total population and therefore far outnumber minorities in absolute terms at every socio-economic level ... For example, of a class of recent medical school applicants from families with less than $10,000 income, at least 71% were white.... Of all 1970 families headed by a [438 U.S. 265, 377] person not a high school graduate which included related children under 18, 80% were white and 20% were racial minorities. Moreover, while race is positively correlated with differences in GPA and MCAT scores, economic disadvantage is not. Thus, it appears that economically disadvantaged whites do not score less well than economically advantaged whites, while economically advantaged blacks score less well than do disadvantaged whites.... These statistics graphically illustrate that the University's purpose to integrate its classes by compensating for past discrimination could not be achieved by a general preference for the economically disadvantaged or the children of parents of limited education unless such groups were to make up the entire class.

Source: U.S. Supreme Court, *University of California Regents v. Bakke*, 438 U.S. 265 (1978), 438 U.S. 265, *Regents of the University of California v. Bakke*, *Certiorari to the Supreme Court of California*, No. 76–811, Argued October 12, 1977, Decided June 28, 1978.

367. Excerpts from Celeste Durant, "California Bar Exam—Pain and Trauma Twice a Year," 1978

The basis of affirmative action is to level the playing field. President Lyndon B. Johnson (1908–1973) initiated economic programs to help minority groups make it in society. He felt that there could not be political and social equality without economic opportunity. President Richard M. Nixon (1913–1994) also supported affirmative action programs believing that a prosperous middle class would vote Republican. Universities and colleges supported affirmative action because they wanted diverse campuses and educated professionals that would serve all Americans. Law schools and medical schools still give preferences to applicants from rural communities that have a shortage of professionals. In the late 1970s, at the time of the Bakke decision, which held that race could not be used as a factor in admitting students, in primary care medicine, there was one white doctor practicing medicine for every 700 whites; the ratio for blacks was 1:3,800; for Native Americans, 1:20,000; and for Latinos, 1:30,000. At this same time, the United States ranked 18th among industrialized nations in health care, primarily because of the low quality of care received by minorities—today, in 2007, the United States ranks 37th. The rationale for admitting minority students to medical school was that as doctors they would return to their communities to practice medicine.

California has about 60,000 lawyers—a ratio of one lawyer for every 385 people. In San Francisco, the attorney Mecca for the state, the ratio is one lawyer for every 100 citizens. In Los Angeles County, the ratio is one for every 363....

Although there are no exact figures, it is estimated that only between 1% and 2% of the state's lawyers are members of minority groups.

According to statistics gathered by the Third World Coalition, a group of minority law school students and faculty members in the state, only 28% of the black and Spanish-named applicants passed the Bar on the first try, compared to a rate of 61% for all applicants in 1975, the most recent year for which data are available.

The coalition says also that as of 1975, there was one Anglo lawyer for every 530 Anglos, one Asian lawyer for every 1,750 Asians, one black lawyer for every 3,441 blacks, one Spanish-surnamed lawyer for every 9,482 Spanish-surnamed persons and one American Indian lawyer for every 50,000 American Indians.

Source: Celeste Durant, "California Bar Exam—Pain and Trauma Twice a Year," *Los Angeles Times*, August 27, 1978, p. C1.

368. Excerpts from an Interview with Ernie Cortés, Jr., 2002

The Alinsky Institute was founded by Saul Alinsky (1909–1972). Community organizer and founder of the Industrial Areas Foundation, Alinksy began organizing in Chicago in the 1930s. He started an institute to train grassroots organizers. Alinsky was extremely influential in the Mexican American community, helping found the Community Service Organization (1947) in California. It, in turn, trained César Chávez and influenced organizers such as José Angel Gutiérrez. Ernesto Cortés Jr., educated at Texas A&M, dropped out of a graduate program in economics at the University of Texas at Austin to help organize Chicano workers in Texas. Wanting to perfect organizing to a science, he moved to Chicago and studied at the Industrial Areas Foundation (IAF). In 1974, Cortés returned to San Antonio where he helped organize the Communities Organized for Public Service (COPS). This civic organization lobbied for essential city services like public sewer, drainage and other public infrastructure for inner-city neighborhoods. COPS was organized though the parish councils of a coalition of interdenominational San Antonio churches. Cortés helped organize twelve IAF groups in Texas and similar groups—such as the United Neighborhood Organizations (UNO)—in Los Angeles, California. In the transcript that follows, Cortés describes his involvement in these and other groups, and his philosophy of organizing people to bring about change.

DT: [Introduction] It's April 12th, year 2002. We're in Austin, Texas, and visiting with Ernie Cortés, who's been involved with organizing and inspiring people to be involved on environmental issues, public health issues, educational fronts, through groups such as COPS [Communities Organized for Public Service], Valley Interfaith, and many others that he's helped build....

EC: Growing up in San Antonio, you saw a lot of things that didn't seem to be quite they way they were supposed to be, so it's hard to say how you develop those kind of interests. The environmental concerns came to me, frankly, out of concern for public health questions, toxicity of water, concern about lack of sewage, impact on health of air quality, and this whole analogy that I like to use, which is not mine originally, but the coal miner's canary, that the environment is like the coal miner's canary. And, so we have to kind of be concerned, about the environment, not only because, for it's own sake, but because of its impact on the quality of human life, or even the viability and the sustainability of human life. It comes from me all kinds of places, the Book of Genesis gives us from early on, believing that, that means that we have dominion or responsibility, or stewardship over the Earth and that means we have to, that means quality of life for other, all living creatures, species. So, I don't know where it came from—my parents, my church, my school, my community.... I never trained with [Saul] Alinsky, per se, I went to the Industrial Areas Foundation, which is Alinsky's training institute, I met Mr. Alinsky, but I never really worked with him that closely. The guy I worked with at the IAF was Ed Chambers, who was the National Director of Industrial Areas Foundation and worked, built IAF organizations in Chicago and [Rash Shash Shaneer] other places. But long before I went to IAF, I knew ... [its] concerns about civil rights issues and I learned an incredible amount of, [things about] issues relating to public health, in organizing farmworkers, and working with the farmworkers in organizing Red River Valley and learning about the impact of pesticides. How [pesticides have an impact] on human beings, on farmworkers, in particular. And, also, on us, from eating, thinking about, you know, the impact of eating foods which have been laced with pesticides, and the dangers—of the carcinogenic impact that they have. So, it was not, I mean, it was, there was a lot of other things that were going on, in the sixties when I grew up and was going to school, which affected how I saw the world, so IAF was, was not, didn't shape my interest in those issues. When I went to IAF, it was to learn how to do something about those concerns, not, not to understand those concerns.

DT: Are there some writers ... people there, alive or dead, people you met or didn't meet, that might've helped influence you.

EC: I can't point to a particular writer who influenced my thinking about environmental questions.... I've read enormous numbers of reports about things like impact of chemical ... petrol chemical products, ... When, ... in Houston area, learning about ... the quality of water in the Rio Grande River and the impact of ... dumping pollutants from whether it's steel plants, or lead plants, or etc., ... it's hard to say any particular writer shaped my thinking about issues in environment and public health.

DT: It seems that one of the techniques that you have for organizing people, or at least understanding why people want to organize themselves, is because you listen to them.... Can you ... give some examples of when you went down to the Valley and you helped put together [a] farmworkers community down there, and how you might have learned from them?

EC: In the Valley I was with the Valley Interfaith ... in organizing that organization ... I [conducted] ... hundreds of relational meetings, one-on-one meetings, listening sessions, ... having conversations with people who are leaders and potential leaders and found out about their concerns, about everything from the burning of toxic waste off the coast of Brownsville, [to] the concerns that people had about the food chain, the impact of burning—there was a chemical waste management corporation ... [it] was gonna ... burn toxic waste and they were concerned about that.... We began to organize around that particular issue, but then there also the question of a lack of sewers in the *colonias*, ... questions of asbestos in the paint in schools, which is making kids sick, molding, ... which is contributing to absenteeism and enormous visits to doctors.... We would meet with people ... connected with clinics in the Rio Grande Valley ... [the people] would talk about the impact of Third World diseases, ... because of the lack of sewers, secondary sewage systems that existed. In El Paso, the same kind of concerns came up, meeting with people with the public health systems and the hospitals.... Before I began organizing, ... I was on the Board of Managers at the Bexar County Hospital District and ... [I] began to hear about [the] kind of impact that things like lead paints [had, and] through a process of conversations and listening to lots and lots of people, you find out ... that they really care ... [and] want to do something about [it]. What they lack is power. And they lack someone to teach them how to act on their concerns.... [Their demands are] very specific and concrete so that they can do something about [these concerns]....

DT: Can you give me an example of your work with COPS [Communities Organized for Public Service]? ...

EC: The organization got heavily involved ... in the whole question of ... degradation of the water supply, by trying to limit development over the sensitive areas of the recharge zone ... it had to do with just zoning questions, and ... making sure that there were the adequate safeguards. [COPS] got involved in elections, they got involved in fights over the kind and quality of development.... unfortunately Texas and San Antonio are notoriously, ... lax and, and unvigilant, lacking in vigilance and diligence in dealing with ... these safeguards ... [mobilizing people] requires an outraged [community which is] effectively organized and mobilized ... to make sure the public officials do what they're told.... The organization ... got involved in fairly significant fights to clean up the toxicity around Kelly Air Force Base ... forcing Kelly to do some major cleanups in the areas around the base.... The organizations that we build, the IAF organizations are political organizations, ... they don't pretend to be faith-based organizations ... However, ... they operate and they act on their ... values ... And their values are shaped by their faith, traditions, whether it be Catholicism, Judaism, Islam, the different forms of ... different Christian traditions, Baptist, Episcopalian, Methodists, etc. So ... they bring to the table a commitment and an understanding—and a hope for realization of these two sets of values ... The values of a free and open society, the political values which come out of understanding the seminal and—and meaningful documents of our tradition: the Constitution and the Declaration of Independence, the Bill of Rights ... various important statements, the Emancipation Proclamation, Northwest Ordinances, which kind of affirm and—and reaffirm, you know, our commitment to certain things which are real important to us ... Freedom of expression. So, there is this kind of ... secular faith, that is part of our tradition and part of what makes us tick and makes us, and ... animates us, and gives us some energy. This faith in ... democratic traditions and institutions. At the same time, ... [there is the] understanding and that commitment and that tradition is also connected to and challenged by and agitated by, hopefully, and shaped by commitment to the values of Judaism and Christianity, particularly those which have to do with concern for the stranger and the Exodus, the stories that come out of the Exodus tradition. A fear of God, as over against the Pharaoh, a fear of God as over against secular authorities, which means a disposition to—to— take the kinds of risks that are, you know, that are, that are, conceptualized, and—and—the stories of the Exodus traditions, whether it be the midwives who refused to yield the Pharaoh's beckon—beckoning, or—or the prophetic tradition, where the prophets go after the muckety-mucks, as I call them, the powerful people, the—the king ... and the land owners who control the institutions ... dispossessing people of their land and of their work and of their very lives ... So, ... there is a strong, powerful tradition which animates and shapes and motivates people, gives meaning to their lives and we draw heavily upon, and are nourished by, particularly in—in battles which require patience and—and constant vigilance and constant endurance. We draw heavily upon those traditions and the resources of those traditions to sustain us over time....

EC: Justice takes on many different dimensions and many different understandings, ... there is the kind of justice which comes out of the biblical traditions. The word *mishpot* comes to mind, which has to do with the concrete realization of certain ideals, in certain municipal institutions, which have to do with the fact that no one should be left out, no one should be deprived of the means to participation in ... the prosperity of the community, and that's, in the prophetic tradition, this notion of mishpot meant that no matter who you were that you were not to be, no one could take away from you the tools that were necessary [for life]—your house, your ... farm implements, ... In order to be able to participate in the shared prosperity of the community. Even so, ... if you owed money to a money lender, if you owed money to a landlord, and even though that debt was legitimate if it meant, in order to pay the debt, if it meant losing your capacity to have shelter, your capacity to own, to make a livelihood, that justice would not allow that to happen, and so therefore it is incumbent upon the people who ran these municipal courts to not deprive you of that, and to—and to rule in your favor ... against the powerful interest of people who were ... the economic power players of that particular lot and community. And so that understanding, that tradition is something which animates us, and frankly, it is reflected in the populace tradition in Texas ... The Homestead Exemption comes out of that understanding, and the notion of a safety net comes out of that understanding that ... there's a level below which people should not ever fall and so you may have an enterprise economy with risk taking and dynamism and etc. and winners and losers, but there's a—there's a level below which people never fall. And, so therefore, that we never deprive people of certain basic things, which are important for their humanity.... Adam Smith and *The Wealth of Nations* said that ... a just society is one where a working person can appear in public without shame, without being humiliated, ... that meant for, in his time, being able to have a decent shirt, pair of shoes.... [It] was important for the people who ran that society to understand that everyone should have the access to those things which are necessary to appear in public without feeling humiliated, and so, then the question for us is, ... in the year 2002, ... what is necessary for a person to be in public without shame? And I always argue, it's more than just clothes, it's also access to health care, it's access to education, it's access ... to running water, ... shelter. In 1949, the Republican controlled Congress, ... led by Sen. Robert Taft, passed a Housing Act ... of 1949 [that] said that every American, no matter who he or she is ... should be given, and should be provided with a decent home and a suitable living environment.

An Israeli scholar by the name of [Avishai] Margalit, wrote a book called *A Decent Society* and he said that there's a difference between a civilized society and a decent society and a just society. A civilized society is where the people of that society are nice to each other and kind and sensitive.... But you can have a civilized society which is not a decent society because that civil [and] decent society requires that the institutions of that society do not humiliate adults. So you could have a society where the institutions humiliate adults ... which treat adults as second-class citizens, even though people are nice to each other.... In South Texas ... with Mexicans, ... and in San Antonio ... institutions ... denied people the right to participate. You had institutions which treated adults as second-class citizens to be seen and not heard. That is not a decent society ... So, in order for there to be a decent society, those institutions, whether it be the school, the workplace, the universities, have got to make it possible for people to feel that they are first-class citizens. They have a right to be heard, a right to participate, a right to deliberate. Now, in order for it to be just, it means that they have to have access ... to the resources of that society which are necessary in order for them to maintain a decent standard of living, health care, education, full employment, which enables them to participate, again, in, we call the shared prosperity, or what the Hebrew community would call the shalom of the community.... San Antonio was not a decent society because there were—and it certainly was not a just society because you had whole communities which were left out of access to public facilities, that did not have flood control in their communities. When it rained, ... people couldn't go out. Their homes were flooded, ... ipso facto unjust society.... It was not a decent society because when they tried to participate, ... there was a resistance to their participation. And it took the organizing of COPS in order to open up ... the institutions, whether it be the political institutions, etc. to enable them to participate. The same thing is true in the Rio Grande Valley, when you have people who live in whole colonias and hovels, who don't have water, who don't have access to sewer.... Then, clearly, you know, that community is not just. If, when you pay people less than a decent standard of living, when you pay people poverty wages and when you subsidize, you know, and give corporate welfare ... to developers ... who sustain poverty wages, then it's clearly you have an unjust system, and in order to change that unjust system, you're going to have—often times, you have to create or enable institutions to develop capacity, and that means, in the process of making it just, you make it decent as well....

BM: COPS is Communities Organized for Public Service, O.K., which is an IAF organization in San Antonio. COPS Metro Alliance, it's made up of about 60 different institutions, congregations, unions, neighborhood groups. All across San Antonio, particularly, in the beginning stages, in the South and West and East sides, in the older areas. Now, it's much—much more expanded and in a much more metropolitan scope, and so it includes areas all over the city of San Antonio, from Helotes on the Northeast, or the Northwest side, excuse me, to congregations on the Southeast side, and so it's a broad coalition of institutions, an organization of organizations whose purpose is to develop capacity to teach people effectively how to participate in the political, social, and cultural life of the community.

EC: [Cortés describes the IAF network] ... One of the greatest leaders of the COPS organization was a priest named Albert Benavides [who] unfortunately drowned in 1984. In Valley Interfaith, you have people like Carmen Anaya, Father (inaudible), Estella Sosa-Garza, O.K. In El Paso, in La Pisa organization. You have enormous numbers of people in Dallas Area Interfaith, Rev. Gerald Britt, here in Austin, Regina Rogaolf. You have a whole range of leaders Jewish, from Jewish congregations to Roman Catholic churches, school leaders, school principals like, Claudia Santa Maria, parent leaders like Lourdes Sanmaron, ... who've been developed and—and they've learned through action and reflection, through research actions, through relational meetings, through house meetings, ... all across the state of Texas they've developed skills and understanding and wisdom ... about public and social life.... Most of them, all of them, had curiosity and imagination and, but they didn't look like they were smart, they didn't look like they were effective, they didn't look like they were people who could—could be significant.... Over the course of a year and out of the thousand, you find ... 50, 60, 75 [emerge] who's got enough talent, and then they go back and look for people among the other people that you met with and so that you begin to create this kind of collaborative group of leaders ... who you mentor and you guide and you teach and you develop, and they, in turn, go out and do the same for others....

The challenge of this work is ... not to organize the community, but to find the people who are going to do the organizing, to find the people who got the energy, the imagination, the curiosity, the talent to do that kind of work, and so that then you then mentor and guide and teach and put them in different situations and develop their capacity to act and develop their capacity to gain recognition and significance. And, so therefore, organizing them becomes really the teaching of these skills and these insights, and—and helping people understand and interpret their experiences, tell their stories in creative and effective ways, tell their stories to news media, tell their stories to political figures, tell their stories to corporate leaders, so that they begin, they begin to create a different kind of conversation.... A different understanding of what is essential to the life of that particular community, whether it is about schools, health care, jobs, etc.... The role of time horizon for a corporate executive is the quarter.... The role of a time horizon for a politician is the next election. The role of a time horizon for—for a hospital, or educational bureaucrat is the budget cycle. But, the role of a time horizon for a grandmother is a generation, because she's concerned about what happens to her grandchildren. So, the difficulty is finding people who understand the role of time horizons ... And, when you have, you know, kind of a faddish, kind of instantaneous kind of ... society where people, again, expect immediate results, ... it's hard to get people to think about what is the role of a time horizon.... [in getting diverse people to work together] If they just want to be comfortable, they feel good, then you just kind of connect to people that you know and feel good about.... If you want to have power, then you got to go beyond just your identity, politics. You got to go beyond your comfort zone and take some risks with people that you don't know very well, that you don't feel so comfortable with, that you can't make small talk with.... The question then is how to teach people how to engage and how to have a conversation with somebody whose background they don't know anything about or they never went to school with or they don't know what to talk about and they feel awkward at first.... And get them over those feelings of awkwardness, or hostility, or fear, or anger, or whatever it is that comes to mind, because people, we're taught, we're taught to be fearful, we're taught to be, to be dismissive, we're taught to—to basically, to be hostile, ... to be other, whether that otherness is sexuality, whether the otherness is religion, whether the otherness is race, whether the otherness is faith … you try to teach people what we call relational power, … and the difficulty is that people operate out of … unilateral power, which is zero sum "I win, you lose." … So, that the gains we get are going to come only at your expense. Well, if you teach people, no, now wait a minute, there is a different way of thinking about this, … there is a concept of relational power which means we can both win.… But that means, by expanding the pie. We can both win by creating more capacity.… If we don't allow … other people to play the prisoner's dilemma on us … where they isolate us or separate us, [i.e.] the prisoner's dilemma; I do it to you before … you do it to me. Rather than … teaching people to know about each other's stories, their histories, their backgrounds, their fears, their anxieties.… So, on the basis of that, we can act on small things and develop some trust and some understanding of reliability and develop what Hannah Wren … calls public friendship, the friendship that emerges among colleagues, or people who fight together, argue, dispute with each other, but always maintain their relationship. And, so to teach people how to do that is the critical thing. Now, we did this in Dallas, … where people like Gerald Britt, an African American minister, coalitioned Dallas Area Interfaith and organized and, with Latinos and people from the … Anglo community, which is not really accurate.… But, you know, Lutherans, and … Methodists, and other Protestant denominations on behalf of after school programs and got the Dallas School Board to vote.… Latinos and African Americans to come together when they had been divided around these after school programs. So the question is, how … can they begin to come together? They were able to recently get bond election passed.… [The] process [was] of [holding] individual meetings, house meetings, research actions, teaching people how to negotiate with each other, teaching them that they could get things for their schools, for their communities … if they collaborated and worked together, and negotiated. I'll work for you on your issue, but you got to work for me on my issue.

DT: When you're trying to organize people, … I hear about the house meetings and the things, yet your organizing in communities where you have multiple adults having to work multiple jobs to make ends meet and the constraints of … the people who need to do and say the most are, by the very institutions that are oppressing them, have the least time of all the commodities to do it. How do you convince them to put in the two hours, four hours, of it's not their own child who's sick, or it's not actually touching them personally, how is [it] made to be worth their time?

EC: It's worth their time because, the ones you start off with, because they want certain kinds of, because they're not satisfied with the life as it is. And so, even though, … it may not directly, immediately impact their child, or immediately impact their community, … it impacts them and the quality of their life as they see it.… You find enormous capacity on the part of people to find dimensions of their lives.… I organize ours around a particular problem, … cleaning up a ditch, etc. But once that was done, they left.… Or, you organize them around getting a new school. And, once they got the school, they were out. The question [or alternative]—to build an organization like COPS, or Metro Alliance, or Valley Interfaith, or Apeaso, [where] you have to find people who want more than that. They want more than just their house fixed, they want more than just a new school, they want more than just a lot, they want those things to be sure, and it has to be about those things, otherwise they won't stay in it. But they also want something else. And those something elses are quite intangible. But they're just as important to them, and they have to do with their ability to understand the world, they have their ability to find meaning in their lives, have to do with their meaning—ability to deal with relationships and to understand relationships and—and to understand what the human condition is all about … and all the questions that plague all of us and have plagued all of us from time immortal.…

DT: Sounds like those are special people.

EC: An optimist is somebody who—who looks, who just kind of looks beyond reality, O.K., in my humble opinion. Hanna Wren put it this way, she said that in order for things to change you need anger and humor. She said, hope, unfortunately in her terms, which I'm going to use optimism, jumps over reality.… And so, you don't engage reality. Anger teaches you how to engage reality, … and humor situates you in a context so that you don't take yourself too seriously and notwithstanding your appropriate anger and so therefore, you can have perspective.… So that combination of hope and anger, that synthesization of it … forces you to engage the world as it is, at the same time situates you in … geological time. So that you don't take yourself too seriously.… And, therefore, don't burn yourself out. That gives you hope, and that's what I mean by hope, … is that understanding of the world as it is, and not recognizing the challenges and the daunting nature of what we are trying to strive for, we can still recognize the possibilities.… The role of the organizer [is to combine] anger and humor and perspective, that maturity to know that anger is not hatred and—and not outrage.…

DT: How [do] you keep activists from burning out? Did they come to some sort of mature outrage, some kind of anger that they can sustain, that's a cold anger that doesn't consume them?

EC: Well, I hope it is. I don't know if I can keep anybody from burning out, I mean, I can keep myself from burning out, and if it helps me, I point out to people what sustains me, and what gives me energy and what gives me the capacity to go on. But, they have to figure that out for themselves. Now, I'll be more than happy—I am more than happy to work with people to help them figure that out. But, everybody's different.… Not everybody does—enjoys what I enjoy. And so, part of the job that I have is to try help people figure out what is it that makes sense to them? What is it that is meaningful to them; where is the joy in their life. Because you can't do this work if you can't find some joy in it. If you don't find meaning in it, if you don't find significance in it, over time, I mean, because it's not enough, I don't think, O.K., to rectify a situation. It's not enough to, you know, even do things that are important, big, I mean, we—to make it possible for people to have a living wage job, that's very significant, very important. To make it possible for people to have water that didn't have it, that's very important. But after a while, it—you know—that's not enough. And so—but people have to figure out what is—what else is it that will sustain them in this work.... We try to teach them these kind of things early on, that a lot of them just would not listen. That you just can't—you can't just exhort and scold people. It doesn't do any good, it just gets their back up. Now I'm not trying to say I don't believe in confrontation, I'm not trying to say I don't believe in tension. I think, unfortunately, that—that's the law of change, you know. That all change comes about either through pressure or threat.... That there is no nice way to get change. What I'm talking about is if you're going to get people to act in such a way that they're willing to bring about pressure, if they're willing to create the tension, then they gotta under—they gotta have some sense of power. And if they're always involved in institutions where they're being told, being told what to do by experts, after a awhile, that's not good—they're not gonna sustain themselves in those kinds of organizations.... We teach, you gotta be selective. You gotta pick and choose your fights. And you gotta pick and choose fights which help you build an organization. So you gotta ask yourself, how does this fight, how does this issue gonna help us build the organization. And then, the activist will say, Yeah, but you're not dealing with this issue, and this issue, and this issue, and all these things. But they all demand immediate concern, we just can't deal with every single one of them at the same time, it just won't happen.... And that's part of the tragedy of life, sometimes the best solution gets in the way of a good enough solution and so sometimes you gotta learn, so that's what I mean by learning how to understand politics.... It's really about learning how to negotiate when you don't have that much power, and learning that sometimes you gotta take, you know, victories, and build for the future. And even though all those victories look like big, huge defeats.... Or so you're in a situation where, yeah, the other guy wins, ... we're not gonna stop development over the Aquifer.... But, we don't have the power to do it right now. So, what do we do then? Well, we try to build, we try to get some concession, some victories, teach our people that at the same time we won, ... that there is still a larger issue out there which we haven't dealt with, and haven't addressed, but we gotta be able to organize and build capacity if we're gonna deal with that issue. I don't know if I'm being clear or not.... So you don't give up on the fight and you teach it, and you don't pretend that there's not a serious problem out there. But you also recognize that we don't have the power to deal with that problem right now. So we gotta build some more power. This victory we got here today was good, it's significant—it's important and meaningful. But, is it the solution? No. [Does] it solve the problem? No. Is it—do the other side, are they still doing some horrible things? ... Then, why are we negotiating with these people? Because we gotta live in the world as it is. And we gotta learn, that if we're gonna be successful, O.K., we're gonna have to figure out a couple of things. One is how to build our organization. Two is turn yesterday's adversaries into today's allies, or tomorrow's allies.... The way to organize around people with environmental concerns is to teach them how they effect public health. And I think that the more effective way to do this is to talk about questions of health and quality of life and viability ... Because otherwise you allow those people who don't care about it to kind of paint you in a picture ... [They] stereotype you as people who are quaint and tree huggers or whatever ... it appears to become the province of very self-absorbed, very comfortable people, who've gotten theirs and don't want anyone else to share in the bounty. They've got their nice home viewing the ocean and they don't want anyone else to have—you know, to disturb their view.... And so you become relegated to people who become self-absorbed and narcissistic. And I think that's the biggest danger. For people who are concerned about the environment, is they gotta figure out a way in which it effects the lives, the quality of lives of people who are in minority communities and low-end communities. The average state, you know, guy who, basically, is just trying to make a buck for his family, O.K. Alright. [End of Interview with Ernie Cortés.]

Source: Ernie Cortes (EC) Interviewers: David Todd (DT) and David Weisman (DW); April 12, 2002; Austin, Texas REELS: 2185 and 2186, LaRed Latina of the Intermountain Southwest. http://www.texaslegacy.org/m/transcripts/cortesernietxt.html.

369. Interview with Antonio González on Willie Velásquez, Southwest Voter Registration Education Project, 2004

In 1974, William C. Velásquez, or "Willie" as everyone called him, founded the Southwest Voter Registration Education Project (SVREP). SVREP became the largest and the most successful national Latino voter registration project. Prior to SVREP's founding, the disparate voter registration projects lacked coordination and research components. Willie, with the help of a professionally trained staff, conducted voter registration drives in 200 cities and Indian reservations. He followed up these drives with extensive polling. Willie was a native of San Antonio, he had been active in La Raza Unida Party, led a farmworkers' strike in south Texas, and contributed to the election of Chicano elected officials. In registering Chicanos and Latinos to vote, he wanted to give them the option of being good citizens and bring about positive changes through the election of Latino elected officials. Willie Velásquez died of cancer at the age of 44. The following interview is with one of the SVREP presidents since Willie's unexpected death.

Willie Velásquez was the charismatic leader behind the Southwest Voter Registration Education Project (SVREP). For 20 years, beginning in the 1960s, he took his cue from African Americans working to secure their full civil rights and applied their tactics to La Raza, the Mexican Americans in his native Texas, and throughout the Southwest. SVREP did not have the high profile of the politically strong La Raza Unida Party or the mainstream organizational pull of the League of United Latin American Citizens (LULAC), but its impact at the ballot box, through the election of more people of color, has been lasting and is still playing out.

The work might have ended in 1988, the year Willie Velásquez suddenly died. But the mission continued. In 1994, Antonio González, 48, took over as president. In the crowded Pico de Gallo restaurant in San Antonio, González spoke with special correspondent Joe Nick Patoski about how the institution has survived in the absence of the man who founded and personified it.

What's the Southwest Voter Registration Education Project and the William C. Velásquez Institute?

González: Southwest Voter Registration Education Project is a nonprofit, nonpartisan [organization] that is dedicated to increasing political participation among minorities, particularly Latinos, throughout the United States.

The William C. Velásquez Institute is another nonpartisan, nonprofit, organization that is dedicated to policy and research towards supporting effective governance by Latino voters and Latino-elected officials and leaders—sort of a spinoff of the Southwest Voter Registration Education Project.

Tell us about Willie Velásquez.

González: Willie Velásquez was a radical youth from San Antonio of working-class origin who was a student at St. Mary's University, which was a hotbed of political activism at that time. The Chicanos were influenced by the black Civil Rights Movement, by Martin Luther King, [Jr.,] particularly by the Student Nonviolent Coordinating Committee, by Malcolm X, and by their own homegrown heroes in Mexican American politics, which had a history, particularly in Texas and New Mexico, that antedated the Civil Rights Movement.

Willie was one of the founders of La Raza Unida, an independent Latino-Chicano third political party that was successful in many places in South Texas. He left Raza Unida [around 1970] to create Southwest Voter. It was finally founded in 1974. It was a tough row to hoe, getting it funded.

Latinos' numbers were declining in political participation until around the time Southwest Voter was founded. The numbers since have gone up consistently and dramatically. Hispanics have been the fastest-growing group in registration in voting in America since 1980, measured by every presidential election, without exception. Willie's contribution was to create the vehicle for that and to believe that we could stimulate this.

What was the initial impact of SVREP?

González: Southwest Voter Registration Education Project and Willie Velásquez are key elements in the transition of the condition of the U.S. Latino community from utter and complete powerlessness to where we are today, which is having some power, but not enough. Clearly, we have changed our condition from being outside the power. Willie Velásquez's context was the era of powerlessness. That's why people were militant and protesting, organizing third parties. They were utterly excluded by policies, practices, barriers, laws, and institutions. Velásquez led the charge. He opened those doors.

Willie died in 1988. He had just begun to reinterpret Latino politics. I remember Willie beginning to agitate that we had to equip ourselves to govern because we were winning. When Southwest Voter started, there were about 1,300 Latino-elected officials in the country and about 2.3 million Latino voters. Ten years later, we nearly doubled the number of Latino-elected officials to about 2,500 and nearly 4 million Latinos were registered to vote.

Willie's whole team was a group of intellectuals, so they would think about these things. Willie agitated to create the capacity to train candidates and train elected officials and come up with new policy strategies, do opinion surveys, the sort of things that 20 years later we all do. Willie saw the Latino community governing. Henry Cisneros was mayor of San Antonio and on Mondale's short list for vice president. The Hispanic caucus of Texas was very powerful. Tony Anaya was governor of New Mexico.

How did the Institute come about?

González: Willie was wrong [to think] that we had broken through and were in a condition of exercising power. It certainly wasn't true across the country, though it was true in Texas and New Mexico. That's why he created the institute, which was called the Southwest Voter Research Institute. We renamed it after Willie died to honor him. The institute started polling and doing international work to take delegations of Latino-elected officials and leaders to Central America. Willie went to Nicaragua and El Salvador. He was interested in revolutions. Willie was a global thinker.

That was the later stage of Willie's career and lifework, pondering "how do we govern?"

Willie saw the immigration reform in 1986, but he didn't get to see the big wave. None of us predicted the impact it was going to have in speeding up our political empowerment.

Was his death a surprise?

González: Totally. He was only 44. He got sick and a month later he died. I was a member of his staff. I'd been there for four years. I came in 1984, and I was involved with the '84 presidential campaign. Then I worked on special projects—an immigration bill, the '87 Texas Legislature, and an international project called the Latin America Project.

How did you deal with the sudden loss of your charismatic leader?

González: I'm from California. When Willie died, I was sent back to California to help [keep] us from collapsing. We were on the verge of bankruptcy. We had the test of fire.

Willie had a number two named Andy Hernandez, who had been with Southwest Voter from the beginning. Fortunately, he was there and was able to step in. He had 14 years of experience with the organization, so he became the president when Willie passed away. We weathered everything that happens when you lose your charismatic superstar. We had to retool the fundraising and reassure the leadership. People thought we were going to disappear. We had a tough couple of years.

How did you keep on going?

González: We had a hard-core group of staff who basically dedicated themselves to Willie's memory and said, "Not on our watch. We're not going to be recorded in history as the group that couldn't make it after Willie died."

It took a lot of hard work. The hardest part was figuring out how to raise money without the superstar doing it. [Before,] Willie would pick up a phone and we'd get money. We had to reestablish relationships with foundations, start raising money from corporations and unions who used to give us nothing, zippo.

Willie enjoyed the largesse. He was the darling of the New York liberals. When he went away, they went away. We had to go to our base. For at least a couple of years there was goodwill, meaning, "We'll do this for Willie. We'll help Southwest for Willie." By the 1990s, we were able to get into "the self-interest cycle," meaning people have a self-interest in seeing the Hispanic vote grow. Once we got past the '92 election, people saw Southwest Voter was going to make it. So they came back.

Andy Hernandez stepped down as SVREP president in 1994. What happened after that?

González: I was surprised when he stepped down. You know, I don't think Andy ever reconciled himself to being Willie's successor and being the head of Southwest Voter without Willie because they were like brothers. [Willie's death] was a personal tragedy for him. I was sort of in position because I was [Andy's] number two, although more focused on the Velásquez Institute, which had grown quite a bit and had a big international program. Andy sort of popped it on me. I didn't really have a choice. He said, "I'm leaving, you're in." The board said, "Yeah, that's right." Been there ever since. How did you lead the organization out from under Willie's shadow, when SVREP had been so much about him?

González: I will tell you, it's the reverse. Southwest Voter now is much bigger than Willie ever was. This year we'll quintuple the budget of Willie's biggest year. We do work in many more states. We're in 16 states, with partnerships that get us into 26 states. When Willie was alive and the Institute and Southwest were together, they raised $1 million. When they were separate under Andy, he raised about $2 million. We'll do $5 million, maybe $6 million, between the two organizations this year.

We're clearly the preeminent Latino vote organization, bar none, registering and turning out people. We're going to hit 10 million [registered voters] this year. We were two-and-a-half million when Willie started. We're at eight-and-a-half million now, and we'll hit 10 million [by the fall 2004 elections], maybe nine-and-a-half, 9.3—it depends.

Our challenge is to keep Willie's memory alive. We're going to pay a lot of attention to that this year. It's our 30th anniversary. There's a book coming out about Willie in April: *The Life and Times of Willie Velásquez* (Arte Publico Press) by Juan Sepúlveda.

We're going to push to create a Willie Velásquez archive. We're preparing to start the process to build a building, maybe a statue, in his honor on the West Side here in San Antonio. There's a Velásquez education building at St. Mary's University and Velásquez mural. There's a Velásquez [Walk]. There's Velásquez schools. We're going to do more because Willie is not known to the younger generation.

What are top priorities for the project?

González: We're setting up voter registration campaigns. We have active projects right now in Little Havana, Kendall, Hollywood, Tampa, and Plant City in Florida; in Hobbs and Las Cruces, New Mexico; four different ones in Maricopa County [Phoenix] in Arizona—it's a big county—and setting up in Tucson and Casa Grande. Seattle, Yakima Valley, the Tri-City area of Washington state, and about 20 more on the drawing board. We've still got to get into Albuquerque, got to get into Santa Fe.

We're shaking and baking. We've got offices of people moving all around. We're setting up the coalitions, contracting organizers. There's training going on in

Albuquerque next weekend, and then two weeks after that, trainings in Miami-Dade and in Tucson. We have to set up 300 of these. Our partners are setting up another 150.

The Velásquez Institute is on a separate but complementary track, getting into the field in April with a national opinion survey. Through our leadership program, we're sending a religious delegation to Cuba. Through our community development program, we're conducting a solar retrofitting initiative with Hispanic businesses in urban Southern California as a policy response to the energy crisis. Energy's very expensive. Through our international program, we do Cuba, Central America. We have a drug policy reform initiative. We're co-sponsoring a national conference in Houston. We have a major research project going in anticipation of the Voting Rights Act [of 1965] reauthorization fight. It's a longitudinal study looking at 30 years of census data. We're seeking to measure the level of social, economic, and political inclusion of native-born Latinos.

There's a debate being argued from these neoconservative academics and Latino academics. They say voting rights is a black-oriented program and Latinos are not excluded like African Americans are. Therefore, the Voting Rights Act should not apply to Latinos, because Latinos are inevitably on a path of social, political, and economic inclusion. It's just a matter of time and overcoming our own cultural barriers; that there are really no substantive barriers to inclusion.

We obviously disagree. And so we have to demonstrate that, based on the data on Latinos. We're looking specifically at native-borns because foreign-borns do show increased inclusion, because they become citizens. So it's a false positive when you look at immigrants.

You had a golf tournament?

González: We do golf tournaments, we do annual banquets—six of them: Miami, Houston, San Antonio, Phoenix, Los Angeles, and the Bay Area. We're doing a small-dollar endowment that we're launching this year where it's basically working folks. We're going to sign up ten thousand $1,000 donors from our network, where they give us $30 a month over three years. It's like dues, but it goes into an endowment.

You have to figure out something for each sector. What do we have? We have a lot of working folks. So that's that sector. And we have a professional sector; you have golf tournaments and fundraisers. Fundraisers include your corporate donors. We have a lot of people in anticipation of the money. Willie had to ask five people. It got harder. So you spend more time raising money, but we raise a lot more.

You can't ask for a better situation. Both parties say they have to have your vote to win. And when your vote is big enough to make a difference, and when you look like you're going to have the resources to mobilize the infrastructure to make a difference, issues that matter to our community are going to bubble up because we have these other things in place. This is the kind of context and scenario that I live for. And it's one that Willie lived for. He didn't get to see it, but a generation after his passing, it's here today.

Source: An interview with Antonio González, President of the Southwest Voter Education Project, June 2004. Voices of Civil Rights, AARP, the Leadership Conference on Civil Rights (LCCR), and the Library of Congress, 2004. http://www.voicesofcivilrights.org/civil3_gonzalez.html.

370. Excerpt from *Enriqueta Vásquez and the Chicano Movement,* 2006

Enriqueta Vásquez is a leader who has lived with the Chicano community and participated in most of its struggles to attain equality. She coedited *El Grito del Norte,* a newspaper in New Mexico, where she wrote about social and economic injustice. Enriqueta was not limited to Chicano issues and expressed solidarity with the Vietnamese and Cuban people. She also sought to bring about needed change within the Mexican American community by writing about racism, sexism, imperialism, and poverty. She introduced these questions in a logical but firm manner and was respected because for her commitment to progressive thought.

LOS POBRES Y LOS RICOS

A while back, I attended a meeting where I heard a man speak about his experience in Washington on the Poor People's March. It was good to hear one of our Raza stand up and speak for the Raza and our life here and the way of the poor.

During the discussion there was a lady present (Raza) that spoke up and said, "I am not poor, I work." Here was a person who has a nice home (mortgaged), two cars (mortgaged) and many beautiful useless things (also mortgaged). If this woman's husband was to become sick and hospitalized for a few months and she was not able to work, you would end up with human beings who would lose all of their material wealth and find themselves quickly changed from "wishfully middle class" to the "poor class." The picture would be changed, but fast.... What would they be?

Let us first of all forget the idea that we will never be poor and by all means let us never look down on the poor. For that matter, the poor are often times better people in that, because they do not have money, they know what to do with themselves and their time. Those with money and things are useless and have no real purpose in life. Take away their money and livelihood (I don't wish this on anyone) and you would find them jumping out of windows.

Now we come to the question, just what is it that we want? Do the poor want money? Do we want to be like the Anglo? What do we really value?

Just looking at the different government machines, I believe that probably the Department of Defense has the provisions for life that the poor people need. Do you know that they take care of their armies from cradle to grave? The entire family of a soldier is taken care of. Now, why can't everyone in this country have this? Isn't this an abundant economy? We have food surplus. Anytime they want, they can solve the job problem by cutting the working hours in half. Really, the amount of money spent for the people of this country is very little. A drop in the bucket in comparison with that which we spend in war killing little people in little countries. Asking for a share of the wealth is not asking too much.

We should also unite with our people, all of us. This stuff about "I made it, you can too," does not sound good to me. It sounds too much like the higher-up talking to the down-there. This competitive (playing one human against the other) way of life is what the "Americano" has given us. They build their lives around competition. And if you don't know what I mean, just watch that lousy TV and see what advertising is all about. They can make you want more fancy junk you don't need than you would ever believe. They have a way of making you build your lives around things and this, Hermanos, is what it is all about. The Anglo society is built on a value system of things, not humans. Once you begin to value things more than humans, it is like an alcoholic that craves more and more and there is no end to satisfying the thirst that wants more.

The Raza in the Southwest is not asking for things so much as being ourselves. Being human. We want our history back. We want our language and culture to be our way of life. We refuse to give in and submit to a hypocritical way of life. This Southwest was built on Indian, Spanish, and Mexican history, not English. Our cities, our mountains and rivers were explored and settled by Indians and Spaniards, not pilgrims and wagon masters. The first cattle raisers, cowboys, and farmers were Raza, we weren't waiting here to be saved by the great white fathers. In Mexico, the Indians had big beautiful cities, they had mathematicians and astronomers and they weren't waiting to be "civilized."

We want to be treated with the dignity that is ours. In matters of jobs, law enforcement, and business we are now second-rate citizens.

In 1968, U.S. defense spending constituted 46.0% of federal outlays, or $81.9 billion versus $96.2 billion on non-defense expenditures. See Harold W. Stanley and Richard G. Niemi, eds., Vital Statistics on American Politics, 4th ed. (Washington, D.C.: Congressional Quarterly P, 1994), 361.

The only place where we are first-rate citizens is in the draft call and I sure don't consider it a compliment to be part of a useless machine. Let's all stop and look at ourselves for what we are. Let's wake up and help each other. Let's look at the issues, let's look at our country, let's look at our communities, let's look at ourselves and our families, let's look at our law enforcement agencies, and let's look at this thing called justice. Let's not sit back and give up. We need YOU now. The time is NOW. Let's all stand up, beautiful people. Let's all stand up. LA RAZA UNIDA.

Despierten mis hermanos, no nos podemos permitir perdernos en la rueda de la vida hipócrita con precios anglos. Para que triunfe nuestra cultura e historia tenemos que hablar y gritar y cantar nuestra historia. La tierra es de nosotros. Defiendanla, ella no se vende ni se compra. Es de nosotros.

Wake up, my brothers and sisters, we cannot loose ourselves in the hypocritical wheel of life with Anglo prices. In order for our culture and history to triumph, we must speak out, yell, and sing about our history. The land is ours. Defend it, it is not to be sold or bought. It belongs to us.

October 5, 1968
Translated by Herminia S. Reyes.

Source: Excerpt is reprinted with permission of the publisher of *Enriqueta Vasquez and the Chicano Movement*, by Enriqueta Vasquez. Edited by Lorena Oropeza and Dionne Espinoza. Houston: Arte Público Press—University of Houston © 2006. pp. 8–10.

371. Excerpts from Elizabeth Martínez, "A View from New Mexico: Recollections of the Movimiento Left," 2002

Elizabeth "Betita" Martínez, Chicana activist, author, and educator, is best known for her 1990 book *500 Años del Pueblo Chicano/500 Years of Chicano History: In Pictures*. She is currently working on a similar volume focusing on Chicanas. Martínez was active in the civil rights movement as a member of the Student Nonviolent Coordinating Committee (SNCC). She worked as a United Nations researcher on colonialism in Africa. In 1968, she joined the Chicano movement in New Mexico, where she coedited the newspaper *El Grito del Norte* from 1968–1976 and cofounded the Chicano Communications Center, a barrio-based organization. In 1982, she ran for governor of California on the Peace and Freedom Party ticket. In 1997, she cofounded and still directs the Institute for Multi Racial Justice in San Francisco and is active in the anti-war movement involving the Iraq War.

If ever there has been a chapter of the U.S. left with deep cultural roots in every sense, it is the movimiento of New Mexico.

The roots include social relations, economic traditions, political forms, artistic expression, and language—everything that defines peoplehood. They are Native American, Spanish, and Mexican mestizo (mixed), and they go back centuries. Migrant workers of the last 150 years have played a crucial part, but "immigrant" does not describe the totality of those roots.

Unlike any other area except southern Colorado, the movimiento in Nuevo Mexico evolved within the framework of a long, popular struggle against U.S. colonization and for land—that is to say, nothing less than the means of production. Its origins lie in the colonization of First Nation peoples like the Pueblos and the Dine (Navajo) in what became Nuevo (later New) Mexico and their long resistance to occupying forces. In 1680, some of the Indians joined with Mexican workers in Santa Fe and drove out the Spanish for twelve years.

The land struggle that came much later, waged by Spanish-speaking mestizo people and sometimes armed as well as underground, could be called nationalist. But if we do so, we should not equate it with the nationalism of many other U.S. movement groups. It was not primarily cultural, not exclusionary of other peoples, not "mi Raza primero" (my people first). And whether or not we call that land struggle consciously left, it directly or indirectly encouraged militant leftism including Marxism during the movimiento years.

New Mexico had remained a territory for over fifty years after the war on Mexico. It did not become a state until 1912, when its Spanish-speaking, Catholic majority had given way to an Anglo majority that made white easterners much less nervous. Before and after that date, Mexicans carried out underground actions against Anglo landowners, mainly in rural areas of the north. Cutting Anglo fences and burning barns were common forms of protest against the continuing land robbery.

After arriving in 1968, I soon learned to respect names like Las Gorras Blancas (White Caps) a longstanding underground resistance group, and La Mano Negra (Black Hand), reputed to be headed by a woman at that time. Resistance nourished by historical, cultural, or religious tradition was also strong. Examples could be found in the Penitentes (a semisecret religious organization), dances and plays performed on certain holidays reenacting key moments in the area's colonial history, the curanderos who cured with herbs not usually known to outsiders, along with other expressions of a long isolated, necessarily self-sufficient society—from building with adobe bricks, to cultivating a unique variety of chilies for cooking. A spirit of collectivity and interdependence ran strong in all this.

Politically, northern New Mexico presented an almost classic example of European colonialism. Anglos stood at the top holding economic and political power while "Hispanos" formed a control or buffer class that included teachers, judges, police, and other local officials, leaving the majority of Mexicans at the bottom. That colonial reality defined the anti-imperialist project and its class contradictions.

The Alianza Federal de Mercedes emerged in the 1960s to initiate a new, militant stage in the land struggle, making national news with its 1967 armed takeover of the courthouse in the mountain village of Tierra Amarilla to protest state repression. Alianzistas, led by Reies López Tijerina, organized to win back communally held land that had been distributed to their ancestors in grants by Spain (which had seized it from indigenous peoples). Their Spanish colonial ancestry, which preceded Mexico's rule, made them probably the only group in the United States today who can call themselves "Hispanic," or Hispano, with some accuracy.

In the 1960s and early 1970s, Alianzistas sympathized with the struggles of other peoples of color, like African Americans (the Alianza welcomed visiting SNCC leaders twice), Puerto Ricans, and Palestinians. Of all the possible alliances with Native Americans at home, the Alianza is best known for supporting the long Taos Pueblo struggle to get back their sacred Blue Lake lands.

The worldview of Alianza's constituency—impoverished, dispossessed, small landowners—could be very conservative. They were not radical in the sense of consciously seeking to restructure the entire society as opposed to achieving justice in one area, recovery of land ownership that the United States had promised to respect under the 1848 Treaty of Guadalupe Hidalgo. At the same time, their goal could hardly be met without that restructuring, any more than the U.S. government was likely to "give it back to the Indians." For some Alianzistas and supporters, who saw that their poverty could not be ended without systemic change, their worldview could certainly be called revolutionary nationalism.

The anticommunist influence of McCarthyism could be found among a few Alianzistas, who equated the word with dictatorship. However, Tijerina himself did not take virulent anticommunist positions. His conservatism in other areas was notable, for example, having an almost entirely male Alianza leadership and expressing male supremacist attitudes. (On the unofficial level, many Alianza women were respected for their wisdom, strength, and leadership in ways similar to what I had found in rural Mississippi in 1964.)

The overall attitude in northern New Mexico toward socialism or communism was not negative. One or two Alianza supporters whom I met had even tried to get to Cuba and join the revolutionary forces there in the late 1950s. A sprinkling of old left members could be found like Vicente Vigil, who became a columnist for the newspaper *El Grito del Norte* (*Cry of the North*). Organizers in the land grant and other movements received frequent support from a small but sturdy number of Anglo socialists and Communist Party (CP) members or sympathizers in New Mexico.

We can also recall the 1951 Silver City strike against Empire Zinc, inspired by proletarian goals with help from committed CP organizers, and made into the movie *Salt of the Earth*. Years later some of the strike leaders did support work for the Chilean resistance after the 1973 coup, which reflected an ongoing radical tradition.

El Grito del Norte, a newspaper I co-founded with movement attorney Beverly Axelrod, began in 1968 as a vehicle to support the Alianza. It soon expanded to cover the Chicano movement in urban areas, workers' struggles, and Latino political prisoners, along with a broad spectrum that ranged from the black liberation movement to Mexican student protest to radical whites. At the same time, *El Grito* encouraged nationalist consciousness and cultural self-respect among Chicanos as sources of strength in sparking a movement, especially among youth.

The paper never abandoned its focus on the land struggle in New Mexico, and linked it with contemporary land struggles in Hawaii, Japan, and Third World countries, thus internationalizing it. This combination of what could be called liberatory or revolutionary nationalism with internationalism made *El Grito* very unusual among the dozens of more nationalist Chicano movement newspapers that covered the Southwest and inspired activists.

El Grito's favorable coverage of Vietnam, Cuba, and China left no doubt that it was pro-Socialist. It sent reporters to all those countries. We also sent a reporter and photographer, along with a carload of supporters, to Wounded Knee during the long, armed American Indian Movement occupation in 1973. All this did not seem to limit the paper's popularity, at least not in the north. Probably we were helped by the fact that the 1967 Tierra Amarilla courthouse raiders were our friends and one, Jose Madril, an editor with *El Grito*. Nobody messed with those guys!

We did encounter some harassment from the police in Española, where our office was located, for example when they detained Antonio Cordova who had photographed them tear-gassing people at a demonstration.

With a predominantly female set of regular columnists, writers, artists, photographers, and production workers like Jane Lougee, Tessa Martinez, Adelita Medina, Kathy Montague, Sandra Solis, Rini Templeton, Valentina Valdes, and Enriqueta Vasquez, together with myself as managing editor, the paper made its feminism clear. This continued a cultural tradition in which numerous Mexican women journalists played a major role during national struggles like the 1910 [Mexican] revolution.

El Grito also sought to encourage and train young Chicanas in putting out a paper. One of the main successes here was a series on Vietnam written by grassroots organizer Valentina Valdes, who had to read a book on Vietnam the first time with a dictionary—and then read it again—for background. Another example: Adelita Medina and Sandra Solis started the publication *Tierra y Libertad*, in Las Vegas, New Mexico, after having been trained at *El Grito*.

In Albuquerque, the Black Berets also followed an internationalist approach. They adopted principles and a program sometimes modeled on the Black Panthers, for example, its breakfast program, that made it less strictly nationalist than Brown Beret groups in Texas and California. The Black Berets also founded the Bobby Garcia Memorial Clinic, committed to the idea that health is a human right, not a privilege. Their main leader, Richard Moore, and others went to Cuba on the Venceremos Brigade. The Berets and *El Grito* were partners, sharing news, analysis and sometimes members like reporter Antonio Cordova, who along with Beret Rito Canales, was assassinated by police in 1972.

In the early 1970s, *El Grito* began looking for a new strategy and tactics, both for the newspaper and the movimiento in general. To do this, we ceased publication of the paper in 1973, and some of us moved to Albuquerque. With other local activists we launched the Chicano Communications Center (CCC) as a multimedia, educational barrio project. Soon after, the CCC established a formal alliance called CLARO (Chicano League Against Racism and Oppression) together with the Bobby Garcia Memorial Clinic and the Cañoncito Wood Cooperative based in a land grant area just outside the city. CLARO had a central committee for decision-making; it set up a study program on Marxism and contemporary socialism, attended by CLARO people.

In 1974, self-identification with the Socialist vision reached a high point. That was the year Richard Moore went to Cuba with another Beret leader, Joaquín Lujan. Marvin García of Cañoncito went with a group to China. A major meeting took place to discuss strategy in the face of what we saw as heightening repression. Over fifty seasoned activists came from all over the state. In a dialogue about our long-range goals, someone asked what was socialism. I explained some basic points and added it was a stage on the way to communism but not the final goal, communism. At that point a Chicana cried out, "Well, in that case, we're Communists!" and everyone clapped to my and others' amazement.

Also in 1974, another group that wanted to focus on mass organizing started and linked up with CLARO. Its name: MAO (Movement Against Oppression). Happily, this name did not mean CLARO had decided there were two equally destructive imperialisms or spend time on endless battles over that and other lines. This was largely because of New Mexico's relative isolation from the national left main-stream, an isolation that proved both a blessing and, over time, a limitation. The Socialist Workers Party (SWP), did exist but in very small numbers, although some members commanded personal respect. The major, crucial exception to that isolation was travel to Cuba, going back to *El Grito* and now the Venceremos Brigade. Richard Moore served on the Brigade's National Committee and went to Cuba every year through the 1970s. That experience is why he could say, as he did recently, "we didn't pull any punches about being for socialism then. We might use slightly different language with grassroots folk but the ideas were there. We were not afraid of saying so." It didn't hurt that Richard was a big, tough-talking guy whose politics came more from the street than books.

It also didn't hurt that we had two beloved, world-famous Latino revolutionary heroes. Emiliano Zapata, whose portrait provided the logo for *El Grito*'s masthead, had raised the cries that echoed all over northern New Mexico: "Tierra y libertad" and "Tierra, Pan y Justicia!" (Land and Liberty; Land, Bread and Justice). The other was Ernesto "Che" Guevara, whose image adorned many public spaces including the waiting room of the Tierra Amarilla clinic started by movimiento activists. Those two icons symbolized the Chicano movement culture all over the Southwest.

If a certain male domination is creeping into this description of our work, then the contributions of various women must be noted. Nita Luna's theatrical genius generated a teatro group for the CCC that rocked Albuquerque, especially with her play about the Watergate scandal. Luci Rios, factory organizer and poet, along with Susana and Cecilia Fuentes, Susan Seymour, Ruth Contreras, and others not only got much of the CCC's work done but were also leading sisters.

It was also in 1974 that some CLARO members, mostly from the CCC, received a series of visitors from national Marxist-Leninist formations to see about possibly affiliating with one of the groups as a way of sharpening our strategy. The only formation to attract serious interest was the August Twenty-Ninth Movement (ATM), founded in 1974 and named after the historic August 29, 1970, Chicano Moratorium against the Vietnam War, in Los Angeles. ATM had emerged from the Labor Committee of the La Raza Unida Party (LRUP) in Los Angeles, which was well to the left of most LRUP chapters. It had a primarily Chicano membership rather than the almost all-white leadership of most other national formations that visited, and it included local activists personally known to the CCC.

What followed was the kind of destructive experience often found on the U.S. left during these party building years when vanguardism and sectarianism ruled the day. ATM's politics, set forth in such publications as "Fan the Flames: A Revolutionary Position on the Chicano National Question" and its "Unity Statement," followed the tendency of denouncing the Soviet Union as revisionist, hailing the leading role of China and Albania, and pledging to unite with all genuine (that tricky word!) Marxist-Leninists. For the Chicano movement, ATM adopted Stalin's definition of a nation and affirmed Chicanos were a nation—not just a national minority, as other left formations believed.

That position was a major reason, I was told later, why ATM rejected the bilingual book published in 1976 by the CCC, *450 Years of Chicano History in Pictures* (reprinted later as *500 Years of Chicano History*). The book did not declare Chicanos to be a nation; the CCC people were not yet convinced of it. That alleged crime and others apparently compelled ATM members, who took over the CCC, to have the entire second printing of the book shredded in 1976.

ATM in New Mexico also severely undermined the struggle of the Cañoncito land grant group, and a labor struggle. Soon after the ATM takeover, the CCC dissolved. Later, members of ATM in northern California expressed concern privately that New Mexico's ATM included one or more government infiltrators. Many activists in New Mexico believe to this day that such infiltration explains the destruction of *500 Years of Chicano History*. That appears to be true.

At the same time, as anyone who participated in the New Communist Movement of the 1970s knows, the cause might have been garden-variety vanguardism, or a power play to eliminate the influence of certain CCC leaders. The CCC itself was not free of vanguardist tendencies, as shown by its Maoist-style "campaign against liberalism" or its attempt to fulfill cadre-type demands that at one point included meeting to discuss whether, given the needs of the revolution, one member could get pregnant (as she wished). Our dogmatic imposition of cadre demands ran against the barrio culture and longtime styles of organizing.

In short, ATM's actions were destructive yet not incomprehensible for the times. In this way, New Mexico's leftism shared qualities with leftism elsewhere. Those qualities, it must be added, included unlimited commitment to La Causa, great personal self-sacrifice, and a spirit of willingness to die if the revolution needed that.

Today, the left tradition can be seen in New Mexico, for example, in the battle against environmental racism where the enemy is so clearly capitalism. The South-West Organizing Project of Albuquerque (SWOP) and the Southwest Network for Environmental and Economic Justice (SNEEJ), with headquarters in that city, confront capitalism and imperialism constantly. Richard Moore of the Black Berets was cofounder of SWOP and coordinates SNEEJ. In the homeland of the atomic bomb and crucial military bases, New Mexican radicals also confront militarism firsthand on many levels including environmental racism. Chicanos/as and other Latinos in New Mexico, as elsewhere, have a long way to go to develop a strategy and tactics for social transformation. Learning from the past is our first crucial step, and calls for much more analysis than this brief essay.

A reason to be hopeful for Chicano left politics across the Southwest is that the fear of being labeled Communist has diminished, especially among urban youth, even though people may not be consciously Socialist or even anticapitalist. One example comes to mind. In 1970, I visited North Vietnam as the first Chicana/o organizer to do so. On returning, I tried to talk other antiwar Chicano activists into going, as I had been invited to do by the Vietnamese. With one exception, they were too worried about the effect of such a trip on their grassroots community organizing. They couldn't afford to be labeled red.

I do not think that would happen today. More and more Chicanos, especially youth, are recognizing that the revolution, of which many speak so passionately, has to be won through anti-imperialist struggle, not with an exclusively or primarily nationalist agenda. Also, Latinos who have come here from Central America, and other arenas of long struggles against U.S.-supported repression, understand imperialism only too well. They are less fearful of the Communist label (setting aside the policies of particular, often sectarian groups).

There are also Chicanos/as committed to moving beyond the "Chicanismo" of the movimiento years, which was often culturally nationalist, sexist, lacking in any class analysis, and defined by its worship of Corky Gonzales, José Angel Gutiérrez, César Chávez, and Reies López Tijerina. "Beyond Chicanismo," a project based on community college campuses in Denver, is setting a bold example with their demand for Chicano Studies to be focused differently. If their politics are not overtly Marxist or Socialist, they are radical and internationalist.

Another trend that has grown strong today is *indigenismo*, embraced by those who identify with the cultures and struggles of the indigenous peoples of the Americas. Its adherents emphasize indigenous expressions of spirituality and respect for all living creatures. At best, they uphold indigenous concepts of communal interdependence and collectivity rather than private property, commodification, and individualism. Philosophically, this puts indigenismo a short distance from communism.

The idea that Marxism is a white philosophy—which somehow prevailed through the years of adoration for Cuba and Che, China and Mao, Vietnam and Ho Chi Minh, and Guinea-Bissau and Cabral, to mention only a few folks of color who found Marxist theory relevant—is not dead. In insisting on an ideology that incorporates a critique of racism, sexism, and heterosexism, as it should, some Latinos reject Marxism because it "ignored" those other -isms. Or, perhaps more often, because of "all those crazies"—sectarian left formations that claim to speak in its name.

Radical Chicano youth today may not embrace the centrality of class or use what they call "old" words like socialism to define the new society. But they still want to go to Cuba, and they do go. They are far less sexist than their predecessors. Their anger is more profound than that of youth forty years ago, their grasp of the fundamental politics of the United States does not take as long to develop. Their rage comes more quickly; it goes from hip to hop.

Source: Elizabeth Martínez, "A View from New Mexico: Recollections of the Movimiento Left," *Monthly Review*, July–August 2002.

PART XX
Latinos, 1980–Present

In 1980 the Latino population was divided with Mexicans in the Southwest, Midwest, and Northwest, and Puerto Ricans in New York and Chicago. Cubans lived mostly in Miami and the Northwest. However, by 2008 the Latino population had spread out and the generalizations that were near true in 1980 no longer applied. Los Angeles, New York, and Miami were still important but now Latinos moved to the suburbs and headed elsewhere. Places like Dallas, Houston, Phoenix, and Sacramento became ports of entry for new immigrants. Atlanta had 24,000 Latinos in 1980; 20 years later it had 268,851; Raleigh-Durham, North Carolina, went from 5,670 in 1980 to 93,868 in 2000. By 2005, 42 million Latinos lived in the United States.

Table 2 shows the numbers of Latinos in the United States. With the exceptions of the Mexican, Puerto Rican, and Cuban most came in sizeable numbers after 1980. Worthy of repetition is that the island of Puerto Rico is part of the United States. The 2000 U.S. Census reported that Puerto Rico's population was 3.8 million with an estimated 3.4 million Puerto Ricans living on the U.S. mainland. Not only because of their numbers and duration in the United States did Puerto Ricans and Cubans dominate the cultural icons of these concluding decades but also because of the vitality of those communities.

Central American migration is traced to the bloody civil wars. From 1980 to 1992 some 72,000 people were killed in El Salvador in a war in which the United States supported the right wing military government at a tune of over a million dollars a day. This caused migration of between 500,000 and one million Salvadorans whose population today numbers over a million in the United States—there were less than 10,000 Salvadorans before 1960.

Although a number of Dominicans had come to the United States during the mid-1960s as U.S. troops invaded the island, most came after 1980. The 1980 census reported 69,147 Dominican-born persons in the United States. The 1980s saw a swift entry of Dominicans and ten years later 506,000 persons of Dominican descent—Dominican-born—lived in the United States. Almost 90 percent settled in the Northeast, mostly in New York.

Like in the case of most immigrants, the voices of these groups remained outside the United States. They were still very much involved with their countries of origin. They sent remittances to Central America in 2004 that amounted to $7.8 billion U.S. dollars. El Salvador accounted for $2.5 billion; $2.6 million were sent to Guatemala. There is a dependency on these remittances without which those countries

Table 2. Latinos at Mid-Decade Detailed Hispanic Origin: 2005

	Number	%	Home Country Population
Mexican	26,784,268	63.9	109 million
Puerto Rican	3,794,777	9.1	4.0
Cuban	1,462,593	3.5	11.0
Salvadoran	1,240,031	3.0	7.0
Dominican	1,135,756	2.7	9.4
Guatemalan	780,191	1.9	13.0
Columbian	723,596	1.7	44.4
Honduran	466,843	1.1	7.5
Ecuadorian	432,068	1.0	13.8
Peruvian	415,352	1.0	28.7
Nicaraguan	275,126	0.7	5.7
Argentinean	189,303	0.5	40.3
Venezuelan	162,762	0.4	26.0
Panamanian	141,286	0.3	3.2
Costa Rican	111,978	0.3	4.1
Chilean	105,141	0.3	16.3
Other Central Americans	99,422	0.2	
Other South Americans	89,443	0.2	
Bolivian	68,649	0.2	9.1
Uruguayan	51,646	0.1	3.5
Other Spanish/Hispano/Latino	3,003,648	7.2	
Spaniard (self identified)	362,424	0.9	

Source: Pew Hispanic Center 2005.

would suffer economic, political, and social collapses. However, the voices of these nationalites within the United States are growing louder as their populations demand quality within the United States forming their unique voices within this country.

372. Excerpts from Bjorn Kumm, "The Loyola Opposition: El Salvador's Rebel Priests," 1978

Even before the fall of Nicaraguan dictator Anastasio Somoza (1925–1980) in 1979, there were movements within El Salvador for reforms. Many priests, especially the Jesuits, were at the forefront of championing land redistribution and demanding more democracy. A landed oligarchy of 2 percent of the population with links to United States businessmen controlled or owned 60 percent of the land. El Salvador was one of the 10 poorest Latin American countries with a third of its population living in poverty. The oligarchy considered the clergy Communists and declared war on them. The excerpts below tell of the involvement of the church during the late 1970s, especially that of the Jesuits and Fr. Rutilio Grande García, S.J. They were at the forefront of liberation theology that essentially taught the peasants that their rewards should be in this life, God did not want them to suffer injustices, and they should act as a community to bring about justice. Fr. Grande, with two other Salvadorans, was assassinated in 1977. This assassination changed Archbishop Oscar Romero (1917–1980), who began to publicly speak out against injustice and demand an investigation into the murder of Fr. Grande. Romero was later assassinated while passing out communion.

In El Salvador, there is a head-on collision between the government, controlled by rich coffee planters, and the Catholic Church, which is today the country's only effective legal opposition.

Catholic priests are unlikely revolutionaries—or at least they were in the Latin America of earlier days, when peasants knew their station and the churchmen considered it their main task to provide the sacraments.... In those days, too, the Church was a trusted ally of the landlords, the oligarchs....

In the past decade, after Pope John XXIII's "Populorum Progressio," the Second Vatican Council, and the 1968 meeting in Medellin, Colombia, of Latin American bishops, things have changed a great deal ... in El Salvador.... "There are priests in this country who talk as if they were Fidel Castro," says Ernesto Rivas Gallont, secretary general of the Salvadorean Association of Industries (and in his spare time honorary consul of Rhodesia and South Africa). "The priests are telling the peasants that everything should be distributed equally.... They side with the peasants. They consider us the bad ones." ... [The oligarchy] with the help of the army has build up a paramilitary organization, called Orden, in Spanish, means "order" ... They are given some military training (the government hesitates, however, to give them guns) and told to keep tabs on possible revolutionaries in their areas especially union organizers and Catholic priests.

One of the Salvadorean priests murdered last year ... Fr. Rutilio, certainly was no Gild-eyed revolutionary. He had spent his formative years at seminaries in Europe and Central America, often in great spiritual anguish, since he did not consider himself a good Christian....

In the early 1970s [Rutilio] ... found that his task in the area almost amounted to missionary work, preaching the gospel all over again to peasants who had been left on their own by the priests, except that they were regularly squeezed for money.... "The peasants around Aguilares are living under medieval conditions," said Fr. Rutilio. "They are serfs under their landlords. The wealthy coffee farmers of El Salvador have ceased being Christian. It is not our Lord they are praising when they get up in the morning. They cross themselves in the name of their lord, Coffee. And when they have prayed to their lord Coffee, then they pray to their lord Sugar." Prophetically, Fr. Rutilio referred to the landowners in the Aguilares area as the "brothers Cain." ... Six months after he and his colleagues started there in the parish, a major strike hit the sugar plantations, organized by two radical peasant organizations with Catholic links.

[Fr. Rutilo was shot down].... the Jesuits were preaching the need for the peasants to organize. A couple of months after Father Rutilio's death, the army moved in force to occupy Aguilares and expel the remaining Jesuits. Aguilares was kept under occupation for eight, days....

Archbishop [Oscar] Romero is an intensely private man who suffers a great deal from the public stand he has been forced to take during the past two years. He says that he would prefer to make his protest by withdrawal, by keeping absolutely silent. But circumstances do not permit. The death of Fr. Rutilio, his close friend, seems to have been the turning point for the Archbishop, who has literally become the voice of the opposition in El Salvador.

Every Sunday morning at eight o'clock the giant cathedral in the country's capital is so packed that the congregation spills out onto the sidewalks. The former cathedral burnt down a few years ago, under mysterious circumstances, and the present structure is hardly impressive, looking like a great unfinished hangar. The government has been contributing toward a new building, but the Archbishop seems uninterested in architecture. "He does not consider it his task to erect buildings," says a Catholic nun in El Salvador. "What the Archbishop is really doing is building the people."

Every Sunday morning, the sermon of the Archbishop, the unwilling leader of El Salvador's opposition, is broadcast from the Catholic University station....

"We are seeing the ugly face of our history," preaches the Archbishop, "It is not the Church which is sowing the seeds of violence. Violence is the fruit of unjust laws.... If the Church is trying to change things and at the same time trying to maintain its identity, keeping true to Christ, this is not communism, it is Christian justice. Our Savior taught us that you must lose you.

"But," adds the Archbishop bitterly, "these men who are ruling us do not want to lose anything at all." Archbishop Romero thinks it is, likely that the government will intervene and slap ban on his sermons.

However, until he is silenced he will go on preaching and presenting to the public the testimonials of peasants who were evicted from their houses and their bits of land during their clashes between Orden and the peasant organizations. Making their way over the mountains, the roads being blocked by the army, hundreds of peasants and their families reached the Archbishop's office in a seminary in San Salvador. It is doubtful that they will ever be able to go home. They will add themselves to the hundreds of thousands of slum dwellers in the capital.

"The clashes in the countryside, in effect, help the landowners to modernize agriculture, as well as rid themselves of agitators," says an observer. "The coffee men made lot of money during the past few years' coffee boom. They need fewer workers on the land, and the population is increasing steadily. But they might need them in the towns, as cheap labor for their new tax-free industries geared for exports. Our oligarchs have always been able to adapt to new circumstances."

"For a little while, the Salvadorean oligarch was running scared. Many members of the leading families (they are popularly known as "the fourteen," but are in fact somewhat more numerous) moved to Miami where a number of them have bought expensive condominiums. Now they are returning. They still worry about the Church and its revolutionary priests, but heartened by the growing presence of U.S. financed Protestant missionaries.

"The Protestants are true Christians," says Alfonso Quiñones Mesa, a leading Salvadorean oligarch and once his country's "coffee ambassador" to London. "They do not mix religion with politics."

Source: Bjorn Kumm, "The Loyola Opposition: El Salvador's Rebel Priests," pp. 738–740. Reprinted with permission from the December 30, 1978 issue of *The Nation*. For subscription information, call 1-800-333-8536. Portions of each week's *Nation* magazine can be accessed at http://www.thenation.com.

373. Excerpts from Maura I. Toro-Morn, "Yo Era Muy Arriesgada: A Historical Overview of the Work Experiences of Puerto Rican Women in Chicago," 2001

The 2000 census counted 113,055 Puerto Ricans in Chicago—they were 15 percent of the city's Latino population. Puerto Ricans lived in barrios scattered throughout the city. Where they lived was greatly affected by Chicago's history of gentrification, which is a big word meaning poor neighborhoods are starved of public funds and allowed to deteriorate through overcrowding and increased crime. This blight becomes a pretext for leveling the area and building new housing for middle-class buyers. Increasing the value of real estate is another way of getting rid of the poor. As the price of property goes up, absentee owners are encouraged to sell to more affluent buyers at prices the residents cannot afford. More often than not, developers are in collusion with elected officials. Together, they designate wards to be redeveloped or cleared. Local government uses the power of eminent domain, the power to condemn property for the public good, to get rid of the residents. When residents fight back, developers burn them out. In Chicago, Puerto Ricans, Mexican Americans, and other Latinos were constantly shifted to make way for so-called progress. Mexicans were moved out of the Near Westside to make way for the University of Illinois at Chicago Circle; Puerto Ricans were moved out of Lincoln Park to make way for Yuppies (young upwardly mobile professionals) who were white middle class buyers. It did not happen by accident; the political machine always intended to lure middle class whites back to the city because they paid more taxes, and development kept the city financiers happy. By the 1960s, sizeable Puerto Rican neighborhoods had formed in Lincoln Park, West Town, and Humboldt Park. Chicago's first Puerto Rican *barrio* was along Division Street near Humboldt Park, which Boriqueños called *la División*. By 1995, "La División" was also called "*Paseo Boricua*." It had a population of close to 10,000 souls—two-thirds of whom were Puerto Rican. It was home to the working poor. Most Puerto Rican men and women had not moved into the middle-class—60 percent worked in manufacturing industries, as laborers, and in the service sector. The following excerpts describe the experiences of Puerto Rican women in Chicago and how they adapted to factory work there. Chicago's rhythms were different from Puerto Rico or New York.

After I got to Chicago my husband didn't want me to work, but I wanted to work. I wanted to work because you can meet people, learn new things, and one can also leave the house for a while. I saw all the women in the family, his sisters and cousins, working and earning some money, and I wanted to work too. They used to tell me that I should be working. But I had four children, and who was going to take care of them? (Rita, 72 years old, Puerto Rican migrant in Chicago).

When I started working at Zenith I started welding. I lied to them, I told them that I knew how to do it but I didn't ... The lady next to me was Italian. I told her I really needed this job, that I had three kids. I told her that I was really interested in learning how to do the job, if she showed me I could learn faster. Within six months I was line inspector, within another six months I was spot checker, and within another six months, I was quality control operator. (Nellie, 52 years old, Puerto Rican migrant in Chicago) ...

The U.S. colonization of Puerto Rico transformed (and continues to transform) the work and migration experiences of Puerto Rican men and women. Historically, Puerto Rican women became part of a labor force that since the United States occupation has shifted from island to mainland to meet the needs of an expanding capitalist and patriarchal system. In Puerto Rico, feminist scholars have documented that Puerto Rican women were integrated into a gender-segregated market closely related to the needs of the U.S. colonial capitalism. Research conducted in Puerto Rican communities in the Northeast shows that, as in Puerto Rico, Puerto Rican migrant women were a source of cheap labor for New York City's needle and garment trades. Puerto Rican women migrants in the Northeast were also subject to gender and racial discrimination at work and were excluded from participating in labor unions....

The first large group of Puerto Rican women workers that migrated to Chicago were [sic] recruited to resolve the shortage of domestic workers that existed in the city in the 1950s. Gender ideology figured prominently in the migration of Puerto Rican women as domestic workers. In Puerto Rico, the government campaigned to move low-skilled single women to the United States as a way to deal with the unemployment and population problems in the Island. Government officials rationalized the migration of young single women as domestic workers by subscribing to the ideology that Puerto Rican women were inherently suited for domestic work. In Chicago, employers relied on racial stereotypes to pay women salaries that were significantly lower than the going rate for domestic work and made women work long hours without days off. Some contract workers broke their contracts and sought employment in the booming industrial sector, which was also in need of low-skilled labor. These early migrants provided information and resources to other Puerto Rican men and women about employment opportunities in Chicago. As a result, since the 1950s Chicago has become a viable destination for Puerto Ricans migrating to the United States in search of work opportunities.... In the 1980s, in keeping with changes in the global economy, many factories closed their operations to relocate to more profitable places in the Caribbean and Central America. Ironically, industries closed their operations in Chicago to open plants in Puerto Rico, thus further cementing the links between Chicago and Puerto Rico. Puerto Rican families in Chicago were hit hard by lay-offs, unemployment, and plant closings. Many families were not able to recover economically and slipped into poverty, a problem that hit the Puerto Rican community hard in the 1980s....

[Meanwhile], in the 1970s and 1980s, Puerto Rico lost to Mexico and other Caribbean countries its comparative advantage as a source of cheap labor, thus leading to rising unemployment and underemployment. Between 1970 and 1985, the overall unemployment rate in Puerto Rico almost doubled to 21 percent. Men and women were affected differently by these shifts. Although men experienced losses in their share of employment, they seemed to have gained in their share of total employment because of the growth of employment in the public sector. But in general, increasing unemployment and declining employment opportunities pushed Puerto Rican families to become dependent on federal welfare programs for survival. Others have resorted to the informal sector, also known as *chiripeo*, as a way to survive. There is a gender dimension to chiripeo, as both men and women engage in this kind of work; however, men's chiripeo includes fruit and vegetable vending, among a range of other activities, whereas women's work include domestic work, and jewelry making, among other characteristic activities....

Typically, the recruitment process proceeded as follows: private citizens in Chicago contacted the agency, filled out a contract request for a domestic worker and paid $210.00 for each employee's transportation as well as a service fee to the employment agency. By signing the contract request, potential employers also agreed to sign a blank employment contract to be delivered to the Department of Labor in Puerto Rico for the signature of the domestic servant and approval of the Commissioner of Labor. In a chart attached to the employer contract, the employer described the desired age, height, weight, and sex of the prospective servant and type of services needed from the domestic worker. Another way employers sought to hire domestic workers was by making informal requests to the U.S. government. For example, a prospective employer in Washington, D.C. wrote in a letter to the Department of the Interior, with the following request: "Boy, how I would like to get a good couple without children, if possible—the man to do yard and furnace work and drive my car and the woman to do the cooking."

The migration of Puerto Rican women as domestic workers is important because it links Puerto Rico and Chicago in distinctively gendered ways.. First, there is the government campaign to move low-skilled single women to the United States as a way to deal with the unemployment and population problems in the Island. Government officials rationalized the migration of young single women as domestic workers by subscribing to the ideology that Puerto Rican women were inherently suited for domestic work. In addition, employers accepted a cult of domesticity that elevated the status of women as mothers and homemakers, yet they made demands on domestics that hindered them from carrying out these responsibilities in their own households. In moving to Chicago as domestic workers, the productive and reproductive spheres of women's work not only intersected in the migration process, but, more importantly, linked Puerto Rico and Chicago in distinctively gendered ways. The migration of the domestics is also important because it led to the migration of other working class families, a topic I address in the remainder of this paper. Finally, the hiring of Puerto Rican women as domestic workers needs to be seen within the larger history of contract labor to the United States; how the United States had relied on Puerto Ricans as a source of cheap labor also requires attention....

Working-class Puerto Rican families in Chicago responded to their dire economic circumstances by sending every working age member in the household out to work.... Josefa describes the demands of industrial employment on women and the relative ease with which women were able to come in and out of work:

Shortly after I got here from Puerto Rico I started working. I started working in a steel factory. We made some car parts.... Men did part of the work and threw it our way and we cleaned it. At the beginning, I cut my hands. They paid me 85 cents an hour. I worked 40 hours a week and sometimes we had to work Saturdays. In that company I worked for 3 or 4 years.... After that I worked in another factory. I stopped working there because I started losing weight and feeling ill. After that I went to General Electric....

The other side of the economic restructuring can be found in the progress made by Puerto Rican women in the white collar sector ... the number of women employed in white collar jobs increased from 12.9 percent in 1960 to 63.6 percent in 1990. In particular, the number employed as clerical workers increased from 8.1 percent in 1960 to 32.6 percent in 1990. In this respect, as shown earlier in this paper, some Puerto Rican women have been able to take advantage of the jobs in the white collar sector, but most of the changes have taken place in sectors that do not pay well, such as clerical work, and that do not offer much opportunity for advancement. In addition, lack of educational opportunities and discrimination continue to prevent women's movement into higher-paying, higher status jobs.

The growth in the number of Puerto Rican women employed in the white collar sector is connected to the migration of middle class and educated Puerto Ricans to the city, a movement that started in the 1980s. In the late 1980s and 1990s, as the city's economic landscape changed, the city began to attract middle-class and educated Puerto Ricans to work in the service sector and in newly developed sectors of the economy. For example, the Puerto Rican Planning Board in San Juan estimates that in the 1990s, about 5,000 Puerto Ricans migrated to Chicago yearly to find jobs in high-tech fields, education, and health care. In my own work, I found that a large segment of the families that migrated to the city in the 1980s were educated women lured by employment and educational opportunities in the city. More recently, the *Chicago Tribune* has confirmed that the migration of educated Puerto Ricans to Chicago continues unabated. For example, Marisol Inesta-Miro and her husband John Lopez-Haage came to Chicago with their three children when they were recruited by Lucent Technologies in Naperville. (Marisol described her situation to a *Chicago Tribune* reporter as follows: "There were not too many opportunities back in Puerto Rico.... A lot of our friends—doctors and artists—also have moved to the States." So Marisol and her family relocated from Puerto Rico to the Chicago suburb Naperville, a pattern that has always fostered a great deal of resentment and tensions between barrio residents and middle-class migrants. In addition, as the community matured, second- and third-generation Puerto Ricans have entered the labor market, thus adding a new chapter to the history of Puerto Rican workers in the city of Chicago. This new generation of workers continues to solidify the transnational labor links that exist between Chicago and Puerto Rico....

Source: Maura I. Toro-Morn, "Yo era muy arriesgada: A Historical Overview of the Work Experiences of Puerto Rican Women in Chicago," *CENTRO: Journal of the Center for Puerto Rican Studies* Volume 13, Number 2, Fall 2001, pp. 26, 27, 30, 31, 32, 39.

374. Excerpts from Silvia M. Unzueta, "The Mariel Exodus: A Year in Retrospect," 1981

From April 15 to October 31, 1980, more than 125,000 Cubans departed from Cuba's Mariel Harbor and landed in South Florida. The United States had broken diplomatic relations with Cuba in the early 1960s and imposed an economic boycott on the island prohibiting Americans from trading with or visiting Cuba. This created an economic hardship and Cubans were barely able to buy necessities. They were forced to rely on the Soviet Union for aid. With growing hunger on the island, many Cubans sought to immigrate to the United States. In 1980, about 10,000 Cubans sought to gain asylum in the Peruvian embassy. Cuban leader Fidel Castro announced that anyone who wanted to leave could leave. With cooperation of Cuban-Americans, a boatlift got under way. It caused almost immediate strains with the United States, negatively impacting President Jimmy Carter as thousands of Cuban refugees landed in Florida. There were accidents as some over-crowded boats capsized and 27 migrants died.

The massive arrival caused problems for local government agencies. While earlier migrations of Cubans had been largely white and middle class, the Marielitos, as they were called, had a larger proportion of Cubans of African origin. Critics accused Castro of emptying out the prisons and sending a large number of homosexuals and convicts. This said more about the critics since regardless of their color or sexual orientation, most Marielitos were only seeking economic stability. The record below shows efforts of Dade County, Florida officials to incorporate the Marielitos and provide them with medical and social services.

Before their [Marielitos] arrival, the population of Dade County was 35% Hispanic, 16% Black American, and 49% White (Reference: Metro Dade County Planning Department, 1979). The Black Americans are about equally divided between those from the [Caribbean] Islands and those from the Deep South. After their arrival, the Hispanic population increased by a half of a percent. More than most other metropolitan areas, Dade County was a city of descendants of immigrants or immigrants themselves.

The exodus of over 125,000 Cuban men, women, and children started when more than 10,800 Cubans moved into the grounds of the Peruvian Embassy in Havana, on April 4, 1980, after the Cuban Government guards were removed from the Peruvian Embassy. The word quickly spread throughout the island. The removal of the guards was Castro's response to a dispute between the Cuban and the Peruvian Governments, when the previous week a small group broke into the Embassy seeking asylum.

At that time, no one predicted that the removal of the Cuban militia guard from the Embassy was to be interpreted as anything but "teaching a lesson," to Peruvian authorities. Instead, in less than twenty-four hours, over 10,800 Cubans jammed into the Embassy grounds seeking political asylum. Dramatic photographs of crowded men, women, and children in trees, and on the Embassy roof without water, food, and basic necessities hit the world press, creating embarrassment, and pressure for their release. After extensive third country negotiations and humanitarian requests from all over the world, the Cuban Government agreed to allow the departure of Cubans holding the Embassy. Peru, Spain, and Costa Rica, along with the United States, agreed to give refuge to the 10,800 Cubans seeking political asylum. During these negotiations, spontaneous demonstrations of support by Cuban Americans throughout the United States, other countries, and the world press, helped to highlight the incident and eventually helped to achieve the release of approximately 1,500 of the 10,800 originally in the Embassy. Upon the arrival of the initial group in San Jose, Costa Rica, and Madrid, the Cubans shared with the world media, the horrors lived while at the Embassy. This exposure generated a negative opinion for the aging Cuban Revolution. A few days later, in a skillful and talented show of strategy, Fidel Castro announced the opening of the Port of Mariel and invited Cuban Americans to come to Mariel, Cuba, and pick-up their relatives who wanted to leave the island. The announcement was well-received by the Cuban American community which immediately began what appeared to be an endless flotilla through the Florida Straits.

After a few weeks, it was evident that the Cuban Government had no intention of fulfilling their promise. Instead, some individuals released from jails and mental institutions became part of the human flow that constituted the Mariel exodus. The "human avalanche" reached unprecedented numbers. During the month of May, 88,817 Cubans arrived. This figure constitutes the largest number of Cubans that arrived in any single previous year.

During May, a number of other factors converged to create a very special situation. President Carter stated that: "We will continue to provide an open heart and open arms to refugees seeking freedom from Communist domination." That statement was qualified less than a week later. Decisions surrounding the handling of the Mariel exodus became entangled in the national political scene.

In Dade County, the initial processing and housing of refugees was skillfully handled by a handful of local, state, and federal officials under the coordination of Metropolitan Dade County Government. At Tamiami Park, a twenty-four hour processing center was set up where more than 1,500 Cubans were scrutinized by Immigration and Naturalization Service, fingerprinted, X-rayed, and released to family, friends, and supportive others. Food, clothing, and shelter were generously donated by individuals, local business, and civic groups. The processing and housing operation involved more than 1,500 volunteers daily, who worked day and night in a unique and heart warming show of care and goodwill. The Tamiami Park opened its doors on Monday, April 21st and operated until the evening of Friday, May 9th, when the process was moved to an old hanger near Opa-locka Airport.

That same month, a state of emergency was declared by the President and the Federal Emergency Management Agency (FEMA) was put into action. FEMA is the arm of the federal government responsible for coping with natural disasters and emergencies. FEMA's efforts were plagued by a lack of staff with knowledge of the language and culture of the people arriving, changes in personnel, policy inconsistencies, lack of clear direction, and clashes among various federal agencies. A Cuban-Haitian Task Force was appointed in an effort to guide federal efforts during the emergency.

Although many errors were committed and several criticisms of the federal management had been voiced throughout this process, many individuals were served because of the work and dedication of workers and volunteers.

FEMA's presence, however, attempted to bring the needed federal dollars and the recognition of the exodus as a national emergency. Meanwhile, the Cuban Government had turned what had been a negative internal situation for them into a serious emergency for some of us in the United States. The masses of humanity continued arriving in Key West and other parts of Florida. In Cuba, one of the results of Mariel was alleviating serious internal administrative and political problems, and exporting a high-risk population to its political rival, the United States. The exodus freed jobs, houses, and prison space for the Cuban establishment, and these were critically needed in the island. The departure of dissidents and other marginal persons relieved Cuba from explosive internal pressure.

At this time, still in May, another phenomenon took place: FEMA opened four refugee camps in Florida, Arkansas, Pennsylvania, and Wisconsin:

1. Eglin Air Force Base in Northwest Florida, housing 10,025. This was the first camp, a city of tents.
2. Indiantown Gap, in Pennsylvania, with a population of 19,094 Cuban refugees.
3. Ft. McCoy, in Wisconsin, housing 14,243.
4. Ft. Chaffee in Ft. Smith, Arkansas, with 19,060 refugees....

Life in camp began another chapter in the lives of these new immigrants. Physical and psychological abuse, beatings, and rapes were happening along with riots as the weeks went by and many Cubans remained tangled-up in the red tape of federal bureaucratic management. At one point in the month of June, more than 62,000 Cubans were in the four camps.... Most of those without relatives and who had broken away from their sponsors or "padrinos", gravitated to areas of high Hispanic populations. California, New York, New Jersey, and Florida became primary targets where homeless Cubans sought refuge.

In the Miami, Dade County area ... The Orange Bowl was opened by the City of Miami in the second week of June. On June 20th, Metro Dade County obtained a special allocation from Washington to feed refugees breakfast and one hot meal a day.... Up to 800 Cubans were housed in Tent City at one time, and more than 4,000 lived there during the two months it was open. Tent City remained open until September 30, 1980....

Although no conclusive figures are available, individuals familiar with the Mariel population place the number of non-Whites as high as 30% to 40%, and males making up approximately 60% to 70% of the population. The average educational level is estimated to be between the 6th and the 9th grade, with few of the arrivals being able to communicate in any language but Spanish.

Perhaps the most serious problem this group faces is a lack of attachment to family and friends outside of Cuba. This lack of a support system has often inhibited effective resettlement efforts....

Dr. Jose Szapocznik, Director of CAMP, Cuban-American Adolescent Management Program, University of Miami, Department of Psychiatry, Spanish Family Guidance Center, which provided services to Cuban unaccompanied minors, reports their total in the camps at 672. Of those, more specific information was obtained on 549 cases; of these....

55 or 10% were females;
43% were non-white;
18% have been or were in a marital or paired relationship;
12% reported coming directly from jail;
50% reported having been in jail at some point of their lives; and
59% reported having some relative in U.S., but only about half of these could give any portion of an address.

Parental occupation and education was reported to be:

70% labor/agricultural,
20% skilled labor, and
10% professional.

Szapocznik reports that a large portion of the interviewees appeared to have poor adjustment to school. Sixty-five percent stated that they had stopped going to school. The rough literacy assessment turned up approximately 8% illiteracy rate.

Six of the 55 female minors stated that they thought or knew that they were pregnant at the time of the interview. Fifty-six, or almost 10% of the respondents reported sexual abuse, venereal disease, or multiple sexual problems in their recent or distant past.

Clinical judgments of a series of psychiatric symptoms and conditions reported the following characteristics:

47% had experienced behavioral problems in Cuba,
14% had experienced hallucinations,

8% had experienced delusions,
31% were or had been clinically depressed,
22% had experienced suicidal tendencies, and
14% had made a suicide attempt.

Much has also been said about the percentage of homosexuals in those arriving from Mariel. However, no data is available as to the actual number of homosexuals in the Mariel population....

Legally, the individuals coming in the Mariel Flotilla have been granted the new administrative category of "entrant." This technicality rendered them ineligible for assistance available through the U.S. Refugee Act of 1980. Many experts believe that the denial of refugee status to these people greatly contributed to the many problems encountered at all levels. It was through the Fascell-Stone Amendment to the Refugee Act of 1980, that special funding was authorized, and in the form of cash assistance, reached the entrants during the latter part of February 1981....

CRIMINAL JUSTICE

The increase of criminal activity has been one of more item often blamed on the Mariel refugees. As of December 26, 1980, Unzueta reports that of 163 Cubans charged and/or convicted felons housed in Dade County's main jail, 103 or 63.9% are Mariel refugees, 11 or 6.8% are Cuban ex-political prisoners, and 47 or 29.1% are Cuban Americans. Mariel refugees represented 9.8% of individuals in the main jail. In the Women's Detention Center, where females either charged or convicted of felonies or misdemeanors are housed, Unzueta reports 8 or 4.6% Cuban American women along with 8 or 4.6% Mariel Cuban females and 7 homosexual Mariel males. Mariel refugee women represent 4.6% of the total females, while Mariel homosexual men represent 4.0% of the total individuals housed in the Women's Detention Center on December 26, 1980. The increase in criminal activity has impacted heavily on the entire Dade County judicial system.

Source: Document 0033 Cuban Information Archives. http://cuban-exile.com/doc_026-050/doc0033.html.

375. Excerpts from Chip Berlet, *The Hunt for Red Menace: How Government Intelligence Agencies and Private Rightwing Counter Subversion Groups Forge Ad Hoc Covert Spy Networks That Target Dissidents as Outlaws*, 1987

In 1979, the Salvadoran military responded to student protests by installing a military junta. The following year saw the rise of extreme right wing Salvadoran Maj. Roberto D'Aubuisson and the Republican Nationalist Alliance (ARENA). The military received a boost with the election of Republican President Ronald Reagan (1911–2001) who gave over a million dollars a day to the Salvadoran military to fight rebels who were demanding democratic elections. Meanwhile, D'Aubuisson's death squads (i.e., military units assigned to assassinate dissidents and church people), with the support of the U.S. Central

Intelligence Agency (CIA), killed thousands. Hundreds of thousands of Salvadorans came to the United States in response to the civil wars in their country in the 1980s and early 1990s. The Salvadoran civil war lasted 12 years, from 1980 to 1992, costing El Salvador 75,000 lives. The United States spent between $4 billion and $6 billion in El Salvador alone. The peace accords of 1992 between the Salvadoran Government and the rebels gave a place in the nation's politics to both the conservative ARENA party and the Farabundo Marti National Liberation Front (FMLN) rebels. While in the United States, many of the exiles helped set up organizations that would bring peace to their country. Because many of these organizations supported the rebels, they came under intense surveillance. The following article discusses government infiltration of the Committee in Solidarity with the People of El Salvador (CISPES) that was based in New York City. It was a national activist organization with chapters in major cities in the United States. It supported the FMLN and the progressive social movement in their home country. It was founded in 1980 and sought support in the United States for the guerrilla army.

The genesis of the FBI probe of CISPES was a complex network of groups and individuals with a common counter-subversive worldview: The underlying theories which prompted the FBI investigation of CISPES were developed at the start of the Cold War, and reflect the same discredited view of subversion that the American public finally rejected to end the McCarthy period. Individuals and groups who hold this discredited view of subversion played influential roles in shaping the policies of the Reagan Administration in this area, and then in some cases moved on to become consultants and staff members in Administration and Congressional posts.

These same groups and individuals then set out to rebuild a private counter-subversion network among conservative and rightist groups with the goal of assisting the government, and specifically the FBI, in investigating subversion. The results of their investigations were published in a range of newsletters and journals in articles which frequently cross-cited each other and often traced back to unsubstantiated charges of Communist subversion made by persons testifying before congressional witch-hunting committees.

Young conservatives from colleges and universities were recruited and trained to participate in monitoring and analyzing the activities of alleged subversive groups through a network of interlocking conservative institutions based in Washington, D.C. Information and documents collected by private right-wing groups were provided to government law enforcement agencies that would otherwise be prevented from obtaining the information by constitutional and legislative restrictions. This biased and unverified information was then used to justify criminal investigations of dissidents in general and the anti-interventionist CISPES in particular.

Many activists involved in Central American issues became aware of ham-handed snooping by Federal Bureau of Investigation agents in the early 1980s. In 1986, the Center for Investigative Reporting in California used the federal Freedom of Information Act [FOIA] to obtain FBI files which suggested a large-scale probe into CISPES. In 1987, testimony by a former FBI informant, Frank Varelli, also suggested a broad attack on CISPES by the FBI. Varelli later told reporters of the involvement of other governmental and private right-wing groups in targeting CISPES.

Some 1,300 pages of additional FBI files released in 1988 by New York's Center for Constitutional Rights (CCR), on behalf of CISPES, reveal in sharp detail the extent and nature of the FBI probe into CISPES. More importantly, the files show that the FBI, to justify its actions, accepted as fact a right-wing conspiratorial world-view which sees dissent as treason and resistance to oppression as terrorism.

The first FBI investigation of CISPES was launched in September of 1981 to determine if CISPES should be forced to register under the Foreign Agents Registration Act. Among the documents used by the FBI to justify this CISPES probe, according to Congressional testimony by FBI official Oliver "Buck" Revell, was a 1981 article by a former FBI informant and ongoing right-wing private spy—John Rees. The Rees article appeared in *Review of the News* a magazine published by the paranoid ultra-right John Birch Society. This FBI investigation was terminated without indictments in December of 1981.

A second FBI investigation of CISPES began in March of 1983. It was premised on the right-wing conspiracy theory that CISPES was a cover for "terrorist" activity. To justify this view, the FBI relied not only on reports from its informant Varelli, but also in part on a conspiratorial analysis contained in a report written by Michael Boos, a staffer at the right-wing Young Americas Foundation. This FBI "counter-terrorism" investigation was terminated without indictments in 1985.

The FBI relying on the malicious musings of paranoid right-wing ideologues to justify probes of the anti-Administration CISPES is rather like the IRS assigning Jerry Falwell to audit the financial records of the American Civil Liberties Union.

THE TERRORIST-BAITING OF CISPES

The June 1984 report on CISPES by Michael Boos, the staff member at the Young Americas Foundation, was titled: "Group in Nation's Capitol to Aid Left-Wing Terrorists." In the report, Boos wrote that the D.C. Chapter of CISPES would "soon launch a fundraising campaign to provide direct military assistance to the Soviet-supported Marxist terrorists seeking to overthrow the recently elected government in El Salvador." This conclusion was reached when Boos made the Kierkegaardian assumption that the shoe factory CISPES planned to help build in El Salvador would not really benefit civilians, but would secretly make and repair boots for rebel soldiers—and thus constituted military aid for "Soviet-supported Marxist terrorists."

Boos wrote his report after attending a public CISPES meeting in Washington, D.C. According to a spokesperson at the Young Americas Foundation, Boos was apparently engaging in a freelance information-gathering activity not directly connected with his staff position. Boos filed his report with the right-wing newsletter *American Sentinel*, and sent an unsolicited copy to the FBI. The FBI promptly distributed it to 32 of its field offices and apparently sent it to other federal agencies as well.

It is ironic that the Boos report on CISPES for *American Sentinel* was revealed in the FBI documents on CISPES since the Young Americas Foundation is only a minor player in the right-wing information network. The [Young Americas] Foundation primarily is involved in recruiting college students into the conservative anti-Communist movement. Boos, while at Young Americas Foundation, circulated a newsletter reporting on campus activists, but it too is not influential in right-wing circles.

The Young Americas Foundation is a haven for aging former members of the right-wing campus-based Young Americans for Freedom (YAF). While it was started by a former YAF staffer, the [Young Americas] Foundation is not formally tied to that group. They are certainly right-wing ideological soul-mates, however, and they cooperate closely. The [Young Americas] Foundation once sent out a fundraising mailing calling former Sen. George McGovern "anti-American," and claimed "our classrooms are full of teachers and textbooks that tear down our system of republican government and free enterprise while glorifying communism and socialism."

The *American Sentinel*, the newsletter which published the Boos report on CISPES (without attribution) is, however, one of the core right-wing outlets for red menace diatribes. The *Sentinel* frequently touts its relationship to law enforcement. The *Sentinel* raised funds to send its blacklist-style report to "723 FBI offices and local police departments," pledging to keep track of "the liberals, the left-wingers, the radicals and the Communists."

PARANOID THEORIES AND THE FBI PROBE OF CISPES

That the views of the paranoid right wing find safe harbor at the FBI is supported by the documents they released under the FOIA concerning the probe of CISPES. As Alicia Fernandez of the Center for Constitutional Rights explained in an article appearing in the Movement Support Network News:

"In order to justify its investigation, the FBI utilized two rationales: it posited the existence of a covert program and it resurrected a 1950s favorite, the concept of a 'front group.' These two notions were extremely useful. By positing a covert program, FBI headquarters was able to reason away the lack of findings in investigations conducted by the field offices.

"When a field office reported that assiduous investigation had revealed that a local CISPES chapter pursued only such projects as teach-ins, slide shows, and pickets, headquarters would remind the field office of the 'covert program.' This, headquarters explained, was known to only a few CISPES members, but represented CISPES' true intentions and activities. Thus headquarters would caution the field office not to be deceived and urge it to dig deeper. The deeper the field office dug, with no results, then clearly, reasoned the FBI, the deeper they needed to dig.

"When field offices cabled headquarters to inform it that they had located no CISPES chapter but had found a Central American solidarity committee, or a Latin American human rights group, or a sanctuary church, headquarters would recommend aggressive investigation and explain that CISPES operated through 'fronts,' in which respectable people were duped for its 'terrorist purposes.'"

In this way, any group which ever worked with CISPES or shared members became a potential "front." "The very logic of these rationales increased the pressure to expand the hunt for fronts and intensify the search for covert activities," Fernandez points out.

The FBI probe of CISPES involved 52 of the 59 Field Offices of the FBI. Dossiers were compiled on hundreds of other organizations which intersected in some vague way with CISPES during the course of the investigation.

Margaret Ratner of the Center for Constitutional Rights called the FBI probe of CISPES a "sweeping and intrusive investigation … the FBI utilized wiretaps, undercover agents, and informants in addition to the type of intensive physical surveillance that is normally reserved for investigation of serious crimes." According to Ratner:

"The investigation, which was begun in 1981 to determine if a violation of the Foreign Agents Registration Act existed, was quickly turned into a 'Foreign

Intelligence/Terrorism' inquiry, even though no basis for such existed. The new category, however, allowed the FBI to utilize 'special techniques,' that are considered illegal when applied to domestic investigations. It allowed the FBI to avoid strictures developed to remedy the abuses that came to light in the post-Vietnam protest era."

Ratner charges that "the investigation was used as one of the pretexts for the harassment and surveillance" being reported by those who oppose the Reagan administration's foreign policy. FBI director William Sessions, however, defended the CISPES investigation as a legitimate probe into criminal activity. But one FBI agent assumed a more sinister motive for the CISPES investigation in a memo which warned:

It is imperative at this time to formulate some plan of action against CISPES and, specifically, against individuals [deletion] who defiantly display their contempt for the U.S. government by making speeches and propagandizing their cause while asking for political asylum.

New Orleans is of the opinion that the Departments of Justice and State should be consulted to explore the possibility of deporting these individuals or at best denying them re-entry after they leave.

Among the many groups named in the CISPES FBI files were: Central American Solidarity Committee, Clergy and Laity Concerned, Church of the Brothers, Chicago Interreligious Task Force, Fellowship of Reconciliation, Friends Religious Society, Maryknoll Sisters, National Education Association, Southern Christian Leadership Conference, United Steel Workers Union, and the United Auto Workers Union. Also named in the files were a number of individual churches, colleges, religious orders, community organizations, women's groups and political groups.

The following excerpt from the Pittsburgh FBI field office file on the local CISPES affiliate, the Central American Mobilization Committee (CAMC), showed the ideological framework which forms the basis of the FBI investigation:

The membership of the CAMC and its affiliated groups appears generally to be of two type groups: the "core" membership and the "affiliate" membership. The "core" membership consists of individuals with strong Communist or Socialist beliefs who have a history of being active in Communist or Socialist political organizations, some since the Vietnam War era. The "affiliate" membership, on the other hand, consists in large part of local college students relatively new to the political scene. It has at least one female high school student member. Some of these younger "affiliate" members appear to be politically unsophisticated in that they know little of current international events save what they read or hear at their political meetings. Pittsburgh has noted at least two of these members or affiliates both were young females.

The CISPES FOIA revelations came on the heels of charges by former FBI informant Frank Varelli that he was pressured into inventing information to show that CISPES was tied to terrorists. Varelli told a Congressional subcommittee in 1987 that his reports were designed to provide an excuse for the FBI to intimidate critics of Reagan's Central America policies.

According to Varelli, "The FBI led me to believe that CISPES was a radical 'terrorist' organization.... Ironically, never once during the next three years of my association with CISPES did I encounter anything even close to the picture painted by the FBI. The CISPES organization was peaceful, nonviolent, and devoted to changing the policies of the United States towards Central America by persuasion and education."

Varelli sued the FBI, alleging they refused to pay him $65,000 in back pay. Varelli was terminated as an informant when the FBI agent controlling him carelessly lost in a car burglary files containing secret information that might have blown Varelli's cover.

Source: Chip Berlet, *The Hunt for Red Menace: How Government Intelligence Agencies and Private Rightwing Counter Subversion Groups Forge Ad Hoc Covert Spy Networks that Target Dissidents as Outlaws*. Revised. Cambridge, MA. Political Research Associates, [1987] 1993. http://www.publiceye.org/huntred/Hunt_For_Red_Menace-12.html.

376. Testimony of Peter Kornbluh, "Congressional Inquiry into Alleged Central Intelligence Agency Involvement in the South Central Los Angeles Crack Cocaine Drug Trade," October 19, 1996

The civil wars in Central America created push factors that drove many Central Americans to the United States during the 1980s and 1990s. In the United States, the nation was divided: one camp condemned U.S. intervention while the other said that it was necessary to stop communism. When Nicaraguans elected the Marxist Sandinistas, CIA involvement was stepped up as it funded and aided the Contras—right-wing Nicaraguan counter-revolutionaries that sought to overthrow the Sandinistas. Seeking to limit U.S. involvement, Congress passed the Boland Amendments in 1982 and 1984, aimed at limiting U.S. government assistance to the Contras. However, this did not stop the involvement of the CIA, which switched to covert actions. Congressional investigations revealed that the United States sold arms to Iran in exchange for the release of hostages taken by Iranian militants in 1979. The profits from arms sales went to the Contras. Further investigations suggested that the Contras received more money through other illegal programs that were coordinated by Col. Oliver North of the National Security Council. President Ronald Reagan (1911–2001) denied knowledge of the affair—even though it was clear his administration circumvented the provisions of the Boland Amendments. Vice President George H. Bush (1924–) and William J. Casey (former director of the CIA, who died in May 1987), were implicated but not charged with violating the Boland Amendments. The following formerly classified redacted document shows that on February 10, 1986, North was informed by his liaison Robert Owen that a plane being used to run materials to the Contras was previously used to run drugs proving U.S. complicity in trying to overthrow the constitutionally elected Sandinista Government. The turmoil throughout Central American was the principal reason for immigration to the United States, and it formed the politics of many of the refugees when in the United States.

Testimony of

Peter Kornbluh
Senior Analyst
National Security Archive

October 19, 1996

Congresswoman Juanita Millender-McDonald, members of the Black and Hispanic Caucus, and the Select Committee on Intelligence, I want to thank you for affording me the opportunity to both testify at, and be witness to, this important hearing.

The name of my organization, the National Security Archive, sounds like the type of government agency that might be involved in this scandal. I can assure you that we are not. We are a public interest documentation center, specializing in obtaining the declassification of internal national security documentation and making it available to Congress, to journalists and to concerned citizens to enhance the public debate over foreign policies that are conducted in our name but often without our knowledge.

The Archive—which is nonpartisan and does not take a position on legislation—often deals with documents that are classified TOP SECRET for national security reasons but that, in truth, have no real bearing on the security of our nation. Today, however, I am happy to have the opportunity to share with you declassified White House documents which indeed address a real and present danger to the national security of this country, to the security of our cities, of our households, and to the health, well-being and personal security of each and every citizen in this room—the scourge of drugs.

Let me say at the outset that I cannot speak to, nor provide evidence for, the allegations that are stated and implied in the *San Jose Mercury News* stories. Internal U.S. government documents on the early years of the contra war that might shed light on the issues reported by Gary Webb have not been declassified. Hopefully, public pressure brought on the CIA, the Justice Department, the National Security Council and the Drug Enforcement Agency will result in the release of those documents.

But I can and will address the central premise of the story: that the U.S. government tolerated the trafficking of narcotics into this country by individuals involved in the contra war.

To summarize: there is concrete evidence that U.S. officials—White House, NSC and CIA—not only knew about and condoned drug smuggling in and around the contra war, but in some cases collaborated with, protected, and even paid known drug smugglers who were deemed important players in the Reagan administrations obsessed covert effort to overthrow the Sandinista government in Nicaragua.

Exactly two years ago this weekend, this issue came up during Oliver North's failed run for Virginia's U.S. Senate seat. The *Washington Post* ran an article which I have included in your packet suggesting that North had failed to give important information on the contras and drugs to the DEA. In response, Mr. North called a press conference where he was joined by Duane Clarridge, the CIA official who ran the contra operations from 1981 through mid 1984, and the former attorney general of the United States, Edwin Meese III. Mr. North called it a "cheap political trick … to even suggest that I or anyone in the Reagan administration, in any way, shape or form, ever tolerated the trafficking of illegal substances." Mr. Clarridge claimed that it was a "moral outrage" to suggest that a Reagan Administration official "would have countenanced" drug trafficking. And Mr. Meese stated that no "Reagan administration official would have ever looked the other way at such activity."

The documentation, in which Mr. North, Mr. Clarridge and Mr. Meese all appear, suggests the opposite. Let me review it here briefly:

1. KNOWLEDGE OF DRUG SMUGGLING

Oliver North's own diaries, and internal memoranda written to him from his contra contact, reveal explicit reports of drugs trafficking.

On April 1, 1985, Oliver North was informed by his liaison with the contras, Robert Owen, that two of the commanders chosen by the FDN to run the southern front in Costa Rica were probably, or definitively "involved with drug running."

On July 12, 1985, Oliver North was informed that the contras were considering the purchase of arms from a supplier in Honduras. The $14 million that the supplier had used to finance the guns, "came from drugs."

On August 9, 1985, Oliver North was informed that one of the resupply planes being used by Mario Calero, the brother of the head of the largest contra group the FDN, was "probably being used for drug runs into [the] U.S."

On February 10, 1986, North was informed by his liaison Robert Owen that a plane being used to run materials to the contras was previously used to run drugs, and that the CIA had chosen a company whose officials had a criminal record. The company, Vortex Aviation, was run by Michael Palmer, one of the biggest marijuana smugglers in U.S. history, who was under indictment for ten years of trafficking in Detroit at the same time as he was receiving more than $300,000 in U.S. funds from a State Department contract to ferry "humanitarian" aid to the contras.

In not one of these cases, Congresswoman Millander-McDonald, is there any record of Oliver North passing this important intelligence information onto proper law enforcement or DEA officials. Out of the tens of thousands of documents declassified during the Iran-Contra investigations, there is not a telephone message slip, not a memo, not an e-mail, nor a letter.

We also know that Mr. North, who you remember thought it was a "neat idea" to use the Ayatollah Khomeini's money to fund the contras, was predisposed to use drug monies to fund the contras when they ran short of cash. In 1984, during a drug sting the DEA was attempting against leaders of the Medellin Cartel, he asked two DEA agents if $1.5 million in cartel money aboard an informants plane could be turned over to the contras. The DEA officials just said no.

2. PROTECTION FOR DRUG SMUGGLERS

The case of José Bueso Rosa demonstrates the lengths to which high White House and CIA officials were willing to go to protect an individual who fit the classic definition of a "narco-terrorist." General Bueso Rosa was involved in a conspiracy to import 345 kilos of coke into Florida—street value $40 million. Part of the proceeds were to be used to finance the assassination of the president of Honduras. I think most people in this room would agree that a major cocaine smuggler and would-be international terrorist such as General Bueso Rosa should be locked up for life. But because this general had been the CIA's and the Pentagon's key liaison in Honduras in the covert war against Nicaragua, North, Clarridge, and others in the Reagan administration sought leniency for him. As North put it in an e-mail message U.S. officials "cabal[ed] quietly to look at options: pardon, clemency, deportation, reduced sentence." The objective of our national security managers was not to bring the weight of the law down on General Bueso, but to "keep Bueso from …

spilling the beans." By the way, he ended up serving less than five years in prison—in a white collar "Club Fed" prison in Florida.

3. COLLABORATION WITH DRUG SMUGGLERS

It is the documentation on U.S. relations with another Latin American general, General Manuel Noriega in Panama, that most clearly demonstrates the shameless attitude of the highest U.S. national security officials toward major drug smuggling into our cities. General Noriega is currently serving 40 years in prison for narcotics trafficking. All of us in this room remember that General Noriega's involvement with the Medellín Cartel was so significant that President Bush ordered the U.S. military to invade Panama to arrest him, at the cost of American lives, Panamanian lives and hundreds of millions of dollars.

The 1989 invasion of Panama was codenamed Operation Just Cause. But in 1986, when U.S. officials had the same evidence of Noriega's career as the Cartel's man in Panama, the Reagan administration appeared to have another kind of "Just Cause" with Gen. Noriega.

Shortly after the *New York Times* published a front page story titled "Panama Strongman Said to Trade in Drugs, Arms, and Illicit Money," General Noriega contacted Oliver North with a *quid pro quo* proposal: help him "clean up his image" and he would have his covert agents undertake major sabotage operations against economic targets inside Nicaragua.

Instead of telling Noriega that he should rot in jail—as most everybody in this room would have done—Oliver North supported this quid pro quo proposal; indeed North even wanted to pay General Noriega one million dollars, yes, one million dollars in money diverted from the sale of arms to Iran, to carry out these sabotage operations (which the contras would have then taken credit for). In one of the most striking, and candid, electronic mail messages ever written inside the White House, North wrote to his superior, National Security Adviser John Poindexter that

"You will recall that over the years Manuel Noriega and I have developed a fairly good relationship.... The proposal sounds good to me and I believe we could make the appropriate arrangements."

And Admiral Poindexter authorized North to jet off to London to meet secretly with Noriega and work out the details on U.S. help to "clean up his image" and collaboration in the covert war. As Poindexter declared in his electronic response: "I have nothing against Noriega other than his illegal activities."

RECOMMENDATIONS

Representative Millender-McDonald and other members of the panel, this is but some of the documented evidence we have of the attitudes and actions of high U.S. officials toward narcotics trafficking and traffickers during the covert war against Nicaragua. While these records do not address the issue of who knew what, when, here in California, they do demonstrate a rather shocking pattern of government behavior that demands an accounting.

The key question, it seems to me, is how that accounting can, and should take place over both the short and long term future. Allow me to conclude with several brief recommendations:

First, members of Congress should call on the President to authorize his Intelligence Oversight Board to conduct a six month inquiry into the questions of official knowledge, tolerance, and complicity in drug trafficking during the covert operations against Nicaragua during the 1980s. With all due respect to the inspector general of the Justice Department and the CIA, an internal investigation is not likely to result in the public disclosure of information required to lay this scandal to rest. The Intelligence Oversight Board is a far more independent body, and far more likely to conduct a thorough investigation that can be declassified along with supporting documentation for a public accounting.

Second, while you, and other Representatives patiently wait on CIA director John Deutch to complete his internal review, you should demand that the CIA immediately declassify a previous internal investigation and report that the agency completed in 1988. This report is already known to exonerate the CIA of wrongdoing. But declassifying it, and all the files on which it was built, is likely to give us a far greater sense of CIA awareness of contra/drug operations, and the action or inaction of Agency officials in the face of this awareness over the course a many years. If the CIA doesn't have anything to hide, it should have no problem releasing this documentation. Its refusal to do so up till now, I suggest to you, should set off the alarm bells throughout the halls of Congress.

Third, a number of files should be released by the Justice Department immediately. Those include files that were not turned over to the Senate Subcommittee chaired by John Kerry in 1987 and 1988, particularly the files related to the so-called Frogman case in San Francisco. Similarly the Justice Department should release its never-filed indictment against Norwin Meneses and all of the supporting prosecution files that went into drafting that indictment, as well as all records relating to why that indictment was never filed and is now locked away in a vault in San Francisco.

Fourth, all DEA investigative records on Meneses and Danilo Blandón should be declassified immediately. In the case of Blandón, the DEA must also release the files on his informant status, including documentation on the deliberations to make him a high-paid informant. The U.S. intelligence community just devoted considerable resources to addressing the scandal of the CIA paying a known torturer and assassin in Guatemala as an informant. Having a major California drug dealer on the U.S. payroll as an informant strikes me as demanding at least as an equal accounting.

Finally, let me say that although the National Security Archive takes no position on legislation, I would personally hope that the political and social organization and mobilization that has been generated by public concern and the commitment of individuals like Rep. Millender-McDonald, Rep. Maxine Waters, Senator Barbara Boxer and others, will address the broader debate over the future of covert operations and intelligence reform. When you think about it, all of the CIA's major covert wars—in Indochina, in Afghanistan, and in Central America—have had as their byproducts drug trafficking and addiction. As the issue we are addressing here today suggests, all too often, covert operations conducted against some obscure enemy abroad have returned home to haunt the very people whose security they are ostensibly designed to protect.

This scandal provides an opportunity—and a challenge—for the American public to protect themselves from their protectors so that five, ten, or twenty years from now, we will not be sitting again in this gymnasium attempting to redress future crimes of state.

Thank you.

Source: National Security Archive Electronic Briefing Book No. 2, http://www.gwu.edu/~nsarchiv/NSAEBB/NSAEBB2/pktstmny.htm.

377. Excerpts from Brittmarie Janson Pérez, "Political Facets of Salsa," 1987

What is amazing is that after over 100 years of colonial rule, Puerto Ricans have maintained their language and traditions, as have most Spanish-speaking Caribbean people. Many people attribute this in part to salsa music and dance that binds youth together. Salsa is a product of many Latin and Afro-Caribbean dances. For instance, Mambo has a pattern of six steps danced over eight counts of music. Whereas Mambo moves generally forward and backward, Salsa moves more from side to side. It creates a mood. There are Cuban, New York, Los Angeles, Dominican, Columbian, and of course Puerto Rican styles. Caribbean music takes 80 percent of its roots from Africa, and it is part of a nightclub life that brings youth together. The following essay excerpts discuss the political aspects of salsa.

Late at night, in a discotheque in a Latin American country whose political system is dominated by the military and is not particularly known for its respect for human rights, a crowd is dancing salsa, a generic term covering Caribbean dance music. The song is Willie Colón's "El General." It starts with a roll of drum beats and a sarcastic description of the general getting up in the morning to put on his uniform and dictate orders to the president. A thrill of fifes follows and a [stentorian] shout: "To the right!" The verse describes citizens as delighted not to have a free press and a dangerous democratic system with its tricky politicians. The military gazette is very enjoyable and it is reassuring to have a regime which puts men with strange ideas behind bars. In the discotheque, the crowd continues dancing. The next stanza says the general is rumored to be about to retire: What will happen to the country and the people without him? "For a long time I've wanted to thank you," is the refrain, "goodbye and thank you, my general."

By this time, one of the dancers is consciously aware of the lyrics and wondering, "what kind of a song are we dancing to?" It is a long song which thanks the general in the name of those who are no longer there, the *desaparecidos* [disappeared]. A chorus which starts by asserting that there is no censorship in the country cleverly turns the refrain into a denouncement: Censura! This is followed by the sounds of an execution. Someone orders: "Aim … Fire!" A spatter of shots is heard followed by a military march and the ominous sound of a siren. Over a megaphone, a male voice with a Chilean accent announces a curfew. The next stanzas are loaded with hypocritical thanks to the *jefe supremo* for all he has done for the people, for what he did for Pablo Pueblo, who came home from the factory to find his family missing. "In the barrio we all toast the general with rum and cold beer, waiting for the day he can rest," the lyrics add. Addressing the general, the song continues: "Either you retire or they retire you, but what a glorious day that will be. How happy I am that you will go…. Goodbye little general, tyrant of my life."

The song is a dramatic composition with bold sound effects and elements in the verse with which people from many parts of Latin America can identify. A proper semiotic analysis is impossible here; only a few examples can be given. A general who dictates orders to the president is compatible with many past and present regimes in Caribbean countries. The missing, the desaparecidos, are a characteristic of dictatorships, but the term is most closely connected with the Argentine and Chilean experiences. The general's early rise and his work routine are reminiscent of Paraguayan radio newscasts which often start with such reports. The apologia for not having a democratic system is a standard one for military regimes in Latin America.

This song, which was brought to my attention by the dancer just referred to, is not unique. There is a trend in many contemporary salsa recordings to include one or two topics, such as poverty and injustice in Latin America or the oppression of Latin Americans living in the United States, and to present them as a product of corrupt regimes, U.S. imperialism, or capitalism. Denouncements of electoral fraud, government censorship and officially-sanctioned drug trafficking are among the themes dealt with in salsa by Panamanian composer and singer Pedro Altamiranda. The proclamation of nationalist causes is seen in the work of other composers from the Caribbean region. The range of issues is broad but the one whose social and political implications is rarely addressed is machismo.

The question of why "El General" could be played under the particular circumstances just described is a fascinating one, but because the permissibility of aesthetic protest is heavily dependent on the country and the prevalent political climate, it will not be broached here. Instead, I want to explore two broader questions: why salsa, an eminently danceable genre, is being used as a medium for powerful political messages; and whether commercial, ideological, and technological impingements threaten salsa's survival.

2. THE GENRE

Politics has rarely been absent from Latin American music Mexico's politicised [politicized] corridos are well known. Puerto Rican composers voiced their independentist concerns in a few boleros, also a Latin American dance genre. The highly committed nueva *canción latino americana* has been amply documented. *Salsa* differs from these, however, in that it is a large-scale capitalist commercial production, a consumer product aimed at all of Latin America and Hispanics residing in the United States but which, nevertheless, contains critiques of capitalism from various viewpoints. The *salsa* of socio-political themes is not the type of protest song sung in demonstrations, rallies, or overtly political contexts. It is protest embedded in everyday life: songs heard over the radio or record player, and music danced to at parties and in nightclubs or discos. The public is in a passive, recipient situation in contrast with, for instance, the U.S. blacks of the civil rights movement who sang "We Shall Overcome" in active resistance. This recipient relationship in popular music, between the product and the consumer, should not be over emphasized, however, since in the end it is the individual who, in accepting or rejecting a song, has the last say as far as commercial success is concerned.

The birth of *salsa* was the product of an eminently political event: the Cuban Revolution of 1959 and the OAS [Organization of American States] boycott of the island which ensued. Until that time, Cuba was the undisputed centre of Caribbean or Afro-Antillean music. Commercial production of popular music in Cuba for export was brought to an end by these events and many prominent Cuban musicians, composers, and singers emigrated to the United States, where New York still had sufficient big bands to be able to assimilate the influx. But the final end of the big band era was in sight by the time the Beatles swept the entire continent in 1964. U.S. recording companies had stopped production of Cuban music several years before. Yet New York was the mecca of Latin American artists as well as the centre of large-scale migration, not only from Puerto Rico but from all Caribbean Basin countries. Marginalized in the new land and consigned to an inferior status not unlike that of U.S. blacks—many of the emigrants were black—the émigrés settled in ghettos of their own, the *barrio*, adjacent to slums such as Harlem. In New York, the musical outcome was the emergence of barrio music and musicians, of small ensembles which played for their barrio brethren and incorporated into their music the sounds and daily problems, the cacophony and violence of the urban slum. The musical roots of these compositions—which were in part a quest for affirming ethnic identity—were eminently Cuban or Afro-Antillean. The clave, a rhythmic time-line of 312 or 213 over two beats, became the pattern not only for the re-interpretation of already existing Caribbean music, but also for new compositions. The use of traditional instruments such as *congas, maracas, güiros, bongos*, the piano, plus trumpets and trombones—which were emphasized to translate the sound of the barrio—was retained as an ideological affirmation of the Caribbean heritage. The new music was heavily indebted to the highly syncopated Cuban *son* [sound or musical style].

In the following years, a most interesting phenomenon occurred: although salsa was still not identified as such, the genre which started in New York was rapidly taken up in the big cities of the Caribbean in a spontaneous process, unconnected with fashion or commercial promotion. Possibly this was because the need for cultural identification felt by the Latins in alien New York was basically the same as that of Caribbean barrio inhabitants; both lacked a musical expression to represent them at a time when radio stations were playing the Rolling Stones and television stations were dominated by canned U.S. serials.

By the early 1970s, *salsa* reached its first stage of maturity in New York and the recording industry made its influence felt. *Barrio* music was given a label, salsa, and actively promoted. The *salsa* boom which followed had its apex in 1974, fuelled by a recording enterprise, Fania, which came to dominate the *salsa* market.

But the boom was double-edged. It gave employment to many Latin American musicians but the enterprise's efforts at "crossing over" into the broader U.S. and European markets had negative effects. In general terms, "crossing over" means validating an economically, politically, or racially subordinate culture before a hegemonic culture. In this case, the goal was commercial: to invade the lucrative big markets with salsa. For this effort to be successful, however, the enterprise's executives deemed it necessary to modify the genre. For the *salsa* industry to become really big-time and surpass the confines of the Latin consumers market, Fania's managers felt that they had to change salsa's image radically. From being the music of the barrio, associated with poverty, delinquency, and marginality, it had to be polished and approximated to the overwhelming U.S. pop culture....

The *salsa* boom would increase sales but eventually it killed the music's feeling and indeed its reason for being. Fania started producing supermarket music which insistently and desperately denied the true essence of salsa and became a Caribbean-type music disguised for "gringo" consumption. An example of such music is *Rhythm Machine* released by Fania with CBS in 1977. Productions such as these were rejected by the Latin public. The boom was exhausted in New York by 1979, at which time Venezuela and Puerto Rico took up the slack. But the demand for new recordings resulted in very poor quality, overnight productions which did not satisfy the public. *Salsa* seemed to be on its way out....

However, in keeping with Raymond Williams' theory of the flux of dominant, emergent, and residual elements in the cultural hegemonic process, an emergent trend arose within salsa—itself the product of an emergent, oppositional, and co-opted element—which was to give new life to the genre in the nick of time. The downward slide of commercial salsa was dynamically broken by what I here term socio-political *salsa*....

3. IDEOLOGY

As already noted, from its earliest days, barrio music contained a number of compositions which in sound and themes provided a meta-commentary on poverty, delinquency, oppression, and domination. These themes were, to a large extent, submerged during the salsa boom but once that boom waned they returned to prominence through the contributions of Willie Colón, Catalino Curet Alonso, and Rubén Blades. These, and other figures, each deserve more individual attention than they can be given here. I have chosen to focus on Rubén Blades, who has played a stellar role in the introduction and popularisation of socio-political themes in salsa and whose co-production with Colón, *Siembra (Planting)*, became the best selling salsa record in 1979, when the end of the boom was in sight....

A Panamanian composer and singer, lawyer, and film star who emigrated to New York in the early 1970s, Blades appears to have a two-fold mission. On the one Hand, his musical compositions are directed at Latin America in an effort to give Latin Americans an identity and to raise their political consciousness. Ideologically, he has identified with the left in Latin America and the left has identified with him. On the other hand, Blades seeks to represent Latin America in the non-Latin world, to validate the Hispanic presence and seek its rightful place in the order of things, particularly in entertainment.

He contrasts in these efforts with Pedro Altamiranda, who is also a Panamanian, has a Ph.D. in linguistics from the University of Paris, and whose socio-political songs seek to capture the language and lifestyle of his fellow countrymen. Altamiranda is strictly focused on his country. He has described himself politically as "oppositional and anti-militaristic" and has refused offers to enter into the glossy international entertainment world.

This, however, is the world in which Blades is eminently successful. In his quest to give Latin Americans an identity and to unify them ideologically, he has been triumphant and has become the idol of Latin American leftists and the public in general. His songs have dealt with the predicaments of the common man in Hispanic America as well as of Latin Americans living in the United States. His most overtly political album, *Buscando America (Searching for America)*, was released in 1984, after Blades had done a stint with various salsa artists and recording companies in New York, and had become the first Latin American artist to be signed by a U.S.

mainstream label, Elektra Asylum.... The songs deal with themes such as emigration because of political repression ("Caminos Verdes"—"Green Roads"); the assassination of Salvadoran Archbishop Oscar Arnulfo Romero ("El Padre Antonio y el Monaguillo Andres"—"Father Anthony and the Acolyte, Andres"); his search for unity, identity, and social and economic justice in America ("Buscando America"— "Searching for America"); the secret police ("GBDB"); difficult decisions in everyday life ("Decisiones—"Decisions"); and missing persons in dictatorships ("Desapariciones"—"Disappearance").

Previously recorded songs which gained him his outstanding position in sociopolitical salsa include "Pablo Pueblo" ("Paul People"), to which Willie Colón referred in "El General," "Pedro Navaja" ("Peter, the Switchblade"), and "Juan Pachanga" ("Juan, the Playboy").

In his second objective, to make the Latin American presence felt in the international entertainment world (or "crossing over," which is the subject of his second film, *Crossover Dreams*, released in 1985), Blades has been no less successful.

He has received extensive media coverage in the U.S., been featured on the cover of *New York* magazine (19 August 1985) and *Current Biography* (May 1986), and been written up in other publications too numerous to mention. His U.S. television appearances have included interviews on the *Johnny Carson Show* and *60 Minutes*. He has been on several world tours, appeared as an opening star in a concert given by Joe Jackson in Baltimore in 1984 and at the Olympia Music Hall in Paris in May 1986. As an actor he has appeared in two films and is in two more scheduled to be released in 1987: *Continental Divide*, directed by Michael Apted and co-starring with Richard Pryor, and *The Milagro Beanfield War*, directed by Robert Redford.

His unqualified success in crossing over (he himself dislikes the term and prefers to use "convergence") may ultimately jeopardize his other role, that of addressing Latin America. To be lionized in the heart of capitalism, starring in Hollywood productions, and being selected as one of the ten sexiest men of the year by *Playgirl* may place him in the situation of playing a discrepant role.... That is to say, his loyal Latin American constituents may ask how, if he represents oppositional sectors, can he be so applauded by the culture which dominates them? In the United States he has announced his intentions of putting Colombian Nobel Prize winner Gabriel Garcia Marquez' stories to music and to compose an album entirely in English, singing calypso under a new name, not his own persona but in that of an alter ego, "Panama Blades".... In a Panamanian television interview, he announced that he would record a two-album series of songs for Panama and by Panamanians and omitted mention of his plans to make the English-language record....

Blades has explained his cinematographic efforts to his constituents—who may some day become his real constituents as he has announced at various times that he may enter into the Panamanian political arena—in the following terms:

Right now, I am in the United States helping to end the stereotype of the Latin in the United States and also helping the 20 million Latins who live in that country for many reasons but generally because of the opportunities it affords. [I am in the United States] also for economic reasons, to make my life more possible to maintain once I return to Panama. [The latter] because in situations where you are economically controlled, money is freedom. That will give me an opportunity when I return to Panama not to have to ally myself with discredited groups and to see in what way I can do my work here....

Blades' situation has been discussed here because it is relevant within the framework of Williams' previously cited work. More will be said about this in a moment. Within salsa, the success of Blades' socio-political songs has attracted a large number of imitators. Some songs, such as Willie Colón's "El General" are of the same quality as Blades' own best productions, while others, such as the work of Pedro Altamiranda, is [*sic*] of an entirely different nature and follows different aims. But there are many imitators of a vastly inferior quality, characterised by trite themes and virtually inaudible lyrics. Oscar D'Leon, for example, a Venezuelan salsa star, recently released an album which contains two socio-political themes, one on the errant street boy and another on poverty, which are wholly lacking in originality, feeling and clarity. In the end, commercial enterprises and imitators may kill off the authenticity and attractiveness of socio-political salsa. In other words, again, what was once a brave ideological and artistic effort may be co-opted by commercialism.

The question which now arises is: What is going to happen to salsa? Such important figures as Willie Colón and Elías López have commented on its current problems.... If its themes are played out, are there other resources that can prevent this genre from falling into the musical fossil pit of tangos, boleros, and other past Latin American genres which are heard today only for reasons of romantic nostalgia? If one looks to either ideology or technology to rescue the genre, there is little cause for optimism for the following reason: ideology is constraining technology.

4. TECHNOLOGY

The very affirmation of ethnic identity in the face of a dominant, hegemonic culture led early and later salsa composers and arrangers to eschew electronic music and rely for the most part on traditional instruments with which they were more comfortable. It was believed that the purity of Latin music would be lost to a technology which was essentially capitalistic. But the use of traditional Caribbean instruments and the cautious introduction of electronic music into salsa have resulted in a sound which is anachronistic from the viewpoint of today's stereophonic record players, equipped as they are to transmit sounds which are far beyond the range of these instruments, particularly in the bass. In the opinion of informed individuals whom I have interviewed, salsa simply cannot compete in sound with rock music. The model for those who advocate change is the Miami Sound Machine, a group of musicians of Cuban origin who seem to have been successful in the crossover quest. They were recent guests at the unveiling of the Statue of Liberty, have played for President Reagan in Miami and in festivals in Chile, Peru, Costa Rica, Mexico, and a number of other Latin American countries.... Although retaining a Latin beat, the Miami Sound Machine is contemporary in its use of electronic instruments. Its clientele in Latin America is formed by a younger generation more in tune with rock, computers, and arcade games than with the legacies of the past. On the other hand, this musical group is [an] anathema to the nationalist left.

This war of ideology embedded in technology is felt at another level, that of composers. Tille Valderrama, a Panamanian composer and arranger who has a degree from Berklee Music College in Boston, expresses the frustration felt by some contemporary composers in Latin America. He feels that salsa is becoming obsolete because of the strictures of those who dominate its commercial production (as, for example, in their insistence on keeping the clave rhythm for the sake of the dancers who, if the rhythm were changed, might reject it). Additionally, they eschew the richness of what Valderrama calls the American drum set and are extremely hesitant to use electronic music.

The whole issue has become ideological: to use electronic music or to change the rhythm is felt to be as much a betrayal of the culture as what Fania enterprises did to the original salsa. If Blades uses electronic music or changes the rhythm it is accepted. If other composers do it, it is ideological treason.

5. CONCLUSIONS

We can see, therefore, that the history of salsa has been one of fluctuation between emergence and co-optation by capitalism. I have not said "by the dominant culture" because that is what the whole issue of "crossing over" involves. Whether or not salsa or the issues raised in socio-political salsa will be accepted by the public who are part of the hegemonic cultures is very open to question. It may depend on the success of the efforts of Blades or someone else, or upon the emergence of yet another saving lifeline. What seems to be clear is that the whole process of the dominant culture's absorption of emerging or oppositional elements is very complex. On the one hand, there are purely commercial efforts to exploit emergent trends. On the other, one sees individuals from emergent trends or subordinate cultures seeking validation through inclusion in the dominant stream. Crossing over may be done with a number of intents and poses a thorny problem. An artist may seek to have his ethnic group represented in the world's entertainment field and be very successful in doing so. On the other hand, he may run the risk of losing his constituency for failing to represent them ideologically. The whole process of the emergent being absorbed by the dominant may thus be seen as an active one on the part of both sides—with certain qualifications and intents on the part of both—rather than as a one-way path in which the dominant makes use of and manipulates the subordinate, emergent, or oppositional.

Another question concerns the use of an eminently danceable genre to transmit powerful political messages. It is here suggested that in the Caribbean and regions influenced by the Caribbean cultures, dance music is a privileged genre. Not only do the cultures which make up this region fall roughly within what one calls oral or residually oral culture.. but there is a strong African heritage whose musical traditions, e.g., the heavy use of drums and syncopation, may also privilege dance music as an aesthetic communicative genre ... explains:

As far as the Caribbean is concerned, far from entailing a sacrifice to dance, music always entailed an emphasis on dance. It is not a question of falling into the mediocre classification of *making music to dance to*; it is simply that music, with all its virtues, innovations, and variations, has dance implicit in it. In this part of the world there is no sense in making music that is not danceable.

As far as *salsa* is concerned, it is not difficult to conceive of a political message being successfully transmitted when heard at home, over the radio or record-player; it is much more difficult to assess its effectiveness in a social context, when a crowd is enjoying itself drinking and dancing.

There is more than one way to approach this subject. One can draw on Maurice Bloch, who declares "you can't argue with a song," because it involves abandonment of the freedom of natural discourse, and no argument or reasoning can be communicated.... In this particular context, the implications might be that the recipients of socio-political salsa receive and accept the message without question. Alternatively, a view held by several research assistants and record salesmen is that people go along with the music and either do not listen to the words, or listen to them selectively. The implication here is that the political effect upon listeners is slight.

However, both the dancer who brought "El General" to my attention and the large number of Blades' followers seem to indicate that some individuals do listen to the lyrics and others, being ideologically attuned to a particular trend or identifying with a particular genre, are indeed highly conscious of the lyrics, even when dancing.

Lastly, one may think of the recipients of the messages of socio-political salsa in terms of Freudian psychoanalytic theory: In the same way tunes that come into one's head without warning turn out to be determined by and belong to a train of thought which has a right to occupy one's mind though without one's being aware of its activity. It is easy to show then that the relation to the tune is based on its text or origin....

From this perspective one could imagine that there is ideological penetration of the listener who, whether he listens to the lyrics or not, is unwittingly having his consciousness raised.

The answer to this question may include all three of these opinions. It is hard to argue with a song and song therefore has a great deal of force. Many people do not pay attention to the lyrics, but it is possible that the lyrics may penetrate their subconscious. Other people identify with the lyrics or with a particular ideology and for them the song has the greatest force. Additionally, if we are dealing with a culture in which dance is not only a comfortable but indispensable and traditional component, the fact that a political message is embedded in a dancing song should not affect these various conditions of receptiveness just discussed.

Source: Brittmarie Janson Pérez, "Political Facets of Salsa," *Popular Music*, Vol. 6, No. 2, Latin America (May 1987), pp. 149–159.

378. Excerpt from "Joint Resolution, Deploring the Actions of President Clinton Regarding Granting Clemency to FALN Terrorists," 1999

Thirty-five House members, and 34 Republicans co-sponsored a resolution denouncing the decision of U.S. President Bill Clinton (1946–) to offer clemency to 16 members of the Puerto Rican nationalist group Fuerzas Armadas Liberación Nacional Puertoriqueña (FALN) or, in English, the Armed Forces of National Liberation, that allegedly set off 130 bombs in New York and Chicago in the 1970s and early 1980s. They had been given sentences ranging from 35 to 90 years. They had served between 14 to 19 years in prison. FALN, commonly known as the Macheteros, operated in the United States during the 1970s and 1980s. The group was dedicated to the independence of Puerto Rico and claimed responsibility for numerous bombings and robberies.

Whereas there is a militant terrorist organization that claims responsibility for the bombings of approximately 130 civilian, political ... (Placed on Calendar in Senate)*

Mr. Lott (for himself, Mr. Coverdell, Mr. Brownback, and Mr. Hagel) introduced the following joint resolution; which was read the first time.

JOINT RESOLUTION

Deploring the actions of President Clinton regarding granting clemency to FALN terrorists.

Whereas the Armed Forces of National Liberation (the FALN) is a militant terrorist organization that claims responsibility for the bombings of approximately 130 civilian, political, and military sites throughout the United States;

Whereas its reign of terror resulted in 6 deaths and the permanent maiming of dozens of others, including law enforcement officials;

Whereas 16 members of the FALN were tried for numerous felonies against the United States, including seditious conspiracy;

Whereas at their trials, none of the 16 defendants contested any of the evidence presented by the United States;

Whereas at their trials none expressed remorse for their actions;

Whereas all were subsequently convicted and sentenced to prison for terms up to 90 years;

Whereas not a single act of terrorism has been attributed to the FALN since the imprisonment of 16 terrorists;

Whereas no petitions for clemency were made by these terrorists, but other persons, in an irregular procedure, sought such clemency for them;

Whereas on August 11, 1999, President William Jefferson Clinton offered clemency to these 16 terrorists, all of whom have served less than 20 years in prison;

Whereas the Federal Bureau of Investigation, the Federal Bureau of Prisons, and 2 United States Attorneys all reportedly advised the President not to grant leniency to the 16 terrorists;

Whereas the Federal Bureau of Prisons reportedly based its decision in part on the existence of audio recordings indicating that some of the 16 have vowed to resume their violent activities upon release from prison;

Whereas the State Department in 1998 reiterated two longstanding tenants of counter terrorism policy that the United States will: "(1) make no concessions to terrorists and strike no deals; and (2) bring terrorists to justice for their crimes";

Whereas the President's offer of clemency to the FALN terrorists violates longstanding tenants of United States counter terrorism policy;

Whereas the President's decision sends an unmistakable message to terrorists that the United States does not punish terrorists in the most severe manner possible under the law, making terrorism more likely and endangering to every American; and

Whereas the release of terrorists is an affront to the rule of law, the victims and their families, and every American who believes that violent acts must be punished to the fullest extent of the law:

Now, therefore, be it

Resolved by the Senate and House of Representatives of the United States of America in Congress assembled,

That President Clinton should not have granted clemency to the FALN terrorists and that in doing so he has made deplorable concessions to terrorists, undermined national security, and emboldened domestic and international terrorists.

Source: SJ 33 PCS, Calendar No. 274, 106th Cong., 1st Sess. S. J. RES. 33, September 9, 1999.

379. Excerpts from Ramona Hernández and Francisco L. Rivera-Batiz, "Dominicans in the United States: A Socioeconomic Profile," 2003

The Dominican Republic shares the island of Hispaniola with Haiti—the western half of the island. Puerto Rico is its eastern neighbor. The Dominican Republic has approximately 5.5 million people. Of the 169,147 Dominican-born residents in the United States at the time of the 1980 census, only 6.1 percent had come to the United States before 1960. More than a third came during the decade of political instability in the Dominican Republic during the 1960s; 56 percent arrived in the 1970s. During the 1980s, Dominican immigration soared as more than 250,000 Dominicans were legally admitted to the United States. While Dominicans are relatively small in numbers in relation to other Latin American nationalities, their numbers are growing and they are active in profiling the community. The following excerpts are from one of the many self-studies done by that community.

SUMMARY OF FINDINGS

This research report presents the first detailed study of the socioeconomic status of the Dominican population of the United States. Using information recently provided by the 2000 U.S. Census of Population, the study concludes that:

(1) The Dominican population in the United States rose from 520,121 in 1990 to 1,041,910 in 2000, making it the fourth-largest Hispanic/Latino group in the United States, after Mexicans, Puerto Ricans, and Cubans. It is estimated that, at current population growth rates, the Dominican population will overtake the Cuban population before the year 2010, making it the third largest Hispanic/Latino population in the country.

(2) The major source of Dominican growth continues to be immigration. Between 1990 and 2000, close to 300,000 Dominicans migrated to the United States on a net basis.

(3) Besides substantial immigration, the Dominican population born in the United States rose sharply in the 1990s. There were 394,914 Dominicans born in the U.S. residing in the country in 2000. This constitutes one out of every three Dominicans.

(4) The largest concentration of Dominicans continues to be located in the state of New York, but there has been a significant spread to other states in the last decade. The state of New York was host to 617,901 Dominicans in 2000; followed by New Jersey, with 136,529; Florida, with 98,410; Massachusetts, with 69,502; Rhode Island, with 24,588; Pennsylvania (13,667); and Connecticut (12,830). There were also budding Dominican communities in almost every region of the country, from Alaska to Hawaii.

(5) New York City continues to dominate the location of Dominicans in the United States. The Dominican population of New York rose from 332,713 to 554,638 between 1990 and 2000. Dominicans are currently the second largest Hispanic/Latino population of New York, following Puerto Ricans. But the Puerto Rican population in the City declined substantially in the last decade. If current

population growth trends continue, Dominicans will overtake Puerto Ricans as the largest Hispanic/Latino population of the City within the next ten years.

(6) The greatest concentration of Dominicans in New York continues to be in Manhattan, where one out of every three Dominicans in the City resided in 2000. But just as the population has spread throughout the country, Dominican New Yorkers have also spread throughout the City. The Dominican population in the Bronx is now almost as large as that in Manhattan, with 32.7 percent of all Dominicans. There has also been substantial growth in Queens, Brooklyn, and Staten Island.

(7) The expanding Dominican population outside New York City has reduced the proportion of Dominicans in the City from 73.4 percent in 1980 to 65.1 percent in 1990 and 53.2 percent in 2000. Following New York City, there are major Dominican populations in the City of Lawrence (Massachusetts), where 22,111 Dominicans reside, the City of Paterson (New Jersey), with 19,977 Dominicans, Providence (Rhode Island), with 19,915 Dominicans, and Boston (Massachusetts), with 19,061 Dominicans. The cities of Jersey City, Passaic, Perth Amboy, and Union City in New Jersey also have substantial Dominican populations, as do the City of Yonkers in New York, and Miami in Florida. Many other cities all over the country have smaller, but rapidly growing Dominican populations.

(8) The mean annual per-capita household income of the Dominican population in the United States was $11,065 in the year 1999. This was about half the per-capita income of the average household in the country that year. It was also significantly lower than the per-capita income of the Black/African American population and even slightly lower than the income of the average Latino household.

(9) There is substantial variability in the socio-economic status of Dominicans in various parts of the United States. Among the most populous states, Dominicans in Florida had the highest per-capita household income, equal to $12,886 in the year 1999. By contrast, Dominicans in Rhode Island had the lowest average per-capita income, equal to $8,560 in the year 1999.

(10) In New York City, the average per-capita income of Dominicans was below the average for the United States. The poverty rate of 32 percent among Dominican New Yorkers was the highest of the major racial and ethnic groups in New York. The overall poverty rate in New York in 1999 was 19.1 percent, while it was 29.7 percent for the overall Hispanic/Latino population.

(11) A high proportion of Dominican families in poverty consist of female-headed families, with no spouse present. In 2000, as much as 38.2 percent of Dominicans in New York lived in this type of family, compared to 22.1 percent for the overall City. Close to half of Dominican female-headed families in New York City were poor, more than twice the poverty rate for other households.

(12) Despite the low relative socioeconomic status of Dominicans in New York City, their income displayed significant growth in the 1990s, rising by close to 16 percent in the decade (adjusted for inflation). The overall increase of per-capita income in the City in the decade was 9.2 percent, but both the Black/African American population and the overall Hispanic/Latino population in the City had lower income growth rates. The White population in the City displayed a growth of over 20 percent in per-capita income.

(13) The labor force participation rate of Dominicans is lower than that for the rest of the population. In 2000, it was approximately 64 percent for men and 53.1

percent for women. The figures for the overall U.S. workforce are 72.7 percent and 58.5 percent, for men and women, respectively.

(14) The unemployment rate of Dominican women and men in 2000 greatly exceeded that of the overall labor force in the United States. In 2000, Dominican men had an unemployment rate of 7.8 percent, compared to an overall unemployment rate of 3.9 percent for men in the country. Among women, the Dominican unemployment rate was 10.7 percent in 2000, compared to 4.1 percent in the country overall.

(15) Despite the comparatively high unemployment rates of Dominicans, these rates declined sharply between 1990 and 2000. In New York City, for instance, the male and female unemployment rates among Dominicans were 15.7 percent and 18.4 percent, respectively, in 1990. These dropped to 8.9 percent and 13.1 percent by 2000.

(16) The comparatively high unemployment rates of Dominicans in New York City are connected to a painful long-term switch in the employment of the Dominican labor force from manufacturing to other sectors. In 1980, close to half of the Dominican workforce was employed in manufacturing. This declined to 25.7 percent in 1990 and to 12.4 percent in 2000.

(17) The Dominican labor force is very young and mostly unskilled. Only 17.3 percent of Dominicans in the United States have managerial, professional, and technical occupations, about half the proportion for the overall United States. As a result, the average earnings of Dominican men and women are substantially lower than those of other workers in the nation.

(18) The overall educational attainment of Dominicans in the United States is among the lowest in the country. In 2000, 49 percent of Dominicans 25 years of age or older had not completed high school and only 10.6 percent had completed college. By contrast, less than 20 percent of the American population had not completed high school in 2000, and 24.4 percent had finished college.

(19) But the educational situation of Dominicans varies enormously when decomposed by immigrant status. Although the educational attainment of Dominican immigrants is very low, the situation for U.S.-born Dominicans is sharply different.

(20) The Dominican second-generation in the United States has educational indicators that suggest a remarkable acquisition of human capital over the last 20 years. This differs from the overall situation of U.S.-born Hispanics/Latinos, whose educational indicators are substantially worse than those for Dominicans. In 2000, close to 60 percent of all Dominicans born in the United States with 25 years of age or older had received some college education, with 21.9 percent completing a college education. By contrast, among U.S.-born Mexicans, only 13.3 percent had completed college, and 12.1 percent of U.S.-born Puerto Ricans had finished college.

(21) The explosive increase of the educational attainment of U.S.-born Dominicans is reflected in the experience of Dominican New Yorkers. For U.S.-born Dominicans in New York, the proportion who attained some college education rose from 31.7 percent in 1980 to 42.8 percent in 1990, and to 55.1 percent in 2000.

(22) Dominicans have school enrollment rates that are higher than those for other minority groups. In New York City, Dominican high school retention rates are substantially higher than for the overall Hispanic/Latino population, and for women, they approach the average New York City high school retention rate.

(23) There were 111,553 Dominican children enrolled in the New York City public school system. This constitutes 10.4 percent of the New York City school student body in 2000. Among public college students in New York City, 8.5 percent are Dominicans, exceeding the proportion among Puerto Ricans, which was 7.7 percent in 2000.

This report presents a mixed picture of the Dominican population of the United States. On the one hand, Dominicans have among the lowest per-capita income in the country, comparatively low labor force participation rates, high unemployment rates, and low earnings. On the other hand, Dominican income and employment indicators did improve significantly in the 1990s, and the Dominican second-generation appears to be accumulating vast amounts of human capital, increasing its educational attainment very rapidly. Therefore, despite facing considerable challenges in its remarkable growth during the last twenty years, the prospects for the future look bright for Dominicans in the U.S.

Source: Ramona Hernández and Francisco L. Rivera-Batiz, "Dominicans in the United States: A Socioeconomic Profile 2000," Dominican Research Monographs, Dominican Studies Institute, City College, City University of New York, November 2003.

380. Excerpt from Roberto Suro and Audrey Singer, "Latino Growth in Metropolitan America: Changing Patterns, New Locations," 2002

Since the Ford Foundation funded the University of California at Los Angeles 1960 census study of Mexican origin people, statistics have become an obsession and an important tool in defining the needs of Latino communities. The Pew Foundation, a public interest charitable fund, established a Hispanic Center housed at the University of Southern California, which generates important data. The Pew Research Center is a self-styled "fact tank" based in Washington, D.C. that provides reports on the issues, public opinion, and trends in the United States and the world. The Pew Hispanic Center has issued the most important studies on Latinos in the past decade. Its 2002 research showed that there were 10 million second-generation Latinos—29 percent of all Latinos. There were 11 million "third generation" Latinos—31 percent of all Latinos. The U.S. Census Bureau projects that by the year 2025, the Latino population will jump from 35 million to 61 million. It will compose 18 percent of the total U.S. population. The following excerpt follows this growth in urban centers.

FINDINGS

An analysis of the U.S. Hispanic population across the 100 largest metropolitan areas finds that:

The Hispanic population is growing in most metropolitan areas, but the rate and location of increase varies widely. Four distinct patterns of growth can be discerned. Established Latino metros such as New York, Los Angeles, Miami, and Chicago posted the largest absolute increases in Latinos between 1980 and 2000. However, new Latino destinations like Atlanta and Orlando charted the fastest growth rates, despite their historically smaller Hispanic bases. Metros with relatively larger Latino bases, such as Houston, Phoenix, and San Diego, meanwhile, became fast-growing

Latino hubs during the past 20 years, with population growth averaging 235 percent. Small Latino places, such as Baton Rouge, posted much lower absolute and relative growth than the other locales.

Fifty-four percent of all U.S. Latinos now reside in the suburbs; the Latino suburban population grew 71 percent in the 1990s. In 1990, the central-city and suburban Hispanic populations in the 100 largest metros were nearly identical, but during the next decade suburban growth so outpaced central-city growth that by 2000 the suburban Hispanic population exceeded the central-city population by 18 percent. New Latino destinations saw the fastest growth of Latino suburbanites.

Hispanic men outnumber Hispanic women by 17 percent in new Latino destination metros where the Latino population grew fastest. By contrast, in slower growing metros with large and well-established Latino communities, more Hispanics live in family households and gender ratios are more balanced....

Source: Roberto Suro and Audrey Singer, "Latino Growth in Metropolitan America: Changing Patterns, New Locations," Center on Urban & Metropolitan Policy and The Pew Hispanic Center, July 2002. © 2002 Pew Hispanic Center, a Pew Research Center project, www.pewhispanic.org.

381. Letter from Dámaso Serrano López, Mayor-Elect of the Municipality of Vieques to President William J. Clinton, November 10, 2000

Vieques Island, population 8,602 in 1990, is 55 square miles and nearly 6 miles off eastern Puerto Rico. Since the 1940s, Vieques was occupied by U.S. military installations. The U.S. Navy used it for target practice. This military occupation rankled land-hungry Puerto Ricans. In 1999, the U.S. Navy admitted using depleted uranium shells on at least one occasion. Puerto Ricans linked this to a high cancer rate on the island. Meanwhile, Vieques native David Sanes was killed by a bomb dropped during bombing exercises. This touched off a series of protests with mass civil disobedience in 2002, during which a large number of celebrities were arrested. Finally after intense confrontations, the Navy agreed to evacuate the island, which was accomplished in 2003. The following is a letter from the mayor of Vieques to U.S. President William Jefferson Clinton (1946–).

November 10, 2000
The Honorable William J. Clinton
President of the United States
The White House
1600 Pennsylvania Avenue, N.W.
Washington, D.C. 20500

Dear President Clinton:
My name is Dámaso Serrano López and I am the Mayor-elect of Vieques, Puerto Rico. I won Tuesday's election with 63.8% of the votes, for a four-year term as Mayor of Vieques. My campaign focused on achieving the immediate and permanent cease and desist of all military activities in Vieques, which is the primary goal and demand of our people.

At the same time, the candidates in the general election in Puerto Rico who support that same goal and demand, won in Tuesday's elections, among them the

Honorable Sila Calderón, Governor-elect of Puerto Rico, and the Honorable Aníbal Acevedo Vilá, elected as Resident Commissioner to the U.S. Congress.

The demand that the U.S. Navy must leave Vieques without dropping one more bomb, of any kind, has been the popular will of the people of Puerto Rico in general, and of Vieques in particular, before you issued your Directives on Vieques, and after you issued those Directives.

President Clinton, now the will of the elected representatives of Puerto Rico, in the Mayoralty of Vieques, in the Governorship of Puerto Rico, in our Representative in the U.S. Congress, in the Puerto Rico Senate and House of Representatives, and in the majority of the mayoralties in Puerto Rico, concerning Vieques is the same as the will of the people of Puerto Rico in general and of Vieques in particular: That the U.S. Navy must be ordered out of Vieques now, without dropping one more bomb, of any kind.

We are calling on you to respect that demand and that, before you leave office ten weeks from now, that you issue an Executive Order implementing that demand.

It was foreseeable that your Directives on Vieques would be changed by a Republican U.S. Congress, especially in an election year. That is why we insisted that you issue the Executive Order that we are demanding once again. You still have some time to do what's right, and the urgency of our plight is accentuated by the fact that the Republicans will control Congress once again.

If you don't issue this Executive Order, your Directives (drastically modified by this Congress and with no guarantee that they will be respected by the next Congress) will be used to say that there is no alternative site to Vieques, that Vieques is indispensable and that the Navy hasn't found another site. Meanwhile, bombing will continue in our island of close to 10,000 people. The only incentive for the Navy to seriously find an alternative site is if they are ordered to stop bombing in Vieques.

Mr. President, on Election Day, during a radio interview with reporter Amy Goodman, you urged the American people to vote for the Gore-Lieberman ticket, for First Lady Hillary Rodham Clinton as Senator from New York, and for John Corzine as Senator from New Jersey. In so doing, you told the American public the following:

"Now, the Republicans in Congress broke the agreement, and instead of giving the Western part of the island to Puerto Rico, gave it to the Interior Department to manage. If I can't find a way to give that island, the western part of the island back to the people of Puerto Rico, and to honor the agreement that the government of Puerto Rico itself made with the support of the local leaders, including the mayor of Vieques, then the people of Puerto Rico I think have a right to say the Federal Government broke its word, and the training has to stop right now."

That encouraging statement, Mr. President, gives us hope that you will not once again let our people fend for ourselves once again before a Republican Congress, especially since you will leave office shortly. It is easy to blame the Republican Congress for what they have done, and may foresee ably do, regarding Vieques. But the constitutional authority to "stop the training right now" lies with you, President Clinton. If you fail to do so, the responsibility for the continuing suffering of our people and the disrespect towards the will of our people and our elected representatives, is solely yours.

I respectfully and emphatically call on you, President Clinton, to heed the will of our people and our elected representatives and issue an Executive Order ordering the immediate and permanent cease and desist of all military activities in Vieques. Please call me in Vieques, or call Flavio Cumpiano in Washington, D.C., to set up a meeting or a conference call in order to provide you with whatever information or assistance we can give, or answer whichever questions you may have, in order to resolve this critical situation and accomplish this essential demand.

Sincerely,

Dámaso Serrano López

Source: In Vieques Protestors Spread Message Atop Statue of Liberty, http://www.endex.com/gf/ buildings/liberty/solnews/solyah110700.htm.

382. Excerpts from Regina Aragón, Jennifer Kates, and Liberty Greene, *Latinos' Views of the HIV/AIDS Epidemic at 20 Years: Findings from a National Survey,* 2001

Latinos in the United States are affected by HIV/AIDS in a greater proportion than their representation in the U.S. population. They are the second highest in the nation, by race/ethnicity. In 2006, there were approximately 1.2 million people living with HIV/AIDS in the United States, including about 200,000 Latinos. As the largest and fastest growing ethnic minority group in the United States, the problem will increase. Although Latinos represent approximately 14 percent of the United States they accounted for 19 percent of the AIDS cases diagnosed in 2005. The following report is a major study of the devastating epidemic of HIV in the Latino community, which until recently was ignored.

Latinos, who now comprise the largest and fastest growing ethnic minority in the United States, continue to be disproportionately affected by HIV/AIDS. Although they represent approximately 14% of the U.S. population, Latinos accounted for 19% of new AIDS cases reported in 2000. The AIDS case rate (per 100,000) among Latino adults (30.4) was almost four times that for whites (7.9), and AIDS is now the fourth leading cause of death for Latinos between the ages of 25 and 44. The epidemic's effect on different subgroups of Latinos is also striking. For example, the AIDS case rate among adult Latinas is 13.8 per 100,000, more than six times the rate for white women (2.2). And although Latino youth represent approximately 14% of U.S. teenagers, they accounted for 20% of new AIDS cases reported among those ages 13–19 in 2000. In addition, in a recent study of young men who have sex with men (MSM), HIV prevalence (the proportion of people living with HIV in a population) for young Latinos was 6.9, compared to 3.3 for whites. Finally, there is growing evidence that the HIV/AIDS epidemic is increasingly concentrated in low-income communities in which people of color are often disproportionately represented. Such communities generally are faced with multiple other health and social issues and limited resources with which to respond to the epidemic.

UNDERSTANDING THE VIEWS OF LATINOS

The disproportionate impact of HIV on Latinos, as well as the continued growth of the Latino population in the United States, point to the need to understand their views and knowledge of the epidemic. Such views can play an important role in how community leaders, health officials, and other policymakers target educational information and design programs that best meet the needs of this community.

This report, based on a national survey, examines Latinos' views of HIV/AIDS, including differences between Latino subgroups. Where data are available, analyses of changing attitudes over time are also provided. The survey indicates that Latinos are concerned about the epidemic and that attitudes toward HIV/AIDS vary significantly by race and ethnicity, with Latinos expressing more concern and urgency about the epidemic than the public overall. In addition, views within the Latino population vary significantly by income, education, language, and age. Although the sample size in this survey does not allow for comparisons of views by national background (i.e., Mexicans, Puerto Ricans, Cubans, etc.), such distinctions are also important given the role ethnic identity and culture play in individuals' beliefs and attitudes....

More than one-third of Latinos (37%) say AIDS is a more urgent health problem for their local community today than it was a few years ago. While the proportion of Latinos who believe this to be the case decreased since 1997 (52%), it is still significantly greater than the proportion of whites (18%). Moreover, almost seven in ten (69%) Latinos say AIDS is a serious problem for people they know, including 54% who say it is a "very serious" problem. The proportion saying AIDS is a serious problem for people they know has declined from 76% in 1995 and 81% in 1997. Nearly four in ten (38%) Latinos also say they know someone who has HIV/AIDS or has died of AIDS. Latinos (38%) are as likely as whites (42%), but less likely than African Americans (57%) to report knowing someone who is living with HIV/AIDS or has died of AIDS.

Latinos also express concern about the impact of HIV/AIDS in their own lives, with a majority (53%) saying they are either "somewhat" or "very" personally concerned about becoming infected with HIV. Personal concern among Latinos has fluctuated over the past five years from 51% in 1995 and 64% in 1997. Personal concern among Latinos (53%) is much greater than that expressed by whites (33%), as is concern among African Americans (56%). More than four in ten (43%) Latinos say that their concern has grown in the past few years (compared to 18% of whites and 35% of African Americans)....

THE FACTS ABOUT HIV/AIDS

Most Latinos understand that a person can become infected with HIV through unprotected intercourse (98%), sharing an IV needle (96%) and having unprotected oral sex (88%); however, as with the general public, misperceptions about the risk of contracting HIV through casual contact persist. For example, 37% of Latinos say that a person can become infected with HIV through kissing; an additional 8% of Latinos do not know whether or not kissing poses a risk of infection. According to the CDC, casual or close-mouth kissing poses no risk of transmission, and even open-mouth kissing in the absence of open wounds or sores in the mouth is considered a very low-risk activity. Nearly three in ten (29%) Latinos incorrectly believe that touching a toilet seat poses a risk for infection or do not know whether this poses a risk. Among Latinos, men (27%) are twice as likely as women (13%) to believe that a person can become infected this way. One in four (24%) Latinos thinks that sharing a drinking glass used by someone with HIV/AIDS poses a risk for infection or do not know whether this activity poses a risk. In general, Latinos, as well as African Americans, are more likely than whites to say that these activities pose a risk for infection.

Source: "Latinos' Views of the HIV/AIDS Epidemic at 20 Years" (#3184), The Henry J. Kaiser Family Foundation, November 2001, pp. 2, 4 and 8. This information was reprinted with permission from the Henry J. Kaiser Family Foundation. The Kaiser Family Foundation, based in Menlo Park, California, is a nonprofit, private operating foundation focusing on the major health care issues facing the nation and is not associated with Kaiser Permanente for Kaiser Industries. http://www.kff.org/hivaids/3184-index.cfm.

383. Excerpt from "3 Who Survived Sinking Won't Be Deported," 1999

Elizabeth González of Cardenas, Cuba, took a raft from Cuba to Florida in late November 1999 with her young son, Elián, and 12 others. The raft capsized, killing most of the passengers and Elián González's mother. Elián and two others survived. Elián had a father in Cuba; however, Elián was placed in the temporary custody of relatives who allowed anti-Castro forces to create the "Cult of Elián." When his father came to claim his son, the Cuban-American community mounted a campaign to keep him from returning. A federal court finally ruled that the father had custody of the child and the Justice Department forcefully took Elián from the cousins and returned him to his father. The following excerpt memorializes when and by whom Elián was rescued at sea. This is a major event in the history of Cuban Americans.

Miami, Nov. 26, (AP)—A 5-year-old Cuban boy and two adults who floated to Florida on inner tubes after their boat sank in the Atlantic Ocean will be allowed to stay in the United States, an official with the Border Patrol said today.

The boy, Elián González, was picked up by fisherman on Thursday morning, shortly after a man and a woman washed up on the beach at Key Biscayne.

Source: "3 Who Survived Sinking Won't Be Deported," *New York Times,* November 27, 1999, p. A11.

384. Attorney General Janet Reno's Statement Regarding the Removal of Elián González, April 22, 2000

On November 25, 1999, Elián González, a five year old Cuban was found by two fisherman, floating in an inner tube in the Atlantic Ocean off Fort Lauderdale, Florida. His mother and ten other people drowned when their raft, which was headed to the United States from Cuba, capsized. The only other survivors were a boyfriend and girlfriend. Elián was placed in the custody of his paternal great-uncle, Lázaro González and Lázaro's daughter, Marisleysis González. The Miami Cuban community heralded it as a miracle. Juan Miguel González, Elian's biological and legal guardian, petitioned the U.S. government for the return of his son to Cuba. The Miami Cuban community blocked this petition claiming it was not his dead mother's wishes that Elián be returned to a Communist dictatorship. Juan Miguel came to the United States, and after a legal battle, the court granted him custody. The problem was that the Cuban community and the Gonzálezes would not surrender him, so the Justice Department raided their home and gave Elián back to his father, who took him back to Cuba. Attorney General Janet Reno explains why they had to raid the González home on April 22, 2000. The controversy caused a split within the Latino community. The following is a press release by U.S. Attorney General Janet Remo explaining why the government seized Elián.

Good morning. Earlier this morning, federal agents in Miami upheld the rule of law and began to reunite Elián González with his father. As I speak, Elián is safe and on a plane headed from Homestead Air Force Base to Andrews Air Force Base where he will be reunited with his father for the first time in 5 months.

When the two are reunited, they will remain together in the United States throughout the appeals process while the injunction is in place. And, in accordance with the Court of Appeals ruling, we will take every step necessary to ensure that Elián does not leave the country while the Court of Appeals injunction is in place.

We have been to great lengths to resolve this case in the least disruptive manner possible. Up until the last [moment], we tried every way we could to encourage Lázaro González to voluntarily hand the child over to his father.

Unfortunately, the Miami relatives rejected our efforts—leaving us no other option but the enforcement action.

Elián Gonzalez is a child who needs to be cherished—he needs to have quiet time, private time, to be with his father. And that is what this case is still all about—the bond between father and son. Juan Miguel González wants to be with his son and that is what has happened now.

More than three months ago, the INS determined that only Juan Miguel González could speak for his son on immigration matters. From that moment, I could have taken action to return Elián to his father. But I did not.

Instead I gave the Miami relatives a chance to challenge my decision in federal district court. They did and the court sided with the government. It ruled that this was a federal case and that the INS was right to say that the father speaks for the child.

Two weeks ago, a state family court turned away the Miami relatives as well. In a strongly worded opinion, the judge said not only that the matter belonged in federal court, but that a 6-year-old boy is far too young to make life altering decisions on his own.

That same week, I traveled to Miami to try to encourage the family members to work out a resolution. The relatives in Miami said all they wanted was a meeting with Juan Miguel González, before turning over the child. But when I arranged that meeting, they still refused to produce Elián.

Every step of the way the Miami relatives kept moving the goal posts and raising more hurdles.

That is why I finally directed the relatives to turn over the child 9 days ago. That deadline carried great significance. When Lázaro González didn't comply, parole and care was revoked. That means that for the past 9 days, Lázaro González has not had lawful custody of Elián.

When the INS places an unaccompanied child into the care of an adult, that adult is required to abide by the directives of the INS. To maintain—as the Miami relatives did—that the INS somehow lacks authority over the immigration parole of a minor in the U.S. simply ignores the law.

So this morning I commenced an operation with the paramount concern being the well-being of Elián and the safety of the agents and others. After negotiating through the night, I informed the parties that time had run out. At that moment, I gave the go-ahead for the operation.

After I had already set the operation in motion, the intermediaries called back to offer one more counteroffer. I indicated that I was willing to continue to engage in dialogue, but time had run out.

I did until the final moments try to reach a voluntary solution. Law enforcement personnel on the scene were authorized to, and did, make the final call as to when to enter the González home.

Eight agents were in the house during the operation. They were there for three minutes. During that time, a female agent picked up Elián, and spoke to him in Spanish.

The agents then took Elián to Watson Island where they boarded a helicopter bound for Homestead Air Force Base. There he [Elián] was examined by a doctor to make sure there were no injuries. At that point, he was boarded onto a U.S. Marshal's plane headed to Washington D.C. where his father is anxiously waiting for his son.

This has been a very emotional case for everyone involved. The most important thing is Elián is safe and that no one is seriously hurt.

As we all await the outcome of the appellate process, I think it is important for us all to accept Elián's long over-due reunion with his father.

It is time to heal the wounds that have divided this community that is so dear to me.

Let us give him and his father the space, the calm, and the moral support they need to reconnect and reaffirm their bond between father and son.

Source: Press Release, Attorney General Janet Reno, U.S. Justice Department, April 22, 2000, http://www.usdoj.gov/opa/pr/2000/April/225ag.htm.

385. Excerpts from Roberto Suro, "Counting the 'Other Hispanics': How Many Colombians, Dominicans, Ecuadorians, Guatemalans, and Salvadorans Are There in the United States?" May 9, 2002

Because of the size and length of time in the United States, communities of Mexican and Puerto Rican origin often eclipse other Latino groups, most of whom came in critical numbers after 1980. The identification of these groups is complicated by the broadness of categories such as Latino and Hispanic that often do not distinguish the disparate nationalities. Due to distance, fewer working class Columbians, for instance, migrated to the United States; it was simply too far and too costly to migrate in large number from there. Even in the case of Central Americans, there were class and racial differences among the refugees. They had different interests depending on their social class. The Salvadoran community was mostly working class, but a large portion was first generation so their focus was in its home country. There were also generational differences, and by the second generation, they focused more on U.S. problems. They were concerned with problems similar to those of second generation Mexican Americans. Some Nicaraguans and Hondurans were middle class with interests similar to those of the Cuban refugees. Middle-class Nicaraguans and Hondurans played a greater role in defining the issues in their communities and were often influential in Republican circles. The later pressured national Latino organizations to support conservative agendas. The Pew and Mumford Centers, academic public interest research foundations, did an excellent job sorting these out. The following report by the Pew Hispanic Center at the University of Southern California, which describes recent Latino immigrants.

Among the key findings using these new estimates:

- The number of Dominicans may have actually increased by some 80 percent between 1990 and 2000 to more than 938,000 nationwide. The Census 2000 count of 764,495 Dominicans yielded an increase of only 47 percent over 1990. In the New York City metropolitan area, the Dominican population may be 25 percent larger than the count in Census 2000.
- The population with origins in El Salvador apparently increased by 65 percent nationally to more than 932,000, compared to a Census 2000 count of 655,155, which would have marked an increase of only 16 percent. The Salvadoran population in the Los Angeles metropolitan area is some 60 percent larger in the alternative estimate than the Census 2000 figure.
- The alternative estimates indicate that Mexican population may have grown by 60 percent nationwide to more than 22 million rather than the Census 2000 count of 20.6 million, which produced a growth rate of 54 percent since 1990.
- In Florida, where the Latino population is increasingly diverse, the Central American population is nearly 55 percent larger in the alternative estimate than the Census 2000 figure and the South American population is 37 percent larger.
- Finally, the new estimates indicate that the unexpected results of Census 2000 are largely the result of changes in the questionnaire from the 1990 Census rather than a dramatic shift away from self-identification by national group in favor of pan-ethnic labels such as "Hispanic" or "Latino."

The Census 2000 count of the "other Hispanic" national origin groups first aroused curiosity and then controversy because the results did not seem consistent with what was already known about immigration flows from those countries. For example, according to Census 2000, the number of persons identifying themselves as Salvadorans had grown by 90,084 for an increase of 15.9 percent since the 1990 census (see Table 3). The Hispanic origin question does not distinguish individuals by nativity or immigration status, and so that number should include native-born U.S. citizens, who identify themselves as being of Salvadoran descent, as well as both legal and illegal immigrants from El Salvador. However, according to the Immigration and Naturalization Service [INS], 215,798 Salvadorans were admitted as legal permanent residents of the United States between 1991 and 2000. All legal immigrants need not necessarily reside here, and many may have been counted in the 1990 Census because they were living here before being admitted for legal residence. Nonetheless, the increase in the INS figures is so much larger than the increase in the census figures—240 percent bigger—that the difference suggests a significant deficit in the census count. In Table 3, the same disparities with INS figures are also apparent in the counts for other national origin groups in the "other Hispanic" category. While the growth rates between the 1990 and 2000 censuses for those national origin groups seemed low, the number of Hispanics not identified with any national group

Table 3. Selected Hispanic or Latino Origin Groups in the United States, Census 2000
Supplementary Survey (C2SS), 2000

	Estimate	Lower Bound of Estimate	Upper Bound of Estimate
Dominican Republic	912,501	855,043	969,959
Central American	2,271,912	2,169,770	2,374,054
Guatemalan	520,233	467,877	572,589
Honduran	306,667	267,150	346,185
Nicaraguan	238,149	204,743	271,555
Panamanian	117,719	96,698	138,740
Salvadoran	932,117	857,339	1,006,895
South American	1,663,329	1,583,994	1,742,664
Colombian	572,032	529,109	614,955
Ecuadorian	337,746	292,351	383,141
Peruvian	271,698	244,163	299,233
Other Hispanic or Latino	3,298,111	3,185,901	3,410,321

increased by an extraordinary 223 percent between the two census counts, nearly four times the growth rate of the Hispanic population as a whole....

Source: © 2002 Pew Hispanic Center, a Pew Research Center project, www.pewhispanic.org. May 9, 2002, pp. 2, 6, 11.

386. Mireya Navarro, "Puerto Rican Presence Wanes in New York," 2000

In the year 2000, 57 percent of Latinos in New York State lived in the borough of the Bronx, and 319,000 were Puerto Ricans. This was a drop from the 1990 census when the Puerto Rican population of the Bronx was 349,115. The 2000 Census counted 7 million Puerto Ricans living on the island and the mainland; 3.6 million were living in the United States. Despite over a hundred years under the American flag, Puerto Ricans still retained the Spanish language and a unique culture. Even though they had fought in at least six major U.S. wars, problems persisted. New York City's Board of Education's Chancellor reported in 2000 that 15 percent of all New York City public school students are in English as a Second Language (ESL) programs, and of them 26 percent are Latinos. Some 60 percent of all incoming Puerto Rican patients to the local hospital had a problem communicating in English. Of concern to some was that with the declining numbers came a decline in political influence. The article shows that hegemony of Puerto Rican numbers in New York City was waning. And it gives a more extensive analysis of the impact of this loss of numerical hegemony.

A stretch of 116th Street in East Harlem—increasingly marked by Mexican restaurants and Dominican bodegas—nonetheless still bears the name "Luis Muñoz Marin Boulevard" after the first native son governor of Puerto Rico. On the blocks around "El Barrio," Puerto Rican music still wafts out of certain storefronts.

And Maria Martínez, 62, hangs no fewer than three Puerto Rican flags from her apartment window and fence. "The truth is," she likes to say with a bit of Puerto Rican defiance, "we got here first."

These days, though, it is hard to resist the sense that Ms. Martinez is hanging her flags with as much a feeling of nostalgia as pride....

In certain ways, city planners say, the trend reflects a traditional immigration pattern: the dispersion of groups from the city to the suburbs and other parts of the country as they make economic headway. But unlike most traditional immigrant groups who came to New York during the early part of the 1900s, more than a third of Puerto Ricans leaving the city have moved to Puerto Rico, including significant numbers of people born in the States....

In the 1900s, the percentage of Puerto Rican households in the city living at or below the poverty line increased despite a strong local economy, to a rate greater than that of any other group. According to the most recent data, about 40 percent of New York's Puerto Ricans qualified as poor, a figure considerably higher than that of African-Americans and worse than the average rate for all Hispanics....

The number of Puerto Ricans in the United States has grown over the last decade or more, up from 27 million in 1990 to 31 million, according to the Census Bureau's latest count in 1997. But in New York City, the Puerto Rican population fell by more than 96,000 residents in roughly the same period, to 800,000 in 1998.

While Puerto Ricans have moved out, however, the city's broader Latinization has increased, its boroughs filling with Central Americans, South Americans, Dominicans and Mexicans. City planners estimate that in about 10 years, Puerto Ricans will be replaced by Dominicans as the city's largest ethnic group by place of origin....

Retirees and successful younger people have also been drawn back to Puerto Rico, where the unemployment rate of 12 percent today is half what it was in the 1980s. Hildamar Ortiz, a lawyer who left New York with her 14-year-old daughter in 1996, said she moved partly to honor her late father's dreams of retiring in Puerto Rico. But she said she had always wondered what it would be like to be Puerto Rican in Puerto Rico....

After a half century, Puerto Ricans in New York have succeeded in carving out electoral districts and Latino studies programs in universities. They have won bilingual education and civil rights battles and congressional, state and municipal posts. They have created a wide array of organizations, from cultural institutions to nonprofit agencies that now increasingly serve other Latinos.

"Puerto Ricans have to be acknowledged as the front line that opened doors for every Latino that came after them," said Susana Torruella Leval, director of El Museo del Barrio, the Puerto Rican and Latin American art museum.

Source: Mireya Navarro, "Puerto Rican Presence Wanes in New York," *New York Times*, February 28, 2000, p. A1.

387. Consuelo López Springfield and Elizabeth Hernández, "Women and Writing in Puerto Rico: An Interview with Ana Lydia Vega," 1994

Ana Lydia Vega (1946–) is a Puerto Rican-born writer who incorporates the history of Puerto Ricans into her prose about everyday life and culture. She is the recipient of both the Premio Juan Rulfo (1982), an international literary prize given by the Cervantes Institute in Paris, and the Premio Casa de las Américas (1981), an annual prize given by the House of the Americas in Cuba. She is a postmodernist, and her writing often deals with gender and sexuality. She is the author of *Virgenes y martires* (1983), *Encancaranublado y otros cuentos de naufragio* (1987), *Pasion de historia y otras historias de pasion* (1987), and *El tramo ancla* (1988). The following is an interview with her where she discusses Puerto Rican literature.

SPRINGFIELD: Let's begin, Ana Lydia, with a broad question. Why do you write?

VEGA: It's something I've been doing since I was a little girl. My father never had a formal education, he never went to school. He was *jibaro* [peasant] from Coamo, an improvisator of *décimas* who always socialized with other oral troubadours. He always performed oral poetry. In time, he taught himself to write; then, he wrote down his poems. I was raised in this environment of listening to oral poetry improvisations and after reading my father's décimas, I yearned to do the same thing. It was a process of imitation. Perhaps, I wanted to gain my father's approval. He always said that the one who inherited his poetic gift was me. Thus it was that I began to write décimas and poetry. I wrote strictly poetry until high school. Then, I began to write short stories and other things. Writing was an integral part of my life. I never decided to write nor did I have any specific reason for doing so. I simply did it, like people who sing from childhood onwards.

SPRINGFIELD: I'd like to ask you about feminism. How has it affected your way of writing?

VEGA: A lot. First of all, I believe that everything we are affects our writing. My being Puerto Rican shows up in my writing. If I'm black, it will be in my writing. If I am a woman, it will be there, too. All that we are is in our writing, and it frames the perspective from which we write, whether one is aware of it or not. It doesn't have to be something conscious. I believe that the experiences that I have had as a woman since my infancy, my experiences with repression, this constant negotiation with a male-dominated world, leaves an imprint on one's self. One does not have to know feminist theories to be a feminist in practice, to arrive at some positions that frame what one chooses to write about. I think that my "feminism" is more practical than theoretical. It is more a response to decisions I have made in my life than to theoretical readings in feminism. While in the university, I read feminist theories; but my feminism grew out of decisions and positions that are lived experiences.

SPRINGFIELD: I believe that your writing and Rosario Ferre's works are changing the attitudes of many young people.

VEGA: I think that at least we are getting through to young people. I don't know if we are transforming them. I don't think that I have as much faith in literature as you do. However, many young people come up to me to show me their writing and say "what you have been writing touched me, made me think of this and that." I have received lots of comments like this and, I suppose, many other women writers have as well. I believe that our function at this historical moment in Puerto Rico is to create "role models" that didn't exist before. There were women writers. From the nineteenth century, there have been many. Twenty-five novelists, at least. But these women writers never gained recognition at the national level. They never arrived at what we call "literary power." They were always marginalized. They had to publish their works themselves and circulate them among friends. They don't appear in the important anthologies of different eras. Only men appear. I think that Rosario Ferre cracked open "the closet." Her first publication was seen as scandalous. Here was the daughter of an ex-governor, a rich woman who broke with the conventions of her class. When she published, she immediately gained national attention. This broke down the barriers. This and the feminist struggles of the 1960s began to change popular consciousness. In turn, it allowed a group of women writers to gain legitimacy in the sense that they appeared in anthologies, achieved critical attention, and reached more readers than men who were publishing then. To me, it is interesting that literature written by women at this time received more popular endorsement than the works of contemporary male writers.

SPRINGFIELD: Another reason for the popularity of women writers is that there are more women reading.

VEGA: Yes, definitely. In general, there are more people reading. You have to remember that in the 1940s, Puerto Rico had a high rate of illiteracy. It was comparable to that of Haiti, for example. Ours is a country that experienced a cultural revolution in the sense that access to schooling and to the universities created a reading audience that flourished in the 1970s and 1980s. There were many women in this audience because there were more women than men in education, in the universities. While more men have been the victims of wars, crime, and unemployment, women have been improving their status through education. This is one of the factors. Another is that women's writing, after the 1960s, is more closely related to life, to the daily life of ordinary people. People can more readily identify with this literature than with a literature that treats, for example, the greatest national problems, the traditional, classical, political problems, the nationalist struggles, the relationship with the United States, etc. People are a bit saturated with this kind of literature. They want to see in literature written by women a reflection of their own lives, a reflection of what is actually happening to them. They want a literature that is more personal. That's what I think. Humor, too. I think that women writers have worked more with humor, with parody, with irony. Rosario, Carmen Lugo Filippi, Magali Garcia, for example. That's what people like. Not a "somber" literature, traditional, patriarchal literature, but one that is humorous, although it may also be patriotic. I think that contemporary Puerto Rican women's writing also has a wider ironic distance. People like that because it responds to our era, a time when no one believes in ideologies anymore. Irony, thus, is a necessary posture. There are other reasons; but I think that these are the most important: a larger reading public, a greater number of women readers, and a stronger identification between the reader and the stance taken by women writers.

SPRINGFIELD: There are many critics who say that women's writing emerges from a collective voice. Perhaps, your voice is communal.

VEGA: That may be so. But I believe that women's literature is more "demythifying." Women have always been seen as marginalized. Throughout their lives from early childhood on, women fight against this marginalization and against repression. One ends up by not identifying with the dominant power. One cannot identify with it because one does not have access to it. You have to identify with those sectors that are marginalized, like you. And from this point of view, we can speak of "the collective voice." Along with this comes irony and aggressive linguistic styles. Women's lives, to be sure, are always more collective because we're mothers, we take care of children, we tend to our parents when they're ill, we are neighbors. Men don't have this kind of life—one that is integrated with the community. Their lives are more public but not necessarily more communal. Women's lives are more private, but perhaps, more collective.

SPRINGFIELD: Let's extend the word "communal." Among women writers today is there much communication? Do you discuss what you are doing, teaching, and trying to develop?

VEGA: Yes, a lot. But I must add that this is not only going on among women but with men, too. There is a small group of close friends who are writing today among whom I may mention Juan Antonio Ramos, Edgardo Sanabria Santaliz, Kalman Barsy, and those whom I mentioned earlier: Rosario, Magali, Carmen. We're all good friends. We call one another on the phone, we go to one another's book openings, we present together at colloquiums and congresses, and we get together at the hotels where we are staying. We share ideas. I think that there is a great deal of communication.

SPRINGFIELD: And what about those who are writing in the United States? I am thinking of Judith Ortiz Cofer, whose poetry is extraordinary.

VEGA: I don't know her personally, although I have read some of her work. We are now beginning to establish communication with those over there. Until recently, there never were meetings held between writers from here and those from there. We knew one another, but only from a distance. For instance, we knew Pedro Pietri, Miguel Algarin, and Tato Laviera, from the 1960s and 1970s. But we knew them little and only a few. And they only knew a few of us, mostly writers of the 1950s—Rene Márquez, Pedro Juan Soto—the "Classics." A few activities, one at Rutgers, brought together some of the writers from there and some from here. Afterwards, Manuel Ramos Otero, who was at Lehman College, put together another. That was about three years ago. Recently, in Mayaguez, the most important one took place. Aurora Levins Morales, who, to me, is very interesting, came. There was a lot of communication. On one hand, it was conflictive because the writers from there have a lot of resentment. They feel rejected there and rejected here. And they're right. It has been that way. But I think that that is changing some because of the communication that now exists between New York and San Juan. That's not the way it was before. Before, there were two totally separate universes. At the Mayaguez conference, where we stayed at the same seaside hotel, we talked a lot. We learned that they felt ill-at-ease for writing in English. Before they came, they were fearful because they thought that as Spanish is now the official language, English would be the "death sentence" for them as Puerto Rican writers. But we told them "no," that this (the official use of Spanish) is part of a process that is politically and historically indispensable in establishing a Puerto Rican identity. But within this process, they have a place. We told them that what is most important is the content of their work, not the language in which it is written. We now see that even though they are writing in English, many of the themes are the same. We are part of the same literature. The group of writers at this last conference came to the conclusion that they are an integral part of Puerto Rican literature. Now, we write to one another, we call one another up on the telephone.

SPRINGFIELD: We were talking about your recent book, *Falsas Cronicas del Sur* [*False Chronicles from the South*]. It's a little different from your previous work.

VEGA: Well, it is and it isn't. You see, I have always been fascinated with history. In fact, when I was at the university, I had to decide whether to study Languages or History. I chose Languages because it offered more opportunities to travel. But I always loved History and continued to read it. I'm a frustrated investigator. In this book, I continued a course that I had initiated in my early work. In *Virgenes y Mártires*, there is a story about Haiti called "Puerto Principe Abajo" ["Down There in Port-au-Prince"] that deals with history. Another, "Ahi Viene Mamá Yona" ["Here Comes Mama Yona"], deals with the history of Puerto Rican nationalism. In the second book, *Encancaranublado*, you'll find a lot that has to do with the history of the Caribbean. And in the long short story, "Sobre Tumbas y Heroes" ["About Tombs and Heroes"] which is about the Grito de Lares, there is a search for the hidden history, a special theme of mine. The only difference is that now the complete book deals with this. It isn't written history but oral history, the history people told me about these towns, especially Arroyo, where my mother comes from. It's about how they see history, lived history or told history.

SPRINGFIELD: That is very "communal" because you are gathering the ideas people have about history, while, concurrently, using your own narrative voice.

VEGA: Exactly. In the first stage, I take oral testimonies. Secondly, I go to the library to verify data. Then, I recreate what people have told me, using my literary imagination. The public imagines the rest in the fourth stage.

HERNÁNDEZ: Why the title, *Falsas Cronicas del Sur?*

VEGA: Because they are chronicles. A chronicle is a reflection of a period one has lived through. They are always "false" because the oral tradition imparts a new history each time one tells it. If I were to interview five elderly people, each would tell me a different "history." And when I go to the library, the written historiography tells other versions, as well. Everyone tells a history in light of his or her own vision, social class, sex, or position. Everything that you are frames your perspective of history. And that constantly changes. Just as I, too, relate history, this history will change in the process of writing it. It's inevitable because I am viewing it from my position as a university professor. So, I thought that the most honest thing to do was to call it "false chronicles." The book sets out to question what is history. History is a story told by people as they see it. There are data that are fixed. We know, for example, that Susan Morse (Samuel Morse's daughter) lived in Puerto Rico for forty years. We know that she married Edward Lind. But the way in which people tell the life of Susan Morse and Edward Lind changes constantly. I changed it, as well.

SPRINGFIELD: This sounds like detective work. You read a lot of detective stories, don't you?

VEGA: It's my "drug." I constantly read detective and horror stories. I'm very morbid. Ha! But I also think that it has a lot to do with my fascination for investigative work which means gathering data in order to arrive at a conclusion.

HERNÁNDEZ: I am interested in your narrators. In the opening tale, the primary narrator is a foreigner, Miss Florence. You move on to an upper-middle class narrator from Ponce, and finally, to one of the "common" people. I'd like to know what you had in mind.

VEGA: To begin with, I related the Lind-Morse family tale from a foreigner's viewpoint to illustrate the situation faced by an emerging Creole class in the nineteenth century, a time when an awareness of a distinctly Puerto Rican culture was just beginning to appear. In the southern region of the island, 3/4 of the landowners—the people with money—were foreigners. They weren't even Spanish. There were very few Spaniards controlling the economy in this region. It was very international. There were British, Dutch, Danes—people from all over Europe as well as those who came via the Caribbean Islands. There was a lot of circular movement within the Caribbean. There were North Americans, too. This world fascinated me, especially the town of Arroyo, an international emporium of great wealth based on the exploitation of sugar. I said to myself, "this world where everything is foreign, where everyone is foreign, must have created special difficulties for the emergence of the Creole, of Puerto Rican consciousness." It appeared to me that in the character of Susan Morse's son, Charles, who commits suicide, we have a tragic figure. I knew—because I had carried out research and had received correspondence from Mr. Overman, a descendant of this same family—that Charles had a great deal of conflict with his father over the issue of slavery. He seemed to be the ideal person through whom I could express this tragic sentiment of the Creoles in an environment dominated by foreigners. I thought to myself, "what better way to tell the tale than through the eyes of a foreign woman? This also allows me distance." If I had told it from Charles' point of view—first, it was impossible because he committed suicide, and secondly Charles was part of the same problem: he was controlled by these terrible contradictions. He couldn't reflect on them as one could who was more distanced from the situation. I also wanted to tell the tale from a woman's point of view because another theme that I wanted to treat in this tale was the theme of slavery, not only the enslavement of blacks but also of women in the patriarchal world of haciendas.

HERNÁNDEZ: The enslavement of all women stands out: slaves, servants, wives—it was really appalling.

VEGA: It was terrible for all women. Black women were raped and impregnated by patriarchs. "Traditional" women suffered constant betrayal in terms of men's promiscuity with enslaved Africans. They were all prisoners—like Susan who came from New York where there was intellectual life that she could no longer have while confined to the hacienda.

HERNÁNDEZ: I see this in Miss Florence.

VEGA: Yes. I wanted to show how an independent woman who had her own career as a tutor, who came from England where feminism was developing at the time (although it was the Victorian Era) could, within the institutions of slavery, fall into a state of psychological bondage. What we see, then, is this process within Miss Florence to liberate herself.

SPRINGFIELD: Can we say that you address internalized sexism in your feminist perspective?

VEGA: Yes, all forms of oppression. It may have different names: racism, sexism, classism. It all comes from being oppressed by a dominant class.

HERNÁNDEZ: We see this in the case of Charles who falls in love with a mulatta.

VEGA: Yes. Everyone told me about the tragic tale of his love for a Creole mulatta. In a way, it relates to Charles' search for Puerto Rican roots. He experimented with this when he went to Paris, to Oller's studio. I invented this part of the tale. Charles had been in Paris studying art. I visited the house where he lived in the artist's section. I checked the *Diccionario Puertorriqueño* and I found that Oller, during this same era, was in Paris, where he had his studio. I thought, "well, why couldn't Charles have visited Oller's studio?" And there he could have experimented with this evasive "Puertoricanness" that he couldn't get a handle on but that he felt.

HERNÁNDEZ: And Dr. Fouchard?

VEGA: I included Dr. Fouchard because I found out that the French, in this world of Arroyo, were very involved with abolitionist causes. You know that in the nineteenth century, the French were liberal thinkers. Betances, a Puerto Rican patriot, for instance, frequented Paris. There were numerous French abolitionists; and I wanted to place them in history. I also wanted to break with the view that all foreigners were at one with the dominant slaveholders. There was also a foreign sector of liberals that worked against these interests. It seemed *chevere* [cool] to establish a romantic intrigue between him and Miss Florence; but in my symbolic treatment, Miss Florence is torn between her own feelings, loyalties to an oppressive system in which she lives and from which she receives her wages and her romantic outlook toward the patriarchal figure. On the other hand, there is the attraction of liberal ideas that are represented in Dr. Fouchard. She is caught in the middle, divided by both. And at the end, we are left with the possibility that they might find one another. This is not developed because I did not want to have a closed ending; I wanted an ambiguous ending where you wonder what'll happen to Miss Florence, where you try to imagine an ending yourself. I wanted at the same time to parody and to break from the nineteenth century narrative model in women's writing which one finds in writers like the Brontes. I wanted to alter that narrative by leaving it open. Those narratives always left everything resolved, everything was nicely tied up at the end. You knew exactly what would happen.

SPRINGFIELD: And there's always a marriage at the end.

VEGA: Not here. Here, you have all the options.

SPRINGFIELD: What are you working on now?

VEGA: I am beginning a project tentatively titled "Chiripas." The "chiripa," you know, refers to the work people do to survive while unemployed. In English, it's called "odd jobs." I am investigating all the strange "chiripas" in Rio Piedras. There is a large Dominican colony in Rio Piedras, for instance, that lives off "odd jobs." There is a student colony that also depends on them. Rio Piedras offers access to public transportation, to the public market. I'm going to use the same methods that I used in *Falsas Cronicas del Sur*. I want to carry out interviews, research the experiences that people relate to me, and write about them within the context of "subterranean" employment.

SPRINGFIELD: Then, will you be interviewing Dominicans?

VEGA: I interviewed a man who came in a small boat from Santo Domingo. He told me about the trip. It was horrible. I interviewed some of the chauffeurs of *carros públicos* [public cars] who are a gold mine when it comes to telling tales about themselves and about others. I really enjoy the world of carros publicos; I've ridden in a lot in them. You hear good stories and you also get to rejuvenate your use of language. It adds to the creative process.

SPRINGFIELD: Talking of creativity, you have taught Francophone Caribbean literature for several years. Has it affected your way of writing or your oral literary trajectory?

VEGA: It has to have influenced my writing. I believe in the theory that everything that excites one's passion and forms part of one's identity has to influence what one writes. While writing, I am not conscious of this. What it has clearly influenced, however, is my thematic content.

SPRINGFIELD: This has to do with your search for roots, for interconnections.

VEGA: Yes. I use themes that treat Puerto Rico's relationship with the rest of the Antilles. In many of my stories, I deal with Haitians, with Dominicans. One story with a Dominican character was very popular in Santo Domingo. And, you know, our works are rarely known there because our books don't circulate well. They aren't sent anywhere but to the U.S.A. Nevertheless, Dominicans who have read the book here have made photocopies of it, they've lent it out, and everyone knows this short story. When I go to literary events in Santo Domingo, people ask me to read the Dominican's story. And, do you know, that people there always tell me that no one, or almost no writers, are dealing with the theme of immigration.

SPRINGFIELD: That's awful because that is the reality in which they now live.

VEGA: So, when I write about it, they are interested because it reflects part of their reality and they don't find it in their contemporary literature. There are Caribbean writers whom I feel passionate about. I like Maryse Conde a lot. I have always liked Aime Cesaire. And there are Haitian writers who fascinate me like Jacques Roumain, who wrote *Gouverneurs de la Rosie*. Also, I wrote my doctoral thesis on Haiti's King Cristophe in Antillean theatre and in Black theatre in the United States. This has allowed me to become quite familiar with the black world, which is well represented in my work, too. You see it in my last book, in the world of the hacienda, in my treatment of slavery. My generation wanted to return to our African roots that have always been hidden by the dominant class in Puerto Rico. We are the children of Jose Luis González and Isabelo Zenon who wrote two books that launched new views on our African roots. Most of the writers of the 1970s and the 1980s, in one way or another, have tried to emphasize this. Because, for us, it has been a fascinating discovery. We were brought up ignorant of all of it, ignorant of history, because in school, history ended with 1898, and you knew nothing of what happened afterwards. And what you knew of history before 1898 was that Columbus discovered Puerto Rico and that Spanish governors ruled over it. But you knew nothing about the internal history of Puerto Rico, of the resistance movements, of anything. We learned nothing of this. On the other hand, you learned absolutely nothing about our African heritage because it was "taboo." It was completely concealed. So, I thought that in order to achieve our own personal liberation, it was mandatory to begin the process here, in the search for the hidden history, a search for our roots, and to underscore these roots as well.

SPRINGFIELD: I would like to know about slaves who fled Puerto Rico for other islands. I am not sure when slavery ended on St. Thomas, which was Danish, or St. Croix, or whether Puerto Rican slaves were able to escape there before slavery was finally abolished in 1873.

VEGA: That's fascinating. What we do know is that they went to Haiti. There are lots of testimonies about those who fled to Haiti. Do you know what really fascinates me, something that I would like to write about someday? When Haiti declared its independence—it was like the Cuba of its time—it had a plan to liberate all the slaves in the Caribbean. It sent secret agents into all the islands to agitate, to raise uprisings, and to organize. In Guillermo Baralt's *Esclavos Rebeldes*, we learn of a Haitian called Chaulette, who came to Puerto Rico on this mission but who later disappeared. We hear nothing more of him. I kept thinking of Chaulette and of how I would like to write about his clandestine life in Puerto Rico among the haciendas. It would be a type of adventure story directed at juvenile readers.

HERNÁNDEZ: It would be a great project, but it would involve a lot of research. You'll need lots of sabbaticals to finish it.

VEGA: That's the problem. Did you know that for twenty years in the university, I have only had two sabbaticals: one that I had about eight years ago and the one that I am about to take now. The first one wasn't for creative writing. That wasn't allowed then. This is the first I'll have for creative writing.

SPRINGFIELD: And what do you think about homophobia in the writing community?

VEGA: I think that themes of homosexuality are very infrequently treated. You find it in the work of Manuel Ramos Otero, a militant for gay rights who was always open. But besides the work of Luz Maria Umpierre and maybe a few of the Newyorican writers, you really don't find it. The topic is very suppressed, very "taboo."

SPRINGFIELD: Do you think that this will continue?

VEGA: No, I think that it has to come out because there has been an evolution in the thinking of people about gay rights. Someday, among some writers who are now beginning to write, this will take off. I am interested in this theme. Sometime, I would like to write about it. I told a gay friend recently that the best friends I have had in my life have been gay men. I think that there is a relationship between gay men and women that is unique because you do not feel threatened by these men. You feel completely at ease and you can communicate well. You can share confidences and you can even have a kind of platonic love.

SPRINGFIELD: And lesbians?

VEGA: My lesbian friends are like any of my friends; their preferences don't enter into the picture nor do mine.

SPRINGFIELD: But there are many women here in Puerto Rico who fear lesbians.

VEGA: Yes, but that is a very medieval mentality. They think that lesbians are going to rape them or something. Absurd, ridiculous thinking! I believe that this mentality is changing. People are beginning to realize that that way of thinking, this fear, is ridiculous. The problem that I see today relates to AIDS. At a time when people are becoming more liberated from these dreadful fears, it has brought distrust once again. Don't you agree? Even though in Puerto Rico, AIDS has more to do with drug addiction. There have been studies. It has been statistically proven. The problem of drugs is severe. Well, I have always wanted to put a gay man into my stories in such a way that would be very positive; he would be a perfect friend. There are lots of interesting things about gay men. They are very "artsy." They are congenial. I think that ultimately, the younger generation of Puerto Rican writers will treat this theme. It's inevitable. It's inevitable. And it's good.

SPRINGFIELD: Thank you very much.

Source: Consuelo López Springfield, and Elizabeth Hernández, "Women and Writing in Puerto Rico: An Interview with Ana Lydia Vega. *Callaloo* 17:3 (1994), pp. 816–825. © Charles H. Rowell. Reprinted with permission of The Johns Hopkins University Press.

388. Excerpts from John R. Logan, "The New Latinos: Who They Are, Where They Are," 2001

The Lewis Mumford Center was established at the University of Albany in 1988 to conduct urban research both comparative and historical in scope. John R. Logan, a professor at Brown University, who has conducted extensive studies of the 2000 Census through the Center. The excerpts below focus on new Latino immigrants—those arriving en masse in the United States since 1980. This is one of the first studies to separate out the groups via the 2000 U.S. Census. As pointed out in the report, there are differences in the groups that delineate obstacles to their receiving equal protection.

As the Hispanic population in America has grown in the last decade (from 22.4 million to 35.3 million), there has also been a shift in its composition. The fastest growth is not in the traditionally largest Hispanic groups, the ones who arrived earliest in the largest numbers (Mexicans, Puerto Ricans, or Cubans), but among New Latinos—people from the Dominican Republic and a diverse set of countries in Central American (such as El Salvador) and South America (such as Colombia). Based on Census 2000 and related sources, the Mumford Center estimates that the number of New Latinos has more than doubled since 1990, from 3.0 million to 6.1 million.

Cubans are still the third largest single Hispanic group in the United States, at 1.3 million. But there are now nearly as many Dominicans (1.1 million) and Salvadorans (also 1.1 million). There are more New Latinos than Puerto Ricans and Cubans combined, and these new groups are growing much more rapidly.

The New Latinos bring a new level of complexity to the rapidly changing complexion of ethnic America. This report reviews what we now know about this important minority: who they are (in comparison to the better known Hispanic groups) and where they live. For those who wish further information about specific metropolitan regions, population counts are now available through the web page of the Lewis Mumford Center.

WHO ARE THE NEW LATINOS?

An outstanding characteristic of the New Latinos is their diversity. Not only do they come from many different countries. More important is that they have a wide range of social and economic backgrounds, some better prepared for the U.S. labor market than any of the older Hispanic groups, and others much less successful. Our best information about their backgrounds is from the Current Population Survey; in order to maximize the size of the sample on which they are based, our figures here are pooled estimates from the CPS conducted in March 1998 and 2000.

Nativity and year of entry. Puerto Ricans are considered by definition to be born in the United States. The majority of Cubans are foreign-born (68%), though relatively few of those entered the country in the last ten years (27%). They mainly represent a pre-1990 immigration stream. In contrast, only about a third of Mexican Americans (36%) were born abroad, but nearly half of their foreign-born members are recent immigrants (49% in the previous ten years).

The New Latino groups are like Cubans in having a majority of foreign-born, ranging from 63% of Dominicans to over 70% for Central and South Americans. But they are like Mexicans in that they represent the most recent wave of immigration—generally 45–50% of their foreign-born arrived in the last ten years.

Education. Mexicans are the least educated of the older Hispanic groups, with an average education of only 10.2 years (for those aged 25 and above). Puerto Ricans average 11.4 years, and Cubans 11.9 years. The New Latino groups range both below the Mexicans and above the Cubans. Salvadorans and Guatemalans have the least education (below 10 years). But Hispanics from most South American origins are better educated than Cubans, averaging 12.6 years.

Income. Compared to Puerto Ricans and Mexicans, Cubans in the United States have always been regarded as economically quite successful. The mean earnings of employed Cubans are above $13,500, compared to about $10,000 for Puerto Ricans and $8500 for Mexicans. Only 18% of Cubans fall below the poverty line, compared to 26% of Mexicans and 30% of Puerto Ricans.

Among the New Latinos, Dominicans stand out for their very low income: mean earnings below $8000 and more than a third in poverty (36%). The major Central American groups are roughly equivalent to Puerto Ricans in average earnings, though they are less likely to fall below the poverty line. On the other hand, Hispanics from South America do considerably better, and on average they earn more and have lower poverty rates than do Cubans.

Unemployment and public assistance. Levels of unemployment among Hispanic groups are generally consistent with what we found to be their average earnings. New Latinos from the Dominican Republic have higher than average unemployment and they are the group most likely to be receiving public assistance (above 8%—in both respects they are less successful than Puerto Ricans). Those from South America have the lowest levels of unemployment and are even less likely than Cubans to receive public assistance....

Counting the New Latinos

The New Latinos are hard to count in Census 2000. Up to now a single "Hispanic question" on the census has served reasonably well to distinguish Hispanics from different national origins. In the last two decennial censuses people who identify as Hispanic were asked to check one of three boxes (Mexican, Puerto Rican, or Cuban), or to write in another Hispanic category. In Census 2000, unlike in Census 1990, no examples of other categories were provided to orient respondents. Probably for this reason an unprecedented number of Hispanics in 2000 gave no information or only a vague identification of themselves (such as "Hispanic" or "Spanish"). These people, 6.2 million or 17.6% of all Hispanics, have been counted in census reports as "Other Hispanics." This is nearly double the share of Other Hispanics in the 1990 census, and a very large portion of them is New Latinos.

The result is a severe underestimate of the number of New Latinos. National studies that rely solely on the Hispanic origin question of the decennial census find only modest growth for such major sources of Hispanic immigration as El Salvador (+16%) and Colombia (+24%). States and metropolitan areas where New Latinos are particularly concentrated are dramatically affected by this problem. In the State of California, for example, the census estimated the number of Salvadorans in 1990 as 339,000; ten years later the estimate is only 273,000. In Miami the census counted 74,000 Nicaraguans a decade ago, but only 69,000 in 2000. It is implausible that these New Latino groups actually fell in this period of intensified immigration. We conclude that their number has been understated as a result of the large Other Hispanic count in Census 2000.

Another reason to be wary of the Census 2000 estimates is that they diverge so widely from the results of other studies conducted by the Bureau of the Census.... The estimates of the number of Central and South Americans are very different in these three sources: 3 million in Census 2000 (which classed 17.6% as Other Hispanic), a million more in the Census 2000 Supplemental Survey conducted at the same time (based on a sample of nearly 700,000 and which classed only 9.6% as Other Hispanic), and almost another million in the March 2000 Current Population Survey (with a sample of about 120,000 and only 6.1% Other Hispanic).

In this report we present improved estimates of the size of New Latino groups, compared to relying solely on the Hispanic origin question in Census 2000. Our procedure uses the Current Population Survey, which has the advantage of being conducted in person or by telephone, as the basis for determining what is the percentage of Hispanics who "really" should be classified as Other Hispanic. We then apply this target to Census 2000 data at the level of census tracts. Where the census has an excessive number of Other Hispanics, we allocate them across specific national origin groups according to a pre-established formula. Details of the procedure for 1990 and 2000 are documented in the Appendix to this report.

New Latinos in the United States, 1990 and 2000

[Table 4] provides a detailed breakdown of the Hispanic population at the national level (not including Puerto Rico) in 1990 and 2000. There are very large disparities between these and the Census counts from the Hispanic origin question, especially in 2000.

In absolute numbers, the Mexicans are the group most affected by our reallocation of Other Hispanics, increasing by 2.4 million from the Census count. In proportion to their number, however, it is the New Latinos for whom the figures are most changed. Taken together the Mumford estimates show that New Latinos more than doubled their number, compared to an increase of about a third reported by the Census Bureau. We calculate more than 350,000 additional Dominicans and Salvadorans, 270,000 additional Colombians, and 250,000 additional Guatemalans.

- By all estimates, Mexicans are by far the largest Hispanic group, about two-thirds of the total and still growing rapidly. The Mumford count is now over 23 million, an increase of 70% in the last decade.
- Puerto Ricans and Cubans remain the next largest Hispanic groups, but their expansion is now much slower, up 35% and 23% respectively since 1990.
- The largest New Latino groups are Dominicans and Salvadorans, both of whom doubled in the last decade and have now reached over 1.1 million.
- There are now over a half million Colombians (nearly 750,000) and Guatemalans (over 600,000) in this country. And three other groups are quickly approaching the half million mark: Ecuadorians, Peruvians, and Hondurans.

States with the Largest New Latino Populations

There are growing numbers of New Latinos in most states, but about three-quarters of them are found in just five states: New York, California, Florida, New Jersey, and Texas.... The Mumford Center webpage provides more detailed breakdowns for all 50 states, including both 1990 and 2000 and both Mumford estimates and counts from the Census Bureau.

- New York State has the most New Latinos (close to 1.4 million, up from 800,000 in 1990). About half (650,000) are Dominicans, who have had a noticeable presence in New York City since the 1950s. Close to half a million are various South American countries, a much newer immigrant stream. Puerto Ricans were once the predominant source of Hispanic immigration. Now they account for barely more than a third of the state's Hispanics, and they are outnumbered by New Latinos.
- California has almost as many New Latinos as New York (also close to 1.4 million), though they are greatly outnumbered by Mexicans. The largest share—over a million—are from Central America, including especially El Salvador, Guatemala, and Nicaragua.
- Florida's Hispanic population is well distributed among many national-origin groups. The Cubans are by far the best known of these at a national level (and they are still the largest, with nearly 900,000 residents statewide). Yet their growth has been slower than other groups, and nearly an equal number now are New Latinos (850,000), weighted toward South American origins. There are also over half a million Puerto Ricans and close to 400,000 Mexicans.
- Because of its proximity to New York, New Jersey's Hispanic population might be expected to mirror that of its neighbor. It is similar, in that Puerto Ricans still are about a third of them (385,000). And Puerto Ricans are now outnumbered for the first time by New Latinos (over 500,000). The difference is that a much smaller share in New Jersey is Dominican; about half of the state's New Latinos are from South America.
- Finally, Texas now has 400,000 New Latinos, more than doubling since 1990. As is true of California, the largest share is from Central America, especially El Salvador. They are barely noticeable statewide, next to 6 million of Mexican origin. But as will be shown

Table 4. Estimates of the Hispanic Population in the United States, 1990 and 2000

	Mumford Estimates			Census Hispanic Question		
	1990	2000	Growth	1990	2000	Growth
Hispanic total	21,900,089	35,305,818	61%	21,900,089	35,305,818	61%
Mexican	13,576,346	23,060,224	70%	13,393,208	20,640,711	54%
Puerto Rican	2,705,979	3,640,460	35%	2,651,815	3,406,178	28%
Cuban	1,067,416	1,315,346	23%	1,053,197	1,241,685	18%
New Latino						
groups	3,019,780	6,153,989	104%	2,879,583	3,805,444	32%
Dominican	537,120	1,121,257	109%	520,151	764,945	47%
Central						
American	1,387,331	2,863,063	106%	1,323,830	1,686,937	27%
Costa Rican				115,672		68,588
Guatemalan	279,360	627,329	125%	268,779	372,487	39%
Honduran	142,481	362,171	154%	131,066	217,569	66%
Nicaraguan	212,481	294,334	39%	202,658	177,684	-12%
Panamanian	100,841	164,371	63%	92,013	91,723	0%
Salvadoran	583,397	1,117,959	92%	565,081	655,165	16%

Table 4. (continued)

	Mumford Estimates			Census Hispanic Question		
	1990	2000	Growth	1990	2000	Growth
Other Central American	68,772	181,228		64,233	103,721	
South American	1,095,329	2,169,669	98%	1,035,602	1,353,562	31%
Argentinian			168,991			100,864
Bolivian			70,545			42,068
Chilean			117,698			68,849
Colombian	399,788	742,406	86%	378,726	470,684	24%
Ecuadorian	199,477	396,400	99%	191,198	260,559	36%
Paraguayan			14,492			8,769
Peruvian	184,712	381,850	107%	175,035	233,926	34%
Uruguayan			30,010			18,804
Venezuelan			149,309			91,507
Other South American		311,353	97,969		290,643	57,532
Other Hispanic	1,530,568	1,135,799	−26%	1,922,286	6,211,800	223%

below they are most heavily concentrated in Houston, where they are about a sixth of the Hispanic population....

The New Latino population lives almost entirely within metropolitan regions....

Some parts of the country deserve special attention:

- The entire region surrounding New York City—including the New York, Nassau-Suffolk, Newark, Jersey City, Bergen-Passaic, and Middlesex-Somerset-Hunterdon metro areas—is the most important focal point for New Latino immigration. The New York PMSA alone has over 1.1 million, and the surrounding and largely suburban metro areas add another half million. Dominicans are about half of these in the New York PMSA. Central Americans (especially Salvadorans) are more than half of the New Latinos in suburban Long Island. In Northern New Jersey, many specific groups are present, but a plurality is South American.
- Los Angeles-Long Beach is the center for New Latino immigration in Southern California, where it has a mostly Central American flavor (300,000 Salvadorans, nearly 200,000 Guatemalans). In nearby metro areas (Riverside-San Bernardino and Orange County) New Latinos are also plentiful, but they tend to be dwarfed by the huge and growing Mexican population.
- In Miami and neighboring Fort Lauderdale there are about 600,000 New Latinos. They are about evenly split between Central and South Americans in Miami, and more tilted toward South Americans in Fort Lauderdale.
- Washington, DC is the next great center for New Latino growth (over 300,000). About two-thirds are Central American (130,000 Salvadorans) and one-third South American.
- Finally, Houston has 200,000 New Latinos, of whom the largest share is Salvadoran (90,000).

NEW LATINOS: PRESENT AND FUTURE

The scale of immigration from less traditional Hispanic sources brings new and less known groups into the United States. Within ten years, we need to become as aware of Dominicans, Salvadorans, and Colombians—people with very different backgrounds and trajectories—as we are of Puerto Ricans and Cubans.

Because they are so highly concentrated in a few regions, and often in a fairly narrow set of neighborhoods within those regions, each group has special local significance in those places. There are two ways in which accurate knowledge about New Latino groups is most critical.

One is in the realm of political representation. Public officials and leaders of political parties need to be aware of changes in their constituencies. Although political redistricting is not required to take into account the internal composition of the Hispanic population, surely some choices about where to draw lines, whom to support for public office, and what issues to highlight in public policy initiatives will depend on whether the constituency remains more Mexican, Puerto Rican, or Cuban, and to what extent it is becoming Dominican, Salvadoran, or Colombian.

The other is in the provision and targeting of public services. Particularly since so many services are now provided through non-profit organization, often seeking to serve specific ethnic populations, it is important for public officials to know who are the clients in a given locale. Again, whether the client base remains more Mexican, Puerto Rican, or Cuban, and to what extent it is shifting toward one or more of the New Latino groups, should reasonably be expected to affect judgments about how to serve the Hispanic community.

The serious inadequacies of the Hispanic origin question in Census 2000 require that alternative estimates be made available. Undercounted can too easily translate into underserved. The Mumford Center offers one approach. Our procedure makes maximum use of publicly available data, it can be replicated, and it offers usable figures at the level of individual census tracts. We encourage others to assess the plausibility of these estimates and to seek better methods of estimation. In particular, we encourage the Bureau of the Census to use the whole range of data that it has on hand for this purpose. Information from the Supplemental Survey or the long form of Census 2000 on country of birth and ancestry, taken together with the Hispanic origin question, would allow the Bureau to create a new composite variable for a large sample of the population. This new composite variable would provide an excellent estimate of Dominican, Central American, and South American populations for the nation and for many states and large metropolitan regions—clearly better than our adjustment procedure.

Such data would also make possible a substantial refinement of our tract-level estimates. We urge the Bureau to begin consideration of these and other ways in which the resources of the decennial census could be more fully applied to understanding the composition of America's Hispanic population.

Source: Excerpt from John R. Logan, 2001. "The New Latinos: Who They Are, Where They Are." Lewis Mumford Center. http://www.s4.brown.edu/cen2000/HispanicpPop/HspReport/HspReport Page1.html.

389. Excerpts from Roberto Suro and Jeffrey S. Passel, "The Rise of the Second Generation," 2003

The Pew Hispanic Center, a public interest "fact" tank, conducts frequent surveys of the Latino population in the United States. It receives funding from The Pew Charitable Trusts, although it categorizes Latinos as Hispanics, its work has been invaluable in placing a face on the individual Latino peoples. It has conducted a wide range of studies which topics are kept up to date. The following excerpts deal with the changing patterns in the second generation Latino. This is important information in tracking attitudes and ties to the old countries. For example, the children of two second generation Latino parents will have slightly different outlooks than one born of a foreign born and a native born parent. The probability of the child speaking Spanish will be higher in the latter case than the former.

Since the 1970s, immigration has represented by far the fastest and the largest source of Hispanic population growth, and, as a result, the first generation—the foreign born—has become more numerous than the second or the third-plus generations—those born in the United States of U.S.-born parents. This demographic equation is now rapidly changing. Consequently, the effects of Hispanic population growth on the nation are shifting in important ways. Most simply, the largest impact over the past 30 years has been measured in the number of Spanish-speaking immigrants joining the labor force. However, in the current decade and for the foreseeable future there will be very sizeable impacts from the number of native-born Latinos entering the nation's schools and in the flow of English-speaking, U.S.-educated Hispanics entering the labor market. Between 2000 and 2020, the number of second-generation Latinos in U.S. schools will double and the number in the U.S. labor force will triple. Nearly one-fourth of labor force growth over the next 20 years will be from children of Latino immigrants....

Between 1970 and 2000 the Hispanic population grew by 25.7 million and immigrants accounted for 45 percent of that increase while the second generation accounted for 28 percent.... As a result, in 2000 the first generation totaled 14.2 million people, or 40 percent of the Latino population, while the second generation counted 9.9 million, or 28 percent. The third plus generation numbered 11.3 million and made up 32 percent of the Hispanic population....

The growth of the second generation accelerated in the 1990s and reached 63% for the decade, up from 52 percent in the 1980s, surpassing the growth due to immigration (55 percent in the 1990s and 78 percent in the 1980s) even as the nation experienced a record influx from Latin America. This pattern was the legacy of the high levels of immigration in the 1970s and 1980s. Young adults have dominated most migrant streams in modern times, and that is certainly true of Latino immigrants who are concentrated in the child-bearing years. The median age of first generation Hispanics in 2000 was 33.4 years old compared to 38.5 in the non-Hispanic white population overall. Fertility rates are higher among Latino immigrants than in any other segment of the U.S. population. In 2000 the fertility rate was 3.51 births per woman for first generation Hispanics compared to 1.84 for non-Hispanic whites overall. It was higher even than the fertility rates among black (2.53) and Asian (2.60) immigrants....

Using a mid-range estimate of immigration flows, the Hispanic population will grow by 25 million people between 2000 and 2020. During that time the second generation accounts for 47 percent of the increase compared to 25 percent for the first.... Moreover, the second generation more than doubles in size, increasing from 9.8 million in 2000 to 21.7 million in 2020. At that point the second generation outnumbers the first generation which totals 20.6 million....

The rise of the second generation will have immediate consequences for the nation's schools. The number of second-generation Latinos aged 5 to 19 years old is projected to more than double from 2000 to 2020, growing from 4.4 million to 9.0 million people.... About one-in-seven of the new students enrolling in U.S. schools over these 20 years will be a second-generation Latino.

Source: © 2003 Pew Hispanic Center, a Pew Research Center project, www.pewhispanic.org, October, 2003, pp. 2, 3, 5, 7.

390. Excerpts from John R. Logan, "Choosing Segregation: Racial Imbalance in American Public Schools, 1990–2000," 2002

The Lewis Mumford Center, housed at the University of Albany, State University of New York, has studied urban trends since the late 1980s. In the following excerpts from his study, sociologist John R. Logan statistically analyzes the extent of segregation in the public schools, and the possible implication for Latinos. Despite the fact that 1954s *Brown v. the Board of Education* was to put an end to de jure segregation, it has increased dramatically among Latinos.

After a period in which desegregation efforts were widespread in American public schools, the average level of segregation has hardly changed in the last ten years, and in some places there is clearly a rollback of progress made before 1990. In many metropolitan regions, desegregation evident in the 1989–90 school year has given way to substantial increases of black–white segregation. In most of these, Supreme Court action in 1991 that relaxed the criteria for rescinding desegregation orders has freed

Table 5. Isolation Experienced by Hispanic Students in Top 50 Metro Areas

1999 Rank	1989 Rank	Area Name	1999 Segregation	1989 Segregation
1	1	Laredo, TX	97.6	95.4
2	2	McAllen-Edinburg-Mission, TX	96.6	95.0
3	3	Brownsville-Harlingen-SanBenito, TX	95.3	93.9
4	4	El Paso, TX	88.7	83.6
5	5	Las Cruces, NM	81.6	75.2
6	8	Salinas, CA	80.2	69.9
7	7	Corpus Christi, TX	75.6	74.1
8	9	Los Angeles-Long Beach, CA	75.5	68.9
9	6	San Antonio, TX	73.9	74.3
10	10	Miami, FL	73.2	67.5
11	12	Orange County, CA	71.1	60.5
12	11	Jersey City, NJ	69.0	63.2
13	13	Visalia-Tulane-Porterville, CA	68.9	58.7
14	18	Ventura, CA	67.6	56.5.
15	14	Fresno, CA	66.4	58.5
16	16	Bakersfield, CA	65.8	57.3
17	15	Albuquerque, NM	62.1	57.4
18	17	Chicago, IL	61.3	60.1
19	20	Houston, TX	60.4	52.6
20	19	Tucson, AZ	59.6	54.2
21	30	Riverside-San Bernardino, CA	58.5	43.2
22	27	Merced, CA	57.8	44.6
23	24	Phoenix-Mesa, AZ	57.1	46.2
24	22	New York, NY	56.6	49.6
25	28	San Diego, CA	56.0	44.3
26	31	Dallas, TX	55.1	42.4
27	25	San Jose, CA	54.8	45.8
28	29	Austin-San Marcos, TX	51.9	43.9
29	34	Denver, CO	50.5	39.7
30	35	Modesto, CA	50.1	37.1
31	21	Hartford, CT	50.0	51.7
32	23	Bergen-Passaic, NJ	48.8	48.2
33	32	Fort Worth-Arlington, TX	48.4	41.8
34	36	San Francisco, CA	46.2	36.1
35	26	Newark, NJ	45.3	44.6
36	37	Stockton-Lodi, CA	44.1	32.4
37	45	Las Vegas, NV-AZ	42.2	17.1
38	39	Oakland, CA	38.1	25.8
39	33	Philadelphia, PA-NJ	37.5	39.9
40	38	Boston, MA-NH	35.7	28.3
41	46	Orlando, FL	31.7	15.0
42	42	West Palm Beach-Boca Raton, FL	30.0	18.5

Table 5. (*continued*)

1999 Rank	1989 Rank	Area Name	1999 Segregation	1989 Segregation
43	49	Salt Lake City-Ogden, UT	29.0	12.4
44	40	Tampa-St. Petersburg-Clearwater, FL	28.9	20.3
45	44	Washington, DC-MD-VA-WV	27.5	18.4
46	41	Nassau-Suffolk, NY	26.6	18.6
47	43	Sacramento, CA	25.6	18.4
48	47	Portland-Vancouver, OR-WA	24.7	14.4
49	48	Fort Lauderdale, FL	24.1	12.9
50	50	Atlanta, GA	19.9	9.3

school officials to pull back their previous steps to achieve racial balance. Consciously or not, Americans in these regions are increasingly making a choice for segregation.

New national data for 1999–2000 show that segregation from whites has edged upwards not only for black children, but also for Hispanic and Asian children. At the same time, they reveal that segregation places black and Hispanic children, on average, in schools where two-thirds of students are at or near the poverty line....

The average white child attends a school that is over 78% white. Only 9% of other children in this typical school are black, 8% Hispanic, and 3% Asian. Though children often do not attend a neighborhood school, the racial composition of schools attended by white kids closely matches that of their own neighborhood. In sharp contrast, the average black child's school is more than half black (57%). Hispanic children also are in majority Hispanic schools (57%). And Asians, despite being only 4% of the elementary population, are in schools that average 19% Asian.

Each minority group's exposure to white children is declining. In 1989–90, 32% of the average black child's schoolmates were white; that has dropped to 28% in 1999–2000. Similar drops were experienced by Hispanics (from 30% to 25%) and Asians (52% to 46%)....

Hispanic children are less segregated than black children (D = 58 in 1999–2000, compared to 65 for blacks). [The standard of segregation is the Index of Dissimilarity (D) which captures the degree to which the two groups are evenly spread among schools in a given city.] However the trend is in the same upward direction, and varies in a similar way across metropolitan regions.... Hispanic segregation dropped by a point (from 52 to 51) in regions where Hispanics are less than 5% of the elementary population. But it increased by 3 points (from 57 to 60) in regions where they are more than 20% of the total. These 20% plus regions are where more than 3 out of 4 Hispanic children live....

Another important factor for Hispanics is their rapid population growth, more than a 50% increase in the last decade, almost equaling the number of black elementary children in metropolitan public schools (about 3.6 million for each group). As their numbers grow, they become more highly concentrated: the average Hispanic attended a school that was 53% Hispanic in 1989–90, increasing to 57% Hispanic in 1999–2000. Unlike African Americans, there has been little court action regarding Hispanic school segregation. As a result, it is uncommon to find a metropolitan region in 1989–90 where school segregation was lower than neighborhood segregation....

Overall trends in Hispanic-white segregation are provided in the following tables. These are the indices for the metropolitan region as a whole, and they include data for the 50 metropolitan regions with the largest number of Hispanic elementary school children in 1999–2000....

[Table 5] provides the values of the Hispanic isolation index. The highest values are extreme: the average Hispanic child in the Texas metropolitan regions of Laredo, AcAllen, and Brownsville is in a school that is more than 95% Hispanic. But in a majority of these metropolitan regions isolation is above 50%, and even where it is relatively low, it is increasing as the Hispanic population grows....

Source: Excerpts from John R. Logan, "Choosing Segregation: Racial Imbalance in American Public Schools, 1990–2000." Lewis Mumford Center for Comparative Urban and Regional Research, University at Albany. Revised March 29, 2002, pp. 3, 4, 11, 14. http://www.s4.brown.edu/cen2000/SchoolPop/SPReport/page1.html.

391. Excerpts from John Ross, "Mexicanizing the Mara," 2004

John Ross, a premier columnist for the *Texas Observer*, a progressive Texas magazine, describes the migration of Central Americans through Mexico, and the problem that they have with gangs who try to shake them down. The political instability in the sending countries (i.e., country that the immigrant came from), has worsened since the United States exportation of gangs as well as the growth of the drug trade. Since the twenty-first century, drug cartels have used Central America, Mexico, and the Western Caribbean as the main corridor for transporting 92 percent of the South American cocaine destined for the United States; drug trade routes are shifting through the nations in these areas. This has coincided with a U.S. policy of deporting Central American gang members who, for the most part, migrated to the United States as war refugees during the 1980s and 1990s civil wars. They were raised in the United States since infancy and were recruited into gangs while in the United States. Many deported youth continued gang affiliation in Central America and became involved in drug traffic. Central Americans did not have the resources to stop either the violence or the traffic. Mara Salvatrucha was the name of one of the largest of the Los Angeles Salvadoran street gangs involved in this activity.

Angel and William had set out the week before from the slums of San Pedro Sula, Honduras, and gotten as far as the Guatemalan-Mexican border on thumb and hoof. "One night, we had to walk until it was light out. We were too scared to stop," confesses William, who claims to be 18 but looks four years younger. Now the boys were determined to reach Houston, where Angel's cousin has promised them jobs. From Tecun Uman, Guatemala, the U.S.A. is a kind of dreamland basking in the golden sunlight with a fortune to be made at the end of the red, white, and blue rainbow or at least that's the way it's depicted in the mural painted inside the Casa de Los Migrantes. The Catholic-run Casa, a run-down hacienda fronting a rutted jungle path that leads to a bend in the slow-moving Suchiate River, is an obligatory pit stop for tired travelers heading north. It's also an invaluable trading post for news of the dangers that lie ahead and the two boys' eyes grew wide as they considered the advice of a grizzled border vagabond: "Watch out for your partners; don't even trust your *cuate* (pal)," he warned ominously. "The coyotes will take your money and then sell you to the Migra. They'll take you to where the train leaves, but watch out! The Mara Salvatrucha owns that train and if they catch you up there without paying, they'll throw you right off."

Then he explained how every week migrants are found dead and dying along the track, separated from their limbs, having lost their grip on a hand-rail or else been tossed bodily from the east-bound freight, the "Mayeb," by the dread Salvatruchas for not anteing up the *cuotas* fast enough. Angel and William seemed to shudder in the tropical heat at the mere mention of the much-feared Salvador-based gang that rules in this no-man's land between Mexico and Guatemala. Yet, despite the lurid warnings, they were among 50 or so very young men and women who lined up at the Casa's big doors by 6 P.M., itching to get on the road north. First, they would wade or swim the Suchiate (more affluent travelers coast across on inflated inner tubes). Then they'd make a beeline for the railroad tracks to catch the evening freight running east out of Ciudad Hidalgo and Tapachula through Chiapas, Tabasco, and Veracruz up to the south Texas border, a route their fathers and mothers and big brothers had followed during the wars in Central America and after the calamitous 1999 Hurricane Mitch, from which the region has not yet recovered.

But in between here and there, as the Casa mural so graphically illustrates, there would be many obstacles "both the Mexican and Gringo Migras, border walls and fences, death in the desert" not to mention the Salvatruchas.

At dusk, the *indocumentados* are strung out all along the train track near threadbare settlements, darting figures camped in the hobo jungles along the right-of-way, ready to leap aboard when "El Gusano de Hierro" ("The Steel Worm") lumbers slowly past. Suddenly, a panicked cry goes up. It's hard to tell whether people are yelling "Migra" or "Mara!" Dull thuds can be heard in the thick underbrush from which tall men with clubs emerge, but their identities are indistinguishable in the moonless dark and my taxi driver wants to leave at once. Maybe they are the Maras beating up on the migrants for chump change, he conjectures. More likely they are agents of Mexico's immigration police.

Mexican immigration authorities deport 100,000-plus undocumented migrants back across the Suchiate to Tecun Uman each year (in 2003, the totals were 146,000), all of whom are deposited across the bridge in Guatemala regardless of where they actually came from. Last year, half of the complaints Mexico's National Human Rights Commission [Comisión Nacional de Derechos Humanos] (CNDH) received from Central American migrant workers and their advocacy groups along the southern border accused the National Immigration Institute (INM) of brutality, extortion, and other crimes against the travelers. The Mexican Migra has such a bad rap that the government has had to invent a second police agency, the Beta-Sur units, to provide some security for the workers.

José Andrés almost made it to Texas. He and his road mates had gotten all the way to Monterrey, a hundred miles from the border, but the hotel owners turned them in when they tried to beat the bill. Now he was borrowing money to call his people back in Honduras. Despite his bruises, he would start out again tonight. "If the police catch me again, I'll only get a beating," he said. "But the Maras could kill me."

Yet he appeared undaunted; he had his *chimba* (lead pipe, the Salvatrucha weapon of choice) hidden out in the jungle beyond the Casa walls and was prepared to use it. "They will think I am one of them," he laughed, flashing a small tattoo on his inner lip as he walked off.

Salvatrucha psychosis is thriving along Mexico's southern border. Tabloid headlines tout the gang's notoriety in big black letters. The Tapachula hotel where I stayed had 24 hour-a-day video cameras in the hallways to keep the Maras out of my room. The Chiapas state police has formed an inter-agency taskforce codenamed "Operation Steel" to keep the gangbangers in check. Last year nearly 700 suspected Maras were caught.

Immigration authorities tend to be alarmist about the Salvatrucha invasion, estimating that 25 to 50 members cross into Mexico each day. The INM has detected Salvatrucha presence in eight states and the Federal District. The agency estimates a total of 5,000 members are in México, 3,000 of them grouped in 200 bands hunkered down in squatter colonies around Tapachula, a sort of tropical Tijuana where anything "stolen cars, kilos of cocaine, pounds of human flesh" seems to be for sale. But xenophobia is a condition of life in this border region and any undocumented kid picked up on the hard road north is apt to be counted into the mix.

The Mara Salvatrucha was born on the mean streets of California in the late 1970s and '80s as refugees from the blood letting in Salvador streamed into the state, seeking sanctuary. Forced to defend themselves from long-established Mexican youth gangs, the older kids organized new arrivals into a respected fighting force that was as much into heavy metal music and stoner drugs as rumbling with the Mexicans. The etymology of the name is open to question. Presumably, the "Salva-" prefix refers to the members' country of origin but it could also mean "save yourself" in Spanish. "Trucha" is a trout, the slippery fish whose agility in navigating troubled waters is a characteristic of these hardened youths' lives. "Mara" is Salvadoran slang for a group of friends but may borrow attitude from the "Mara Bunta," a particularly virulent Central American ant army. In the Salvatrucha lexicon, the "mara" is a tattoo, mandatory ID for members.

By the '90s, with the war in El Salvador winding down, the Salvatruchas began to drift home. Some, doing time in California prisons, were deported directly back to a country they barely remembered. Others were sent back by their families to keep them out of trouble. They coalesced in a post-war El Salvador where chaos reigned and everything was up for grabs. Recognizing themselves as "jomies" ("homeboys"), the Maras strong-armed their way into the street rackets, pushed dope, and were accused of dozens of kidnappings for ransom. Half the homicides in El Salvador were pinned on them. In 2002, the Salvadoran legislature passed an anti-Mara law; the crackdown soon spread to Honduras and Guatemala, where the Salvatruchas have branch offices. The Salvadoran police's Operation 'Mano Duro" (Hard Hand) collared 5,000 suspect' truchas in its first hundred days.

Then the Maras started to turn up horribly dead, decapitated and eviscerated on the city streets. The police attributed the butchery to the gang's brutal nature. But the truth may be more diffuse. Some victims were found cruelly disfigured by tortures such as being hung up by their thumbs, a practice emblematic of the work of military and police death squads during a war that took 100,000 lives before a peace agreement was signed in 1992. "Homies United," a California group that seeks to rehabilitate repentant Maras, sees the hand of the "Sombra Negra" (Black Shadow), purportedly a death squad composed of ex-soldiers.

But whoever is responsible for the killings, the clean-up campaign is scattering the Salvatruchas. According to a recent piece in the Mexican daily *La Jornada*, the

Salvatruchas are sandblasting off their tattoos and swimming north again for their own safety.

Today, the Maras are an international conglomerate with functioning organizations in three Central American countries, Mexico, and the United States, including such unlikely locations as Somerville, Massachusetts; Dodge City, Kansas; and Nashville, Tennessee (where Salvadoran labor built a new football stadium for the Titans).

The Mareros divide roughly into three tribes "the Mara Salvatruchas (MS)" or original gangsters; the M-13s or "Calle 13s" ("M" is the 13th letter of the alphabet); and the "M-18s," once part of the network of cliques that gathered in the 18th Street Gang, Los Angeles's largest, with an estimated 20,000 members. Each of the Salvatrucha clicas is governed by a council of "Macisos" ("tough guys") and lives by a lethal code that does not tolerate traitors and informers; internal strife is dealt with harshly. Initiation in the M-13s consists of a brutal 13-second beating with lead pipes. Elaborate gang hand-signals and face tattoos are Salvatrucha "trademarks" some add a tattooed teardrop for every kill and others a cross to body tattoos. Removing a tattoo is considered a grave violation of the Mara code although, as gang members travel north, they reportedly remove them to avoid police detection or else engrave them on interior body surfaces like Jose Andres [had].

Because of heavy Mexican immigration controls that try to keep the Maras bottled up in Chiapas, the Mexican-Guatemalan border has become a temporary concentration point for the Salvatruchas. Sleepy border towns during the day, Ciudad Hidalgo and Tecun Uman (a city with an unusually large number of one-legged men begging on its dusty streets) turn violent in the dark, with whorehouses and cantinas running full blast.

Maras who take up residence in the squatter colonies along the Tapachula border soon become role models for impoverished farm kids, wannabe "M-13s" and "M-18s" who decorate schoolhouse walls with gang graffiti, do house burglaries, beat on hapless migrants, and occasionally tangle with each other.

Meanwhile, the true-blue Salvatruchas are moving on to more fertile fields the moment they are able to get away from the border, a phenomenon that has made its way into Latin American literature. Rafael Ramírez Heredia's new novel, *La Mara*, is a magic realist tale featuring a drag queen who controls the traffic across the Suchiate with the assistance of brutal Salvatrucha lieutenants. Ramírez researched Mara lore in Tecun Uman, Honduras, and Salvador. The real dimensions of the Salvatrucha phenomenon are grossly underappreciated, according to Ramírez.

"There are 300,000 hungry kids coming north to this border every year," he writes. "Every one of them is a potential Mara."

Source: John Ross, "Mexicanizing the Mara," *Texas Observer*, June 18, 2004.

392. Excerpts from Stacey Chapman, "Yo Soy Boricua, Pa' que Tu Lo Sepas! (I'm Boricua, Just So You Know!): An Interview with Rosie Pérez," June 12, 2006

Dancer and actress Rosie Pérez was born in Brooklyn of Puerto Rican parents. She started dancing with Soul Train when she was spotted by a producer while dancing at a night club. Later Spike Lee saw her in another club and cast her in *Do the Right Thing* (1989). Pérez worked as a choreographer on *In Living*

Color and was nominated for an Oscar in 1993 for her performance in *Fearless*. Pérez is one of dozens of Puerto Rican entertainers and sports heroes from Puerto Rico and the mainland. Pérez has a strong sense of identity and has been vocal in defense of the rights of Puerto Ricans and other Latinos. She starred in the 2006 documentary film *Yo Soy Boricua! Pa' Que Tu Lo Sepas! (I'm Boricua, Just So You Know!)* and has made documentaries on AIDS awareness. The following is an interview with Pérez regarding her motivations in making the 2006 documentary.

Rosie Pérez: I wanted to do a motion picture narrative piece and the places where I went kept telling me that, this isn't true. I was like, "What do you mean it isn't true?" "Well, it didn't happen." I said, "What do you mean it didn't happen?" "They went voluntarily." I was like, oh my God and I just couldn't believe it! I said, "Why were there sterilization clinics placed in factories?" "Well?" That was the response. I said, "Well, if they're major corporations and they're placing sterilization clinics in factories, and the factories are only hiring predominately women, you don't think that there's something funny about that? "Well" I said, "There's legislative Act 136 that passed and says sterilization should be practiced on the poor and the malfunctioned people who are not able to raise children and educate them in a proper manner. That's a government legislative act passed! There's nothing funny about that?" "Well, uh." Those things did happen. Nobody wanted to make that movie, and I just couldn't believe it. So, I kept pressing on and doing other projects, but it was always on the back of my mind.

Then this ex-boyfriend of mine called me up and said, "You know, I hear you're doing the Puerto Rican Day parade. I hear your people all the way over here in Brooklyn, all the way across the river. Y'all are so damn loud! What the hell are y'all so damn loud about?" I said, "Cause we're proud." He goes, "What the hell you guys got to be proud about?" Ha, ha, ha. I hung up the phone on him....

I called my agent that day, and I said I got it. I'm going put all of those things to rest. I'm going to prove it. I'm going to spell it out, and I'm going to tell our whole (Puerto Rican) history. I'm going to wrap it around with people's personal stories, because I was so touched by those women that were interviewed. I said I'm going show how political policy can affect people.

My co-director, Rory Kennedy, called me in her office, and said, "Listen, I feel that you need to be a character in the movie." I said, "Oh hell no! No, hell no! Oh, No No No!" And um, she's like, "I really think you should be, and if you want to be a viable director and make this movie something special, you have to let go and just be in it." And um, I think I told her off. And then finally I gave in....

I really like the Young Lords section. Pablo Guzman was a former Young Lord, and it's interesting to see that you got into that. I really like that part of the film.... I always had an affection for it, because I remember my cousin Titi, God rest her soul. I remember the day when I was a little girl, and she came barreling into the house one day. "Mami mami, oh my god, you should have seen these Puerto Ricans. They're walking in the street, and they had these berets, and everything. I told you, and now they're on TV. I told you. They're gonna be on the news tonight." She was always so fascinated by them, and I was fascinated by her. So I always remember that....

I have [other issues like] my AIDS activism. We just protested in front of the UN yesterday. Got minimal news coverage, which is sad.

Source: Stacey Chapman, "Yo Soy Boricua, Pa'que Tu Lo Sepas!" (I'm Boricua, Just So You Know!): An Interview with Rosie Pérez, June 12, 2006. http://www.blackfilm.com/20060609/features/rosieperez.shtml.

393. Rodolfo F. Acuña, "The Inquiring Mind and Miguel Estrada," 2002

There are differences within the Latino community as to class and consequently the interests of the group. For example, some of the exiles that have arrived since 1980 are middle class and do not understand the civil rights history in this country. Their views differ from those of working-class Latinos. The Puerto Rican community, for instance, is five times as large as the Cuban American community and has a lower median age and income. Mexican and Central Americans have large first-generation groups and a median age of around 25 whereas the median age among Cubans is 40. Moreover, status of Latinos in Los Angeles and New York differ from Miami where there is still a Cuban American political and social hegemony. Not every Latino supports the Cuban American anti-Cuban government politics. And not every Latino supports the other Latinos' views of their native countries. What binds them culturally should not necessarily be confused with what binds them politically where class and race interests are more important than art or music or language. The following article deals with attorney Miguel Estrada (1961–), a Honduran American whom President George W. Bush (1946–) sought to appoint to the 4th Circuit Court of Appeals. The appointment met with strong opposition by progressives and many in the Latino community because of his ultra-conservative views and history of supporting right-wing organizations.

The hearings on the nomination of Miguel Estrada, 41, to the Circuit U.S. Court of Appeals, District of Columbia, are nearing a close. But despite the high stakes involved in selecting the wrong person to the federal bench, Latino moderates and liberals have remained quiet, seemingly oblivious to its consequences. A bad appointment would rank on a par with the impending war in the Middle East. Right-wing Latino organizations and Republicans have stepped into the void and accused Democratic members of the Judiciary Committee of racism for preventing a vote on the nomination of Miguel Estrada.

If confirmed, Estrada would be in line for the U.S. Supreme Court, something the Latino community considers a barometer of its political influence. It would follow the historical tradition of the appointment of Jewish, African American, and women justices who were expected to represent more than just their own interests. By raising the race card, conservative forces have made race an issue—which is unfortunate.

In a previous article I posited that Estrada, Honduran-born and raised, could not be called a U.S. Latino if we apply the test of the civil rights movement and ask who is an oppressed minority. I would have to agree with African American Harvard sociologist Orlando Patterson that by stretching the definition of Latino and qualifying anyone with a Spanish surname to entitlements, giving affirmative action a bad name.

In the case of Estrada, he has no record that indicates or suggests that he identifies with the working Latino community. This does not make him a bad person nor is he unique. Many Latin Americans from privileged backgrounds come to the United States and do not understand the civil rights histories of Mexican Americans and Puerto Ricans.

The truth be told, Estrada comes from a privileged background. His family in Honduras did not relate to the issues of working-class Latinos there. Instead of addressing the question of what comes under the definition of a definable or disadvantaged minority, I have received angry letters from Hondurans accusing me of being divisive and even anti-Honduran. These critics suggest that because a person is a Honduran American or a Cuban American, this automatically makes them Latinos and should be supported by members of that fantasy heritage.

What in fact is divisive is supporting Estrada based on his surname and it has opened this Pandora's box. Does it mean that if Mexican billionaire Carlos Slim, the world's third-richest man, were to take up residence in the United States, he would be a Latino entitled to affirmative action?

Let us not play games; there are millions of upper- and middle-class Latinos who immigrate to this country who, like Estrada, have received good educations in their own country and do not relate to poor immigrants or U.S.-born Latinos. It is easy for them to become Republicans and associate with organizations such as the Federalist Society who pursue right-wing policies that are damaging to Latinos.

Reacting to the claims of Estrada's supporters that he is a Latino Horatio Alger, a Latino who turned adversity into opportunity by going from rags-to-riches, I have delved into his background. He came to this country at 15, and two years after immigrating to the United States, Estrada took the SAT in English and was accepted to Columbia University in New York, from which he graduated magna cum laude. A remarkable feat. More amazing since his supporters infer that he knew no English at the time he immigrated to this country.

What contributed to this phenomenal accomplishment?

Well, these questions have not been asked or answered by the media and the Department of Justice or Estrada's supporters. My independent sources reveal: Estada's father is a lawyer and owns land in the south of Honduras. He is wealthy but does not appear to be a *latifundista*. His father does not have a notoriously bad reputation such as links to military or conservative politicians.

Estrada is not a working-class Honduran by any means who through hard work made it in this country. According to a fellow Honduran, Estrada "is a middle- to upper-class Honduran, from urban professional background, and probably was already highly educated before he came here." Given this background, Estrada probably grew up learning English in elite private schools.

These facts would not be important if his supporters had been honest and forthcoming. It is a disservice to many poor immigrant children who have to attend ghetto schools and live below the poverty line to use Estrada as a role model.

Class is the defining factor in academic success in America. Hence it is intellectually dishonest to claim that Bush nominated Estrada solely on his qualifications. George Bush would not have nominated Estrada if he were not a Latino and an ultraconservative.

Further, Estrada is not uniquely qualified. There are literally scores of lawyers who have graduated cum laude from Harvard Law School, and who, unlike Estrada, have published. For example, Clinton nominated Jorge Rangel (*Harvard Law*

Review) from Corpus Christi, Texas, for the Court of Appeals. Rangel was not confirmed. Moreover, there are thousands of Latinos who have graduated from premier law schools; Harvard is not the only good law school in the U.S. So, beyond his law school transcript, what makes Estrada so eminently qualified?

The problem is that because Estrada was never a judge, he lacks a paper trail establishing his views, forcing critics to make assumptions based on what could be called circumstantial evidence. Estrada is known to be a conservative, but he has made few public comments expressing his legal views.

Lacking a public record, his associations take on greater importance. For instance, Estrada is a partner at Gibson, Dunn & Crutcher, a Los Angeles–based law firm that represented President George W. Bush before the Supreme Court during the contested 2000 election. Estrada also worked for then-Solicitor General Kenneth Starr during George W. Bush's father's administration and was a law clerk for Supreme Court Justice Anthony Kennedy. As mentioned, Estrada is a member of the Federalist Society, an ultra conservative group formed at the University of Chicago in 1983 with Antonin Scalia, the future Supreme Court justice, and Robert Bork as faculty advisers.

Because of these associations, members of congress want to take a closer look at the record. Estrada could eventually become a Supreme Court Justice.

So the Senate Judiciary Committee has requested internal memos written by Miguel Estrada from 1992 to 1997 while working in the Office of the Solicitor General, a branch of the Justice Department. This branch is charged with arguing cases before the Supreme Court. Disingenuously the Bush administration has claimed executive privilege and prudence, in other words, Bush claims confidentiality, something denied to former President Bill Clinton.

Given the slimness of Estrada's public record, and the testimony of a former supervisor that Estrada advocates extreme positions that aligned with ideological biases more than Constitutional reasoning, raises a "red flag." What is Bush trying to hide? Since Estrada has never served as a judge on a lower court, the memos would offer an opportunity to see how he would analyze cases as a judge.

Although my own superficial findings did not uncover any connection with the Honduran-Bush Family and the funding and support of the Contras [Nicaraguan counter revolutionaries], it is disconcerting that the media ignored the possibility. The confirmation fight of U.N. ambassador John D. Negroponte, who served as ambassador to Honduras from 1981–85, was sent to the senate at the same time as Estrada's nomination. Given Negroponte's secret arming of Nicaragua's Contra rebels, the CIA-backed Honduran death squad, and the Iran-Contra deal, this should have been an area of inquiry.

It is unfair to the nation and Estrada to leave these issues in the limbo of speculation.

What makes all of this so unpleasant is the silence of Latino civil rights organizations. I would have expected Latino Civil Rights organizations and Latino politicos to be proactive, opposing this nomination until more was known about Estrada. The Hispanic Congressional Caucus has rolled over. The truth be told, the only reason that we are entitled, is that large sectors of our community are poor and oppressed. Our entitlements are not based on our surnames.

Source: Rodolfo F. Acuña, Urban Archives, September 2002, California State University at Northridge.

394. Council on Hemispheric Affairs (COHA), "Guatemala's Cursed Armed Forces: Washington's Old Friend Is Back in Town," March 16, 2006

Guatemala, a country of 10 million people, is the largest Central American nation. Sixty percent of Guatemala's population is Mayan Indians. From the Spanish colonial period, it has been a leader in the region. In the twentieth century, American corporations, such as the United Fruit Company, have invested heavily in that country, and thus Guatemala has suffered from U.S. involvement and U.S. support of military regimes. For the past 30 years, the Guatemalan military has brutally suppressed popular movements among the indigenous people resulting in the deaths of more than 150,000 people. Much of the U.S. support for the Guatemalan military has come under the guise of the war on drugs. The following is a report by the Council on Hemispheric Affairs (COHA), an independent, non-profit, non-partisan, tax-exempt research and information organization that has been in existence since 1975. The state of Guatemala is important because political instability is a major factor in sending immigrants to the United States. According to the 1990 Census there were 268,779 Guatemalans in the United States—225,739 were foreign-born. In 2000, there were 463,502 Guatemalans. Migration does not happen by accident.

One can be forgiven for arguing that Defense Secretary Donald Rumsfeld, who demonstrably is losing the war in Iraq, is now trying to achieve an easy win in Latin America, where he is presiding over the rehabilitation of what he sees as the Latin American military's sense of honor. But the murderous reputation of that institution was established not due to invention or superficial judgment, but because of the fact that during the 1970s and 1980s, tens of thousands of innocent civilians were tortured and murdered throughout the region at the hands of local armed forces.

Under such conditions, restoring one's good name is no easy task. But due to Rumsfeld's spirit of generosity, all has been forgiven at the Pentagon. At the cost of tens of millions of dollars, it has been staging periodic ministerial meetings with Rumsfeld's counterparts from throughout the hemisphere since 1995, as well as funding the successor to the infamous School of the Americas at Fort Benning. Furthermore, the Secretary of Defense has made an on-site visit to seemingly obscure Paraguay, ostensibly to thank the local leaders for the possible U.S. usage of the Mariscal Estigarribia airstrip, and for allowing U.S. national guardsmen to rotate into the country. In addition, Rumsfeld has facilitated the sale of F-16 fighter jets to Chile, the major military sale from the U.S. to Chile since the end of the Pinochet era, in a deal first arranged by Lockheed lobbyist Otto Reich, and which could ultimately spark an open arms race between Chile and hostile neighboring countries like Peru, Bolivia, and Argentina.

Guatemala's newly appointed defense minister, General Francisco Bermudez, is currently in Washington D.C., for a four day visit that began on March 13. On his agenda is an appointment with the Secretary of Defense. In that meeting, Rumsfeld is expected to address the matter of a renewal of U.S. military aid to Guatemala, and possibly the construction of a DEA [Drug Enforcement Administration] base in the Guatemalan rainforest to help combat drug trafficking in Central America. The relatively high visibility of Bermudez' visit is not adventitious, but represents a long-standing Rumsfeld policy of upgrading ties with some of Latin America's most reprehensible and unsavory military establishments, who during the 1970s and 1980s savaged their nations' constitutions and citizenry, including in Chile, Argentina, El Salvador, and, perhaps most of all, Guatemala.

THE GUATEMALAN MILITARY: *PRESENTE*

Bermudez's visit comes as a follow up to last October's defense conference, "Security and Economic Opportunity," which took place in Key Biscayne, Florida. At that reunion, Rumsfeld met with Central American defense ministers and representatives from different branches of the region's armed forces. It was during this gathering that the then-Guatemalan defense minister, General Carlos Aldana, called for the creation of a Central America peacekeeping force, which putatively would promote political stability, as well as provide emergency relief to civilians after natural disasters such as hurricanes. Secretary Rumsfeld said the talks were a "unique moment in the Americas." But, what Rumsfeld didn't say out loud, was that by attempting to revive the Latin American military, he could be putting to risk the very civil governance whose creation is at the heart of what he says is his Iraq policy.

It was ironic to hear Guatemalan military officers discussing political stability. The armed forces of that Central American nation have long had a reputation for their covert behavior and unqualified brutality, whether they were overthrowing de facto governments almost at will, setting up infamous death squads, staging massacres of indigenous communities in Guatemala's highlands in their "beans and bullets" crusade, and torturing tens of thousands of civilian victims. Dating back to 1960, it is estimated that almost 200,000 civilians have been put to the sword by the Guatemala military, as part of Washington's "Cold War"-abetted national security hemispheric policy. The country's 1960–1996 civil war, which featured unspeakable cruelty, has been sometimes referred to as the "silent Holocaust," for its mindless slaughter. Unfortunately, the end of military rule and civil war did not bring about a new era featuring highly professional, law-abiding, loyal-to-the-nation armed forces. Nor has the Guatemalan government had the temerity to implement some of the most important of the requirements listed by the country's "Truth Commission" in 1999. Despite the Guatemalan military's notorious reputation for drug trafficking, contrabanding, and harsh treatment of the indigenous population, the U.S. is once again involving itself in the internal affairs of the country, extending a growing amount of military aid in exchange for the country's participation in the "war against drugs." In that war, Washington's best friend in Central America is the Guatemalan military, closely followed by the Salvadoran and Honduran armed forces. Ironically, the DEA will remind you that in recent years, the Guatemalan military—particularly its G-2, was the prime drug trafficking cartel in the country.

WASHINGTON'S DRUG STRATEGY

At the same time, the *Boston Globe*'s Indira Lakshmanan ("Cocaine's New Route," November 30, 2005), cited interviews with senior Guatemalan officials who said that they would ask for stepped-up U.S. military cooperation and a permanent

DEA base in the country's dense jungle bordering Mexico. This will not make Mexico City, nor that country's military, particularly happy in having the U.S. as its neighbor, not once, but twice. Such activities could also mark a return to the early 1990s, when the DEA had a fleet of helicopters stationed in Guatemala for purposes of surveillance and interdiction. Since then, "enforcement efforts have shifted to other areas," leaving a dearth of resources for enforcement in Central America. This was revealed by DEA director of operations Michael Braun, in his November 9 testimony before a Congressional subcommittee. The *Boston Globe* article also mentions that Guatemalan convictions of traffickers, whether private citizens or officials, are rare. None of the 16 alleged Guatemalan traffickers wanted in the United States have been extradited in the last dozen years since warrants against them were issued, allegedly because of delays in that country's judicial process, noted Michael P. O'Brien, the DEA's representative in Guatemala.

The most striking example of this new counter-drug relationship occurred last year, when Rumsfeld declared that the U.S. will lift its ban on military aid to that country's armed forces. In March 2005, Washington gave $3.2 million to initiate a modernization process of Guatemala's military capacities. Assistance had been withdrawn in 1990, after it was learned that Guatemalan military forces had been involved in the killing of U.S. citizen Michael Devine. Rumsfeld's repeated expressions of concern for Americans fighting in Iraq apparently doesn't easily transfer to the fate of U.S. nationals Michael Devine in Guatemala or Lori Berenson in Peru. The alleged murderer of Devine, in fact, was Col. Julio Roberto Alpirez, who attended the School of the Americas and was reportedly on the CIA's payroll for many years. While the case remains unsolved, the Bush administration has apparently decided to overlook this, as well as the cold-blooded murder of tens of thousands of Guatemalans during the civil war, in favor of more pressing issues like the war on drugs and Washington's need to erect a thin line of allies to fend off the seepage of the "pink tide" to the north.

MILITARY VS. THE WORLD

Washington was very active in creating the monster that is the Guatemalan military and which terrorized the country during the 1960–1996 Guatemalan conflict. It is ironic, but not entirely surprising, that the U.S.—which has always been fully knowledgeable regarding the face of the Guatemalan beast—now praises the country's ersatz democracy and begins anew to pour money into its corrupt leadership, this time with the help of the newly authorized Millennium Account, which is the White House's new slush fund to fund pro-U.S. personalities and projects throughout Latin America. This is a way to tell President [Oscar] Berger (1946–) "thank you" for his support on issues like CAFTA [Central American Free Trade Agreement]-DR.

Guatemalans deserve a military that they can be proud of, but that does not seem likely to be a fact of life in the immediate future. At best, they will have to wait another generation, when a new group of military officers come to power, who might just be disgusted enough with what their predecessors have done to bring the desperately needed positive change to their pariah institution.

Source: http://www.coha.org/2006/03/16/guatemala%e2%80%99s-cursed-armed-forces-washington%e2%80%99s-old-friend-is-back-in-town.

PART XXI

Chicanas/os and Mexican Americans in Contemporary Society

If Mexican Americans were a nation, they would constitute the fourth largest nation in Latin America—behind Mexico, Columbia, and Argentina and in a dead heat with Peru and Venezuela with populations approaching 30 million. The dramatic growth has been in great part driven by the Mexican immigration of the 1980s and 90s. In 2004 Mexicans accounted for 29 percent of the 34 million foreign-born persons living in the United States. They themselves numbered 28 million. And just over 41 percent of Mexicans were first-generation immigrants. Along with other Spanish-language immigrants they listened to Spanish-language radio and television media. The television giant Univisión had a market capitalization of $10 billion and variety shows such as Don Francisco's *Sabado Gigante*, broadcast throughout Latin America and Europe.

In 1980, the U.S. Census counted 8.8 million Mexican origin residents of the United States in just two states, California and Texas. Illinois and Arizona together contributed another 9 percent, to account for 82 percent of the total Mexican-American population. Of Mexican Americans counted in the 1980 census, 74 percent were native born. By 1990, the Mexican-American population is projected to increase to 14.5 million. Meanwhile, the increase of Latinos along with the enforcement of the 1965 Voter Rights Act brought about the election of more Mexican Americans and Latino elected officials. This created an illusion of power and a shift away from the civil rights history forged by the Mexican American, Chicano, and Puerto Rican movements. Heroes such as César Chávez were replaced by the "beautiful people," who appeared on magazine covers.

The deindustrialization of the economy brought bad times to many Americans in the 1980s. Light industry replaced well paid jobs in heavy industry. Attracted by jobs that Euro-Americans would not take, the foreign-born population increased from 9.6 million in 1970 to 22.8 million twenty-four years later. Mexican immigrants were 43 percent of documented immigrants from Latin America in 1988—joined by waves of Central Americans driven from their homes by civil wars. At least 300,000 Salvadorans and 50,000 Guatemalans lived in Los Angeles alone by the mid 80s. Nativists responded in Californian by passing the "English Is the Official Language" proposition in 1986. That same year Congress passed the Immigration Reform and Control Act (IRCA), which included employer sanctions, stronger border enforcement, and amnesty for undocumented immigrants. By the end of the decade, some 2.96 million had applied for amnesty (about 70 percent were Mexican).

As the Berlin Wall came down in 1989, the United States began building its own walls between it and Mexico. In 1990, the Defense Department built an

11-mile fence in the San Diego area as part of this war on drugs. Two years later, the Army Corps of Engineers announced plans to place scores of floodlights along a 13-mile strip of border near San Diego to "deter drug smugglers and illegal aliens." President Bill Clinton launched "Operation Gatekeeper," sealing the western San Diego County border and forcing undocumented immigrants to cross the suicidal terrain to the east.

Trade union membership declined nationally, with overall private sector union participation falling below 15 percent. In contrast, the new immigrants flocked to labor unions. They brought a militancy that converted the historical anti-immigrant policies of the labor internationals to a pro the foreign born advocacy. They filled the ranks of the Hotel and Restaurant Employees Union (HERE), the International Ladies Garment Workers Union (ILGWU), and Justice for Janitors and fought back. The struggle took on a historic dimension when on May 15, 1990, 150 armed officers attacked janitors and their supporters—a police riot that resulted in 40 arrests and 16 injuries, with two women having miscarriages.

The protection of the foreign born became a priority among Mexican American and Latino activists. Casa Autónoma-Hermandad General de Trabajadores (CASA-HGTC) and La Raza Unida in Texas were training grounds for these activists—many of whom became elected officials and union organizers. In California tens of thousands turned out to protest Proposition 187 (1994) that denied immigrants public services, Proposition 209 (1996) that killed affirmative action, and Proposition 227 (1998) that abolished bilingual education. The perfect storm occurred when the "[Jim] Sensenbrenner Bill," H.R. 4437 (2005), passed the House of Representatives. A million marchers took to the streets in Los Angeles and hundred of thousands in the streets of cities across the country in spring 2006. Among other things the bill would have made living here without documents a felony. Nativists called for the deportation of the 12 million undocumented workers and their families—the cost would be at least $230 billion or more to deport 9 million.

During the 1990s Mexican origin peoples spread through the United States. However, Los Angeles had 4.2 million Latinos; Harris County, Texas that includes Houston and the Chicago areas with over a million each. The median age of Mexicans was just over 24 years well behind the national median of 36 years. Latinos nationally was 25.9, almost ten years below the national median of 35.3. Although the second-generation Mexican-Americans are much more likely to have completed high school than Mexican immigrants, they still lag behind Euro-Americans. At least one-fourth of second- and third-generation Mexican Americans had not completed high school. Poverty still took its toll with poor housing and bad schools being the rule in predominately Mexican and Latino neighborhoods. Lastly, the American labor offers limited opportunities to the unskilled. What is missing is the stairway to the middle class followed by European immigrants as they worked in well paying heavy industry. And although Mexican Americans had one of the highest work participation records among American residents they were perceived in a national poll in 1990 as being second only to blacks as to being lazy and living off welfare.

As mentioned, the Mexican American community was larger than Ireland (4.5 million), Israel (6.5 million), Sweden (9 million) and Norway (4.6 million) combined in terms of numbers. Because many Mexicans had been in the United States before the 1848 takeover, the community developed long term institutions and an identity. In terms of organizations, it had the largest network of any of the Latino groups, as well as a tradition of fighting for civil rights. Because of the struggle of the Mexican American and then the Chicano generations, Mexican and Latino immigrants were able to assimilate into an environment where there were entitlements for them to go to school and equal access to many institutions. For example, the number of Latino university students was negligible in 1968, but because of intense struggle, thousands were attending universities in the twenty-first century—but it must be remembered, it was not given to them.

There was also a greater acceptance of Mexicanas and Latinas who in greater numbers were elected to public office and headed trade unions and other organizations. The struggles of the late 1960s had politicized the community and many of the feminist leaders came out of the activist core. Finally, Chicano Studies had evolved as a field of study with major university accrediting Chicano studies departments and programs. In recognition of the equality of women, the name of the National Association for Chicano Studies was changed to the National Association for Chicana and Chicano Studies (NACCS). The feminist movements of the past had a profound influence on Mexican American and immigrant women.

By 2007 the voices in these communities were diverse. They were not only in Los Angeles, San Antonio, and Chicago but also in the Yakima Valley and the Deep South. By the year 2020 it is estimated that there will be 60 million Latinos in this country; by 2080 160 million.

395. Excerpts from David Reyes, "GI Forum Address," 1980

Congressman Edward R. Roybal (1916–1905) was the dean of Chicano politicos—a legend in his time. In 1980, he responded to the hype of the Decade of the Hispanic, the popular notion among Many Mexican Americans that the Sixties had been the decade of African Americans and that the 1980s would be the Decade of the Hispanic. They had arrived at the gates of the promised land and the economic and political fruits of the nation belonged to Latinos. Roybal was the head of the Hispanic Caucus in Congress and from a generation where Mexican Americans were called greasers and could not swim in public swimming pools except for designated days. The following article reports on his speech before the American G.I. Forum, the leading Mexican American veterans organization that had been around since the mid-1940s, took issue with the decade of the Hispanic questioning the thesis that had arrived and if their organizations were making a difference in the lives of poor Mexicans and others in the United States. It was an important admonition coming from a respected politico of the old school.

ANAHEIM—Rep. Edward R. Roybal (D-Los Angeles) said Wednesday that many of the nation's 12- to 16-million Latinos still occupy the lowest rungs of the economic ladder despite claims that the 1980s would be better.

"We have been told over and over again that the 1980s will be the decade of the Hispanics," the California Democrat told 300 American GI Forum members attending their 32nd annual convention here. "But we all remember that we were told the same thing at the start of the ... the '70s.

"The real answer, my friends," Roybal told the predominantly Mexican-American audience, "is that we have no clout."

He said Latinos are found at the lowest levels of education, health and income, and "our senior citizens live in poverty and deprivation."

Roybal made the statements on opening day of the American GI Forum convention. The 20,000-member organization was originally founded by a group of Mexican-American veterans in Texas. The convention is expected to draw at least 2,000 participants to the Anaheim Convention Center....

Source: David Reyes, "GI Forum Address," *Los Angeles Times*, August 7, 1980, p. OC_A1.

396. Excerpts from Judy Aulette and Trudy Mills, "Something Old, Something New: Auxiliary Work in the 1983–1986 Copper Strike," 1988

On April 7, 1982, Phelps Dodge, the world's largest copper producer, announced the lay-off of 3,400 workers in Texas and Arizona. The next year, it took a hard line in negotiations with the United Steelworkers, and the union agreed to a freeze of members' wages for three years, only asking for Cost of Living Adjustments (COLA). The other copper corporations agreed to these terms, but Phelps Dodge refused to settle. The hard line of Phelps Dodge forced Morenci, Clifton, Ajo, and Douglas, Arizona, miners to walk out. Law enforcement supported Phelps Dodge. Firings and evictions followed as the Arizona Criminal Intelligence Systems Agency flooded the camps with undercover agents. In August 1983, Phelps Dodge announced that Morenci strikers would be permanently replaced by strike-breakers. Injunctions limiting picketing and demonstrations at the mine were enforced and Arizona Gov. Bruce Babbitt sent military vehicles, tanks, helicopters, 426 State Troopers, and 325 National Guardsmen in Morenci to break the strike. The strike grew bitter as women took over the picket lines. In October 1984, the company held an election to vote for a union or not. Only the 1,055 replacement workers and the 1,345 union members could vote. The National Labor Relations Board, controlled by Republicans, rejected appeals from the unions to halt decertification. Overnight, the area went from being overwhelmingly Mexican to overwhelmingly white; overwhelmingly Democratic to Republican. The following article excerpts describe the role of women during the strike.

The MMWA [Morenci Miners Women's Auxiliary] was formed nearly forty years ago as part of the community support network for copper miners and their unions. The copper miners were regularly drawn into strikes when their contracts came up for renegotiation, and the auxiliary was reactivated for each of those strikes. In 1983, the auxiliary was once again reactivated to support the strike against Phelps Dodge ... Although still committed to this aspect of the auxiliary in the 1983–86 strike, members prided themselves on being an important political organization. In contrasting the "new" auxiliary with the old, [Fina] Román told us that, "the membership is different now. We don't just do what the auxiliary used to do.... When Gov. Babbitt sent in the National Guard and the police to suppress the people who were fighting for an equitable contract, then it became political....

MMWA members also participated in work that is not associated with the "traditional female role," and they were especially animated when they spoke about this.

The maintenance of a picket line in Clifton is the most important example of what the women saw as the new political work of the auxiliary. The unions maintained an official picket line in Morenci at the gate of the mine. The impact of this line was limited because Phelps Dodge obtained legal restrictions on the pickets and made it physically difficult to picket by removing a picket shack and moving in piles of dirt to make it impossible to gather many people in this area.... Auxiliary members also worked to bring the strike to the attention of people outside of Arizona [criss-crossing the country, speaking to labor and community groups]....

As one member put it: Women are more aggressive when they see something harming their kids.... When the strikebreaker or scab, he's taking her husband's jobs away, taking the food away from your kids, taking the shoes off their feet, I think women are the first to respond to that.... They're seeing the destruction of the family, and they are going to come out with tooth and claw.

Source: Judy Aulette and Trudy Mills, "Something Old, Something New: Auxiliary Work in the 1983–1986 Copper Strike," was originally published in *Feminist Studies*, Volume 14, Number 2 (Summer, 1988): 251–268, by permission of the publisher, *Feminist Studies*, Inc.

397. Memo from John Tanton to WITAN IV Attendees, October 10, 1986

The major issue for Mexican Americans and other Latinos during the 1980s and into the next century was immigration. Pro-immigrant groups faced a lobby of well-financed foundations. The following memo is from John Tanton, a physician, who was the founder of anti-immigration groups such as the Federation of American Immigration Reform (FAIR) and U.S. English, and published the *Social Contract Press*, a quarterly devoted to anti-immigrant pieces. In 1986, Tanton signed a memo that caused an uproar. He charged that Latino immigrants brought a culture of political corruption to the United States, and were unlikely to become good citizens. He stated that the power of whites was being diluted by Latinos. Tanton laid out an agenda for anti-immigrant groups and called for an investigation of the Mexican American Legal Defense and Education Fund (MALDEF). He drew a picture of two Americas—the white property owners and the propertyless blacks and Hispanics. For many, the Tanton memo raised the question of racism within the ranks of the anti-immigrant organizations, something that was vehemently denied. Some members of English Only resigned in protest, but most tacitly agreed.

TO: WITAN IV Attendees
FROM: John Tanton
DATE: October 10, 1986

Here is a set of questions and statements that I hope will help guide our discussion of the non-economic consequences of immigration to California, and by extension, to the rest of the United States. These are not highly polished; I ask your indulgence.

These notes are based on reading Bouvier's and related papers, on the WITAN III Meeting, and my own thinking over several years on the topic of assimilation and the character of American society. The assignment of subtopics to the main categories is a bit arbitrary; many of them could be moved around.

I. POLITICAL CONSEQUENCES

1. The political power between the states will change, owing to differential migration [in] six immigrant-receiving states. The heartland will lose more political power.

2. Will the newcomers vote Democratic or Republican, liberal or conservative, and what difference does it make? A lot, if you're one or the other.

3. *Gobernar es poblar* translates [to] "to govern is to populate" (Parsons' [Thomas Malthus] paper, p. 10, packet sent May 8). In this society where the majority rules, does this hold? Will the present majority peaceably hand over its political power to a group that is simply more fertile?

4. Does the fact that there will be no ethnic majority, in California, early in the next century mean that we will have minority coalition-type governments, with third parties? Is this good or bad, in view of the European and other experiences?

5. Shall illegal aliens be counted in the census and used to apportion congressional and statehouse seats, thereby granting them political power?

6. Is apartheid in Southern California's future? The demographic picture in South Africa now is startlingly similar to what we'll see in California in 2030. In Southern Africa, a White minority owns the property, has the best jobs and education, has the political power, and speaks one language. A non-White majority has poor education, jobs, and income, owns little property, is on its way to political power and speaks a different language. (The official language policy in South Africa is bilingualism—the Blacks are taught in Zulu and related tongues.)

In California of 2030, the non-Hispanic Whites and Asians will own the property, have the good jobs and education, speak one language and be mostly Protestant and "other." The Blacks and Hispanics will have the poor jobs, will lack education, own little property, speak another language and will be mainly Catholic. Will there be strength in this diversity? Or will this prove a social and political San Andreas Fault?

7. Illegal aliens will pay taxes to the Federal Government; their costs will mostly be local.

8. The politicians are way behind the people on these issues. This brings to mind the story told of Gandhi: he was sitting by the side of the road when a crowd went by. He said, "There go my people. I must get up and follow them, for I am their leader!"

9. Griffin Smith's point from the *Federalist Papers*: It was argued that the colonies would make a good nation, as they shared a common culture and language. Nineteen eighty-seven is the celebration of the adoption of the Constitution, 1988 its ratification, and 1989 the setting up of the first Federal Government. Can we tie into these discussions?

II. CULTURAL

1. Will Latin American migrants bring with them the tradition of the *mordida* (bribe), the lack of involvement in public affairs, etc.? What in fact are the characteristics of Latin American culture, versus that of the United States? See Harrison's *Washington Post* article in the September 3 packet.

2. When does diversity grade over into division?

3. Will Blacks be able to improve (or even maintain) their position in the face of the Latin onslaught?

4. How will we make the transition from a dominant non-Hispanic society with a Spanish influence to a dominant Spanish society with non-Hispanic influence?

5. Do ethnic enclaves (Bouvier, p. 18) constitute resegregation? As Whites see their power and control over their lives declining, will they simply go quietly into the night? Or will there be an explosion? Why don't non-Hispanic Whites have a group identity, as do Blacks, Jews, Hispanics?

6. Note that virtually all the population growth will come from immigrants and their descendants.

7. Is there a difference in the rates of assimilation between Asians and Latins?

8. Should something be said about the competing metaphors of the salad bowl and the melting pot?

9. What exactly is it that holds a diverse society together? Gerda's paper said that in our case, it was a common language.

10. Is assimilation a function of the educational and economic level of immigrants? If so, what are the consequences of having so many ill-educated people coming in to low paying jobs?

11. We're building in a deadly disunity. All great empires disintegrate, we want stability. (Lamm)

12. Enclaves lead to rigidity. (Hardin)

13. The theory of a moratorium: the pause in immigration between 1930–1950, combined with the assimilating experience of fighting side-by-side in the trenches in World War II, gave us a needed pause so that we could assimilate the mass of people who came in the early years of the century. Do we again need such a pause?

14. Concerning the moratorium, here are some phrases that could be used: "The pause that refreshes." "A seventh inning stretch." "Take a break, catch-up, eliminate a backlog, take a breather."

15. Perhaps mention should be made of Pacific Bell's move to install *completely separate* Spanish and Chinese language phone systems in California (see May 27 packet).

16. Novak's term "unmeltable ethnics" is probably better than some of the others that have been suggested. Similarly, ethnicity is a more acceptable term than race. It should also be noted that 50% of all Hispanic surname people on the census forms designate themselves as White. So perhaps we should speak of Hispanic Whites and non-Hispanic Whites, to further diffuse the issue. Is Anglo a better term that White? Language is *very* important here.

III. CONSERVATION AND DEMOGRAPHY

1. What will be the effect on the conservation movement, which has drawn its support in the past from other than the minorities, and which has relied on the political power of the majority to pass legislative measures? As the people that groups like the Sierra Club represent go into opposition (minority political status), will many of the things they've worked for be lost because the new majority holds other values?

2. Can *homo contraceptivus* compete with *homo progenitiva* if borders aren't controlled? Or is advice to limit one's family simply advice to move over and let someone else with greater reproductive powers occupy the space?

3. What are the consequences to California of the raw population growth that is coming, the ethnic change aside?

4. What is the conservation ethnic [*sic*] of the Asian and Latin American newcomers? Will they adopt ours or keep theirs?

5. The Sierra Club may not want to touch the immigration issue, but the immigration issue is going to touch the Sierra Club! (To mention just one group.)

6. On the demographic point: perhaps this is the first instance in which those with their pants up are going to get caught by those with their pants down!

7. Do you agree with Teitelbaum's statement, "International migration has now become an important point of intersection between the different demographic profiles of developing and developed countries"? (*Fear of Population Decline*, p. 134—see also pp. 111–115.)

IV. JURISPRUDENCE

1. What are the consequences for affirmative action of the ethnic change coming along? Will the non-Hispanic Whites (NHW) have a limited number of spots in professional schools, etc. proportionate to their numbers? Or will affirmative action go beyond this (as it does now in Malaysia) to cut spots to below their proportionate share, to enable other groups to "catch-up?"

2. Anything to be said about drugs and the border?

3. Will we get more of the Napoleonic Code influence, and does it make a difference?

4. What do we demand of immigrants—or more correctly, what should we demand of them:

    a. Learn our language.
    b. Adopt our political ideals.
    c. Assimilate and add their flavoring to our stew.

V. EDUCATION

1. What are the differences in educability between Hispanics (with their 50% dropout rate) and Asiatics (with their excellent school records and long tradition of scholarship)?

2. Where does bussing fit into the picture? Keep in mind that by 1990, over 50% of all the people under 15 years of age will be of minority status. They will also be heavily concentrated in certain geographic areas.

3. The whole bilingual education question needs to be mentioned.

VI. RACE/CLASS RELATIONS

1. What will be the fate of Blacks as their numbers decline in relationship to Hispanics? As they lose political power, will they get along with the Hispanics? Relations are already heavily strained in many places.

2. What happens when we develop a new underclass, or a two-tiered economic system? Especially if the two groups can't speak the same language! (See Bouvier and Martin Chapter 5.)

3. Is resegregation taking place, in the Southern part of the state in particular?

4. Phil Martin's point: In agriculture, the Whites and Asiatics will own and manage, but will not be able to speak to the Hispanic field workers. They will need bilingual foremen. Does this sound like social peace? Or like South Africa? Keep in mind the poor educational level of the field hands.

VII. THE ECONOMY

I don't think we should dwell much on the economy: I think we should try to make our contribution by talking about the non-economic consequences of immigration. Nonetheless:
1. Do high levels of immigration cut back on innovation (Bouvier, p. 27)?
2. Does it reduce the tendency and need of employers to hire current minority teens (Bouvier, p. 27)?
3. Is there a downward pressure on labor standards in general (Bouvier, p. 28)?
4. Phil Martin's point on the colonization of the labor market. (Chapter 5.)

VIII. RETIREMENT

1. Since the majority of the retirees will be NHW, but the workers will be minorities, will the latter be willing to pay for the care of the former? They will also have to provide the direct care: How will they get along, especially through a language barrier (Bouvier, p. 40)?
2. On the other hand, will the older and NHW groups be willing to pay the school taxes necessary to educate the burgeoning minorities?
3. The Federal Government may have to pay for the care of the elderly in schools—will it?

IX. RELIGIOUS CONSEQUENCES

This is the most difficult of all to tackle, and perhaps should be left out. Nonetheless:
1. What are the implications of the changes for the separation of church and state? The Catholic Church has never been reticent on this point. If they get a majority of the voters, will they pitch out this concept?
2. Same question for parochial schools versus public schools.
3. Same question for the topic of abortion/choice, birth control, population control.
4. Same question for the role of women.
5. Will Catholicism brought in from Mexico be in the American or the European model? The latter is much more casual.
6. Keep in mind that many of the Vietnamese coming in are also Catholic.
7. Is there anything to be said about the Eastern religions that will come along with the Asiatics?

X. MEXICO AND LATIN AMERICA (CHAPTER 7, BOUVIER & MARTIN)

Perhaps the main thing to be addressed here is whether or not shutting off the escape valve will lead to revolution, or whether keeping it open can avert it.

XI. ADDITIONAL DEMOGRAPHIC ITEMS

Teitelbaum's phrase, "A region of low native fertility combined with high immigration of high-fertility people does not make for compatible trend lines!"

Finally, this is all obviously dangerous territory, but the problem is not going to go away. Who can open it up? The question is analogous to Nixon's opening of China: he could do it, Hubert Humphrey could not have. Similarly, the issues we're touching on here must be broached by liberals. The conservatives simply cannot do it without tainting the whole subject.

I think the answers to many of these questions depend on how well people assimilate. This, in turn, depends heavily on whether the parent society has made up its mind that assimilation is a good thing (we're confused on this point now), whether it works at assimilating newcomers (as Canada and Australia do by following them longitudinally), whether the people coming *want* to assimilate (not all of them do), and, even if all the factors are favorable, whether the numbers are small enough so as not to overwhelm the assimilative process.

Good luck to us all!

Source: John Tanton to WITAN IV Attendees, October 10, 1986. Intelligence Report Summer 2002 Southern Poverty Law Center, http://www.splcenter.org/intel/intelreport/article.jsp?sid=125.

398. Excerpt from a Summary of the Immigration Reform and Control Act (Simpson-Mazzoli Act), 1986

The 1965 Immigration and Nationality Act was a defeat for nativists committed to the ideals of National Origins, strict quotas for immigrants from—according to restrictionists—the least desirable nationalities. It kept Third World immigrants, with the exception of Latin Americans, out of the country. But the act was only a partial loss for nativists because, for the first time, Latin Americans immigrants were put on a quota. As non-white immigrants poured into the country beginning in the 1970s, nativists sent up an alarm and pressured politicos to pass anti-immigration laws. The most obvious immigrant was the Mexican whose undocumented immigration accelerated in the 1970s. By the mid-1980s the nativists gathered momentum as right-wing think-tank foundations married this issue with campaigns against bilingual education, English only, and affirmative action. These nativist forces made immigration restriction a political wedge issue. In Congress, legislators such as Sen. Alan Simpson from Wyoming and Congressman Peter Rodino of New Jersey sponsored nativist bills in their respective chambers. In 1986, Congressman Romano Mazzoli of Kentucky had replaced Rodino in the House of Representative as co-sponsor, and the Simpson-Mazzoli Act, also known as the Immigration Reform and Control Act (IRCA), passed amendments to the Immigration and Nationality Act of 1952. Anti-immigrant forces won: those knowingly employing undocumented workers would face financial and other penalties, and additional funds would be used for border patrol. The law also provided amnesty for undocumented residents who had been in the country for a certain period of time. The following are excerpts from that important law that gave documents to 2.7 million immigrants.

SUMMARY AS OF:

10/14/1986—Conference report filed in House. (There are 4 other summaries) (Conference report filed in House, H. Rept. 99–1000)

IMMIGRATION REFORM AND CONTROL ACT OF 1986

Title I: Control of Illegal Immigration—Part A: Employment—Amends the Immigration and Nationality Act to make it unlawful for a person or other entity to: (1) hire (including through subcontractors), recruit, or refer for a fee for U.S. employment any alien knowing that such person is unauthorized to work, or any person without verifying his or her work status; or (2) continue to employ an alien knowing of such person's unauthorized work status.

Makes verification compliance (including the use of State employment agency documentation) an affirmative defense to any hiring or referral violation.

Establishes an employment verification system. Requires: (1) the employer to attest, on a form developed by the Attorney General, that the employee's work status has been verified by examination of a passport, birth certificate, social security card, alien documentation papers, or other proof; (2) the worker to similarly attest that he or she is a U.S. citizen or national, or authorized alien; and (3) the employer to keep such records for three years in the case of referral or recruitment, or the later of three years or one year after employment termination in the case of hiring.

States that nothing in this Act shall be construed to authorize a national identity card or system.

Directs the President to monitor and evaluate the verification system and implement changes as necessary within 60 days after notifying the appropriate congressional committees (within two years for a major change). Prohibits implementation of a major change unless the Congress provides funds for such purpose. Authorizes related demonstration projects of up to three years.

Limits the use of such verification system or any required identification document to enforcing this Act and not for other law enforcement purposes.

Directs the Attorney General to establish complaint and investigation procedures which shall provide for: (1) individuals and entities to file written, signed complaints regarding potential hiring violations; (2) INS investigations of complaints with substantial probability of validity; (3) Department of Justice–initiated investigations; and (4) designation of a specific INS unit to prosecute such violations.

Sets forth employer sanction provisions. Provides for a six-month period of public education during which no employment violation penalties shall be imposed.

Provides for a subsequent 12-month period during which violators shall be issued warning citations. Defers enforcement for seasonal agricultural services.

Provides, at the end of such citation period, for graduated first- and subsequent-offense civil penalties, injunctive remedies, or criminal penalties (for pattern of practice violations). Subjects violators to graduated civil penalties for related paperwork violations.

Directs the Attorney General to provide notice and, upon request, an administrative hearing in the case of a disputed penalty. States that: (1) judicial review of a final administrative penalty shall be in the U.S. court of appeals; and (2) suits to collect unpaid penalties shall be filed in U.S. district courts.

Makes it unlawful for an employer to require an employee to provide any type of financial guarantee or indemnity against any potential employment liability. Subjects violators, after notice and hearing opportunity, to a civil penalty for each violation and the return of any such amounts received.

States that such employer sanction provisions preempt State and local laws.

Requires the General Accounting Office (GAO) to submit to the Congress and to a specially created task force three annual reports regarding the operation of the employer sanction program, including a determination of whether a pattern of national origin discrimination has resulted. States that if the GAO report makes such a determination: (1) the task force shall so report to the Congress; and (2) the House and the Senate shall hold hearings within 60 days.

Terminates employer sanctions 30 days after receipt of the last GAO report if: (1) GAO finds a widespread pattern of discrimination has resulted from the employer sanctions; and (2) the Congress enacts a joint resolution within such 30-day period approving such findings.

Amends the Migrant and Seasonal Agricultural Worker Protection Act to subject farm labor contractors to the requirements of this Act, beginning seven months after enactment.

Directs the Attorney General, in consultation with the Secretary of Labor and the Secretary of Health and Human Services, to conduct a study of the use of a telephone system to verify the employment status of job applicants. Requires related congressional reports.

Directs the Comptroller General to: (1) investigate ways to reduce counterfeiting of social security account number cards; and (2) report to the appropriate congressional committees within one year.

Directs the Secretary of Health and Human Services, acting through the Social Security Administration and in cooperation with the Attorney General and the Secretary of Labor, to: (1) conduct a study of the feasibility of establishing a social security number validation system; and (2) report to the appropriate congressional committees within two years.

Makes it an unfair immigration-related employment practice for an employer of three or more persons to discriminate against any individual (other than an unauthorized alien) with respect to hiring, recruitment, firing, or referral for fee, because of such individual's origin or citizenship (or intended citizenship) status. States that it is not an unfair immigration-related employment practice to hire a U.S. citizen or national over an equally qualified alien.

Requires that complaints of violations of an immigration-related employment practice be filed with the Special Counsel for Immigration-Related Unfair Employment Practices (established by this Act) within the Department of Justice. Prohibits the overlap of immigration-related discrimination complaints and discrimination complaints filed with the Equal Employment Opportunity Commission.

Authorizes the Special Counsel to: (1) investigate complaints and determine (within 120 days) whether to bring such complaints before a specially trained administrative law judge; and (2) initiate investigations and complaints. Permits private actions if the Special Counsel does not file a complaint within such 120-day period. Sets forth related administrative provisions.

Makes it illegal to fraudulently misuse or manufacture entry or work documents.

Part B: Improvement of Enforcement and Services—States that essential elements of the immigration control and reform program established by this Act are increased enforcement and administrative activities of the Border Patrol, the Immigration and Naturalization Service (INS), and other appropriate Federal agencies.

Authorizes increased FY [fiscal year] 1987 and 1988 appropriations for: (1) INS; and (2) the Executive Office of Immigration Review. Obligates increased funding in FY 1987 and 1988 for the border patrol.

Directs the Attorney General, from funds appropriated to the Department of Justice for INS, to provide for improved immigration and naturalization services and for enhanced community outreach and in-service personnel training.

Authorizes additional appropriations for wage and hour enforcement.

Revises the criminal penalties for the unlawful transportation of unauthorized aliens into the United States.

Authorizes a $35,000,000 immigration emergency fund to be established in the Treasury for necessary enforcement activities and related State and local reimbursements.

Permits the owner or operator of a railroad line, international bridge, or toll road to request the Attorney General to inspect and approve measures taken to prevent aliens from illegally crossing into the United States. States that such approved measures shall be prima facie evidence of compliance with obligations under such Act to prevent illegal entries.

Expresses the sense of the Congress that the immigration laws of the United States should be vigorously enforced, while taking care to protect the rights and safety of U.S. citizens and aliens.

Requires INS to have an owner's consent or a warrant before entering a farm or outdoor operations to interrogate persons to determine if undocumented aliens are present.

Prohibits the adjustment of status to permanent resident for violators of (nonimmigrant) visa terms.

Title II: Legalization—Directs the Attorney General to adjust to temporary resident status those aliens who: (1) apply within 18 months; (2) establish that they entered the United States before January 1, 1982, and have resided here continuously in an unlawful status (including Cuban/Haitian entrants) since such date; and (3) are otherwise admissible.

Authorizes similar status adjustment for specified aliens who entered legally as nonimmigrants but whose period of authorized stay ended before January 1, 1982. (States that in the case of exchange visitors, the two-year foreign residence requirement must have been met or waived.)

Prohibits the legalization of persons: (1) convicted of a felony or three or more misdemeanors in the United States; or (2) who have taken part in political, religious, or racial persecution. Requires an alien applying for temporary resident status to register under the Military Selective Service Act, if such Act so requires.

Directs the Attorney General to adjust the status of temporary resident aliens to permanent resident if the alien: (1) applies during the one-year period beginning with the 19th month following the grant of temporary resident status; (2) has established continuous residence in the United States since the grant of temporary resident status; (3) is otherwise admissible and has not been convicted of a felony or three or more misdemeanors committed in the United States; and (4) either meets the minimum requirements for an understanding of English and a knowledge of American history and government, or demonstrates the satisfactory pursuit of a course of study in these subjects. (Authorizes an exemption from such language and history requirement for individuals 65 years of age or older.)

Specifies circumstances in which the Attorney General may terminate an alien's temporary resident status. Permits travel abroad and employment during such period.

Authorizes the filing of status adjustment applications with the Attorney General or designated voluntary or governmental agencies. Directs the Attorney General to work with such agencies to: (1) disseminate program information; and (2) process aliens. Provides for the confidential treatment of application records. Establishes criminal penalties (fines, imprisonment, or both) for: (1) violations of such confidentiality; and (2) false application statements. Provides for application fees.

Waives numerical limitations, labor certification, and other specified entry violations for such aliens. Permits the Attorney General to waive other grounds for exclusion (except criminal, most drug-related, and security grounds) to assure family unity or when otherwise in the national interest.

Requires the Attorney General to provide an alien otherwise eligible but unregistered who is apprehended before the end of the application period, an opportunity to apply for the legalization program before deportation or exclusion proceedings are begun. States that such alien shall be authorized to work in the United States pending disposition of the case.

Provides for administrative and judicial review of a determination respecting an application for adjustment of status under this Act.

Makes legalized aliens (other than Cuban/Haitian entrants) ineligible for Federal financial assistance, Medicaid (with certain exceptions), or food stamps for five years following a grant of temporary resident status and for five years following a grant of permanent resident status (permits aid to the aged, blind, or disabled). States that programs authorized under the National School Lunch Act, the Child Nutrition Act of 1966, the Vocational Education Act of 1963, chapter 1 of the Education Consolidation and Improvement Act of 1981, the Headstart-Follow Through Act, the Job Training Partnership Act, title IV of the Higher Education Act of 1965, the Public Health Service Act, and titles V, XVI, and XX of the Social Security Act shall not be construed as prohibited assistance. Continues assistance to aliens under the Refugee Education Assistance Act of 1980 without regard to adjustment of status.

Requires the Attorney General to disseminate information regarding the legalization program.

Establishes procedures for the status adjustment to permanent resident of certain Cuban and Haitian entrants who arrived in the United States before January 1, 1982.

Updates from June 30, 1948, to January 1, 1972, the registry date for permanent entry admissions records.

Authorizes FY 1988 through 1991 appropriations for State legalization impact assistance grants. Permits States to spend unused funds through FY 1994. Prohibits offsets for Medicaid and supplemental security income costs. Bases State amounts on the number of legalized aliens and related expenditures. Permits States to use such funds to reimburse public assistance, health, and education costs. Limits reimbursement to actual costs.

Title III: Reform of Legal Immigration—Part A: Temporary Agricultural Workers—Separates temporary agricultural labor from other temporary labor for purposes of nonimmigrant (H-2A visa) worker provisions.

Requires an employer H-2A visa petition to certify that: (1) there are not enough local U.S. workers for the job; and (2) similarly employed U.S. workers' wages and working conditions will not be adversely affected. Authorizes the Secretary of Labor to charge application fees.

Prohibits the Secretary from approving such petition if: (1) the job is open because of a strike or lock-out; (2) the employer violated temporary worker admissions terms; (3) in a case where such workers are not covered by State workers' compensation laws, the employer has not provided equivalent protection at no cost to such workers; or (4) the employer has not made regional recruitment efforts in the traditional or expected labor supply.

Provides with regard to agricultural worker applications that: (1) the Secretary may not require such an application to be filed more than 60 days before needed; (2) the employer shall be notified in writing within seven days if the application requires perfecting; (3) the Secretary shall approve an acceptable application not later than 20 days before needed; and (4) the employer shall provide or secure housing meeting appropriate Federal, State, or local standards, including making provision for family housing for employees principally engaged in the range production of livestock.

Provides that for three years, labor certifications for specified employers shall require such an employer to hire qualified U.S. workers who apply until the end of 50 percent of the H-2A workers' contract work period. Requires the Secretary, six months before the end of such period, to consider the advisability of continuing such requirement and to issue regulations (in the absence of enacting legislation) three months before the end of such period.

States that employers shall not be liable for specified employment penalties if H-2A workers are dismissed in order to meet such 50 percent requirement.

Permits agricultural producer associations to file H-2A petitions.

Provides for expedited administrative appeals of denied certifications.

Prohibits the entry of an alien as an H-2A worker if he or she has violated a term of admission within the previous five years.

Authorizes permanent appropriations beginning with FY 1987 for the purposes of: (1) recruiting domestic workers for temporary labor and services which might otherwise be performed by nonimmigrants and agricultural transition workers; and (2) monitoring terms and conditions under which such individuals are employed.

Authorizes permanent appropriations beginning in FY 1987 to enable the Secretary to make determinations and certifications.

Expresses the sense of the Congress that the President should establish an advisory commission to consult with Mexico and other appropriate countries and advise the Attorney General regarding the temporary worker program.

Establishes a special agricultural worker adjustment program. Provides for permanent resident adjustment for aliens who: (1) apply during a specified 18-month period; (2) have performed at least 90 man-days of seasonal agricultural work during the 12-month period ending May 1, 1986; and (3) are admissible as immigrants. Sets forth adjustment dates based upon periods of work performed in the United States. Authorizes travel and employment during such temporary residence period.

Authorizes applications to be made inside the United States with the Attorney General or designated entities and outside the United States through consular offices. Provides for confidentiality and limited access to such information. Establishes criminal penalties for false application information, and makes an alien so convicted inadmissible for U.S. entry.

Exempts such admissions from numerical entry limitations.

Permits waiver of exclusion (except for specified criminal, drug offense, public charge, Nazi persecution, and national security grounds) for humanitarian or family purposes, or when in the national interest.

Provides for a temporary stay of exclusion or deportation (and authority to work) for apprehended aliens who are able to establish a nonfrivolous claim for status adjustment.

Provides for a single level of administrative appellate review of such status adjustment applications. Limits such review of the order of exclusion or deportation.

Defines "seasonal agricultural services" as the performance of fieldwork related to growing fruits and vegetables of every kind and other perishable commodities as defined in regulations by the Secretary of Agriculture.

Directs the Secretaries of Agriculture and of Labor, jointly before each fiscal year (beginning in FY 1990 and ending in FY 1993) to determine whether additional special agricultural workers should be admitted because of a shortage of such workers in the United States. Sets forth factors to be considered in making such determinations.

Authorizes associations and groups of employers to request additional admissions due to emergency or unforeseen circumstances. Authorizes groups of special agricultural workers to request decreased admissions due to worker oversupply. Requires the Secretaries to make request determinations within 21 days.

Sets forth numerical limitations for such admissions beginning with FY 1990.

Provides for the deportation of newly admitted special agricultural workers who do not perform 60 man-days of seasonal agricultural work in each of the first two years after entry. Prohibits naturalization of such workers unless they have performed 60 man-days of such work in each of five fiscal years.

Treats temporary agricultural workers and special agricultural workers as "eligible legalized aliens" for purposes of Federal assistance to State and local entities for specified costs associated with such workers during their first five years in the United States.

Establishes a 12-member Commission on Agricultural Workers to review the special agricultural worker provisions, the impact of the legalization and employer sanctions on agricultural labor, and other aspects of agricultural labor. Requires a report to the Congress within five years. Authorizes appropriations. Terminates the Commission at the end of the 63-month period beginning with the month after the month of enactment of this Act.

States that specified agricultural workers shall be eligible for legal assistance under the Legal Service Corporation Act.

Part B: Other Changes in the Immigration Law—Increases the annual colonial quota from 600 visas to 5,000 visas.

Includes within the definition of "special immigrant": (1) unmarried sons and daughters and surviving spouses of employees of certain international organizations; and (2) specified retirees of such organizations ("I" status) and their spouses.

Grants nonimmigrant status to: (1) parents of children receiving "I" status while they are minors; and (2) other children of such parents or a surviving "I" status spouse.

Authorizes the three-year pilot visa waiver program for up to eight countries providing similar benefits to U.S. visitors. Requires such visitors to the United States to: (1) have a nonrefundable roundtrip ticket; and (2) stay in the United States for not more than 90 days.

Authorizes an additional 5,000 nonpreference visas in each of FY 1987 and 1988 with preference being given to nationals of countries who were adversely affected by Public Law 89–236 (1965 immigration amendments).

Includes the relationship between an illegitimate child and its natural father within the definition of "child" for purposes of status, benefits, or privilege under such Act.

States that for suspension of deportation purposes, an alien shall not be considered to have failed to maintain continuous physical presence in the United States if the absence did not meaningfully interrupt the continuous physical presence.

Prohibits for one year the admission of nonimmigrant alien crew members to perform services during a strike against the employer for whom such aliens intend to work.

Title IV: Reports—Directs the President to transmit to the Congress: (1) not later than January 1, 1989, and not later than January 1 of every third year thereafter, a comprehensive immigration-impact report; and (2) annual reports for three years on unauthorized alien employment and the temporary agricultural worker (H-2A) program.

Directs the Attorney General and the Secretary of State to jointly monitor the visa waiver program established by this Act, and report to the Congress within two years.

Directs the President to submit to the Congress an initial and a second report (three years after the first report) on the impact of the legalization program.

Directs the Attorney General to report to the Congress within 90 days regarding necessary improvements for INS.

Expresses the sense of the Congress that the President should consult with the President of Mexico within 90 days regarding the implementation of this Act and its possible effect on the United States or Mexico.

Title V: State Assistance for Incarceration Costs of Illegal Aliens and Certain Cuban Nationals—Directs the Attorney General to reimburse States for the costs incurred in incarcerating certain illegal aliens and Cuban nationals convicted of felonies. Authorizes appropriations.

Title VI: Commission for the Study of International Migration and Cooperative Economic Development—Establishes a 12-member Commission for the Study of International Migration and Cooperative Economic Development to examine, in consultation with Mexico and other Western Hemisphere sending countries, conditions which contribute to unauthorized migration to the United States and trade and investment programs to alleviate such conditions. Requires a report to the President and to the Congress within three years. Terminates the Commission upon filing of such report, except that the Commission may function for up to 30 additional days to conclude its affairs.

Title VII: Federal Responsibility for Deportable and Excludable Aliens Convicted of Crimes—Provides for the expeditious deportation of aliens convicted of crimes.

Provides for the identification of Department of Defense facilities that could be made available to incarcerate deportable or excludable aliens.

Source: http://thomas.loc.gov/cgi-bin/bdquery/z?d099:SN01200:@@@L&summ2=m&|TOM:/bss/d099query.html.

399. "In Memory: Remembering César Chávez," c. 1990

César Chávez (1927–1993) is the best-known Chicano/Mexican American civil rights leader. He is the symbol of David taking on Goliath—a small Chicano man taking on the large and powerful agribusiness. As head of the farmworkers he earned $5.00 a week—working over 100 hours a week in an effort to bring social, political, and economic justice to the most underpaid and exploited sector of the U.S. economy. The death of César Chávez in 1993 was a huge loss for the millions who labor on U.S. farms and vineyards and for working people of all colors. Chávez was more than a labor leader, he was an icon, and immediately after his death there were campaigns to name streets in his honor and to have a national holiday designating his birthday. In 1984, Chávez said, "Once social change begins, it cannot be reversed. You cannot uneducate the person who has learned to read. You cannot humiliate the person who feels pride. You cannot oppress the people who are not afraid anymore.... And [as] you cannot do away with an entire people, you cannot stamp out a people's cause. Regardless of what the future holds for our union, regardless of what the future holds for farmworkers, our accomplishments cannot be undone." The following document from the César E. Chávez Foundation provides a compilation of Chávez quotations from throughout his lifetime. Chávez was not only leader but also a teacher.

"People who have lost their hunger for justice are not ultimately powerful. They are like sick people who have lost their appetite for what is truly nourishing. Such sick people should not frighten or discourage us. They should be prayed for along with the sick people who are in the hospital."

"The love for justice that is in us is not only the best part of our being, but it is also the most true to our nature."

"Preservation of one's own culture does not require contempt or disrespect for other cultures."

"If you are going to organize and ask for commitment, you cannot go to the most desperately poor. They are not likely to take action. If you stand on a man's head and push it into the dirt, he may not even see the heel of your boot. But if his whole face is already above ground, he can see your heel and he can see freedom ahead."

"Years of misguided teaching have resulted in the destruction of the best in our society, in our cultures, and in the environment."

"If you really want to make a friend, go to someone's house and eat with him ... The people who give you their food give you their heart."

"Our very lives are dependent, for sustenance, on the sweat and sacrifice of the *campesinos* [farmworkers]. Children of farmworkers should be as proud of their parents' professions as other children are of theirs."

"What is at stake is human dignity. If a man is not accorded respect, he cannot respect himself, and if he does not respect himself, he cannot demand it."

"Non-violence, which is the quality of the heart, cannot come by an appeal to the brain."

Non-violence is a very powerful weapon. Most people don't understand the power of non-violence and tend to be amazed by the whole idea. Those who have been involved in bringing about change and see the difference between violence and non-violence are firmly committed to a lifetime of non-violence, not because it is easy or because it is cowardly, but because it is an effective and very powerful way."

"We cannot seek achievement for ourselves and forget about progress and prosperity for our community … Our ambitions must be broad enough to include the aspirations and needs of others, for their sakes and for our own."

Source: César E. Chávez Foundation. "In Memory: Remembering César Chávez," http://multinationalmonitor.org/hyper/issues/1993/05/mm0593_02.html.

400. Jorge R. Mancillas, "At UCLA, the Power of the Individual— Chicano Studies: The Hunger Strike Was a Morally Justifiable, Politically Reasonable Use of the Tactic," 1993

Throughout the 1980s, Chicano and Chicana students at the University of California at Los Angeles (UCLA) sponsored workshops on how to establish a Chicano Studies department. They formulated plans and a rationale for having a department rather than a program, which was what UCLA proposed. This campaign intensified under the leadership of Marcos Aguilar, Minnie Fergusson, and Bonnie Díaz. Finally, in 1993, believing that all procedures had been exhausted, led by Marcos and Minnie, nine Chicanas and Chicanos began a two-week hunger strike that was supported by Latino students throughout the Los Angeles Basin. The strike was vehemently opposed by white administrators and faculty members, as well as a number of Chicano and Latino faculty members. When the strike successfully concluded, UCLA historian Robert Dalleck alleged that the university negotiated with a gun to its head. Dalleck stated that the compromise, "happily ends the threat to the protesters' health. But it diminishes UCLA's integrity, inflames social tensions, and contributes to what historian Arthur Schlesinger, Jr., has aptly described as 'the disuniting of America.'" The following article by Jorge Mancillas, a UCLA Biology professor at the time who became part of the hunger strike and later was denied tenure, explains why he joined the hunger strike and the significance of this action.

When on the misty morning of Tuesday, May 25, a group of students and I began a hunger strike in front of Murphy Hall at UCLA, we announced that ours was not a symbolic act. We knew that we would either succeed or we would die. We did not die, and now people feel free to criticize us.

Our action has been characterized in many ways, from inspiring to irresponsible, from courageous to suicidal, but to us, it was above all an act of faith and an assumption of responsibility. We had faith in the substance and moral force of our argument. An interdepartmental program in Chicano Studies, taught by professors from traditional departments as "community service" could not fill what has become an urgent necessity in light of the racial strife tearing our society apart.

The hunger strike was decided on and led by a large, multiracial group of students; some participated in it, others organized its logistics and support activities, and others who represented us in negotiations. In a city where so many adults focus on the infantile pursuit of "fun," these young people displayed the highest sign of maturity: the willingness to assume responsibility for the solution of our social and educational problems. The young people who led me into that tent displayed more maturity than many of my elders, and I was willing to follow their lead.

In spite of our success, we have been criticized for our use of "too heavy a tactic," the use of maximal action for an issue of smaller magnitude that "was solvable by other means." This reveals a complete ignorance of history and political strategy. Gandhi used the same tactic, but he did not gain India's independence through a hunger strike. He used the tactic at specific moments within the struggle, in a given context and to achieve defined, measurable goals.

Our hunger strike had a successful outcome because we used it in support of a morally sustainable cause, at the crest of a movement and to focus other ongoing efforts, when other methods had been exhausted. Most important, we applied it in the pursuit of an objective achievable within the time frame of the limits for human survival. Ours was a morally justifiable, politically reasonable, intelligent use of the tactic.

It is ironic that our action was compared to "putting a gun to someone's head." At a time when guns are continuously [*sic*] pointed at heads and triggers pulled in the streets of our cities because of lack of understanding between people of different backgrounds, we resorted to a nonviolent approach.

Our efforts were aimed at enriching the academic curriculum for all UCLA students, regardless of their major. Upon graduation, they must not only have technical expertise in their chosen fields; they also must understand the realities of the world in which they will work.

Our society is being torn apart by tension, confrontation, and violence because of the pursuit of the politics of self-interest. Our message was that we must embrace a different approach, and be willing to give of ourselves, whatever is necessary—our lives if need be—for the collective interest, for the common good. We must pursue life, liberty, and happiness for all of us, not for some of us at the expense of others. We must leave behind the "trickle down" approach to empowerment, the belief that all will benefit in a given community if an individual representative climbs the ladders of economic and political hierarchies. We must give democracy its true meaning and all become participants in the steering of our common economic and political destiny.

The most powerful message of our hunger strike is the illustration of the power of the individual: A small group of individuals with no political power, wealth, or influence was able to play a significant role in influencing the course of events. All it takes is clarity of mind, strength of convictions, and determination.

We may have made many mistakes, and will probably make more. But as Edward R. Murrow once said, "No one makes a bigger mistake than he who did nothing because he could only do a little." Each of us can do more than we realize. Each of us alone, can only do a little. Together, we can make history.

Source: Jorge R. Mancillas, "At UCLA, the Power of the Individual Chicano Studies: The Hunger Strike Was a Morally Justifiable, Politically Reasonable Use of the Tactic," *Los Angeles Times*, June 11, 1993, p. 7.

401. "Declaration of War," December 31, 1993

El Despertador Mexicano (the *Mexican Awakener*) is the Ejército Zapatista de Liberación Nacional (Zapatista Army of National Liberation—EZLN) newspaper representing the Zapatistas. This newspaper issued the following proclamation in response to the North American Free Trade Agreement (NAFTA). The EZLN opposed globalization, or neoliberalism, arguing that it severely and negatively affected the peasant way of life of its indigenous support base by accelerating the demise of small village farms. It marked the Mexican government's abrogation of the Mexican Constitution of 1917 and the destruction of indigenous *ejidos*, communal lands. NAFTA also accelerated the migration to the United States as more peasants were uprooted because their property was privatized. The following is a declaration of war printed in *El Despertador Mexicano* on the day the North American Free Trade Treaty was to go into effect.

DECLARATION OF WAR

[from a photocopy of the original]
Lacandona Jungle, December 31, 1993

Today We Say Enough Is Enough!

TO THE PEOPLE OF MEXICO:
MEXICAN BROTHERS AND SISTERS:

We are the product of 500 years of struggle: first against slavery, then during the War of Independence against Spain led by insurgents, then to avoid being absorbed by North American imperialism, then to promulgate our constitution and expel the French Empire from our soil, and later the dictatorship of Porfirio Díaz denied us the just application of the Reform Laws, and the people rebelled and leaders like Villa and Zapata emerged, poor people just like us. We have been denied the most elemental preparation so that they can use us as cannon fodder and pillage the wealth of our country. They don't care that we have nothing, absolutely nothing, not even a roof over our heads: no land, no work, no health care, no food, no education. Nor are we able to freely and democratically elect our political representatives, nor is there independence from foreigners, nor is there peace nor justice for ourselves and our children.

But today, we say ENOUGH IS ENOUGH. We are the inheritors of the true builders of our nation. The dispossessed, we are millions, and we thereby call upon our brothers and sisters to join this struggle as the only path, so that we will not die of hunger due to the insatiable ambition of a 70-year dictatorship led by a clique of traitors who represent the most conservative and sell-out groups. They are the same ones who opposed Hidalgo and Morelos, the same ones who betrayed Vincente Guerrero, the same ones who sold half our country to the foreign invader, the same ones who imported a European prince to rule our country, the same ones who formed the "scientific" Porfirista dictatorship, the same ones who opposed the Petroleum Expropriation, the same ones who massacred the railroad workers in 1958 and the students in 1968, the same ones who today take everything from us, absolutely everything.

To prevent the continuation of the above, and as our last hope, after having tried to utilize all legal means based on our Constitution, we go to our Constitution, to apply Article 39, which says:

"National Sovereignty essentially and originally resides in the people. All political power emanates from the people and its purpose is to help the people. The people have, at all times, the inalienable right to alter or modify their form of government."

Therefore, according to our Constitution, we declare the following to the Mexican Federal Army, the pillar of the Mexican dictatorship that we suffer from, monopolized by a one-party system and led by Carlos Salinas de Gortari, the supreme and illegitimate federal executive who today holds power.

According to this Declaration of War, we ask that other powers of the nation advocate to restore the legitimacy and the stability of the nation by overthrowing the dictator.

We also ask that international organizations and the International Red Cross watch over and regulate our battles, so that our efforts are carried out while still protecting our civilian population. We declare now and always that we are subject to the Geneva Accord, forming the EZLN as the fighting arm of our liberation struggle. We have the Mexican people on our side, we have the beloved tri-colored flag, highly respected by our insurgent fighters. We use black and red in our uniform as a symbol of our working people on strike. Our flag carries the following letters, "EZLN," Zapatista National Liberation Army, and we always carry our flag into combat.

Beforehand, we reject any effort to disgrace our just cause by accusing us of being drug traffickers, drug guerrillas, thieves, or other names that might by used by our enemies. Our struggle follows the Constitution, which is held high by its call for justice and equality.

Therefore, according to this declaration of war, we give our military forces, the EZLN, the following orders:

First: Advance to the capital of the country, overcoming the Mexican Federal Army, protecting in our advance the civilian population and permitting the people in the liberated area the right to freely and democratically elect their own administrative authorities.

Second: Respect the lives of our prisoners and turn over all wounded to the International Red Cross.

Third: Initiate summary judgments against all soldiers of the Mexican Federal Army and the political police who have received training or have been paid by foreigners, accused of being traitors to our country, and against all those who have repressed and treated badly the civilian population, and robbed, or stolen from, or attempted crimes against the good of the people.

Fourth: Form new troops with all those Mexicans who show their interest in joining our struggle, including those who, being enemy soldiers, turn themselves in without having fought against us, and promise to take orders from the General Command of the EZLN.

Fifth: We ask for the unconditional surrender of the enemy's headquarters before we begin any combat to avoid any loss of lives.

Sixth: Suspend the robbery of our natural resources in the areas controlled by the EZLN.

To the People of Mexico:

We, the men and women, full and free, are conscious that the war that we have declared is our last resort, but also a just one. The dictators have been waging an undeclared genocidal war against our people for many years. Therefore we ask for your participation, your decision to support this plan that struggles for work, land, housing, food, health care, education, independence, freedom, democracy, justice and peace. We declare that we will not stop fighting until the basic demands of our people have been met by forming a government of our country that is free and democratic.

JOIN THE INSURGENT FORCES OF THE ZAPATISTA NATIONAL LIBERATION ARMY!

General Command of the EZLN
December 31, 1993

Source: "Join the Insurgent Forces of the Zapatista National Liberation Army!" General Command of the EZLN, December 31, 1993, El Despertador Mexicano, December 31, 1993, Zapatistas Documents of the New Mexican Revolution, Courtesy of Robert McCaa, Professor, Department of History, International Projects Coordinator, Minnesota Population Center, University of Minnesota. http://www.hist.umn.edu/rmccaa/la20c/index.htm.

402. California Proposition 187: Illegal Aliens. Ineligibility for Public Services, 1994

Jean Stefancic and Richard Delgado in their 1996 book, *No Mercy: How Conservative Think Tanks and Foundations Changed America's Social Agenda* analyze the conservative right's rise to power in the United States. The conservative sector out-organized progressive and civil rights groups in influencing the country's political, social, and education agendas. They have formed conservative think tanks and foundations that systematically affected a conservative revolution. Their method was to fund a variety of issue-oriented studies and programs. Not by accident, well endowed right-wing groups funded anti-immigrant programs and leglislation such as English Only, California's Proposition 187 (which denied public services to undocumented immigrants when passed in 1994), and race and eugenics studies aiming to prove that intelligence could be racially determined. Attempts were also mounted to water down affirmative action, restrict welfare, manipulate tort reform, and slow campus multiculturalism. Campaigns against immigrant and minority groups such as Latinos were a win–win situation because undocumented immigrants were poor and they could not vote. California's "Prop 187" was called Save Our State (SOS), which was, according to racist nativists, a long-overdue distress signal. The number 187 is also the numeric code for the crime of murder, which is used by law-enforcement to designate when this type of crime is in progress. Two-thirds of Latino voters voted against the proposition and an equal proportion of white Americans voted for it. The successful passage of Proposition 187 backfired because many Latinos saw it as a racist attack on the entire community and voted against Republicans. The following is a voter analysis of the proposition. Although it passed, much of Proposition 187 was stricken down by the courts. Nevertheless, Proposition 187 was the prototype for similar bills in other states.

PROP 187: ILLEGAL ALIENS. INELIGIBILITY FOR PUBLIC SERVICES

The Way It Is Now:

About 1 in 5 Californians were born in another country. Most of these 7 million people have become citizens or have official approval to be here. There are about 1.6 million illegal immigrants in California who are not authorized to be here. They are also called illegal aliens.

It is against the law to hire an illegal immigrant, but many find jobs anyway. Illegal immigrants are not eligible for programs like welfare, but can get emergency and prenatal health services. A child born in California to illegal immigrants is a citizen and has the same rights as other citizens.

What Prop 187 Would Do:

- Stop state and local agencies from providing any public education, health care, or other social services to illegal immigrants except for emergency health care.
- Government agencies and schools will have to verify the legal status of anyone receiving services. They are required to report anyone suspected of being an illegal immigrant.
- Make it a felony to make or use a false ID that tries to get around this law. Note: part of Prop 187 may be overruled by a U.S. Supreme Court ruling that all children must be allowed to go to public school.

What It Will Cost:

- About $200 million per year would be saved from not providing health and social services to illegal immigrants.
- It could cost about $100 million to set up the systems needed to check everyone's legal status, especially for schools who have never had to check this before. After that, it might cost $10–20 million per year to verify status.
- There is a risk of losing up to $15 billion in federal funds for Medi-Cal, AFDC, and education because of conflicts with federal privacy laws.

Pros:

"Prop 187 will stop the services that are attracting illegal immigrants across our border. A lot of California's population growth is because of illegal immigrants."

"We don't have enough money to provide important services to legal citizens. We cannot afford to offer services to illegal immigrants."

"The federal government is not doing a good job of stopping illegal immigration. Prop 187 takes action instead of waiting for the Feds."

Cons:

"Prop 187 runs against state and federal laws and the Constitution. The answer to illegal immigration is to tighten our borders and crack down on employers who hire illegals."

"Prop 187 does not send illegal immigrants home. It will pull 400,000 students out of school and leave them on the streets."

"Prop 187 will make California a police state and increase racism. People will be suspected as illegal based on how they look and talk."

Source: California Voter Foundation, 1994, http://www.calvoter.org/archive/94general/easy/meas/187.html.

403. Glynn Custred and Tom Wood, "California's Proposition 209," 1996

California voters approved Proposition 209 in 1996. This legislation prohibited California institutions from discriminating on the basis of race, ethnicity, or gender. In reality, its purpose was to protect white males, and it set the stage for copycat efforts to abolish affirmative action. Unlike Proposition 187, which passed in 1994 and refused public services to undocumented immigrants, Proposition 209 had allies in the civil rights and women's movement. It passed by a margin of eight percentage points, which was not overwhelming. The "Yes on 209" Campaign outspent opponents 3–1. Like 187, it was heavily funded by right-wing foundations and think tanks. The result was that it drastically cut minority enrollment in higher education. The following document provides the text of this initiative.

Following is the text of the California Civil Rights Initiative, Proposition 209 on the November 1996 ballot, which was passed on November 5th by 54 percent of California voters.

(a) The state shall not discriminate against, or grant preferential treatment to, any individual or group on the basis of race, sex, color, ethnicity, or national origin in the operation of public employment, public education, or public contracting.

(b) This section shall apply only to action taken after the section's effective date.

(c) Nothing in this section shall be interpreted as prohibiting bona fide qualifications based on sex which are reasonably necessary to the normal operation of public employment, public education, or public contracting.

(d) Nothing in this section shall be interpreted as invalidating any court order or consent decree which is in force as of the effective date of this section.

(e) Nothing in this section shall be interpreted as prohibiting action which must be taken to establish or maintain eligibility for any federal program, where ineligibility would result in a loss of federal funds to the state.

(f) For the purposes of this section, "state" shall include, but not necessarily be limited to, the state itself, any city, county, city and county, public university system, including the University of California, community college district, school district, special district, or any other political subdivision or governmental instrumentality of or within the state.

(g) The remedies available for violations of this section shall be the same, regardless of the injured party's race, sex, color, ethnicity, or national origin, as are otherwise available for violations of then-existing California anti-discrimination law.

(h) This section shall be self-executing. If any part or parts of this section are found to be in conflict with federal law or the United States Constitution, the section shall be implemented to the maximum extent that federal law and the United

States Constitution permit. Any provision held invalid shall be severable from the remaining portions of this section.

Source: California Civil Rights Initiative, Proposition 209, State of California.

404. Ron K. Unz and Gloria Matta Tuchman, "Initiative Statute: English Language Education for Children in Public Schools," 1998

California passed Proposition 227, abolished bilingual education, in 1998. States like Arizona mimicked California with similar legislation in the year 2000. This attack on bilingual education was disheartening since bilingual education was a fundamental part of the Latino and Mexican American civil rights struggle. The California model was aimed at banning bilingual education for virtually all children learning English as a second language. Arizona's English-only schools initiative was called Proposition 203. Like the California measure, it was spearheaded by Ron Unz, a Silicon Valley millionaire. It mandates English language achievement tests for all Arizona students, regardless of their English proficiency. The following is a copy of the California model.

SECTION 1

Chapter 3 (commencing with Section 300) is added to Part 1 of the Educational Code, to read:

CHAPTER 3. ENGLISH LANGUAGE EDUCATION FOR IMMIGRANT CHILDREN

Article 1. Findings and Declarations

300. The People of California find and declare as follows:

(a) WHEREAS the English language is the national public language of the United States of America and of the state of California, is spoken by the vast majority of California residents, and is also the leading world language for science, technology, and international business, thereby being the language of economic opportunity; and

(b) WHEREAS immigrant parents are eager to have their children acquire a good knowledge of English, thereby allowing them to fully participate in the American Dream of economic and social advancement; and

(c) WHEREAS the government and the public schools of California have a moral obligation and a constitutional duty to provide all of California's children, regardless of their ethnicity or national origins, with the skills necessary to become productive members of our society, and of these skills, literacy in the English language is among the most important; and

(d) WHEREAS the public schools of California currently do a poor job of educating immigrant children, wasting financial resources on costly experimental language programs whose failure over the past two decades is demonstrated by the current high drop-out rates and low English literacy levels of many immigrant children; and

(e) WHEREAS young immigrant children can easily acquire full fluency in a new language, such as English, if they are heavily exposed to that language in the classroom at an early age,

(f) THEREFORE it is resolved that: all children in California public schools shall be taught English as rapidly and effectively as possible.

Article 2. English Language Education

305. Subject to the exceptions provided in Article 3 (commencing with Section 310), all children in California public schools shall be taught English by being taught in English. In particular, this shall require that all children be placed in English language classrooms. Children who are English learners shall be educated through sheltered English immersion during a temporary transition period not normally intended to exceed one year. Local schools shall be permitted to place in the same classroom English learners of different ages but whose degree of English proficiency is similar. Local schools shall be encouraged to mix together in the same classroom English learners from different native-language groups but with the same degree of English fluency. Once English learners have acquired a good working knowledge of English, they shall be transferred to English language mainstream classrooms. As much as possible, current supplemental funding for English learners shall be maintained, subject to possible modification under Article 8 (commencing with Section 335) below.

306. The definitions of the terms used in this article and in Article 3 (commencing with Section 310) are as follows:

(a) "English learner" means a child who does not speak English or whose native language is not English and who is not currently able to perform ordinary classroom work in English, also known as a Limited English Proficiency or LEP child.

(b) "English language classroom" means a classroom in which the language of instruction used by the teaching personnel is overwhelmingly the English language, and in which such teaching personnel possess a good knowledge of the English language.

(c) "English language mainstream classroom" means a classroom in which the students either are native English language speakers or already have acquired reasonable fluency in English.

(d) "Sheltered English immersion" or "structured English immersion" means an English language acquisition process for young children in which nearly all classroom instruction is in English but with the curriculum and presentation designed for children who are learning the language.

(e) "Bilingual education/native language instruction" means a language acquisition process for students in which much or all instruction, textbooks, and teaching materials are in the child's native language.

Article 3. Parental Exceptions

310. The requirements of Section 305 may be waived with the prior written informed consent, to be provided annually, of the child's parents or legal guardian under the circumstances specified below and in Section 311. Such informed consent shall require that said parents or legal guardian personally visit the school to apply

for the waiver and that they there be provided a full description of the educational materials to be used in the different educational program choices and all the educational opportunities available to the child. Under such parental waiver conditions, children may be transferred to classes where they are taught English and other subjects through bilingual education techniques or other generally recognized educational methodologies permitted by law. Individual schools in which 20 students or more of a given grade level receive a waiver shall be required to offer such a class; otherwise, they must allow the students to transfer to a public school in which such a class is offered.

311. The circumstances in which a parental exception waiver may be granted under Section 310 are as follows:

(a) Children who already know English: the child already possesses good English language skills, as measured by standardized tests of English vocabulary comprehension, reading, and writing, in which the child scores at or above the state average for his grade level or at or above the 5th grade average, whichever is lower; or

(b) Older children: the child is age 10 years or older, and it is the informed belief of the school principal and educational staff that an alternate course of educational study would be better suited to the child's rapid acquisition of basic English language skills; or

(c) Children with special needs: the child already has been placed for a period of not less than thirty days during that school year in an English language classroom and it is subsequently the informed belief of the school principal and educational staff that the child has such special physical, emotional, psychological, or educational needs that an alternate course of educational study would be better suited to the child's overall educational development. A written description of these special needs must be provided and any such decision is to be made subject to the examination and approval of the local school superintendent, under guidelines established by and subject to the review of the local Board of Education and ultimately the State Board of Education. The existence of such special needs shall not compel issuance of a waiver, and the parents shall be fully informed of their right to refuse to agree to a waiver.

Article 4. Community-Based English Tutoring

315. In furtherance of its constitutional and legal requirement to offer special language assistance to children coming from backgrounds of limited English proficiency, the state shall encourage family members and others to provide personal English language tutoring to such children, and support these efforts by raising the general level of English language knowledge in the community. Commencing with the fiscal year in which this initiative is enacted and for each of the nine fiscal years following thereafter, a sum of fifty million dollars ($50,000,000) per year is hereby appropriated from the General Fund for the purpose of providing additional funding for free or subsidized programs of adult English language instruction to parents or other members of the community who pledge to provide personal English language tutoring to California school children with limited English proficiency.

316. Programs funded pursuant to this section shall be provided through schools or community organizations. Funding for these programs shall be administered by the Office of the Superintendent of Public Instruction, and shall be disbursed at the

discretion of the local school boards, under reasonable guidelines established by, and subject to the review of, the State Board of Education.

Article 5. Legal Standing and Parental Enforcement

320. As detailed in Article 2 (commencing with Section 305) and Article 3 (commencing with Section 310), all California school children have the right to be provided with an English language public education. If a California school child has been denied the option of an English language instructional curriculum in public school, the child's parent or legal guardian shall have legal standing to sue for enforcement of the provisions of this statute, and if successful shall be awarded normal and customary attorney's fees and actual damages, but not punitive or consequential damages. Any school board member or other elected official or public school teacher or administrator who willfully and repeatedly refuses to implement the terms of this statute by providing such an English language educational option at an available public school to a California school child may be held personally liable for fees and actual damages by the child's parents or legal guardian.

Article 6. Severability

325. If any part or parts of this statute are found to be in conflict with federal law or the United States or the California State Constitution, the statute shall be implemented to the maximum extent that federal law, and the United States and the California State Constitution permit. Any provision held invalid shall be severed from the remaining portions of this statute.

Article 7. Operative Date

330. This initiative shall become operative for all school terms which begin more than sixty days following the date at which it becomes effective.

Article 8. Amendment

335. The provisions of this act may be amended by a statute that becomes effective upon approval by the electorate or by a statute to further the act's purpose passed by a two-thirds vote of each house of the Legislature and signed by the Governor.

Article 9. Interpretation

340. Under circumstances in which portions of this statute are subject to conflicting interpretations, Section 300 shall be assumed to contain the governing intent of the statute.

Ron K. Unz, a high-technology entrepreneur, is Chairman of One Nation/One California, 555 Bryant St. #371, Palo Alto, CA 94301.

Gloria Matta Tuchman, an elementary school teacher, is Chair of REBILLED, the Committee to Reform Bi-Lingual Education, 1742 Lerner Lane, Santa Ana, CA 92705.

Source: Ron K. Unz and Gloria Matta Tuchman, "Initiative Statute: English Language Education for Children in Public Schools," 1998, Center for Multilingual, Multicultural Research, University of Southern California, http://www-rcf.usc.edu/cmmr/Unz_text.html.

405. Patrisia Gonzales and Roberto Rodríguez, "Aztlán Draws Ire of Anti-Immigrants," 1998

Aztlán is the legendary ancestral home of the Nahua peoples, one of the main cultural groups in Mesoamerica. According to legend, the Nahua people were from an area that some have located in Utah. Nativists claimed that Chicano folklore appropriated the name for that portion of Mexico that was taken by the United States after the Mexican-American War of 1846. Far from appropriation, it was adopted at a time of intense racism when Chicanos and other Latinos made demands for human and civil rights. Aztlán was a reminder to racist nativists that Chicanos and Latinos were in North America long before the nativists who told them to go back to where they came from. Accordingly, Chicanos had a historic right of being in the United States. However, nativists persisted with the claim that Aztlán was a symbol for nationalism and meant Chicanos wanted to reconquer the Southwest, a claim that has no basis in fact. In the following article, two respected Chicano columnists and scholars discuss Aztlán and give historical evidence of its existence.

About once a week, someone calls us "Aztlanistas." It's supposed to be some sort of McCarthy-type insult. Aztlán, according to our accusers, is another Quebec.

Accordingly, we're also accused of supporting the "separatist" organization, MEChA, or Movimiento Estudiantil Chicano de Aztlán—a national student organization that promotes education and defends the rights of Chicanos/Mexicans and Central and South Americans. We find their work honorable and their philosophy misunderstood.

Aztlán as a 1960s political idea sought to reclaim the original homeland of the indigenous Mexica or Mexican/Chicano people. Thirty years ago, Aztlán was symbolically represented by the lands lost by Mexico when the United States warred on its neighbor in 1846. A generation later, a new idea of Aztlán is emerging, particularly among the young members, that they're part of a pan-indigenous spiritual nation, not necessarily part of a geopolitical entity. As an anonymous Xicana from Michigan wrote to us last year: "Aztlán is everywhere I've ever walked."

While some still cling to the 1960s expression of Aztlán, its new adherents are not nationalist, nor do they support patriarchal ideas that relegate women to supporting roles. Many are women who spell Chicana with an X, symbolizing their indigenous roots. Theirs is not a separatist movement. Aztlán has re-emerged in response to this population, Mexican/Latinos, being dehumanized to the point where today many of this country's problems are attributed to them. This feeling of being under siege has created a spirit of unity and a spiritual kinship with people from all of the Americas. To some, the idea of Aztlán indeed sounds like Quebec's separatist movement. Yet, this population did not elect to be designated and treated by the government as a permanent lower caste of minorities and aliens. Nor have they chosen to be segregated by corporations as the "Hispanic market." Interestingly, this "segmentation," because it involves hundreds of billions of dollars, is not seen by mainstream society as separation, but rather as part of the American way.

For those who have been marginalized, viewing themselves as part of a spiritual nation is both dignified and liberating. Many view themselves as partaking in a process of self-identity, not bound by government or corporate definitions, which they see as contributing to the systematic eradication of their culture. Many consider the U.S. Census Bureau's designation of this population as "white" a throwback to an era of shame and a continued effort to obliterate the Indian or African within them. To outsiders, the aforementioned ideas may seem unintelligible, but they aren't. All it takes is a little knowledge to understand why this population gets angry when the government and school textbooks erase their history. They view the ripping away of their roots as the first step toward their delegitimization and as lending credence to the idea that they're foreigners.

For many, Aztlán is simply about bringing a dignity to themselves at a time when they perceive a full-scale attack against their culture via an encirclement of forced assimilation policies. And the irony is that these policies—which manifest themselves in national movements against immigration, affirmative action, bilingual education and ethnic studies, plus the militarization of the U.S./Mexico border—are essentially fueling that quest for dignity.

Having a MEChA background should be a source of pride, not consternation. For example, not long after Norma Chávez led a six-mile march on behalf of the United Farm Workers Union—in 110-degree heat in El Paso, Texas—she was elected to the state House of Representatives in 1996. And Antonio Villaraigoza, Joe Baca, and Gilbert Cedillo—MEChA members at UCLA in the 1970s—are now California Assembly members. Villaraigoza, the speaker of the assembly, who is being honored at this year's national MEChA conference at UCLA this month, runs one of the nation's most powerful state bodies. And yet, he's been derided by foes as undeserving of the post because he was once a MEChista. Antonia Hernandez, president and general counsel of the Mexican American Legal Defense and Educational Fund (and former MEChA member), will be keynoting the conference.

All are examples of human beings who have not betrayed their principles and who today carry on their human rights battles in halls of power. There's no dishonor in that or in believing in Aztlán.

Source: Patrisia Gonzales and Roberto Rodríguez, "Aztlan Draws Ire of Anti-Immigrants," Universal Press Syndicate, Week of April 10, 1998. Column of the Americas.

406. Excerpts from Rakesh Kochhar, Roberto Suro, and Sonya Tafoya, "Report: The New Latino South: The Context and Consequences of Rapid Population Growth," 2005

Although the overwhelming majority of Mexican immigrants has been concentrated in the Southwest, by the 1990s, Mexican and other Latino immigrants were moving heavily into the American South. This migration was encouraged by the modernizing of the southern economy and a shortage of labor that was of crisis proportion. This encouraged Latino immigrants, both documented and undocumented, to fill the gap. The 1990s saw the Latino population in the South increase more than 200 percent. Some counties experienced more than 1,000 percent growth. It has been estimated that some 80 percent of those immigrants are undocumented. The following excerpts concern the growth of the Latino immigrant population in the South.

The Hispanic population is growing faster in much of the South than anywhere else in the United States. Across a broad swath of the region stretching westward from North Carolina on the Atlantic seaboard to Arkansas across the Mississippi River and south to Alabama on the Gulf of Mexico, sizeable Hispanic populations have emerged suddenly in communities where Latinos were a sparse presence just a decade or two ago. Examined both individually and collectively, these communities display attributes that set them apart from the nation as a whole and from areas of the country where Latinos have traditionally settled. In the South, the white and black populations are also increasing and the local economies are growing robustly, even as some undergo dramatic restructuring. Such conditions have acted as a magnet to young, male, foreign-born Latinos migrating in search of economic opportunities. While these trends are not unique to the South, they are playing out in that region with a greater intensity and across a larger variety of communities—rural, small towns, suburbs, and big cities—than in any other part of the country. Understanding the interplay of Hispanic population growth and the conditions that attended it helps illuminate a broad process of demographic and economic change in the South and in other new settlement areas as well. To varying degrees, communities scattered from New England to the Pacific Northwest are also seeing surging Hispanic populations. The South, different in so many ways for so much of its history, now offers lessons to the rest of the country. Most of the Latinos added to the population of the new settlement areas of the South are foreign born, and their migration is the product of a great many different policies and circumstances in the United States and their home countries. But there is a local context as well, and it is different in the new settlement areas of the South than it is in states such as California and New York, where migrants join large, well-established Latino communities. Given its distinctive character, Hispanic population growth in these parts of the South will also have distinctive impacts on public policy, and those impacts have only just begun to be felt. This report focuses on six Southern states—Arkansas, Alabama, Georgia, North Carolina, South Carolina, and Tennessee—that registered very fast rates of Hispanic population growth between the censuses of 1990 and 2000 and continue to outpace the national average in the most recent census estimates.... This report also examines 36 counties in the South that are experiencing especially rapid Hispanic growth. Some of these counties contain metropolitan areas such as Atlanta, Georgia; Birmingham, Alabama; and Charlotte, North Carolina; that registered huge increases in their Hispanic populations—for example, Mecklenburg County, North Carolina, which includes Charlotte, was up 500 percent. But other counties are predominately rural or contain smaller cities. Their total population in 2000 ranged from fewer than 37,000 (Murray County, a carpet manufacturing community in northwest Georgia) to almost 900,000 (Shelby County, Tennessee, home to Memphis). Thirty-six of these counties, all with an increase in their Hispanic population of 200 percent or more, had enough statistical information available to be studied in detail for this report. And in every case, the Hispanic population was relatively small before it surged. Fewer than 7,000 Hispanics were counted in Mecklenburg in 1990, but by 2000 there were nearly 45,000. Gordon County, Georgia, had just 200 Latinos in 1990 and saw its Hispanic population soar to more than 3,200 by the 2000 census....

Several features distinguish the kind of Hispanic population growth taking place in the new settlement areas of the South: its speed, its relation to the growth of other population groups and the characteristics of the Latinos settling there. In the six southern states with the fastest Latino growth, the Hispanic population quadrupled between 1990 and 2000. That rapid growth reflects the fact that the Latino numbers started quite small, but it represents an extraordinarily quick demographic change nonetheless. And Latinos are not the only group that is growing. In most areas of the South experiencing very rapid Latino growth from a very small base, the numbers of whites and blacks are also increasing, albeit at slower rates. That is not the case in many other parts of the country, where the non-Hispanic populations are static or declining. Finally, the Latino population added to the new settlement areas of the South is younger, more immigrant, and more male than the Hispanic population overall. This has all the characteristics of labor migration in its early stages....

Aside from its speed, Hispanic population growth in these six states is distinctive because it occurred against a backdrop of simultaneous growth in the rest of the population. In other words, although Latinos are a rapidly growing presence in these six states, they are only one factor in an overall pattern of population growth, and in fact they are a relatively small factor in the broader picture. Both whites and blacks contributed greater numbers to the total population increase in these six Southern states, and this trend has held steady since at least 1990. These states are drawing not just Latinos but others as well, and very fast Hispanic population growth is for the most part happening in places where the whole population is growing robustly.

The total population of these six southern states grew by nearly 5.2 million between 1990 and 2000, and Hispanics made up only about 900,000 or 17 percent of that increase. Meanwhile, growth in the white population (2.3 million) accounted for 45 percent of the total increase and added numbers of blacks (1.3 million) accounted for 26 percent. Thus, even if not one Latino had been added to the population of this region, it still would have experienced notable growth.

This picture of rapid Latino growth amid overall growth distinguishes these southern states both from the nation as a whole and from California, New York, New Jersey, and Illinois, states that have large, well-established Latino populations....

Mexico is the country of origin for more Hispanic immigrants in the United States than all other nations put together, accounting for 64 percent of all Latino immigrants. That dominance is even stronger in the six new settlement states in this study, where those born in Mexico make up 73 percent of foreign-born Latinos.... Recent data also suggest that some new settlements in the South may be drawing a relatively larger share of migrants from regions of Mexico that have only recently begun sending large numbers of immigrants when compared with the traditional settlement states of California, Illinois, New Jersey, and New York....

The growth in the employment of Hispanic and non-Hispanic workers in the new settlement states and counties was well in excess of the nationwide rate. Data from the decennial censuses show that total employment in the U.S. for Hispanic workers increased by 48.6 percent between 1990 and 2000. However, the increase in employment of Latinos in the six new settlement states was much higher than the nationwide rate. The smallest increase was in Alabama, but even so, the employment of Latino workers there increased by 244 percent. The largest increase, 495 percent, occurred in North Carolina. In the six new settlement states combined, Latino employment was 349 percent higher in 2000 than in 1990. The employment of non-Hispanic workers increased by 14.9 percent in the six Southern states. This was well above the national average growth of 9.1 percent for non-Hispanics in the

1990s. Georgia led the way for non-Hispanic workers as their employment increased by 19.8 percent in that state. However, the new South was more critical to the growth in jobs for non-Hispanic than for Hispanic workers. While the percentage increases in the employment of Latinos are astounding, the absolute increases in number are more modest. In the six southern states combined, the total increase in Hispanic employment was just over 404,000, and that accounted for less than 10 percent of the nationwide increase of 4.4 million in Latino employment. All together, these six states added jobs for 1.9 million non-Hispanic workers between 1990 and 2000. That amounted to 20 percent of the nationwide increase of 9.7 million in non-Latino employment. Overall, more than 80 percent of the new jobs created in these states in the 1990s were filled by non-Hispanic workers and fewer than 20 percent by Hispanics. The Hispanic share of new jobs was much higher on a nationwide basis as Latinos captured 31 percent of the 14 million new jobs created nationally between 1990 and 2000....

Hispanic workers in diverse counties are also likely to be found in management, professional, and related occupations but their representation in these occupations (13.2%) in diverse counties was below their national average (16.1%) in 2000. Similarly, Latinos were far less likely (6.9%) than the national norm (13.7%) to be found in office and administrative-support occupations in diverse counties. These tendencies are, no doubt, a reflection of the fact that Latinos in the new South are far more likely to be foreign born than in the rest of the country.

White and black workers are also far more likely to be found in white-collar occupations in diverse counties in comparison with other counties. In fact, 40.1% of whites could be found in management, professional, and related occupations alone in the diverse counties, well above their national average of 31.6% in 2000. Conversely, white workers were less likely than the national average to be employed as construction or production workers in diverse counties....

Nationally, Latinos were earning 61 percent as much as whites in 2000. The situation was approximately the same in manufacturing oriented counties, as Latinos earned 64 percent as much as whites in manufacturing counties and 58 percent as much in transition counties. But the median income of whites in diverse counties is significantly higher than in the other counties—$34,100 versus $26,000 or less in the other county groups. This reflects the far greater opportunities in white-collar occupations for white workers in diverse counties. Consequently, Hispanic workers earned only 47 percent as much as white workers in diverse counties in 2000....

Source: © 2005 Pew Hispanic Center, a Pew Research Center project, www.pewhispanic.org. Prepared by the Pew Hispanic Center for presentation at "Immigration to New Settlement Areas," July 26, 2005, pp. i–ii, 1, 6, 13, 25, 33–34.

407. Excerpts from Stuart Silverstein, "Racial Issues Lose Urgency, Study Finds; UCLA Survey Shows That a Record High Percentage of College Freshmen Believe Discrimination Is No Longer a Major Problem in the U.S.," 2005

In a 2005 University of California at Los Angeles (UCLA) survey, freshman Karina Hernández said she did not recall ever having been discriminated against as a Latina; she was not particularly concerned with the issue of race and ethnic relations. The UCLA survey found 22.7 percent of freshmen believed that racial discrimination no longer is a major problem. Race did not seem to matter as much as in the previous generation. This was reflected in other national surveys. The following excerpts provide a summary of the UCLA survey. The survey is interesting because raises the questions of whether racism exists in our present day society or if we just don't recognize it. It is not as blatant as in the 1940s when Mexicans were called greasers and were not allowed to use public facilities or in the 1960s when greater numbers were drafted into the army and fewer attended institutions of higher learning. What form does racism take today?

[National survey results found that:]

- Freshmen were more polarized politically. Students describing themselves as "middle of the road" remained the biggest group, at 46.4%, but that percentage was the smallest in more than 30 years and was down from 50.3% in 2003. Liberals accounted for 26.1% and conservatives 21.9%. Students describing themselves as "far left" climbed to 3.4%, and those as "far right" rose to 2.2%—both record highs.
- A record high 47.2% of freshmen said there was a very good chance that they would have to get a job during the year to pay for college expenses, versus a low of 35.3% in 1989.
- Students who reported frequently being bored in class during their last year of high school climbed to a record 42.8%, up from 40.1% a year earlier and from a low of 29.3% in 1985.

The survey—titled "The American Freshman: National Forms for Fall 2004"— was conducted by the Cooperative Institutional Research Program, a unit of UCLA's Higher Education Research Institute.

The findings were based on responses to a four-page questionnaire filled out last summer and fall by 289,452 entering freshmen at 440 four-year colleges around the country. The margin for error is 0.1% for the national results and 0.3% for the California results.

Source: Stuart Silverstein, "Racial Issues Lose Urgency, Study Finds; UCLA survey shows that a record high percentage of college freshmen believe discrimination is no longer a major problem in the U.S.," *Los Angeles Times*, January 31, 2005, p. 3.

408. Testimony of María Elena Durazo before the Subcommittee on Employer–Employee Relations, Committee on Education and the Workforce, U.S. House of Representatives, July 21, 1999

The highest-ranking officer in the Los Angeles Federation of Labor is the secretary/treasurer. The first Mexican American to hold this position was Miguel Contreras, who died in 2005. Under Contreras' leadership the County Federation had been more proactive in promoting the political interests of Latinos. His wife, María Elena Durazo, a long-time leader of the Hotel Employees and Restaurant Employees (HERE) International Union, was elected to her late husband's former post in 2006, making her the most powerful Latina in Los Angeles. She is a strong advocate of immigrant rights, and as a youth had been active in Movimiento Estudiantil Chicano/a de Aztlán (MEChA), student groups, and the Centro de Accion Social Autonoma (Center for Autonomous Social Action—CASA), an organization for immigrant rights. Both MEChA and CASA trained a generation of political, civil, and labor leaders. At the time of her testimony before Congress in 1999, Durazo was the president of the Hotel Employee Restaurant Employees International Union. The following document gives us an insight into one of the Mexican American community's leading figures and how she helped build the union.

My name is María Elena Durazo, V.P. at large of the HERE International Union and I am also the elected President of HERE Local 11 in Los Angeles, California.

My parents are immigrants from Mexico and our family of 10 children worked in the fields of California as migrant farmworkers until I was in high school. I started in the labor movement as an organizer in the garment sweatshops with the then ILGWU [International Ladies Garment Workers Union].

I got hired as an organizer at Local 11 in 1983 and for 4 years I witnessed a Union deteriorate right before my very eyes. The leadership of that Local had a policy of exclusion. Seventy percent of the members are immigrants from Mexico and Central America. The meetings were held in English only; the publications were sent out in English only, and members rarely attended meetings. The office closed down at 4 P.M.—the time most members were getting off their shifts.

As a result of their exclusion, the members had no voice in their Union and on the job. They had no training to know their rights. The Union was weak because the members did not participate, and therefore the Union did not have the ability to negotiate fair contracts.

In 1987, I led a rank and file effort to change the leadership and direction of our Union. We were inexperienced and we had a very weak Union of which the employers took full advantage. During the internal election period, charges were made back and forth about the campaigning. The incumbent asked for the [HERE] International Union to step in and a Trusteeship was declared.

Needless to say I was angry and skeptical; I suspected that the International Union was only intervening to save the incumbent from being kicked out. One thing was sure: I was unwilling to give up on our goals—that our members participate in the decisions of the Union because those decisions impact their lives and that employers treat the members with respect, whether they are dishwashers or front desk clerks, or housekeepers.

As it turned out, the International assigned some of their best staff, former organizers with César Chávez and the United Farm Workers Union. The International Union started making the changes we fought for:

- Shop steward system to train the rank and file on their rights;
- Worker participation in negotiating contracts with their employers; and
- All meetings and publications were bilingual (Spanish and English).

Congress and President Reagan had just signed the IRCA [Immigration Reform and Control Act], which created opportunities for members to legalize their status. The International Union gave the local $100,000 to assist our members through the amnesty process.

While Western Regional Director, President John Wilhelm twice negotiated our citywide hotel contract covering more than 4,000 members, we won historic collective bargaining agreements, the best wage increases in decades; we won a pre-paid legal plan with a panel of attorneys to provide free legal services to members, and we protected free family health insurance.

In 1989, the Trusteeship ended, I ran for President, and our entire slate won. I was fortunate that the International continued to provide staff and resources for several years until we could get back on our feet, and learn how to run the Local.

We have built our health, welfare, and pension funds to make major improvements; we quadrupled the pension benefits from the miserable level it had been at for 25 years. President Wilhelm taught us to work hard to establish partnerships with employers and we have succeeded. We also learned that we must fight back if that partnership is rejected and if our members' livelihood is threatened.

In 1996, I am proud to have been elected the first Latina to the National Executive Board of HERE.

Today, Local 11 is a strong, financially viable Union, with a strong presence in Los Angeles; specifically we are known for standing up for issues of concern to the Latino community. We are also known in the broader circles of business and political leadership in the city to promote responsible economic development that includes the needs of workers. Under both Democratic and Republican mayors, I have been appointed to serve on key City Commissions and Boards.

I have learned that it is easier to tear down than to build. During the last 12 years we have worked hard to rebuild this Local. Cooks, dishwashers, and housekeepers participate in negotiating their own contracts and their co-workers vote on whether or not to accept those contracts. Our monthly meetings have grown in numbers because we work hard to make sure the members participate in our Union's daily activities and because our meetings are held in both Spanish and English. The overwhelming majority of our new hires for positions as organizers and Union representatives come from the membership. We have monthly training for shop stewards and committees. We are vibrant. We depend on the participation of our members to make decisions about what is important to them and their families. There is no doubt in my mind that without the help and resources of our International Union, and the training we received personally from President Wilhelm, we would not have gotten this far.

Source: http://edworkforce.house.gov/hearings/106th/eer/ud72199/durazo.htm.

409. Linda Lutton, "Old-Time Chicago Politics Aren't Dead Yet— Just Ask 'Chuy' García," 1998

Before entering politics, Jesús García was a community activist and prominent member of the Centro de Accion Social Autonoma (Center for Autonomous Social Action—CASA). A native of Durango, Mexico, García, like so many Mexicans in Chicago, arrived in Chicago at an early age. In 1986, he was elected as alderman and committeeman for the 22nd Ward as one of the city's first Mexican American aldermen. He became an Illinois state senator in 1992, representing the Pilsen and Little Village Districts, which were heavily Mexican American. It surprised his supporters that García lost his state senate seat in 1998. He had gotten his first office as a supporter of Chicago reformer, Mayor Harold Washington. García became the executive director of the Little Village Community Development Corporation (LVCDC). The following article discusses his loss and was written at the time of García's state senate defeat.

Jesús "Chuy" García looked like a shoo-in. The incumbent Illinois state senator had a long history of work in the Latino neighborhoods he represented; he had 14 years of legislative experience, first on the Chicago City Council and then in the state Senate; he was respected at home and had won a reputation nationally and even internationally as a dedicated progressive and an advocate for the poor, labor, and immigrants. "He's the most admired Mexican American candidate in the entire state," says Cook County Clerk David Orr, a fellow progressive who served with García on the City Council during Mayor Harold Washington's administration in the mid-'80s. "He's been a good organizer, he's never a guy with a big ego, he's always willing to help other people ... a wonderful record, well liked, well respected—in my mind, he's really one of the most outstanding elected officials in the state." He lost anyway. García and his supporters are still reeling from his defeat by a no-name candidate—Antonio "Tony" Muñoz, a Chicago cop with no legislative or community experience—in the Democratic primary last March. García admits that his campaign made some strategic mistakes, but he's also clear about the biggest factor in his defeat. "There is a machine in this town," he says. "It's a new type of machine ... but it still does what the old machine was capable of doing." That old machine reached its height under Richard J. Daley, who served as mayor from 1955 until he died in 1976. Daley controlled 40,000 city jobs as well as nearly all 50 aldermen and Democratic committeemen. Gary Rivlin wrote in *Fire on the Prairie* that Daley's Cook County Democratic Party central committee "ran city government just as the Communist Party's politburo ran the Soviet Union.... It was no wonder that people outside the city's borders looked on Chicago with awe and horror. It was home to not only the last of the great big-city machines but also the most awesome of them all." Just as ward committeemen and aldermen were beholden to Daley, they had armies of precinct workers beholden to them. It was at the ward level that patronage jobs and favors were passed out: Knocking on doors and bringing out the vote for the machine slate on Election Day could get you a promotion and perks; losing your precinct could mean having to join the unemployment lines. Daley's death and the internal fight over who would succeed him weakened the machine in the late '70s and early '80s, but the organization took its first real hit when Harold Washington won the Democratic mayoral primary in 1983, beating Mayor Jane Byrne and Richard M. Daley, Richard J.'s son, who split the machine vote. Washington was an African American, progressive reformer who promised to be "fairer than fair." A coalition of blacks, Latinos, and progressive whites swept him to victory, and he became Chicago's first black mayor, serving until he died in 1987. Richard M. Daley was waiting in the wings; right after his father's death he had been mentioned as a possible heir to the mayoral throne. Washington's death, and the almost immediate dissolution of his progressive coalition, offered the younger Daley his chance. He was first elected as mayor in 1989. Since then, García says, "We've witnessed probably the most rapid consolidation of power that any large city has experienced within the last 40 or 50 years. The influence that the Daley group exerts is vast: City Hall, County Board, the agencies—CTA, Park District, Board of Education—they control it all. And we've witnessed the evolution of the machine from relying on the precinct captain to deliver, to relying on direct mail and utilization of the electronic media to stay in power. The precinct captains aren't that key anymore, but they still decide races like mine. They can still produce." Daley has paid particular attention to Latinos; who are Chicago's fastest growing and soon-to-be largest ethnic minority. As one *Chicago Tribune* political reporter noted in 1994, "The old line 'regular polls' are grooming some younger talent. These emerging new players are Hispanic, predominantly Mexican-Americans, and the mutual hope is that a white–Latino coalition can maintain hegemony over Chicago." The Latino arm of the Daley machine proved in the García race that old-time machine tactics haven't been shelved quite yet. "Patronage is alive and well in the city of Chicago even though [we] have Shakman," says Miguel del Valle, a progressive state senator from Chicago's Northwest Side and the only other Latino in the Illinois Senate. The Shakman decree is the federal court ruling that prohibits patronage hirings and firings. "Someday people will understand that this administration in many respects functions the way that the old administrations functioned," del Valle says. García gave the machine plenty of reasons to pick him as a target. While the mayor has been able to win over or eliminate nearly all of his opposition—more than a third of the current City Council was originally appointed by Daley—García has been steadfast in pursuing a progressive agenda. He's been consistently critical of Daley's development policies for the city, protesting the upscale development of near-downtown neighborhoods that is displacing long-time and poor residents. His name also has been on the short list of potential challengers to Daley in the upcoming February 1999 mayoral elections. "Chuy is about neighborhoods and he's about people and he's therefore a threat," says Alton Miller, Harold Washington's second-term press secretary and biographer. Miller says García was "absolutely the target of a machine attack. Anytime anybody raises his head a little bit higher, the Daley folk want to knock it down. He was and is a real threat to their long-term aims, because ... he's a person who's going to be out there blowing the whistle and keeping people mindful of what the real priorities are." But it wasn't just the old Daley machine that took out García. A newly organized Latino wing of the machine, the Hispanic Democratic Organization (HDO), made up of Latino leaders loyal to Daley and an army of Latino patronage workers, joined forces with white ethnic machine bosses to bridge a generation and ethnic gap and bring out the vote for Muñoz. Most HDO members are city workers who got to their positions by politicking and understand that's how they'll get promoted as well. While they may like García, they're fundamentally concerned about getting what's theirs, and they believe that the way to do that is to support those in power and wait for the perks. The combination of new and old that the machine put together for the primary does not bode well for other Latino progressives. Topping the hit list: 22nd Ward alderman and García protégé Rick Muñoz (no relation to Tony) is up for re-election in February. García-mentored state Rep. Sonia Silva won the primary by just 55 votes and in November faces a Republican challenger with Democratic machine ties. U.S. Rep. Luís Gutiérrez is also vulnerable. If these three were replaced with machine Latinos it would almost completely wipe out independent Latino voices in public office. And Daley's Latinos have proven a loyal bunch: In an analysis of key City Council votes, for instance, *Illinois Politics* concluded that "Hispanic aldermen provided near unanimous support for the mayor, with only nine dissenting votes out of 157 cast by the seven Latinos." The First District on Chicago's Southwest Side has a greater number of immigrants than any other district in Illinois. It is an odd mix of old white ethnic neighborhoods—parts of Daley's home ward are in García's district—and the largest, most concentrated Mexican and Mexican American neighborhoods in the Midwest.

March 17 was an Election Day that brought back memories of the way things used to be. Old machine veterans and their well-taught Latino brethren brought out the works for Muñoz: campaigning city workers, job promises and city services galore. Despite a cold rain that fell all Election Day, the streets of the district had the air of a fiesta. There were so many precinct workers out that in some places they stretched from one polling place to another, like part of a long parade snaking through the district. "This was probably the most effective mobilization of the city–county patronage army in a long time," García says. "I don't think I've seen it like this in my 14 years in elected office." Precinct workers were 10 deep. City building inspectors, off-duty cops, and community policing volunteers huddled around polling places. Muñoz campaign workers wore yellow City-issued raincoats and warmed themselves beside portable Streets and Sanitation heaters. City trucks drove slowly down streets with loads of brand-new garbage cans. If it hadn't been for the rain, voters in one precinct would have had to practically step over city workers laying new sidewalks outside the polling place. Weeks before the election, campaign workers went door to door and made phone calls asking residents if they needed a tree cut down, new garbage cans, a street light turned on, and encouraging them to vote for the machine slate. People who had filed applications for employment with the city received anonymous phone calls and were told not to vote for García. City services were so critical to the Munoz campaign that even Muñoz seemed duped by the tactic. When Spanish-language TV news asked him what he planned to do in the Senate, he answered in English—he doesn't speak Spanish—that he'd make sure residents got their city services, sounding more like he'd just clinched an appointment as a ward superintendent rather than the Democratic nomination for the state Senate. Going up against the machine should have been nothing new to García. He came of age at a time when the political consciousness of Latinos and blacks in the city was being jolted awake. By his mid-twenties, he was involved in some of the strongest anti-machine, progressive neighborhood organizing going down in Chicago. In the late '70s and early '80s, García and other progressive Latinos built what would prove to be the most efficient independent political organization in the city and began to form coalitions with their progressive minded African American neighbors, a formula that eventually led to Harold Washington's victory. García spent much of his time before the March primary stumping for two candidates for state representative in his district. "There wasn't really a campaign focusing on my re-election," he admits. García lost by 960 votes out of nearly 13,000 cast, his support dropping in every ward, including two of the most heavily Latino wards. "We took our eye off of the formula that's enabled us to get elected against great odds, to get re-elected, and then to expand," García says. "That was framing the election as a fight between the neighborhood versus power brokers who want control—the machine. That's how we first got elected, that's how we got re-elected, and this last time that wasn't the message that we had out there. As a matter of fact, the message was pretty vague." García's supporters had no reason to think that their candidate would lose. "Our voters were asleep on Election Day, and that's why we lost," says García. "If we had felt threatened, and if we would have communicated that to our volunteers and to our voters, we would have had higher turnout. We didn't. They stayed home." It's hard to fault him for being overconfident. The machine looked almost desperate. No one had heard of Tony Muñoz. He had no legislative experience and didn't speak Spanish. But García ran headlong into a recurring problem for the left: While he was debating immigration and Welfare reform issues, gentrification and neighborhood development, the machine was passing out city services and counting votes. "We see things politically," says Larry González, García's press secretary. "[But] people just say, 'Hey. These guys came and they gave us something.'" García has blamed his defeat on the traditional machine wards, arguing that voter turnout among whites was higher than in previous elections while Latino turnout was lower. Why would whites be any more likely to vote for someone named Muñoz than for someone named García? "They did their precinct captain a favor," says Richard Barnett, who's been involved in independent politics in Chicago's black community for the past 44 years. "Years ago, the precinct captain used to go around and tell the people in his precinct, 'Could you do me a favor?' In 1964, we elected a dead man for Congress, we sure did. Because the people did their precinct captain a favor." As is his custom, Daley never officially endorsed Muñoz. But witnesses say his choice in the race and the importance he put on it was obvious to everyone from Springfield lobbyists to his Latino underlings. "This mayor has a reputation for being hands-off and for staying out of ward races and other kinds of races," del Valle says. "What people don't realize is that there's this roving band of City Hall Latino patronage workers who will go wherever they're are assigned. This last time around, they were assigned to concentrate on defeating Sen. García." The "roving band of Latino patronage workers" is the HDO. HDO has been registered as a PAC in Illinois since 1993, with the avowed purpose of promoting "the goals and ideals of the Hispanic Community through the exercise of the right to vote." HDO's top guns have expensive City Hall jobs (head of the Mayor's Office of Inter governmental Affairs, commissioner of Human Services, deputy commissioner of Streets and Sanitation, director of personnel at Human Services, etc.) and refuse to comment on the group's structure or activities. Muñoz was apparently a founding member of the group, but denies it has any political purpose, despite its name. "It's just a bunch of guys who get together, that's all," he says. "We basically talk. We've had picnics and stuff." Insiders paint a picture of a large group of mostly city workers, 85 percent Hispanic. "HDO's 1,500 strong," says one Muñoz campaign worker at the Streets and Sanitation outpost where he's employed. "You're looking at that many city employees from various departments. When issues come up as far as services, we can touch bases on just about every department—Streets and Sanitation, whatever. When I knock on your door you can be sure of one thing: That when I ask you for the vote, 90 percent of the time you're gonna go my way.... I got a lady here last night called me, 'Someone dumped a load of tires in my alley, what do I have to do to get 'em out?' First thing I'm gonna do this morning is make sure a truck goes over there. The people won't forget that." HDO's win against García will likely strengthen the organization significantly. The group took a huge bite out of García's base in the Latino community. "The fact that they beat Chuy means more attention is going to be given to them from the administration," says one political consultant who's worked against HDO on the North Side. But he doesn't think García-allied politicians up for re-election in the near future should throw in the towel just yet. "I think you're going to witness a backlash to Chuy's loss," he says.

"There's a growing 'Remember Chuy' type of fever." It's unclear how many voters actually rejected García for his politics. A conservative block of Chicago Latino voters definitely exists: To them it may not be important that a candidate speaks Spanish—they may speak only English themselves. Bilingual education and immigrant rights are not on their list of priorities. They have no intention of allying themselves with blacks and are most concerned with getting what's theirs. As one Latino machine precinct captain puts it, "If you're not supportive of the people that are in power, then you can just about count yourself out as far as getting that piece of the cake." But despite the media talking about "a message from Latino voters," it would seem impossible to deduce voter opinion on García's politics in an election where city services and job promises played a bigger role than what either candidate thought about any given political issue. For del Valle and García, the loss of the Senate seat to a machine candidate is a shot at the heart of the fight for Latino self-determination, political representation, and democracy. "The irony here is that it's the same individuals we went to court to fight to gain Latino political representation when we had nothing," del Valle says. "These days, it's not that they're electing someone who is non-Latino, but they're still around, determining which Latino." "That's what you wind up with in machine politics—control," García says. "The cost that you pay is the ability to control your representatives and to make them work for you. What differences are there between the mayor and his allies? There can't be differences. If there are differences you negotiate through jobs, contracts, things of that sort. It's about keeping total control of elected officials. And it's about eliminating opposition that may get complicated. And I guess that complication is the swing factor. If Latinos aren't under control, it makes governing risky and uncertain. It makes it democratic." Adds David Orr: "Fighting for democracy in a place like Chicago—I'm not gonna compare it to a place like Guatemala—but it's a struggle. It's not like Wisconsin or Minnesota. If people forget that for a moment, that's when these kinds of things can happen."

Source: Linda Lutton, "Old-Time Chicago Politics Aren't Dead Yet—Just Ask 'Chuy' García," *In These Times,* October 4, 1998, p. 17.

410. Rodolfo F. Acuña, "Latino Leaders Take a Holiday," 1999

Police and Mexican American relations have always been contentious, especially between Los Angeles police and civil rights leaders. Since before the Sleepy Lagoon Case of 1942—when almost two dozen Mexican American youths were rounded up and tried for the murder of José Díaz—Mexican Americans have complained about disparate treatment at the hands of police. Another landmark case was the Bloody Christmas case of 1951 when seven young Chicanos were beaten to a bloody pulp by 50 police officers. The pattern continued in the 1950s as Los Angeles police and deputy sheriffs attacked a peaceful crowd of 30,000 protestors on August 29, 1970, and beat the members of the crowd, killing three. The so-called Ramparts case of 1999 deserved equal billing. On September 8, 1999, Los Angeles police officer Rafael Pérez, 32, was caught stealing a million dollars' worth of cocaine from police evidence locker facilities. Pérez made a plea bargain to rat out corruption within the Los Angeles Police Department. He was in a special police unit that was supposed to be combating gangs in Rampart district, just west of downtown L.A. Pérez told a tale of bogus arrests, perjured testimony, and the planting of weapons on unarmed civilians. In all, Pérez implicated about 70 officers in wrongdoing. The following article criticizes Mexican American elected officials for not displaying moral outrage at the police and raises the question of whether this was because a great many residents in the Ramparts Division were of Salvadoran extraction. Would the elected officials have acted different if the victims had been Mexican American voters?

The other day, a TV-media reporter asked me why Latino politicians and leaders had been so silent on what was happening in the Ramparts Division. I was at a loss for words, realizing that I myself had said absolutely nothing about this blatant abuse of police power.

In stark contrast to the silence of Latino leaders, the brutal beating of Rodney King by four LAPD officers touched off a torrent of moral outrage that paralyzed the city. As a result, Mayor Tom Bradley convened what became known as the Christopher Commission that, after extensive hearings, produced small reforms. The fallout, however, proved so devastating that Chief of Police Daryl F. Gates was forced to resign and, for the first time in recent history, the city brought in a chief from outside the department.

In testimony before the Christopher Commission, late Asst. Chief Jesse A. Brewer stated, "We know who the bad guys are. Reputations become well known...." Police authorities promised to weed out the bad cops. Yet the election of Richard Riordan as mayor wiped out hard-fought gains of the community. His law-and-order rhetoric energized the police. And, although the police continued knowing who the bad cops were, they kept the bad apples in the barrel.

Given that the Rodney King beatings were outrageous, the events surrounding the Ramparts Division of the Los Angeles Police Department pale it. Indeed, if they had happened in any other community in L.A., Black and white leaders would have been rightfully up in arms. In contrast, Latino leaders have allowed police officers with the power to kill or destroy lives to hide behind a wall of secrecy.

What happened at the Ramparts Division is part of "L.A.'s Dirty Little War on Gangs." Its particulars became known in September 1999 when LAPD officer Rafael A. Pérez spilled the beans after being caught stealing eight pounds of cocaine from police evidence lockers. He turned whistle blower: In return for a plea bargain agreement, Pérez implicated fellow officers. What unfolded was a story of police brutality, perjury, planted evidence, drug corruption, and attempted murder.

Much of the narrative revolves around the anti-gang unit, known as CRASH (Community Resources Against Street Hoodlums). In July 1996, CRASH raided an apartment house on Shatto Place in the heart of the MacArthur Park district of Los Angeles, near the old headquarters of the American Civil Liberties Union. Its target was the notorious 18th Street Gang, L.A.'s biggest and admittedly most violent gang. LAPD's finest assaulted the building in warlike fashion, killing one gang member and wounding another.

Although the LAPD's own report showed that police fired all the shots, the cops who staged the raid claimed the gang bangers were armed. Two pistols, believed to have been throw downs, were found on the scene. A survivor, José Perez initially denied having a gun. He later pleaded guilty to assault. José Pérez [no relation to Rafael Pérez] later explained that he pleaded guilty to avoid a long prison sentence;

he had no gun at the time of the raid. As usual, a department investigation found nothing wrong.

The story did not end there. Officer Rafael Pérez, labeled a rogue cop by the media, triggered an internal investigation and the FBI looked for civil rights violations. So far, over a dozen Ramparts Division police have been fired or relieved of duty.

In another case, in 1996, Pérez and his partner Nino Durden, shot Javier Ovando, leaving him paralyzed and in a wheelchair for life. Ovando was allegedly unarmed when he was shot. The officers then planted a semiautomatic rifle on the unconscious suspect and claimed that Ovando had tried to shoot them during a stakeout. Their testimony put Ovando away for 23 years for assault. Because of what has come out, Ovando has been freed from prison. He has filed notice of a $20 million suit against the city, Pérez and other cops. He was allegedly the dealer through whom Pérez and Durden sold their drugs.

After spending more than two years behind bars, Rubén Rojas, 30, is expected to have his drug conviction overturned because authorities now believe it was based on fabricated evidence and false testimony by Pérez. They arrested Rojas on March 5, 1997, after Pérez and Durden allegedly watched him sell rock cocaine to two men near Marathon and Dillon streets. They allegedly saw Rojas make two sales before calling for backup. After the arrest, Pérez planted powder cocaine in Rojas' front pants pockets.

Rojas pleaded no contest. He said: "I was informed that I was facing 25 years to life by my defense counsel and that there was no way I could have won my case because I was up against a police officer ..." Rojas claimed the police officers framed him after he told the officers that he did not know the whereabouts of a gang member. (The real motive appears to have been that Rojas was seeing a girl friend of Officer Pérez.)

Because of Pérez's whistle blowing, Los Angeles District Attorney Gil Garcetti has been forced to release at least three prison inmates jailed by the Ramparts Division. The DA admits that another forty cases could be reversed because of false testimony by police. Investigators are looking into allegations involving the Ramparts Division, ranging from illegal shootings and drug dealing to excessive use of force and "code of silence" offenses.

The reaction of Los Angeles Mayor Richard Riordan is predictable. His spokespersons said that the mayor had complete confidence that LAPD Chief Bernard Parks would implement the reforms passed after the 1991 King beating. There is no need for an oversight commission. Just a couple of rotten apples. Ironically, it was this mayor who called for an entire reshuffling of the Los Angeles Unified School District and instigated the crude coup of Superintendent Rubén Zacarías because the "code of silence" was too imbedded within the culture of the school system. Apparently, there is one standard for teachers and another for police officers.

One only has to look at Los Angeles' media coverage and compare it with its treatment of the Rodney King uprisings to realize the disparate treatment of the incidents. All of this is, however, predictable. What is not, is the reaction of Latino politicians and leaders who are mute in the face of this gross violation of L.A.'s civil rights. From a historical perspective, Ramparts ranks with the Sleepy Lagoon case of 1942 and is more heinous than the Blood Christmas beatings of the early 1950s.

While I know that term limits have forced Latino políticos constantly to play musical chairs, and I realize that the community itself is so anti gangsters as to intimidate políticos, we cannot afford to be silent. The políticos' silence is almost sanctioning a situation like that which occurred in Brazil a few years back. In 1993, a death squad of off-duty Rio de Janeiro police officers executed eight children as they slept on the steps of the Candelaria Church in downtown Rio. Three years later, they were still shooting children in Brazil. On Rio's Ipanema Beach, an 11-year-old street kid was found dead, hanging by the neck, a sign around his neck that read: "I had to be killed because I didn't go to school. I was worthless to society and my only expectation as a grown up was to be a criminal." Some 85 percent of Brazilians polled supported the police even after a police officer shot an apprehended youth three times, point-blank, in the back of a head at a shopping center.

I guess that I naively believed that Chicanos, having experienced the civil rights struggle of the sixties, would be different. Most of us have experienced injustice and know its meaning. We are also bright enough to know that the problem is more systemic than a couple of bad apples. Perhaps we should inspect the barrel. For us to remain silent is so much worse than for others; more is expected of us.

Source: Rodolfo F. Acuña, "Latino Leaders Take a Holiday," December 12, 1999. In Urban Archives, California State University, Northridge.

411. David Bacon, "Crossing L.A.'s Racial Divide: City Could Elect Its First Latino Mayor in More Than a Century," 2001

Like so many of his contemporaries, Los Angeles Mayor Antonio Villaraigosa was active in MEChA (el Movimiento Estudiantil Chicano/a de Aztlán), a nationwide Chicano student organization fighting for equal treatment on college and university campuses. He was later a member of the Centro de Acción Social Autónoma (Center for Autonomous Social Action—CASA) that defended the rights of undocumented immigrants. He worked as an organizer for the United Teachers Los Angeles (UTLA), a teachers' union, and was elected to the California Assembly where he became Speaker. He was later elected to the Los Angeles City Council before being elected L.A. mayor in 2005. The following document describes Villaraigosa's unsuccessful run for mayor of Los Angeles in 2001.

Fifty years ago, Bert Corona had a dream. Latinos in California—the field workers and factory hands, the kids in school forbidden to speak Spanish—could win real political power. Transforming the excluded and marginalized into power-brokers in the state with the largest population in the country seemed a task so gargantuan that only a visionary like Corona—social radical, labor militant, Chicano activist, and father of the modern Latino political movement—could consider it achievable.

Yet on June 5, Antonio Villaraigosa, one of Corona's disciples from the heady days of the '60s, may be elected mayor of Los Angeles. Villaraigosa learned politics in that era, becoming a community activist in an early left-wing immigrant rights organization founded by Corona, the Centro de Accion Social Autonóma [Center for Autonomous Social Action] (CASA). From those radical roots, Villaraigosa went on to get a law degree at Los Angeles' People's College of the Law, a unique project creating community lawyers from community activists. He worked as an organizer for the city's huge teachers' union, United Teachers Los Angeles. And he began running for office. Villaraigosa eventually became speaker of the State Assembly, one of California's most powerful political positions.

The June 5 election is a runoff, pitting Villaraigosa against James Hahn. Both are Democrats, itself a notable change in a city governed for eight years by Republican Richard Riordan. If Villaraigosa is elected mayor, he'll be the first Latino in that position in more than a century.

The election is partly the story of changing demographics. Los Angeles has the largest urban population of Mexicans outside of Mexico City, and racial minorities in California now make up a majority of the state's population. Most of this demographic shift is due to immigration, and the state is home to as many as half of the nation's undocumented residents.

But the changing population only provides a base. And in California, it took former Gov. Pete Wilson to transform it into a formidable voting force. In 1994, Wilson won re-election by betting his political future on Proposition 187, which sought to exclude the undocumented from schools and medical care.

It was a Pyrrhic victory. Proposition 187 passed, but in the election's wake, thousands of immigrants became citizens with the express intention of never again being excluded from the political process. They then set out to administer a punishment to the Republican Party from which it's still reeling. Democrats today control both houses of the state legislature, and a Democrat sits in the governor's mansion. The new immigrant vote has become the decider in race after race, especially in Los Angeles.

But having a Spanish surname alone isn't enough to get elected in Los Angeles. Although minorities make up 60 percent of city residents, they account for only 39 percent of its voters—14 percent are African American, 20 percent are Latino, and 5 percent are Asian American. Class issues are increasingly the glue holding together a new progressive coalition, bringing together progressive whites with a new generation of leaders in minority communities. "I think the big issues are economic," says Kent Wong, director of UCLA's Labor Center. "People are voting for things like a living wage, affirmative action, and an economic development policy that promotes growth based on good jobs, and which pays attention to underserved communities."

The city has become a hotbed of labor activity. In the past five years, Los Angeles has seen major strikes and organizing drives by immigrant janitors and hotel workers. While immigrants have been the most visible part of that upsurge, African American and Asian American union members have been very much a part of labor's rise.

The Los Angeles County Federation of Labor, which elected its first Latino secretary, Miguel Contreras, five years ago, has put these issues on the political agenda. In a series of bruising electoral fights, it has built up a core of precinct walkers and phone callers, and used them effectively to win upset victories for pro-labor Latinos against more conservative ones, like Hilda Solis, who beat longtime Congressman Marty Martinez last November. The Villaraigosa campaign is the biggest test yet for the federation because it has to be won citywide, involving a larger labor turnout than ever before. "It was a very big risk for the labor movement to step out front and endorse Villaraigosa in the primary," Wong says. "But it has a lot of boldness and daring, and it has built up an incredible ground operation involving hundreds and hundreds of people each weekend."

Unlike Villaraigosa, who has been a high-profile community activist and legislator, Hahn has been a quiet member of an old guard his father helped build. He has been an elected official for 16 years, first as controller and then as city attorney.

Hahn's father, Kenny, was a county supervisor for 40 years, during the era when Mayor Sam Yorty was notorious for racist scare attacks directed at white voters. Hahn was a leading white liberal who stood up for the African American community in South Central Los Angeles. People definitely remember Kenny Hahn, but few voters can point out initiatives taken by his son.

In the local press, the Villaraigosa–Hahn battle is being portrayed as a conflict between blacks and Latinos. "But there's a whole political realignment taking place here," says Anthony Thigpenn, chairman of Agenda, a South Central community organization, and a leading activist in the Villaraigosa campaign. "It's happening in the African American community, like everywhere else, and many of us are looking to be part of it."

Karen Bass, executive director of South Central's Community Coalition, says that Latinos and African Americans have more issues in common than ones that divide them. "Ninety percent of the kids in the criminal justice system and in foster care are African American and Latino," she says. "The most important factor here is that we're neighbors."

In the first election, while Hahn got a majority of black votes, Bass says Villaraigosa still won 26 percent in South Central precincts, while rolling up big majorities in heavily Latino neighborhoods. She predicts the African American vote for Villaraigosa will go higher in the runoff as people become more familiar with him.

"Villaraigosa has a long record, not just supporting the issues important to all of Los Angeles' locked-out communities, but leading many of the efforts to put them into practice," Wong adds. "If he becomes mayor, those communities will have access to power. The ability to turn our issues into real policy will increase dramatically."

Source: David Bacon, "Crossing L.A.'s Racial Divide: City Could Elect Its First Latino Mayor in More Than a Century," *In These Times,* June 11, 2001, p. 5.

412. Dane Schiller, "Castro Upholds Family's Involvement Tradition," 2001

In Los Angeles there is a link between MEChA (the Movimiento Estudiantil Chicano/a De de AztlánAztlan), a national Chicano student organization, CASA (Centro de Accion Social Autónoma or Center for Autonomous Social Action), a pro-immigrant rights organization, and the LRS (the League of Revolutionary Struggle) a national Marxist organization, all of which have been active from the early 1970s to the time of this writing. A high proportion of their membership became union organizers, civic leaders, and politicians. The same can be said of La Raza Unida Party of Texas, the Chicano political party of the 1970s that ran statewide candidates in Texas. Many of today's heads of old-time Mexican American organizations, school board members, judges, and politicos were once members of the Raza Unida. The following is the story of Rosie Castro, who in the 1970s ran unsuccessfully for a seat on the San Antonio, Texas, City Council. Conceding defeat, she told everyone that she would be back and 30 years later she was—to witness one son sworn in as state senator and the other as a member of the city council.

A recent Harvard Law School graduate was sweeping a crowded field Saturday to take the reins of City Council District 7. Julian Castro, 26, who watched election returns from his West Side home, appeared to be easily defeating five other candi-dates, garnering about 60 percent of the vote. Although the post would be his first elected office, Castro has long been groomed for politics by his mother, a well-known grassroots activist. She unsuccessfully ran for a council post 30 years ago but has remained active in politics. "My victory is the product of hard work of many people," said Castro, who was born and raised in the district, which covers the West and Northwest sides. "We had an excellent early vote return and even better Elec-tion Day results," he said. Castro was trailed by Fred Rangel, a business consultant, and John Coleman, a retired Air Force officer. Others in the race were Raul Quiroga Jr., Michael Gonzales, and John García. Surrounded by about 80 supporters, Castro vowed to bring a bold brand of leadership to the district and carry on the style of Ed Garza, who has served two terms. Castro ran on a platform of preserving the charac-ter of neighborhoods, enhancing accountability at City Hall and bringing more avia-tion and technology jobs to San Antonio. "I'd be ready for a mini-vacation, but I'll be back at the law office Monday," said Castro, a business litigation attorney with the Akin, Gump, Strauss, Hauer & Feld law firm. Rosie Castro, his mother and unofficial campaign manager, said her son will carry on the family's tradition of po-litical involvement. "I'm excited," she said. "That was 30 years ago we lost, but today, my son has won City Councilman District 7. "I'm real confident he will be an excellent representative," she said. She said her son, who spent about $30,000 on the race, has the tools to find innovative solutions to problems. She pointed to his coast-to-coast experience, including graduating from Harvard in 2000 and earning a bachelor's degree from Stanford University. Castro, whose twin brother Joaquín served as his treasurer, was a White House intern in 1994. Coleman, who planned to call and congratulate Castro, said he got in the race too late. His contributions of less than $800 were no match for Castro's war chest, he said.

"It is unfortunate I didn't start earlier," Coleman said. "I think I could have won this thing."

Source: Dane Schiller, "Castro Upholds Family's Involvement Tradition," *San Antonio Express-News* (Texas), May 6, 2001, p. 18A.

413. Rodolfo F. Acuña, "Lessons from Vietnam," 2003

The Vietnam War was still fresh in the minds of many Chicanos as the United States invaded Iraq in 2003. They were critical not only on the wisdom of start-ing a war in an area that was explosive, where Sunnis and Shiites and Kurds, had centuries-long grievances against each other. Soon the debate turned to who would fight and who pay for the war. With the schools in shambles in mi-nority neighbourhoods across the nation, many speculated that education would suffer even more as resources were shifted to the war. California, with the largest Latino population, would be heaviest hit. California had one in eight "Americans," but only two of 50 senators. It paid $1.8 trillion in taxes. New York, also with a large Latino population, paid $145 billion in taxes. A large share of these contributions went to paying for the war. The following ar-ticle raises the question of the burden of the war—an issue among Latino acti-vists that rivaled immigration.

A lesson learned from Vietnam is that Americans will not tolerate too many body bags; the latter caused a revolt of middle-class white youth in the sixties and bought down at least two presidencies. Another lesson was that fear of the Communist bogeyman lasts only so long.

It should, therefore, not be surprising that the proposed length of President George Bush's "war on terrorism" has begun to worry some Pentagon officials. Americans are conditioned to pay on credit; though they expect quick results, especially if their sons and daughters are those who are killed.

Not surprisingly, military recruiters have turned to the most vulnerable sector of society—Latinos—for long-term solutions. They are easy targets since most Americans have the notion that Latinos are lawbreakers and should be grateful for the opportunity to be Americans, even if it means dying for that privilege.

Recruiting Latinos as soldiers has become like shopping for organ transplants in Third World countries. The market is unlimited; there is a huge pool of Latinos willing to transport themselves to the United States and fight for Uncle Sam. So, Americans who have more important things to do—like Vice President Richard B. Cheney—can go on with their lives.

No one would deny that things are desperate in Mexico. Rumors that if immigrants volunteer for U.S. military service they will automatically be eligible for citizenship draw the hungry masses. Eager recruits flood the American Embassy and consular offices with inquiries. I am certain that there would also be a similar flood of "volunteers" if there was an offer of $10,000 for a kidney.

Tales of over-zealous recruiters in San Diego tracking youths in Tijuana high schools fan these rumors.

At least five Mexican-born soldiers have been killed in Iraq. A Pew study shows that Latinos are relatively underrepresented in the military when compared to their numbers in the civilian workforce; yet they are overrepresented in combat units, comprising 9.49 percent of the enlisted personnel, but 17.74 percent of those directly handling guns. Of the 60,000 immigrants in the U.S. military about half are non-citizens. More than 6,000 Marines are non-citizens, with the largest group, 1,452, from Mexico.

The practice of recruiting non-citizens as mercenaries is not a new phenomenon. Since the Republican takeover of Congress in 1995, the military has pushed the schools to give it wider access to student records for recruitment purposes. The 1996 Solomon Amendment denied federal funding to institutions of higher learning that prohibited or prevented ROTC (Reserve Officers' Training Corps) or military recruitment on campus. ROTC targets Latino serving institutions (universities that have more than 25 percent Latinos).

Under Bill Clinton, Secretary of the Army Louis Caldera set in motion the Hispanic Access Initiative by which ROTC targeted Latinos and forced universities to hand over personal data to recruiters.

President George W. Bush's "No Child Left Behind Act" pretends to benefit Latinos and other minorities by closing the education gap between rich and poor. Instead the Act tracks minorities into the military, insuring that fewer go to college. It violates students' privacy. Section 9528 of the act is "ARMED FORCES RECRUITER ACCESS TO STUDENTS AND STUDENT RECRUITING INFORMATION." Upon request, school authorities hand military recruiters the names, addresses, and telephone numbers of high school students.

The U.S. military spends between $8,000 and $11,000 to recruit a single soldier; a figure that is climbing as the war takes more casualties. Recruiters are active in the barrios. Many recruiters in the Los Angeles area advocate the lifting of restrictions on enlisting undocumented Latinos. Among young people ages 18–24, Latinos are a prime recruiting market, Latinos make up 14.3 percent of the nation's youth, but only about 10 percent of new recruits.

I believe in affirmative action. But this is carrying things too far. I wish that the universities would be as zealous in protecting Latino students. The same people who are pushing to get more Latinos into the military are the same people who want to push them out of school.

Source: Rodolfo F. Acuña, September 12, 2003, Urban Archives, California State University Northridge.

414. David Bacon, "Los Angeles Turns Out for Amnesty," 2000

The struggle over immigration into the United States continued into the twenty-first century. In 1986, Congress passed IRCA (the Immigration Reform and Control Act), which gave several million undocumented Latinos amnesty, the right to apply to stay in the country permanently. It was supposedly a compromise bill, which criminalized the act of knowingly hiring an illegal immigrant and established fines and other penalties for those employing undocumented workers. The theory was that drying up jobs would reduce undocumented immigration. The law established a one-year amnesty program for undocumented immigrants who had already worked and lived in the United States since January 1982. An estimated 2.7 million undocumented workers were legalized. IRCA did not stop the flow of undocumented immigrants that today are estimated to be as many as 12 million. The reasons are continued poverty in Mexico and Central America, a decline in peasant farming, and political instability—all of which the United States has played a part in creating. Residents without documents have been active in pursuing other amnesty programs that would stabilize their status in the United States. This culminated on May 1, 2006, in a march of close to a million people in Los Angeles and millions more throughout the country. The following is an article by activist photographer and freelance writer David Bacon describing a huge 2000 pro-immigrant march in which undocumented workers demanded amnesty. The importance of the march was that desperate poor people were demanding human rights. The quotations are those of participants in the march.

Los Angeles (6/12/00)—Immigration amnesty for people crossing the border without papers is hardly a new idea in California. In fact, the first one came with San Francisco's earthquake and fire of 1906, which destroyed the records keeping track of immigrants brought from China to work on the railroads.

"A hundred years ago my grandfather and his brother crossed the Mexican border into California illegally, buried in a hay cart," Katie Quan remembers her parents telling her. They had to sneak in, because after the rails were laid, the door to further immigration from China was slammed shut. "The Chinese Exclusion Act, passed in 1882, brings bitter memories for Chinese Americans to this day, because it barred Chinese, and only Chinese, from entering the U.S."

When the fire burned down San Francisco's City Hall, it destroyed the immigration records of the city's Chinese residents. The whole community became undocumented. And when everyone was undocumented, anyone could say they had arrived legally and had their papers go up in flames. Quan's father became a legal resident as a result. Other immigrants brought relatives from China, claiming they were "paper sons," whose documents had perished in the fire.

"That is the way a very high percentage of Chinese Americans came to the U.S., including my mother's family," Quan says.

Quan, a former garment union leader, now works at the Center for Labor Research and Education at UC Berkeley. She recalled her family's history in one of a series of hearings held to gather support for the AFL-CIO's recent proposal that the country needs a new amnesty.

As the hearings, which started in March, moved across the U.S. from New York to Atlanta, Chicago, Silicon Valley, Portland, Salinas and Fresno, the crowds turning out to back the demand swelled. Amnesty has immense support among immigrants, a fact impossible to ignore last Saturday in Los Angeles when over 16,000 people poured into the L.A. Sports Arena, chanting *Que queremos? Amnistia, sin condiciones!*—"What do we want? Unconditional amnesty!" Thousands more gathered outside, unable to get in through the doors.

The last immigration amnesty was contained in the Immigration Reform and Control Act, passed in 1986. It allowed about three million people, who came before January 1, 1982, to gain legal status. But those who've arrived without documents since then have been trapped in the same illegal status the law fixed for those who came before.

The Urban Institute estimates there were as many as 5 million undocumented people in the U.S. just before that amnesty. Afterwards, it dropped to 2–3 million. But by 1992, it was rising again to 2.7–3.7 million. Today, most estimates place the number around 6 million, but no one really knows. Fear of deportation makes undocumented people hesitant to be counted.

Neither sending the National Guard to patrol the high metal fence in Tijuana, nor beefed-up raids in immigrant communities, have been able to halt this flow of people. Nor has anti-immigrant legislation, from California's Proposition 187 to the immigration reform acts passed in 1986 and 1996.

California's experience is no different from Western Europe and Japan. And when the AFL-CIO changed its position on immigration this February, it recognized that continued immigration reflects a new world reality. The UN High Commissioner for Refugees estimates that over 80 million people today live outside their countries of origin, with the U.S. home to only a small percentage. Because of growing economic inequality on a global scale, people increasingly leave and seek survival elsewhere when they cannot feed their families at home.

The AFL-CIO's reversal in position has shifted the political climate around immigration in Washington D.C. dramatically. Suddenly a handful of immigration bills have been introduced, ostensibly intended to legalize at least some people. Just a year ago, even discussion of limited amnesty was considered laughable among beltway lobbyists.

"It's really obvious that the change by the labor movement has made a whole new discussion possible," says Victor Narro, a staff attorney at the Coalition for Humane Immigrant Rights in Los Angeles. "Now we have a labor movement that's on the side of immigrants, rather than one bent on trying to stop immigration, as we had in 1986." At that time, the AFL-CIO argued against immigration amnesty, and for employer sanctions, that section of the law which makes it illegal for undocumented immigrants to work.

When the AFL-CIO announced at its October convention here that the old attitude needed to be changed, it set up a hearing process to advise immigrant workers of their rights, to gather testimony about how immigration law has undermined those rights, and to forge a new labor/community/religious coalition to change the law. In addition to unions, the L.A. hearing was sponsored by ten churches and community organizations, from the Hermandad Mexicana Nacional (the National Mexican Brotherhood) to the Catholic Archdiocese, each kicking in at least $2,500 to help pay for the huge event, and bringing bus loads of people to fill the arena.

"Labor can open some doors," says Miguel Contreras, secretary of the Los Angeles County Labor Federation, "but we need community allies and a grassroots base. We have to build a rank-and-file movement for amnesty, and this huge turnout shows not only that it can be done, but that politicians who want the Latino vote had better take note."

"We really need amnesty," says Mateo Cruz, a day laborer who marched into the sports arena with 2,000 other workers from L.A.'s street corners, mobilized by the Union of Day Laborers. "People hire us and don't pay us. Three years ago I worked for 40 days cleaning restaurants for a contractor, and when I finally told him I couldn't go on being put off about my wages, he called the police and threatened to have me deported. I was humiliated and handcuffed. Not having papers makes bosses and police treat you really badly. I filed a complaint for my wages with the Labor Commissioner, and after 2 years I'm still waiting. Many day laborers won't even do that, because they're afraid that if they make trouble they'll be picked up by the *migra* [Border Patrol]."

Inside the sports arena, a procession of workers recounted similar experiences to a panel of union leaders. María Sánchez described the way managers at the Palm Canyon Hotel in Palm Springs fired a number of workers after they joined the Hotel and Restaurant Employees Union. When forced to rehire them, the hotel suddenly decided to check their immigration status and refused to put them back to work. The workers, both documented and undocumented, responded by staying off the job until everyone was rehired. "I lost my house and my car. I sold some of my possessions so I could survive," Sanchez declared. "But we woke up. We gained self-confidence. I know that I have value and that I have rights!"

Carmen, a seventeen-year old farmworker from the Central Valley, broke down in tears as she stood before thousands of strangers, admitting that her lack of legal status kept her from going to college. "We can't even move [to a bigger house] because we don't have a Social Security number to put down a deposit and turn on utilities ... Even if we could afford a nice home, we can't rent one because we are undocumented.

"Our future depends on a new amnesty," she cried out.

Ofelia Parra, a worker in Washington state's apple-packing sheds, described the mass termination of 700 undocumented workers in the midst of a Teamsters Union organizing drive, at the demand of the Immigration and Naturalization Service. The drive was broken. "We've had to accept jobs at lower wages. I earned $7.51/hour at the packing plant, and now I earn minimum wage," she said. "We contribute to this society just like the people who have papers. We need an amnesty so we can work in peace and organize to improve conditions."

In Los Angeles, in an election year, the demand for amnesty has clear political repercussions. According to Fábian Nuñez, the county labor federation's political director, one million of California's 1.1 newly registered voters are Latino, and 44% of them are new immigrants. "Before 1986, a lot of these people were undocumented themselves, so they know what amnesty means and how important it is," he explains. Politicians like Assemblyman Gil Cedillo and past Assembly Speaker Antonio Villaraigosa were not only partly elected with those votes, but are former immigrant rights activists themselves.

Contreras emphasizes that L.A. labor doesn't see immigration law in a vacuum. "Amnesty is a means to an end—the elimination of poverty and a better redistribution of wealth. L.A. is a county in crisis. Fifty wealthy families have assets of $60 billion, more than the wages of 2 million of the city's lowest-paid workers, who are mostly immigrants. But in the midst of this crisis, we also have a crisis of leadership. Elected officials see amnesty as too controversial. This hearing is a signal to them that amnesty is important to this community. It's a message to all of L.A."

It's also a message that puts the Clinton administration in Washington into a quandary. It seeks to appear Latino-friendly on the one hand, while not appearing to ease up on the immigration enforcement program it's touted for seven years on the other. To at least partly solve this problem, a meeting was convened in Washington in mid-April by Henry Cisneros, past Secretary of Housing and Urban Development and mayor of San Antonio, now CEO of the Spanish-language TV network Univision and a Democratic Party heavyweight.

The meeting sought to craft a compromise short of a general amnesty and the repeal of employer sanctions—the bedrock AFL-CIO positions. Instead, Cisneros joined Republican Jack Kemp in urging participants to support lifting the cap on the recruitment of foreign high-tech workers. In return, they predicted, pro-immigrant groups could get some limited reforms. Those include extending to Haitians and other Central Americans the liberal procedures Cubans and Nicaraguans have for getting asylum, allowing late applicants for the last amnesty to receive one now, moving the registry date for amnesty forward from the old one of January 1, 1982, and removing a provision which forces undocumented workers to return to their countries of origin, often separating their families for years, just to apply for legal status.

The number of people eligible for legalization under these proposals depends on the new registry date, but no one denies it would be far short of the 6 million undocumented people currently in the country. Some immigration activists, while acknowledging the importance of those reforms, are wary of the deal, fearing it will cut short the effort to achieve a broader amnesty.

In Silicon Valley, reservations were voiced for another reason. The computer industry's scheme to recruit more foreign high-tech workers, the H-1B visa category, is a form of contract labor tying workers' immigration status to their employers. If a contract worker is fired, they not only lose their job, but can lose their right to stay in the U.S. as well.

"I was hired by a software company in Los Angeles that sponsored my visa," Kim Singh, a former H-1B worker, told the AFL-CIO's Silicon Valley hearing. "In every paycheck the company would deduct 25% of my salary. When I questioned this practice, I was told that I would get this money when I left. But I never got it." At another company in Torrance, Singh's H-1B co-workers labored seven days a week with no overtime. A third company in Silicon Valley rented an apartment for Singh and three other contract workers for $1,450/month, and then deducted $1,450 from each of their paychecks.

While Singh was able to change jobs and eventually obtain a normal visa, "other programmers stayed at the company because the employer had their passports and they were intimidated."

"Why aren't the companies training workers here for those jobs?" asks Linda Chavez-Thompson, AFL-CIO executive vice-president. While H-1B workers are paid considerably more than the minimum wage, "it still is like the old *bracero* program," she asserts. "Companies use this program to keep workers in a position of dependence. And because they're often hired under individual contracts, U.S. labor law says they don't even have the right to organize." Eliseo Medina, executive vice-president of the Service Employees International Union, was at the Cisneros meeting, and says the AFL-CIO doesn't support the H-1B program.

But both political parties are competing to woo the huge campaign contributions flowing from the computer industry, and in Congress there's overwhelming support for giving Silicon Valley employers the workers they want.

Other industries are not far behind. Employers around the country complain they can't get their labor needs supplied with just citizens, or legal residents already here. Growers have bills in Congress to expand their "guest worker" program, and remove restrictions protecting workers. The garment industry and others dependent on immigrants also want contract labor.

Last year in Nebraska, the INS itself conducted its largest workplace enforcement program ever, intended to build support for these programs. After driving over 3,000 undocumented workers from the state's meatpacking plants, INS Midwest director Mark Reed stated in an interview that "we depend on foreign labor, and we have to face the question—are we prepared to bring in workers lawfully? If we don't have illegal immigration anymore, we'll have the political support for guest worker [contract labor programs]."

The political problem for labor, as defined by its political strategists in Washington, is that some employer support is necessary to get a pro-immigrant bill through Congress. But if the price for that support is a chain of contract labor programs, instead of an immigrant workforce legalized by amnesty and freed from employer sanctions, immigrant workers could wind up more chained than ever.

"I'm not convinced there is a labor shortage," says Medina, one of the main AFL-CIO leaders pushing for the new immigration policy. "We don't support lifting the cap on H-1B. If companies were willing to pay fair wages, they'd have all the workers they want.

"What we do need," he continues, "is workplace enforcement of worker protection laws, instead of employer sanctions. We want a general amnesty, covering all the people who are here now. In addition, many Mexicans would rather stay at home, but companies pay starvation wages in the *maquiladoras*, and wind up creating the very conditions forcing people to come here. So as long as people continue coming, we need to deal with that. One idea is a rolling date, so that people who have been here a certain amount of time could apply for amnesty. The AFL-CIO hasn't adopted this yet—so far we're just talking."

Despite its limitations, Medina called the Cisneros meeting "a good first step," because it brought together a widely disparate group of employers and unions, political conservatives and immigrant rights advocates.

"This is the time to be bold," urges John Wilhelm, president of the Hotel Employees and Restaurant Employees International Union. "I'm not against incremental steps, but we have to push amnesty and get rid of sanctions. In the legislative process we'll wind up bargaining, and what we get will depend on how strong our coalition is. But if someone had told me 3–4 years ago that we'd be taking this position today, I'd have thought they were out of their minds."

That describes pretty well the experience of at least one speaker at the L.A. forum, the grandfather of the immigrant rights movement, Bert Corona. In one of the most emotional moments of the huge rally, Corona was helped across the stage, in steps made haltingly by his age, and given credit for years spent trying to convince the labor movement that defending immigrants was in its best interest.

Corona started campaigning against employer sanctions and immigration raids in the 1960s, long before the 1986 law was passed. He got a cold shoulder from the AFL-CIO's former leaders in Washington. During those years, a rally like Saturday's hearing would have been inconceivable. Corona would certainly never have been an honored guest.

"There is no mine, no bridge, not a row in the fields nor a construction site in all the United States that hasn't been watered with the tears, the sweat, and blood of immigrants," Corona reminded the huge crowd in Spanish. "We demand an amnesty for the workers who have made the wealth of this country possible. Amnesty is not a gift, but a right, for those who have contributed so much, and should be free of any conditions reinforcing the hard exploitation of our past. It means achieving real equality."

Source: David Bacon, "Los Angeles Turns Out for Amnesty," June 12, 2000. http://dbacon.igc. org/Imgrants/14LAAmnesty.htm.

415. Testimony of Commissioner Richard M. Estrada, U.S. Commission on Immigration Reform, "Agricultural Guest Worker Programs," December 7, 1995

A notion that has been picking up momentum in the United States is that an immigration reform bill must have a provision for a guest worker program. The fact is that without Mexican and other Latino labor, U.S. agriculture would suffer huge losses. Already the United States is buying vegetables from China to offset the diminishing supply. In 1942, the United States entered a similar contract to bring workers to the United States as temporary guest workers. The program ended in 1964 and was fraught with corruption and abuses. This renewal of the *bracero* program of World War II vintage was the cornerstone of President George Bush's immigration policy. The rationale is that in this way, Mexican workers could be contracted for temporary periods and returned to their country of origin once their labor was no longer needed. The following is the 1995 testimony of the deceased and ultra conservative columnist Richard M. Estrada, who argued against the bracero program because of its abuses and the lack of provisions enabling workers to, in time, become permanent residents. He saw worker conditions as the same as rented slaves. Estrada's testimony seems as relevant in 2007 as it did then. Estrada frames his argument against the guest worker program in terms of "unfree" labor. Free labor has the right to organize and gain from the fruits of its labor; unfree labor has no rights.

FREE VS. UNFREE LABOR

I oppose new or expanded agricultural guest worker programs because they represent "unfree" labor.

Doubtless, some will immediately object to the use of this term because all the workers in question would presumably come to America willingly. Despite uncertainty about the circumstances under which guest laborers in such programs are selected, let us concede for the sake of argument that all guest workers do in fact come willingly.

One must still insist that the absence of slavery does not imply the presence of freedom. As commonly understood, the term *free labor* also implies that an individual can sell his or her labor on the open market to whomever will contract for it. It is in this regard that guest worker programs are, by definition, unfree labor arrangements or, at the very least, not totally free labor arrangements.

To be specific, the agricultural guest worker is explicitly obligated not to sell his or her labor anywhere else but to the agricultural employer who sponsors entry. Employers tend to prize guest workers for their abilities, true. But they also value them because they have no options and are, therefore, more malleable. (Employers tend to prefer the term "disciplined.")

This basic characteristic is the ugly underbelly of any and all agricultural guest worker programs: the foreign worker is virtually indentured to the agricultural employer, with an important exception. Unlike indentured servitude as practiced in America in the eighteenth century, the guest worker has no expectation based in the legal provisions of his or her entry that he or she will be able to become a free laborer in America.

In addition, guest worker programs tend to have no worker protections. When it comes to housing and health care, uneducated and often illiterate guest workers, who often do not speak English and who have little or no disposable income, are left to fend for themselves. There are thousands of such people roaming the agriculture-based communities of America today. Reasonable and honorable people may disagree about guest worker programs in general, but the specific practice of providing no meaningful worker protections in this manner is unacceptable. It is wrong. It is immoral.

Finally, Congress should consider that the "bracero" guest worker program was implemented in 1942 under extremely unusual conditions. With millions of native-born rural workers suddenly called off to war, turning to foreign labor through a temporary guest worker program was justified. Even so, the fact that it took more than twenty years to end the bracero program, long after the end of the Second World War, should give Congress pause about reintroducing it. Cheap, unskilled foreign labor has proven to be an opiate to agricultural employers. Congress should dispense it sparingly, if at all.

Source: U.S. Commission on Immigration Reform, http://www.utexas.edu/lbj/uscir/120795.html.

416. Enrique C. Ochoa and Gilda L. Ochoa, "Governor's Comments Reveal the Depth of Sexism and Racism," 2006

Mexican Americans and Latinas had, like almost everything else in society, been commoditized at the turn of the twenty-first century. As a "product," they were categorized and stereotyped. The following is an article by Professors Enrique C. Ochoa and Gilda L. Ochoa from California State University Pomona and Pomona College, respectively. This article was written in response to a 2006 remark by California Gov. Arnold Schwarzenegger that Latinas were sexually "hot."

There is nothing new about Gov. Arnold Schwarzenegger's description of state Assemblywoman Bonnie García as "very hot" because of her "black blood" and "Latino blood." Even García's claims—that the governor's comments are just an inside joke and that she is "a hot-blooded Latina"—are not surprising.

It was just two years ago that Mexican President Vicente Fox made similar offensive comments about African Americans. These "jokes" or "slips of the tongue" are part of the enduring legacy of gendered racism that is woven into the fabric of society. And their ramifications are real.

Schwarzenegger's comments are reminiscent of beliefs that were rampant through the early 1900s. These beliefs equated status in society with genetic, innate differences between groups. Northern Europeans were assumed to be biologically superior to all other groups—including Southern and Eastern Europeans, blacks, Native Americans, Asian Americans and Latin Americans.

Such genetic determinism helped to justify 250 years of enslavement of African Americans, attempts at cultural genocide against Native Americans, and segregation and U.S. imperial expansion.

Schwarzenegger's remarks also echo dominant thinking throughout the nineteenth century where the "mixing of blood" was negatively perceived. The first Anglo Americans who came to what is now the Southwest perpetuated the belief that Mexicans in the region were inferior to Anglos precisely because of their mixed heritage. Such biological thought fueled attempts to maintain "white racial purity," and with the exception of Vermont, all U.S. states introduced legislation banning interracial unions.

Not only should Schwarzenegger's comments be seen in the context of this enduring history of racism, but they also suggest the specific ways that most perceptions have interacted with sexism to justify the denigration, sexualization, and exploitation of women of color. During the period of U.S. invasion and domination of Mexico and Central America, popular music and travel literature written by Anglos stereotypically cast Latinas as sexually promiscuous, available, or "hot blooded." At this time, Asian women were similarly depicted as sexually immoral. As with African Americans during slavery, these characterizations of women of color had significant ramifications. They justifies kidnapping and rape, and for Chinese women, they resulted in the Page Law in 1875, where women were excluded from immigrating to the United States until 1943.

Despite attempts to forget this history, its manifestations run deep, and Schwarzenegger's comments reveal the insidious ways that such beliefs continue to shape public consciousness and institutional practices. Central to the anti-immigrant movement today is the mistaken belief that Latinas' sexuality leads to too many children and an overuse of public services. In the current War on Terror, Middle Eastern women are often viewed as repressed victims of a backward culture that need to be saved by a superior U.S. culture.

Communities of color have long challenged these discriminatory attitudes and actions. History is replete with examples, from African American resistance to slavery, Asian American struggles for citizenship, to the civil rights movements of the 1960s and 1970s. By teaching their children counter-histories, maintaining their cultures and languages, and fostering solidarity within their communities, women of color have engaged in multiple forms of resistance. The recent immigrant-rights marches are part of the contemporary ways that Latinas/os are countering anti-immigrant movements and white supremacist ideologies.

We should not let this moment pass as an isolated slip. Political leaders should be held accountable for their statements.

Source: Enrique C. Ochoa and Gilda L. Ochoa, "Arnold's Latina Slip Must Spark Dialogues," [Valley Edition], *Los Angeles Daily News*, September 12, 2006. p. N13.

417. Excerpts from Roberto Suro, Sergio Bendixen, and Dulce C. Benavides, "Billions in Motion: Latino Immigrants, Remittances, and Banking," 2002

Latin Americans working outside their countries sent $60 billion home in 2005, an estimated $45 billion sent by Latino immigrants in the United States. Most studies suggest that without these remittances there would be serious upheavals in Mexico and Central America where these remittances represent a significant portion of these countries' revenue. The Pew Hispanic Center at the University of Southern California, "a fact tank" focusing on Hispanic issues, has written several reports on money sent back to Mexican and Central American home countries whose economies would have collapsed without this support. Remittances in Mexico bring in more money than the tourist industry—second only to oil revenues. Such remittances are one of the major sources of revenue for these countries, which do not receive much money from the United States during a time that the 1994 North American Free Trade Agreement (NAFTA) and the 2004 Central American Free Trade Agreement (CAFTA) have worsened the economic plight of working people in these countries.

Until recently, the money management practices of Latino immigrants in the United States aroused little attention outside their own communities. That changed as the remittance flow doubled in size during the second half of the 1990s. Although the size of the average remittance transfer is miniscule—$200 to $300—in the world of international finance, the cumulative sums have now captured the attention of government policymakers and bankers in the United States and Latin America. Remittances to Latin America and the Caribbean totaled $23 billion in 2001, according to estimates by the Multilateral Investment Fund.... In 2000, remittances to Mexico, El Salvador, Guatemala, Honduras, and Nicaragua—nations that receive almost all their money transfers from the United States—totaled some $10.2 billion. This year, that figure could reach $14.2 billion or more, a flow of $39 million a day. By 2005, the sum, which does not capture all remittances to Latin America, will go beyond $18 billion, according to projections by the Pew Hispanic Center....

Across the United States in communities with large Mexican immigrant populations, a scenario that would have been unthinkable not long ago is now playing out on a regular basis: In a strip mall storefront, on a school parking lot, or in the offices of a community organization, a Mexican "mobile consulate" sets up shop. *Matrículas* are available on the spot. But that is not all. Often, there is someone there who helps the new recipients of the ID card apply for an Individual Taxpayer Identification Number (ITIN). This nine-digit identifier issued by the Internal Revenue

Service (IRS) looks like a social security number, but there are important differences. While a social security number is available only to citizens or people lawfully admitted to the United States, getting the taxpayer number does not require a showing of legal status. Also on the scene is an account manager from a local bank that has decided to accept the *matricula* and the taxpayer number as valid identification. In just minutes, an unauthorized Mexican immigrant can overcome the documentation barriers and be on his or her way to opening a bank account.

U.S. banks are moving aggressively to capture a greater share of the remittance market, and they are getting encouragement, even assistance, from both the U.S. and Mexican governments. In principle, these developments should increase competition and, hence, lead to lower fees, greater investments in technology, and a more efficient remittance flow. In principle, engagement with banks, credit unions, and other financial institutions should produce benefits beyond the remittance flow for both the senders and receivers. However, ensuring these outcomes will require specific efforts by all the parties involved to overcome some substantial obstacles.

The results of this study and the initial success achieved by banks that have targeted Latino immigrants clearly indicate that a large segment of the remitting population is willing, even eager, to explore new methods of sending money home. But this study also shows that familiarity, convenience, and simplicity have kept remitters going back to the old methods, chiefly wire transfer services like Western Union ... even when they are concerned that they are paying excessive transaction fees and foreign exchange costs. This study also shows that there is a widespread wariness of banks among remitters, especially when it comes to managing a household's month-to-month or week-to-week finances, primarily because of minimum balance requirements and the fees charged.

These findings suggest that a wholesale move by remitters to banking channels will only take place if banks can match or surpass the services provided by wire transfer firms at significantly reduced costs. And, given the intimate family connections between remittance senders and receivers, the convenience, reliability, and safety of the services provided in Latin America will have to meet or exceed those currently available there. In effect, U.S. banks will need to guarantee competitive pricing and quality of service at both ends of the remittance transaction. This will involve more than simply putting an effective product on the market and letting it go head-to-head with existing products. This study and others show that most remittance senders and receivers do not currently have bank accounts of any sort and probably never have. Banks, therefore, must successfully convince two populations—Latino immigrants in the United States and their families in Latin America—to trust their money to institutions that are unknown at best and might actually be viewed with some suspicion. Substantial challenges also face the remitters. The reliance on cash, the lack of knowledge about fees, and the minimal efforts put into investigating alternatives for remittances ending that were reported by participants in this study all bespeak low levels of financial literacy. Failure to understand the fundamental workings of a bank account, such as the need to keep track of a balance, can spell disaster for the neophyte in the form of bounced checks, cancelled accounts, and the rapidly mounting fees that result. Such problems prove the undoing of many an American college student every year and could prove all the more daunting to a Latino immigrant trying to manage international money transfers. In addition to learning the basic rules of managing a bank account, remitters will have to change some deeply imbedded behaviors in order to make effective use of U.S. banks. Fixed transaction fees are already emerging as a standard feature of some of the new remittance products. For example, Bank of America's Safe Send charges $10 or $15 per deposit, up to a maximum single deposit of $500 [de]pending on the type of account, each time a remitter in the United States deposits money into an account that the recipient can draw on with an ATM card in Mexico. A remitter who sticks to old habits of repeatedly moving small amounts—recall that the average is now $200 to $300—will pay far more than one who accumulates funds and makes a single transfer for the maximum amount. Similarly, such programs allow subscribers to make a minimum number of withdrawals without a fee. Safe Send, for example, allows one free ATM withdrawal for each deposit. Thus, the recipients will have to change their behavior as well to minimize costs in programs that favor a small number of transactions.

If Latino immigrants were to break the financial cycle of living from month-to-month, paying off bills, and then sending what remains home, they would reap benefits that go beyond economizing on the costs of remittance. The habit of accumulating money in a bank account is the first step toward full engagement with the U.S. financial system. There are a variety of potential benefits, including reduced banking costs, interest-paying savings accounts, the responsible use of credit, and, ultimately, financial practices that are rewarded by the tax system, such as home ownership and retirement savings accounts. If remittances are the point of entry for such engagement in the U.S. economic structure, the long-term benefits for the Latino immigrant population, and for the nation as a whole, could be quite substantial. Newcomers start out as remitters, but many settle here, become permanent residents, and start families as parents of U.S.-born children.

Remitters will need help in accomplishing this evolution. Currently, some banks offer financial literacy training to new customers. For example, the North Shore Bank of Brookfield, Wisconsin, has mounted registration drives with Mexican consular officials to get matriculas for immigrants and sign them up for bank accounts. Every new customer is offered … free training on the skills necessary to manage checking and savings accounts. Some Latino groups, such as the National Council of La Raza (NCLR) through its network of 270 affiliate organizations around the country, have made financial literacy training a major priority. NCLR has determined that the most successful programs have the following elements: (1) they use materials tailored to a specific audience, like recently arrived immigrants; (2) they are tied to a specific product or service; and (3) they are delivered by groups or individuals well known and trusted by the target community…. Greatly expanding these efforts is essential to ensuring that the remitters' engagement with the financial industry is a success. Indeed, failure to adequately educate Latino immigrants who open bank accounts could produce unnecessary setbacks for all concerned….

Source: © 2002 Pew Hispanic Center, a Pew Research Center project, www.pewhispanic.org. Report produced in cooperation between The Pew Hispanic Center and The Multilateral Investment Fund, pp. 2, 16, 17, 18.

418. "An Interview with Sub-Comandante Marcos of the Zapatista Army of National Liberation," 1995

Subcomandante Insurgente Marcos (1957–), is the spokesperson for the Ejercito Zapatista de Liberación Nacional (Zapatista Army of National Liberation—EZLN), a revolutionary army in Chiapas, Mexico. Marcos wears a mask to conceal his identity. The EZLN has pursued a nonviolent revolution and has garnered the sympathy of the world while he holds Mexican officials at bay. The Zapatistas are fighting for the rights of the Mayan people to preserve their culture and way of life. The 1994 North American Free Trade Agreement (NAFTA), which opened the Mexican economy to U.S. industries and promoted the privatization of the Mexican economy, threatened Mayan villages, prompted the destruction of communal lands, and hastened the commercialization of agriculture. In the following interview, Marcos explains why the Mayans revolted against the Mexican government. This message has been the movement's greatest defense and has attracted worldwide support up to this time in history.

San Cristobal

Mexico

He is among the few whose face is covered and is armed with a machine gun. He is not indigenous. While he speaks, he pulls a pipe from a pouch, puts it in his mouth through the opening of the Ski mask, but does not light it. He expresses himself with the clarity of the intellectual accustomed to communicating with the poor. He is surely Mexican, but it is not possible to identify the accent. A young woman with Asian eyes in a black mask stands next to him throughout the interview.

Comandante Marcos, you occupied San Cristobal on January 1st, 1994, who are you?

We are part of the Zapatista Army of National Liberation and we demand the resignation of the federal government and the formation of a transitional government which convenes free and democratic elections in August 1994. We want that the major demands of the peasants of Chiapas be met: food, health, education, autonomy, and peace. The indigenous people have always lived in a state of war because war has been waged against them and today the war will be in their favour. Whatever the case, we will have the opportunity to die in battle fighting instead of dying of dysentery, as the indigenous people of Chiapas usually die.

Do you have relationships with some political organisation of peasants?

We have no such relationships with any open organisation. Our organisation is exclusively armed and clandestine.

Were you formed out of nothing? Improvised?

We have been preparing ourselves in the mountains for ten years; we are not an improvised movement. We have matured, thought, learned, and made this decision.

Do you have racial and ethnic demands?

The Committee of Directors is made up of indigenous Tzotziles, Tzeltles, Choles, Tojolabales, Mames, and Zoques, all of the major ethnic groups of Chiapas. They all agree, and apart from democracy and representation, they demand respect, respect which white people have never had for them. Above all, in San Cristobal the residents, insult and discriminate again them as a daily occurrence. Now white people respect the Indians because they see them with guns in their hands.

How do you think the government will respond?

We do not worry about the response of the government. We worry about the response of the Mexican people. We want to know what this event will provoke, what will move the national consciousness. We hope something moves, not only in the form of armed struggle, but in all forms of struggle. We hope this will put an end to this disguised dictatorship.

Don't you have confidence in the PRD as an opposition party in the next elections?

We don't distrust the political parties as much as we do the electoral system. The government of Salinas de Gortari is an illegitimate party, product of fraud, and this illegitimate government can only produce illegitimate elections. We want a transitional government and that the government hold new elections—but with a capacity that is genuinely egalitarian, offering the same opportunities to all political parties. In Chiapas, 15,000 Indians per year die of curable diseases. It is a statistic of the same magnitude that the war produced in El Salvador. If a peasant with cholera comes to a rural hospital, they will throw him out so that no one will say there is cholera in Chiapas. In this movement, the Indians who form part of the Zapatista Army want to first dialogue with their own people. They are the real representatives.

Excuse me, but you are not an Indian.

You must understand our movement is not Chiapaneco. It is national. There are people like me, others who come from other states, and Chiapanecos who fight in other states. We are Mexicans, that unifies us, as well as the demand for liberty and democracy. We want to elect genuine representatives.

But now are you not afraid of heavy repression?

For the Indians, repressions exist for the past 500 years. Maybe you think of repression in terms of the typical South American government. But for the Indians, this kind of repression is their daily bread. Ask those who live in the surrounding communities of San Cristobal.

What development would you consider a movement?

We would like others in the country to join this movement.

An armed movement?

No, we make a broad appeal which we direct towards those who are active in civil, legal, and open popular movements.

Why did you choose January 1st to attack San Cristobal?

It was the Committee of Directors which decided. It is clear the date is related to NAFTA, which for the Indians is a death sentence. Once it goes into effect, it means an international massacre.

What do you believe the international response will be? Are you not afraid the United States will intervene like it has in other parts of Latin America?

The U.S. used to have the Soviet Union as a pretext, they were afraid of Soviet infiltration in our countries. But what can they make of a movement which claims social justice? They cannot continue to think we are being manipulated from the outside, or that we are financed by Moscow gold, since Moscow no longer exists. The people in the U.S. should be aware that we struggle for those things that others struggle for. Did not the people of Germany and Italy rebel against a dictatorship? Does the rebellion of the Mexicans not have the same value? The people in the U.S. have a great deal to do with the reality which you can observe here, with the conditions of misery of the Indians and the great hunger for justice. In Mexico, the entire social system is based upon the injustice in its relations with the Indians. The worst thing that can happen to a human being is to be Indian, with all its burden of humiliation, hunger, and misery.

This is a subversive movement. Our objective is the solution of the principal problems of our country, which necessarily intersect with problems of liberty and democracy. This is why we think that the government of Salinas de Gortari is an illegitimate government which can only convene illegitimate elections. The solution is a call to all citizens and to the House of Deputies and Senators and to comply with their patriotic duty and remove Salinas de Gortari and all his Cabinet and to form a transitional government. And the transitional government should call elections, with equal opportunity for all political parties.

Based on that, the compañeros say other demands can be negotiated: bread, housing, health, education, land, justice, many problems, which within the context of indigenous people, are very serious. But the demands for liberty and democracy are being made as A call to all the Mexican Republic, to all the social sectors to participate, not with guns, but with the means which they have.

We have been isolated all these years, while the rest of the world rebelled against dictatorships or apparent dictatorships and this was viewed with logic. In this country, however, a series of dictatorial measures were being adopted and no one said anything. We believe there is an international consensus that only the Mexicans were missing, who have suffered under an absolute dictatorship by the Party and now by one person, who is Carlos Salinas de Gortari, now through Luis Donaldo Colosio. I think that at the international level they will see that a movement with demands like these is logical.

There is not in the movement of the Zapatista Army of National Liberation an ideology perfectly defined, in the sense of being Communist or Marxist-Leninist. There is a common point of connection with the great national problems, which coincide always, for one or the other sector, in a lack of liberty and democracy.

In this case, this sector has used up any other method of struggle such as the legal struggle, the popular struggle, the economic projects, the struggle for Sedesol [La Secretaria de Desarrollo Social, federal office in charge of local development of indigenous people], and it ends following the only method which remains, the armed struggle. But we are open to other tendencies and to other forms of struggle, in the enthusiasm to generate a genuine national and revolutionary movement which reconciles these two fundamental demands, liberty and democracy. On these grounds a movement can be formed which will create a genuine solution to the economic and social problems of each sector, whether indigenous or peasant, workers, teachers, intellectuals, small business owners of the small and medium-sized industry.

The repression on the indigenous population has been present for many years. The indigenous people of Chiapas suffer 15,000 deaths per year, that no one mourns. The great shame is that they die of curable diseases and this is denied by the Department of Health.

We expect a favourable reaction from Mexican society toward the reasons which give birth to this movement because they are just. You can question the method of struggle, but never its causes.

Source: Revolutionary Democracy. Vol. I, No. 2, September 1995, http://www.revolutionarydemocracy. org/rdv1n2/marcos.htm.

419. Suzanne López, "The Dense, Impenetrable Adobe Ceiling," 2003

In 2004, in the United States, white women earned 73 cents for every dollar earned by a white man; Asian women, 68 cents; African American women, 64 cents, Native American women, 58 cents, and Latina women earn 51 cents per dollar. Latina girls left high school at a much higher rate than any other group. The major factor was teenage pregnancy but close seconds were marriage, gender roles, stereotyping, family demands, and economic status, as well as attitudes of teachers. These stereotypes continued even after many had made it through college. The article talks to leading Chicana professionals about the operation of an adobe ceiling that has limited their upward mobility. It interviews Cencilia Burciaga who experienced discrimination at various universities.

While White women are said to encounter a glass ceiling that prevents them from progressing in their careers, Latinas face a more formidable barrier—an adobe ceiling—an obstacle far more challenging to overcome because a glass ceiling at least provides a vision of what lies ahead, said a higher education leader in California.

"With a glass ceiling, you are allowed to see the next level," said Cecilia Preciado Burciaga, former associate vice president for student affairs at California State University at Monterey Bay (CSUMB). "At least you can see through it and practice for the promotion. But an adobe ceiling is dense, impenetrable, and it doesn't allow you to see to the next level. I would like that luxury to see what's next. Once Latinas do break through it, they are often surprised by the personal and professional costs."

Burciaga, who has a master's degree in sociology policy studies from the University of California at Riverside, has spent the last few years developing her theory about the adobe ceiling and has spoken about the subject at public forums. This summer, during a speech at Pima County Community College District in Tucson, Ariz, she shared her thoughts on the ceiling and what it takes to break through it. The event had many co-sponsors: the International Women's Film and Speaker Series of the Dean's Interdisciplinary Education Grant, the Crossing Border Speaker Series of the Dean's Minority Education Grant—both funded through the community college, the Arizona Association of Chicanos for Higher Education, Desert Vista Campus, the CSUMB foundation, and its Equal Employment Opportunity Affirmative Action Office.

Burciaga, 57, has 28 years of administrative experience in higher education. She served on the White House Commission on Educational Excellence for Hispanic Americans (1994–2001) and has been named one of the "Top 100 Most Influential Latinas of the Century" by *Latina* magazine.

She speaks of the adobe ceiling from personal experience. Burciaga recently won a discrimination lawsuit she'd filed against CSUMB with two other Latinas. As part of the settlement, she agreed to leave the University early this year, but CSUMB paid $1 million in damages shared among the defendants and an additional $1.5 million for scholarships to Salinas County area students. University officials said they could not comment, as part of the settlement terms of the lawsuit.

"Our population deserves more respect," said Burciaga, adding that she was surprised to have encountered the adobe ceiling at Monterey Bay because more than half of the population in the area is Latino.

Burciaga said she worked for 20 years at Stanford University where she also encountered the adobe ceiling. She climbed through the ranks and held a variety of positions while at Stanford, including director of the Office of Chicano Affairs, associate dean, and director of development in the Office of the Vice President for

Student Resources. When she joined Stanford in 1974, the student body was just 2 percent Mexican American, and there were few Chicano faculty or staff. She worked diligently to increase the numbers of Latinos on the campus so she "wouldn't be the only one there." By 1992, the student body had grown to 11 percent Chicano, and the faculty was increasingly diverse, for which Burciaga said she feels she could take some credit. When she was at Stanford, her staff recruited more women and minorities into the University's PhD programs.

In an interview with the *Christian Science Monitor*, Burciaga said that she did not find open resistance to affirmative action at Stanford, but she did have to fight against apathy.

"It is the faculty that hire faculty," she said in that interview. "They know best how to find their own animals. That means faculty members have got to want it."

In the 1970s, she worked for the U.S. Civil Rights Commission and was named by then-President Jimmy Carter to a National Advisory Committee for Women and on the International Commission on the Observance of International Women's Year.

"Cecilia is one of the people I look up to," said Mickie Solorio Luna, California state president of LULAC [League of United Latin American Citizens]. "She's always in the trenches."

While Latinas and White women face different types of ceilings in the workplace, their home lives widen the gap between the two even further. Anglo women can escape the glass ceiling once they leave their workplace at the end of the day because their spouses, parents, and siblings often enjoy the benefits of being part of the "elite culture," said Burciaga. Latinas, on the other hand, have families who are all generally part of the "non-power" group.

Burciaga said she believes that the personal and social connections Anglo women enjoy through marriage or through their parents and siblings help them get through the glass ceiling but Latinas lack those familial connections, making the adobe ceiling virtually impenetrable.

Another aspect of the glass ceiling analogy is the saying that Anglo women also encounter a sticky floor in their efforts to advance their careers, but Burciaga said the sticky floor provides traction. Latinas encounter a dirt floor under their adobe ceiling, a floor that she said allows Latinas to be swept away.

"It's so true what she said," said Luna. "We're on a slippery floor. We're pushed aside, pushed out the door. Latinas always fight for equality for everybody else. We don't get recognition. Latinas are very humble, and we don't ask for recognition."

Burciaga's theory is backed by numbers. A recent study on corporate America by the Hispanic Association on Corporate Responsibility (HACR) found that Hispanic women are grossly underrepresented. They hold only 0.3 percent of all board seats and represent 0.08 percent of all executive officer positions in Fortune 1,000 companies. Of 141 Hispanic board members at Fortune 1,000 companies, only 21 are women, and of 110 Hispanic executive officers, only eight are women.

"Hispanic women, in particular, have encountered a 'concrete ceiling' in corporate America," said HACR President and CEO Anna Escobedo Cabral. "Even though there are more Hispanic women professionals and the number of businesses owned by Hispanic women is one of the fastest growing sectors, Hispanic women continue to be excluded from contributing as board members and executive officers of the largest companies in the nation."

Burciaga said she feels that Latinas not only encounter the adobe ceiling and dirt floor in corporate America but also in higher education. Anglo women are making strides in becoming college presidents and vice presidents, and she said it is important they not forget their Latina *hermanas* as they create leadership teams for their institutions of higher education.

"This is an opportunity for them to manifest deeper change in the women's movement," said Burciaga. "The question is 'are they diversifying their leadership teams any more than Anglo males?'"

Burciaga expressed concern that the women's movement in general failed to clearly convey the message to women that their advancement carried a responsibility to bring about positive change for all women in the workplace. All women have a responsibility to younger women to help them move forward because any progress that has been made by the women's movement is always at risk and those freedoms can be lost, she said.

But, Burciaga said Latinas must also be more proactive in advancing their own careers, in highlighting their professional successes, a skill that traditionally has been difficult for many Latinas to carry out.

"I tell Latinas not to believe in the good tooth fairy, that if we're good, someone will put a promotion under our pillows," said Burciaga. "Part of our culture is not to be boastful. We're not comfortable with self-promotion. It is important to learn to talk about your accomplishments in a way that is not offensive. To not talk about your accomplishments is deadly."

Amalia Mesa-Bains, director of the Institute for Visual and Public Arts at CSUMB, said she is optimistic about the future for young Latinas. Older Latinas have been striving to develop a model that provides a balance between the family demands of Latino culture and the demands of professional career. Younger Latinas struggle with the Anglo version of having to choose between family and professional aspirations to be successful and the model evolving among Latinas brings the two aspects together.

"I think the young girls are going to kick in the ceiling," said Mesa-Bains. "They are very connected to the goals of the [Latino] community. The unique model we have created for them springs from our family-based and community-based experience. I see us at the adobe ceiling, and I see us finding an opening. We want to open the adobe ceiling, but we do not want to forget the adobe itself."

Burciaga said she feels she is making a contribution, chipping away the adobe ceiling Latinas encounter by filing her lawsuit, mentoring young women, speaking out about the adobe ceiling, and pushing her career forward.

"Cecilia stood her ground for what she believes in, and she never felt sorry for herself," said Luna. "She made a difference and gained the respect from everybody around her. I hope other women will learn from this and stand up for younger women."

Mesa-Bains, co-chair of the Chicano-Latino Faculty and Staff Association at CSUMB, praised Burciaga for her heroic efforts to bring about change at the University.

"We need to recognize the heroism of someone who is willing to sacrifice her own career to force a university to live up to the vision it espouses and to commit the resources necessary to realize that vision."

Burciaga hopes other Latinas are working with her on drilling through the adobe ceiling. Having a network of Latinas to rely on helps make the process of breaking through the adobe ceiling easier, she said. She praises the network of Latinas she relies on and has befriended over the years, saying that they show her that there is a peephole of light and hope through the adobe ceiling.

"Too often we work alone, but we must come together to conquer," Burciaga said. "I have made a commitment to keep chipping away."

Luna said she too believes that if Latinas keep chipping away, eventually the walls will come down.

Burciaga is a first-generation Chicana of parents who were natives of Jalisco, Mexico. She and her late husband, Jose Antonio Burciaga, a poet and artist, have two children, María Rebeca and José Antonio.

Source: Suzanne López, "The Dense, Impenetrable Adobe Ceiling," *The Hispanic Outlook in Higher Education*, Vol. 13, No. 10, February 24, 2003–March 9, 2003, pp. 16, 17.

420. Chip Jacobs, "Return of the Native," 2005

Probably the person most responsible for the California Latino Political Revolution, the election of a critical number of Chicanos to the California State Legislature and the Los Angeles City Council, was Richard Alatorre. Alatorre was elected to the California Assembly and Los Angeles City Council during a time in the early 1980s when there were no Mexicans on those bodies. He served on reapportionment committees in the state legislature, made deals, and was always controversial. However, he always kept East Los Angeles in his heart, and although the deals were often in his interests, they rarely went against the interests of the area. Alatorre, along with State Sen. Richard Polanco, who was chair of the Legislature's Latino Caucus for a 12-year reign and tripled its membership, molded a new generation of Latino politicos that became a force in California politics. The following article, based on an interview with Alatorre, explains the process in which Latinos are a third of the Los Angeles City Council and a majority of the Democratic Party Caucus in the California Assembly.

The 200 folks squished into the VIP lounge of the Henry Fonda Music Box Theater were grinning and yipping as the early poll results blinked on the big screens. It was primary night, March 3, and the Antonio-Villaraigosa-for-Mayor bandwagon resembled a Winnebago. A Motown band crooned, the liquor went fast, and if you noticed it, off to the side of the victory buzz, a gaggle of small-town mayors, party operatives, and various believers were embracing a dark-eyed legend many were afraid to be seen with a few years ago. Richard Alatorre was touchable again.

"He was getting hearty hugs, unsolicited, and people wanted their picture with him," recalls Don Justin Jones, a Democratic activist from Pasadena who has known Alatorre since the 1960s. "There's a saying, 'You don't shake hands with a dead man or he'll pull you down with him,' and the establishment was treating Richard like the long-lost prince of the city. You know he was happy when he was calling people, 'Babe.'"

Had a few things gone differently, it might've been Richard José Alatorre taking the oath as Los Angeles' first Latino mayor in modern times, not the slick, cherubic-faced Villaraigosa (should he unseat Jim Hahn May 17). Had Alatorre not tried to house a little girl who lost her mother nine years ago, some grand building might now bear his name.

Destiny, however, had other ideas. His storybook ascent from barrio kid to Hispanic political royalty collapsed in soap-operatic disgrace in 2001 with a graft conviction and drug allegations. He was banished to the Siberia of house arrest, his legacy tarnished no matter the heartfelt tributes from senators and do-gooders.

Should Villaraigosa need a primer on toughness, the man who has been his unofficial campaign *consigliere* can go one better. He knows history can be viciously ironic.

In 1992, in a recession-flattened, riot-torn Los Angeles, it was Alatorre, the mainstream Democrat, whom the conservative Richard Riordan most feared as his opponent in the mayor's race. It was Alatorre who masterminded the district reapportionment that enabled Villaraigosa to win Alatorre's old seat that he has used to challenge Hahn. And it was Alatorre, along with County Supervisor Gloria Molina, his longtime nemesis, who hoed the path for a fresh crop of Mexican American politicians. One of them was Richard Alarcón, the defeated mayoral candidate and Valley Councilman who liked stressing he was no Alatorre (read: *corrupt*).

Having jogged through hell and back, Alatorre is in his salad days now—happier, healthier, and holier, those close to him say. The impatient snarls that seemed to bubble from a tormented soul—what writer Hunter S. Thompson once called a politician's *inner werewolf*—surface less often. At 63, he is a family guy and elder statesman, both felon and community icon, living sorry for the shame he caused yet convinced that he was hunted.

"I don't condone what I did, but I did it out of desperation," Alatorre explains, slitting his eyes at Camilo's Bistro, one of his Eagle Rock hangouts. "I made a mistake and paid for it. It was a very humiliating experience for my family and friends and the institutions that I was part of. It made me assess the role I'd played in things.

"For five years, I had to wake up wondering what the next story was coming up," he adds. "Because of what happened, I'm the sum of the end of my career, when things were bad. I've got that asterisk on my resume that overshadowed 28 years of work."

That episode now seems like yesterday and never-happened. Peers don't worry anymore if they're being taped when they call him. A grayer, chubbier Alatorre gets warm smiles at City Hall. Politicians frequently call him for advice, or to help settle feuds. He's also not skating fast over the thin ice of insolvency anymore. Working quietly, tooling around in his steel-gray Jaguar, he consults for the Affordable Housing Development Corp., the Los Angeles Port Police, the city of Alhambra, and others. Clients chase him, though he refuses to lobby because of disclosure rules that once got him in hot water as a politician.

"I'm making more money than I ever have," Alatorre confirms. "But I'm not trying to chase the buck. All I want is to support my family and live as privately as humanly possible."

Alatorre, unlike the impeached Bill Clinton or a defrocked televangelist, took his lumps old school: he suffered quietly. Sequestered at home, calling in to his probation officer, he didn't court votes or campaign dough. He's learned to make beds, empty the garbage, and enjoy the peace of not having to attend endless meetings. There was no image-revival campaign, no weepy appearance on Oprah, even if he believed that the media had unfairly portrayed him as a sleazebag.

"I wasn't going to let reporters know I had little respect for them driving me out of town," he says.

THE NATURAL

Before he died, José Alatorre left his son with a nugget: Use your head to make a living, because "you aren't any good with your hands." Young Richard embraced that advice, becoming student body president at Garfield High and part-time collection agent for a Whittier Boulevard jewelry store—a job that taught him when to intimidate people and when to back off.

He was an outgoing teenager, slightly rebellious, sure to attend Mass to check out the girls or pray that his jump shot fell during basketball season.

"I was the typical Catholic hypocrite," Alatorre chuckles. (Today, he's hard-core devout.)

At Cal State Los Angeles, Alatorre majored in sociology and then got his master's in public administration from USC, no small feat. While teaching college courses, he happened one day to run into East L.A. Assemblyman Walter Karabian, who knew potential when he saw it. He gave the kid a staff job.

Itching to be the man, Alatorre soon ran and won the assembly seat vacated by David Roberti. His timing sparkled, and he nuzzled in with a fun-loving set of heavy-hitters led by Speaker Willie Brown and his lieutenant, Mike Roos. Brown so liked Alatorre's preternatural cunning that he gave him the committee chairmanship overseeing juiced gambling and liquor interests. Picketing with Chávez, as Alatorre did in 1966 to protest farmworkers' conditions, fed the soul. Working at the state capital during the Chicano era on pesticide regulation and rent control fed his conviction that the little guy needed protection.

But it wasn't heaven. Being in Sacramento meant he saw little of his two sons, who were living in Alhambra with his divorced first wife, Stella. He was terrified of flying, and distances required he do it constantly. He had a few harrowing experiences, including one occasion when the plane's nose cone blew off. To soothe his nerves, he drank.

Tired of flying and jonesing to put his stamp on local politics, he ran for L.A. City Council in 1985. He won, oiled by special interest money, joining the flamboyant Nate Holden, the stately John Ferraro, and erudite Zev Yaroslavsky at the Council horseshoe. In a portentous act, he paid a record $142,000 settlement to the City Attorney's office for failing to disclose contributors.

Alatorre savored the pothole politics that Brown had laughingly warned him he'd come to despise. He was the king of a fiefdom that ran from Boyle Heights to the Glendale border. In that district's volatile immigrant neighborhoods and yuppified hills, everybody recognized his swarthy, rutted complexion and sandpaper voice.

Mayor Tom Bradley also found his Council point man in Alatorre, even if the two couldn't be any different personality-wise. Alatorre proved to be masterful at three-dimensional thinking and lining up votes—without an excess of silky oratory.

Yaroslavsky, now a Westside supervisor, felt a kinship with Alatorre because they both grew up in the same destitute area and understood tough personalities. Their similarities made for some electric combat.

"I judge people in politics by whether their word was good and whether you can depend on them hunkered down in battle, and yeah, I could trust him," Yaroslavsky said. "The thing about him that I always appreciated, even though we don't always agree … he always was the real deal. He cares about people on the margins.… I'm not going to defend what he did, [but] when I was up against him, I knew I was in the fight of my life."

By the 1990s, Yaroslavsky's portrait was the general impression of Alatorre: a fighter and even a bully. He'd holler at building officials who weren't moving fast enough to get repairs done. He'd sometimes unload on his own staff, exploding like a volcano while aides were left quivering.

Alhambra Mayor Daniel Arguello was part of Alatorre's assembly staff from 1977 to 1982. He remembers him for his odd mix of tenderness, agile thinking, and combustibility.

"As a boss, he was the most fun I've ever had, and there were other times when I wanted to kick in the door," Arguello remembered. "I'd worked for Tom Bradley, and his control was his presence. When Richard Alatorre was angry, everybody knew it."

This explosiveness, Alatorre now believes, was evidence of buried emotions. He was a "dry drunk" who missed his dad terribly. He couldn't uncork his feelings. He regretted what kind of father he'd been. Here he was out at ribbon-cuttings, defending the LAPD, shepherding a budget deal, and yet lost inside.

"People had this impression that I was ruthless, or had no blood in my veins," Alatorre said. "I gave nothing up about my emotions, so they said I was mean, cutthroat, backstabbing. You hear that time in, time out, and you become hardened. You become isolated if you've never taken stock of yourself. I didn't realize that I was bleeding internally."

LITTLE HOUSE IN EAGLE ROCK

The world would find out about his hemorrhaging maybe before he did.

In 1997, this reporter wrote a lengthy story in the *L.A. Weekly* about Alatorre's connections to Samuel Mevorach, an Arcadia-based real estate operator who'd bedeviled L.A. housing officials with his dilapidated properties. Among Mevorach's holdings was the Wyvernwood Apartments, a sprawling, once-tidy Boyle Heights complex that had degenerated into blistered, crime-infested units coated with dangerous flaking lead paint; a number of children were poisoned from it. Feeling the heat from inspectors, Mevorach needed Alatorre's sway to grease a $91-million, city-subsidized sale of the property.

Alatorre unluckily needed Mevorach just as much as the slumlord needed him.

The previous year, Belinda Ramos, the sister of Alatorre's third and current wife, Angie, had died of colon cancer. Ramos left behind an adorable, seven-year-old girl whose father was named Henry Lozano. An older man, Lozano was chief of staff to a Democratic congressman and staunchly aligned with Gloria Molina's political machine.

Ramos' dying wish was for Melinda to live with the Alatorres. Melinda loved them, and they loved her back. Two months later, the Alatorres decided to sell their Monterey Hills condo and relocate to an Eagle Rock house with a yard and floor plan roomier for a child.

About this same time, Lozano, who hadn't had much involvement with Melinda, got upset when the little girl didn't want to spend time with him. Lozano's next move was to initiate a custody fight. It exposed a lot more than parenting techniques.

Soon, the *Los Angeles Times* began writing about how the Alatorres had financed their move into the Spanish-style house. The paper found that Mevorach had given Alatorre tens of thousands of dollars under the table and arranged a sham lease on the condo. Stories about money exchanges at greasy restaurants, bagmen, and mysterious new roofs tied to one of Alatorre's political contributors had a Raymond Chandler feel. When those articles subsided, Alatorre's alleged coke use snatched *Times* headlines.

By 1998, it was unclear whether Alatorre would survive the onslaught. The judge overseeing the ongoing custody fight ordered a surprise drug test, and Alatorre was found to have coke in his system despite his proclamation he was clean. The same judge who'd once praised the Alatorres for their care of Melinda ordered her out of their presence. Alatorre's credibility, the judge scolded, had been "totally shredded."

He'd ignited the biggest ethics scandal to hit L.A. since the final term of the Bradley administration. Bradley's plunge began when it was revealed that he was a paid adviser to a bank doing business with the city. Alatorre's crisis, by comparison, gave the public an excruciating glimpse into his narcotics use and personal relationships.

Alatorre had once vowed he wouldn't wind up like Bradley had—a broken man sadly walking away from a job after overstaying his welcome—but suddenly Alatorre was lunch meat in a media feeding frenzy. So many television news crews clogged his new front porch that a fence had to be installed. FBI agents pried into his affairs, with the District Attorney's office not far behind. Supposed friends shunned him, unaware of his sinking health or tattered finances. Family members were sucked into the chaos, as well.

For Angie Alatorre, who'd stood by her husband during the squall, having Melinda removed was the low point. She'd felt guilty that it was her side of the family that had caused her husband's spiral. The drugs, however, were his doing.

"The only time I" got angry "was when we lost Melinda because of Richard's really dumb behavior and the judge sent her to go to my mother's for a week," she recalls. "I told (Richard) that if we didn't get her back, 'I'll never forgive you for this.' I didn't have to say anything else for him to know things had to change."

The next year, Alatorre stunned his backers when he announced he would not seek re-election. He knew that while he'd probably win the election, it'd be a nasty contest that'd cut deeper into his kin. The fact that Melinda was too young to understand the fireworks above her was a blessing they didn't want to exploit.

RIDDEN TO THE GROUND

Today, private-citizen Alatorre looks healthier than the public one, who often slouched enigmatically at meetings in his fine suits.

Darrell Alatorre, Richard's youngest son, said many people disbelieve him when he says how vibrant his dad has become. With the pressure off, he has time for chatty lunches, USC football games, walks around the Rose Bowl, and doting on Melinda, now a high school junior. Just don't give his dad a home fix-it project because he is all thumbs, Darrell Alatorre laughs.

The late-1990s, conversely, was a wagon-circling time the Alatorre clan would rather forget. The grand jury hauled lots of frightened people before it. Darrell Alatorre lost business clients worried about the stigma. His older brother, Derrick, relocated his family out of the area to relieve the pressure. Alatorre tried reassuring his family he was okay, but he wasn't sleeping well or looking good. The stress contributed to a ruptured diaphragm requiring surgery in 1997 and 1998. Two years later he got prostate cancer. Today he's healthy.

"I didn't worry about his sanity. I worried about his health!" Darrell Alatorre says. "Did I see fear in his eyes? Did he ever break down? Yeah, a couple times. Is that a picture a son wants to see in his father? No! The whole ordeal he went through was bullshit, though there was some truth to his past addiction. I remember asking him during the custody battle why he was doing all this, and he said, '*Mijo*, Melinda has nowhere else to go.'"

Meanwhile, as the subpoenas and the stories about him flew, his friends and colleagues were puzzled. Why wasn't he fighting back? His inner circle was baffled that he wasn't holding a press conference to defend himself or announce a libel suit from accusations that many of them believed were untrue or sensationalized. Alatorre was a lot of things, but passive wasn't part of the package.

The *Times*, among other charges, had accused Alatorre's cronies of paying him off through his wife's event-planning business and charities. Where was the context about why they'd wanted the house, his backers asked. Where were the questions about why Richard was abusing? And where was the lowdown on Mevorach, who'd copped a deal with the feds, telling them that Alatorre had "extorted" him for cash when Mevorach had been currying Alatorre's favor for years?

Darrell Alatorre says he was ready to take on the *Times* when a writer friend at the paper tipped him off that it'd budgeted $500,000 for stories about the family and had hired private investigators to dig up dirt. A reporter who worked on the stories says there was no such budget item for these stories and no investigators were retained.

"I couldn't believe it," Darrell Alatorre said. "It seemed such an astronomical amount of money. Later, I'd never seen the paper so demonize somebody."

Angie Alatorre says she and her husband's longtime confidante Lou Moret didn't always agree on tactics, but they thought their man should counterpunch. Moret, though, found that Alatorre just wanted out, and didn't believe blood-smelling reporters with preconceptions about ethnic politicians would listen to him.

"He didn't think he took money for anything more improper than anyone else had," says Moret, who ran Alatorre's 1972 and 1974 Assembly campaigns. "He knew he'd been treated differently, and partly that's because he's Mexican and partly because of his reluctance to sell his viewpoint, philosophically. That's how the cookie crumbles…. Richard wasn't forced out. He wasn't defeated. He wasn't recalled…. But for the *L.A. Times*, he was an easy target."

For his part, Alatorre says it wasn't until he left office and reflected back that he realized his spin into coke, self-doubt, and silence had been building for 30-odd years.

Early on April 15, 1964, Alatorre's first son, Derrick, was born at a Boyle Heights hospital. Ten hours later, the ecstasy crumbled when Richard's father suffered a heart attack while painting a crib for his infant grandson and died. For José's boy, the loss was ironic, wrenching, and most of all, lasting.

José Alatorre, stove repairman and seventh-grade dropout, had always preached hard work and keeping personal problems private. While stoic, he prized ideals. If the national anthem were [*sic*] playing on TV, he'd make young Richard stand, though he didn't always.

In passing away so abruptly, José never saw his string-bean son, then 21, mature from a student leader with a 60-hour-a-week job to one of the nimblest minds in a mostly white state legislature. Nor was he around to dispense wisdom when Richard's weaknesses roared.

"I never knew how much I blamed my dad for dying," Alatorre confides. "It forced me to become something I wasn't ready to be. I had to become head of a household, but I was still a kid. I had no constructive outlet for being hurt later in life. You don't stuff things down in your soul and expect be happy."

Alcoholics Anonymous helped open his eyes, and he accepted that his addictive personality had shown even at age 14, when he chug-a-lugged some wine. By his 20s, liquor quieted his rage. He finally quit in 1988 after getting treatment, not allowing himself to lapse when the graft investigations revved up.

It was the drug all over L.A.—cocaine—that he sought. (Drugs, it's worth noting, are the one subject Alatorre refuses to detail except to say stories about him snorting at City Hall or with a buddy looking for city contracts were mostly false.)

"Through AA, I now understand I am a grateful alcoholic," he says. "We're not normal. A normal person can have one drink and not 10 to 15. I know that if I took one drink, the run would be on.... I had so much happening in my life then, when the [stories hit], I didn't know I was powerless."

Nor, some say, did he realize his baggage was slowly entombing him.

"He started locking out friends who would've told him, 'Don't do that! What the f—— is wrong with you?'" Moret adds. "He became a refugee. He wasn't making the right decisions. He got in trouble because he's an addict. Even when he was drinking, it wasn't because he liked it. It wasn't wine or fine Scotch he used. It was Seven-and-Seven. Who drinks that?"

THE AL CAPONE TREATMENT

Thick pride may have also contributed to his troubles. By 1996, Alatorre's machinations to funnel government work to Hispanic-run ventures struck many as heavy-handed, as did his connections to the East Los Angeles Community Union, Corboda Corp., and various MTA contractors seeking a piece of a $1-billion rail line through his district. Newly elected Council members didn't fear him as others once had. In what turned out to be his last campaign, a political novice forced him into a runoff.

"He didn't want to give his detractors the pleasure of seeing the mighty stag taken down," says Jones, the Pasadena activist. "He didn't want to let folks in on the pain, and maybe that got him into trouble. Fidel Castro said in his famous speech: 'You can find me guilty, but history will absolve me.' When you look back at this period, people will appreciate that Richard didn't cry when his enemies kicked him in the ass, but I guarantee you that his boots were full of blood."

Even after he left office, the bloodletting continued. When Alatorre was lined up with consulting work typical for ex-politicians with the L.A. Department of Water and Power and the Compton Community College District, the *Times* wrote about it, and officials nixed what could have been $70,000-a-year in income. A $114,000-a-year post with a state unemployment insurance board ended, too, when Alatorre settled with the Justice Department.

His legal-defense bills topped $100,000, and to pay them he had to bust open his IRA and pay a $100,000 penalty for early withdrawal. This somewhat undercuts the notion he'd been stashing away money as a guy-on-the-take, as detractors suspected; there were no secret bank accounts. Because he'd always spent what he made, Alatorre says he "didn't have the luxury of not working" and launched his consulting business.

Dine with him and you glean four things: His cell phone never stops jangling, he wolfs bacon like air, and he can spice cuss words into the most delicate topic. The other f-word—"felon"—he doesn't use. The idea that he is one scalds him. It just doesn't seem to obsess him.

If he has any satisfaction about his demise, it's that a four-year, federal-led investigation of his links to people trying to buy his influence did not result in a major corruption charge. Instead, he pled to not disclosing $42,000 in illicit income on his ethics commission and tax filings. Some call this the "Al Capone" treatment: nailing a high-profile figure on a relatively incidental charge. No other big fish was nabbed, either.

"By prosecuting me, I was making somebody's career," Alatorre says. "We ran the city—me, Zev [Yaroslavsky], and John Ferraro—when Bradley was in trouble. Even the *Times* said that. But certain people did not feel like I was the kind of guy who should be mayor, and what's ironic is that I never wanted that."

Maybe not, but that doesn't mean he's short on ideas about how to get it. Still very much on his game, Alatorre will unleash a torrent of expletive-laden opinion about this year's race. And if he's really talking to Villaraigosa as much as he says he is, current Mayor Jim Hahn's ears are burning.

"Jimmy is like the T-ball mayor. I go back to when Jimmy first ran for City Controller, and I had the distinct impression he fell into politics. It's not where his gut is," Alatorre says. "Jimmy is a very honest guy. It's just that he's always around the edges on issues. If you asked his ex-aides, they'd say he's lazy. He doesn't live and breathe politics like his sister [Councilwoman Janice Hahn] does. [Former Gov.] Gray Davis was evil. He was driven. Jimmy isn't driven. He's just blah."

Alatorre does sees promise in Villaraigosa, saying, "I recognize Antonio's shortcomings, but he has the best chance of getting done what L.A. needs," adding: "We need someone who will work well with the City Council and Sacramento, someone who will get L.A. the goodies."

For instance, he notes that Hahn hasn't even taken advantage of L.A.'s respected police chief, William Bratton, to get more cops or anti-terrorism money. "Bratton likes the notoriety here, but he's so far up Jimmy Hahn's butt, and Jimmy is so far up his, neither of them can see.... If I were mayor, I'd go put my arm around President Bush and say how much I liked his dad if it got us resources."

That is the kind of thinking that got results, and both the residents who recognize him strolling down Garfield Avenue and the powerful remember. Sympathy is another thing.

"Richard Alatorre was clearly the smartest guy on the City Council when I was there; I admire and love him, but I don't feel sorry for him," says former Mayor Richard Riordan, now California's Secretary of Education. "Judge him as he is today. [After all], we forgive murderers."

The family's saga has ended better than any of them could have imagined four years ago—happily. Alatorre has work aplenty and time with his family. Melinda, now a spunky teenager, worships "pops," as protective of him as he is of her. Henry Lozano is a non-factor in their lives. The family even reads the *Times*.

There probably won't be a beach house he had dreamed about as a young man, but c'est la vie.

"I wake up in the morning," he adds, "happy to be alive."

Source: Chip Jacobs, "Return of the Native," *Los Angeles City Beat*, April 7, 2005 http://www.lacitybeat.com/article.php?id=1887&IssueNum=96. Courtesy of Chip Jacobs, http://chipjacobs.com/a_returnof.html.

421. Excerpts from Erica Frankenberg, Chungmei Lee, and Gary Orfield, "A Multiracial Society with Segregated Schools: Are We Losing the Dream?"

The Harvard Civil Rights Project originally produced the following report. Since then, Professor Gary Orfield has moved this project on segregated schools to the University of California Los Angeles. This project brings with it countless reports on the state of Latino education and the progress, or lack of it, that it has made since *Brown v. the Board of Education* (1954) that did not end segregation in the United States. In 2005, Latino students were more segregated than in 1954. And segregation was worsening. The effects of segregation are devastating in that schools in minority areas are invariably inferior to those in white middle-class areas. The school buildings are older and not maintained with the same care, and the teachers are less experienced and less qualified. The following original Harvard study is on the state of Latino education in the twenty-first century. It is important because without this and similar data it would be difficult to change education for the better. It establishes needed guideposts.

The growth in the Latino student population is happening throughout the country. Although the four primary states in [Table 6] with Latino enrollments greater than 150,000 in 2000 are in the West, there are also two states in the South, two in the Northeast, and one in the Midwest. Florida, for example, has had the highest rate of growth in Latino student enrollment in the last thirty years with an unparalleled increase of 614%; Illinois shot up 304% during the same time period. With an increase of almost 2 million since 1970, California has had the largest absolute change in Latino enrollment, a 270% increase.

Unlike black students who have been the focus of hundreds of desegregation orders and Office for Civil Rights enforcement efforts, Latinos have remained increasingly segregated, due, in part, to demographic changes in the population and limited legal and policy efforts targeted to increasing desegregation for Latinos. Latinos were not included in most desegregation court orders due to their small presence in most Southern districts during the 1960s. As a result, Latino students have, until recently, consistently been more isolated from white students than the average black student [see Table 7]. Currently, the average Latino student goes to school where less than 30 percent of the school population is white....

The percentage of Latino students in predominantly minority schools has steadily increased since the 1960s and actually exceeded that of blacks in the 1980s. In the last decade, with the dismantling of desegregation orders and the resegregation of blacks, the level of black segregation is now comparable to that of Latinos: seven out of ten black and Latino students attend predominantly minority schools. The

Table 6. Growth of Latino Enrollments, 1970–2000

States	1970	2000	Enrollment Change (1970–2000)	Percent Change (1970–2000)
California	706,900	2,613,480	1,906,580	269.7
Texas	565,900	1,646,508	1,080,608	190.9
New York	316,600	533,631	217,031	68.6
Florida	65,700	469,362	403,662	614.4
Illinois	78,100	315,446	237,346	303.9
Arizona	85,500	297,703	212,203	248.2
New Jersey	59,100	201,509	142,409	240.9
New Mexico	109,300	160,708	51,408	47.0
Colorado	84,281	159,547	75,226	89.3

Source: DBS Corp. 1982; 1987; 2000–2001 NCES Common Core of Data Public School Universe.

Table 7. Most Segregated States for Latino Students, 2000–2001

Rank % of Latinos in Majority White Schools		Rank % of Latinos in 90–100% Minority Schools		Rank % Whites in School of Typical Latino	
1 New York	13.3	1 New York	58.7	1 New York	18.4
2 California	13.3	2 Texas	46.9	2 California	21.0
3 Texas	16.6	3 California	44.0	3 Texas	22.5
4 New Mexico	17.4	4 New Jersey	40.7	4 New Mexico	27.5
5 Rhode Island	20.0	5 Illinois	40.0	5 Illinois	28.7
6 Illinois	25.5	6 Florida	30.0	6 New Jersey	28.8
7 New Jersey	25.8	7 Pennsylvania	27.6	7 Rhode Island	30.5
8 Arizona	28.2	8 Connecticut	27.1	8 Arizona	32.6
9 Florida	29.3	9 Arizona	25.6	9 Florida	32.7
10 Connecticut	29.6	10 Rhode Island	25.4	10 Connecticut	35.7
11 Maryland	31.1	11 New Mexico	24.8	11 Maryland	36.0
12 Massachusetts	35.2	12 Maryland	21.1	12 Massachusetts	39.6
13 Pennsylvania	35.3	13 Massachusetts	18.8	13 Pennsylvania	40.3
14 Nevada	39.1	14 Wisconsin	16.7	14 Nevada	41.9
15 Georgia	44.5	15 Colorado	15.2	15 Georgia	45.8
16 Colorado	46.0	16 Georgia	12.6	16 Colorado	46.3
17 Louisiana	47.8	17 Indiana	11.2	17 Louisiana	48.8
18 Virginia	49.6	18 Louisiana	10.3	18 Virginia	49.5
19 Kansas	52.7	19 Michigan	10.3	19 Delaware	52.4
20 Washington	55.3	20 Nevada	8.3	20 North Carolina	52.7

Source: 2000–2001 NCES Common Core of Data Public School Universe.

percentage of Latinos in predominantly minority schools is slightly higher than that of blacks (76% for Latinos, 72% for blacks).

More Latinos than ever before are also now in intensely segregated schools (90–100% minority), rising from 462,000 in 1968 to 2.86 million in 2000, an increase of 520% in a little over 30 years. After a low of 23% in the late 1960s, the percentage of Latinos attending these schools has consistently increased to reach an unprecedented 37% in 2000....

Source: Erica Frankenberg, Chungmei Lee, and Gary Orfield, "A Multiracial Society with Segregated Schools: Are We Losing the Dream?" The Civil Rights Project, University of California at Los Angeles, January 2003, p. 32–33, 44, 52. http://www.civilrightsproject.ucla.edu/research/reseg03/resegregation03.php.

422. Pew Hispanic Center, "Fact Sheet: Latinos and the War in Iraq," January 4, 2007

The Pew Hispanic Center at the University of Southern California continues as the premier think tank on Latino-related studies. The following study examines the attitude of Latinos toward the war in Iraq. This study shows that two out of three Latinos believe that U.S. armed forces should be brought home. Unlike in other wars, the Latino population has been critical, with more Latinos disapproving of the war than has the general population. It is significant because in past wars Latinos, especially Mexicans and Puerto Ricans, believed that they had to pay society with their blood. The report is important because it memorializes why Latinos are against the war.

Two out of every three Latinos now believe that U.S. troops should be brought home from Iraq as soon as possible and only one in four thinks the U.S. made the right decision in using military force, according to a new survey by the Pew Hispanic Center.

Hispanics have generally expressed more negative views toward the war compared with the rest of the population. The latest survey, however, shows an even stronger opposition on the part of Latinos, especially when it comes to keeping troops in Iraq.

Two-thirds of Hispanics (66%) now favor bringing troops home as soon as possible, up from 51% in January 2005 [see Table 8]. Conversely, the share of Latinos who favored keeping troops in Iraq until the situation there has stabilized has declined from 37% to 19%.

Native-born Hispanics are generally more supportive of the war than their foreign-born counterparts. But in the latest survey, the native born are almost as adamant about bringing troops home as the foreign born (62% vs. 68% respectively).

The general public also is more inclined to bring the troops home, but not to the same extent as Hispanics. A survey of the general population by the Pew Research Center for the People & the Press in December found that one in two Americans (50%) favored bringing troops home as soon as possible, up from 41% in January 2005.

The changing attitude toward the war is also evident in the answer to a basic question: Do you think the U.S. made the right decision or the wrong decision in using military force against Iraq? Since 2004, a third or more of Latinos responded that using military force was the right decision. In the latest survey, only 24% of

Table 8. Do You Think the U.S. Should Keep Military Troops in Iraq until the Situation Has Stabilized, or Do You Think the U.S. Should Bring Its Troops Home As Soon As Possible?

	January 2005			December 2006		
	Total Latino	U.S. Born	Foreign Born	Total Latino	U.S. Born	Foreign Born
Keep troops in Iraq	37	47	29	19	28	15
Bring troops home	51	46	55	66	62	68
Don't know/ no answer	12	6	15	15	10	17

Latinos agreed with that assessment [see Table 9]. That is down from 39% in April/June 2004 and from 31% in August/October 2006.

By comparison, 42% of the general public believes the U.S. made the right decision in using military force, according to the survey by the Pew Research Center.

The Pew Hispanic Center survey was conducted by telephone from December 5 to 20, 2006, among a nationally representative sample of 1,006 Hispanics age 18 and older. The sample was drawn using a stratified Random Digit Dialing methodology. Interviews were conducted by bilingual interviewers in English or Spanish, according to the respondents' preferences. The results for the full sample have a margin of error of +/− 3.1%. All fieldwork was conducted for the Center by International Communications Research of Media, PA.

LATINO ATTITUDES ON THE WAR IN IRAQ

The Pew Hispanic Center has regularly tracked Latino public opinion on the war in Iraq since February 2003. As with the rest of the American public, Hispanic views on the war have shifted over time, often in direct response to developments in Iraq. The quick end to the first phase of combat produced a spike, for example, but the subsequent violence and the mounting casualties in 2003 eroded support among Hispanics. The capture of Saddam Hussein in mid-December 2003 rallied Hispanic public opinion, but not to the levels seen shortly after the war started. Since then, Latino views on the war have been marked by increased pessimism.

This fact sheet uses three questions that have been asked in surveys to track how the perception of the war in Iraq has changed among Latinos in the U.S.

While support for keeping troops in Iraq has eroded across the board, the decline has been especially steep among Latinos.

In January 2005, a majority of Hispanics (51%) were in favor of bringing troops home, compared with 41% among the general population. In the latest survey, two-thirds of Latinos (66%) were in favor compared with half (50%) among the general population.

Fewer than one in five (19%) of Hispanics now favor keeping troops in Iraq, a decrease from 37% in January 2005 and 50% in January 2004, when the question was asked in a slightly different way. The Pew Research Center survey in December

Table 9. Do You Think the U.S. Made the Right Decision or the Wrong Decision in Using Military Force Against Iraq?

	April–June 2004			January 2005			August–October, 2006			December 2006		
	Total Latino	U.S. Born	Foreign Born	Total Latino	U.S. Born	Foreign Born	Total Latino	U.S. Born	Foreign Born	Total Latino	U.S. Born	Foreign Born
Right decision	39	50	32	37	48	28	31	40	26	24	40	15
Wrong decision	48	42	51	51	46	54	56	52	59	50	42	55
Don't know/ no answer	13	8	17	12	5	18	12	7	16	26	18	30

Table 10. How Well Do You Think the U.S. Military Effort in Iraq Is Going?

	December 2003			January 2004			December 2006		
	Total Latino	U.S. Born	Foreign Born	Total Latino	U.S. Born	Foreign Born	Total Latino	U.S. Born	Foreign Born
Very well	16	15	17	30	25	33	8	11	6
Fairly well	26	33	21	32	46	23	11	17	7
Not too well	32	35	30	24	21	25	26	33	23
Not well at all	17	14	19	9	6	11	42	34	46
Don't know/no answer	9	4	13	5	2	8	13	5	17

2006 found that among the general population 44% were in favor, down from 54% in January 2005.

Described another way, the share of Latinos who favored keeping troops in Iraq declined by 18 percentage points between January 2005 and December 2006. Among the general population, the drop was 10 percentage points.

Even among Latinos who said the U.S. made the right decision in using military force against Iraq, 43% still supported bringing troops home as soon as possible.

Native-born Latinos were roughly split on this question in 2005. However, in the latest survey, the native-born have significantly swung in favor of bringing troops home. Almost two in three (62%) are now in favor of withdrawal, up from 46%. A solid majority of foreign-born Hispanics (55%) were in favor of bringing troops home in 2005 and that share has now increased to more than two-thirds (68%).

Support for bringing the troops home is stronger among those with lower incomes and lower levels of education. Three out of four (75%) Latinos with household incomes of $25,000 or less favored this option, as did 72% of those with a high school education or less. By comparison, among those with household incomes of $75,000 or more, 42% supported bringing troops home. And among Hispanics with college degrees or higher, 57% favored this option.

Perceptions of the war in Iraq vary depending on nativity, with foreign-born Hispanics in general more disapproving. In 2004 and 2005, for example, a plurality among native-born Latinos believed the U.S. had made the right decision in using military force. Even as attitudes toward the war turned negative, 40% of native-born Latinos still felt this way in the two surveys taken in 2006. Among foreign-born Hispanics, however, a majority has said using military force was the wrong decision and that number has pretty much held steady since 2004.

The latest survey also shows an increase in the number of Latinos who express uncertainty on this question. About one in four said they did not know whether the U.S. had made the right decision or the wrong decision or they simply refused to answer, an increase from 12% in the survey conducted between August and October 2006. The uncertainty is more prevalent among foreign-born Hispanics.

Hispanics by a wide margin believe that the U.S. military effort is faring poorly in Iraq. More than two-thirds (68%) said it was either going not too well or not well at all [see Table 10].

Latinos are generally of a mind with the American public in this negative assessment of the military effort in Iraq. In the December 2006 Pew Research Center poll of the general population, 64% of Americans agreed that the military effort was going not too well or not well at all. But while relatively few Hispanics (19%) said the military effort was going either very well or fairly well, in the general population almost a third (32%) cast the military effort in a positive light.

This question was asked of Latinos in December 2003, after a period when American casualties were high and the war was not going well and then again a month later, in January of 2004, shortly after the capture of Iraqi leader Saddam Hussein. As with the rest of the American public, the capture produced a significant spike in support among Latinos. A majority (52%) said in January 2004 that the U.S. military effort was going either very well or fairly well, up from 42% just a month earlier. Today, two years later, only about one in five Hispanics agree with this assessment.

Source: Fact Sheet, Latinos and the War in Iraq, Pew Hispanic Center, January 4, 2007, © 2007 Pew Hispanic Center, a Pew Research Center Project, www.pewhispanic.org. http://pewhispanic. org/factsheets/factsheet.php?Factsheet ID=27.

423. Jorge Mariscal, "They Died Trying to Become Students—The Future for Latinos in an Era of War and Occupation," 2003

Jorge Mariscal is a professor of literature at the University of California at San Diego. Mariscal is a Vietnam Veteran and has written frequently on the topic of the war in Iraq. Like many Latino and Chicano academics he is concerned about the military targeting Latinos for military recruitment. In the following article, Mariscal says why he is against the war, basing much of his opinion on his own war experience.

With the U.S. assault on Iraq moving from the invasion to the occupation phase and the saber rattling continuing to echo out of the Pentagon, it is time to reflect on where the Latino community in the United States finds itself within the larger context of the New World Order.

Like many working class youth, Latinos and Latinas who buy into the vision of military service as a short cut to college or job training are simply looking for a way to grab a piece of the American Dream. But the reality of that dream continues to be relatively distant for the Chicano/Mexicano community. More specifically, alternatives to military service available to Mexicano youth are significantly fewer than for other groups. Until this fact is understood, the fundamental injustice of Mexican and Chicano youth dying to "liberate" Iraq (or any other developing nation) cannot be fully grasped.

One of the more remarked-upon facts during the early days of the war was the number of Spanish-surnamed soldiers and marines killed or missing in action. The sense that Latino communities were disproportionately sacrificing their youth once again, as they had in Viet Nam, was widespread. Media outlets began to comment on the fact that Latinos in the military are over represented in combat and supply units (especially in the Army and Marines) and thus more likely to see hazardous duty.

The American public learned that thousands of non-citizens were now in the U.S. military (approximately 3% of enlisted personnel, a third of whom are from Latin America). The Bush administration had established a fast track naturalization process for foreign recruits in July 2002, as part of the "war on terror." Instead of waiting three years before applying for citizenship, green-card holders in the armed forces who entered after September 11, 2001, could apply immediately for citizenship.

Such offers are often granted in limited form during periods of "military hostilities." (At the time of this writing, John McCain, Ted Kennedy, and eight other senators introduced a bill that would reduce permanently the waiting period from three to two years and provide benefits for non-citizen spouses of non-citizen soldiers killed in action.)

Although the Bush Executive Order contained no guarantees that citizen status would be granted or even expedited, the rumor that automatic citizenship was being granted for military service began to circulate in Latino communities both here and abroad. The number of permanent resident enlistees jumped from 300 a month before the fast track reform to 1,300 a month. Mexican nationals reportedly flooded consulates attempting to volunteer.

Both citizen and non-citizen recruits most often enlist as a way to get an education, seduced by the recruiters' promise of technical training or money for college contingent upon an honorable discharge. For the permanent residents who found themselves in Iraq, their circuitous path to college carried them from Latin America to the U.S. to Baghdad, al-Nasiriyah, and Mosul. Some of them will not be attending classes as they and their families had hoped. Instead they died in the line of duty and subsequently received posthumous citizenship amidst much fanfare and flag waving.

Many in Latino communities, including some parents of the fallen soldiers, sought refuge in traditional patriotic sentiments. The father of Colombiano Diego Rincón, an Army private killed in a suicide bombing, was quoted as saying, "The only thing that keeps me going now is to make sure that he's buried as an American. That will be my dream come true" (*USA Today*, 4/9/03).

Writing on the HispanicVista.com website about the death of Guatemalan national José Gutiérrez, Gil Contreras wrapped himself in the flag, "honor," and "Semper Fi" before criticizing Chicano and Chicana antiwar protestors for complaining too much. The subtitle of Contreras's article made the cynical assertion that Latino casualties proved that "Latinos can be more than gang members and criminals." Not unlike assimilationists from earlier periods, Contreras apparently prefers dead heroes to living and productive citizens.

For other Latinas and Latinos, the bestowal of posthumous citizenship was bitterly ironic. Did Mexican or Central American immigrants have to die to win the approval of the majority of American society? Or as an old Chicano ballad from the Viet Nam war put it: "Now should a man/Should he have to kill/In order to live/ Like a human being/ In this country?"

If Latinos were good enough for military service (so much so that the military academies continue to employ affirmative action policies), why were they not good enough to receive a decent education?

Finally, how could one reconcile the fact that foreign nationals from Latin America were fighting with the U.S. military in Iraq at the same time that armed vigilante "ranchers" hunted Mexican workers along the Mexico-Arizona border for sport?

Despite the fact that Latino communities were divided on the issue, initiatives for expedited citizenship began to proliferate.

Two senators from Georgia, where the Latino population increased by 299.6% during the decade of the 1990s, introduced a bill that would make posthumous citizenship automatic. Leaders in the Catholic Church made similar recommendations. Little was said about the fact that posthumous citizenship was a purely symbolic gesture with no rights or privileges accruing to the deceased person's family (last week, Rep. Darrell Issa [R-Ca] proposed automatic citizenship for the surviving spouse and children of non-citizen soldiers killed in battle and given posthumous citizenship).

WHY LATINOS AND LATINAS ENLIST

"Why should you consider getting an education in the Navy?" [cut to aerial shot of aircraft carrier] "This is one of your classrooms."—U.S. Navy television ad, April 2003. On one level, Latino and Latina GIs are no different from other poor youth drawn into the web spun by military recruiters. It has been widely reported that former POW Jessica Lynch, the daughter of a poor family from Appalachia, joined because she wanted to be a teacher. According to his former mentor, the young man from Guatemala, José Gutiérrez, joined the Marines to get an education. Twenty-one year old Francisco Martinez Flores, killed when his tank fell into the Euphrates, enlisted so that he could go to college and become a stockbroker or an FBI agent, according to his friends (Betsy Streisand, "Latin Heroes," *U.S. News and World Report*, 4/14/03). In short, what motivated these young people to enlist was less the defense of "our freedom" or "honor" than it was simply to increase their access to a decent education and a better life.

The myth that the primary mission of the armed forces is education was given a boost by former Secretary of the Army Louis Caldera during the Clinton years. Throughout the 1990s, the Army was not meeting its enlistment quotas. Caldera and Pentagon planners realized that Latinos were the fastest growing population in terms of young people of military age, and they began to pitch the Army's program offering to pay for GED certificate training (roughly equivalent to a high school diploma). The goal, according to Caldera, was to increase access to the "Hispanic market" as a major recruiting pool. Aircraft carriers became "classrooms."

The promise of education sat in an uneasy relationship to other more traditional messages having to do with what the Pentagon perceived to be Latino "machismo." The racializing undertones of this approach cannot be ignored. An article in the *ArmyLink News* pointed out that many of the surnames on the Viet Nam Memorial were Spanish and that three soldiers captured during the Kosovo conflict were of Mexican descent. The author's conclusion? "By these and many other measures, Hispanics are one of America's more martially inclined ethnic groups" (Sydney J. Freedberg, Jr., "Not Enough GI Josés," *ArmyLink News*, August 1999).

Some recruiters reported that even those Mexican American recruits who "tested out of the infantry" (i.e., scored high enough to qualify for other military jobs) opted to enter the infantry anyway (this despite a 1999 Rand study that explained low numbers of minorities in Special Operations units because of their "preference for occupations with less risk"). Caldera himself claimed that Hispanics were "predisposed" to military service even as he argued that the Army provided the "best education in the world."

And so the Pentagon launched a massive publicity campaign targeting the Hispanic market. "$30,000 for college" claimed the glitzy ads although the fine print did not point out that very few veterans would ever see such amounts of money. Nor was it mentioned that longitudinal studies show that people who go directly to college earn more money over the length of a career than those who enter the military first. "Education" became the recruiter's buzzword because the Pentagon had learned from studies contracted out to the Rand Corporation and other think tanks that Latino and Latina recruits joined the military primarily in search of "civilian job transferability."

With the possible exception of careers in law enforcement, however, small arms expertise and truck driving did not translate well into civilian success. Military service does not close the economic gaps separating the majority of Latinos from the rest of society but potentially widens them.

CHICANOS/MEXICANOS AND THE LACK OF OPTIONS

According to the September 2002 Interim Report of the President's Advisory Commission on Educational Excellence for Hispanic Americans, ethnic Mexicans in the United States fall below every other Latino group "on almost every social and economic indicator." First-generation Mexican immigrants, who make up 54%

of all legal Latin American immigrants, have significantly reduced life chances than their U.S.-born Mexican American counterparts. High school drop-out rates of around 30% for U.S.-born Mexican Americans are bad enough, but the rate more than doubles to 61% for new immigrants. Although Mexican Americans do better in the field of education than their recently arrived counterparts, when their educational achievement is compared to every other Latino subgroup they lag behind. Among all Latinos over the age of 25, for example, only 10.8% of ethnic Mexicans hold a bachelor's degree or higher compared to 13.9% for Puerto Ricans and 18.1% for Cuban Americans (2002 Interim Report). Although Latinos have a high rate of participation in the labor force, over 11% of Latino workers live in poverty. About 7% of Latinos with full-time jobs were still living below the poverty line in 2001 (compared to 4.4% of African Americans and 1.7% for whites). Among all private sector employees in the U.S., 41.5% are considered blue collar, but 63.5% of all Latinos hold blue-collar jobs (U.S. Equal Employment Opportunity Commission 1998). In 2002, 61% of all workers in agricultural production were Latinos, the vast majority of Mexican descent. While nearly 11% of non-Hispanic whites earn more than $75,000 a year, only 2% of all Latinos earn as much. Among all high school graduates who attend graduate and professional programs, Latinos make up only 1.9% (compared to 3% Black, 3.8% Whites, and 8.8% Asian). One could elaborate further this bleak picture of what the future holds for Latino communities. The paucity of good union jobs and the decline in public funding for cultural workers only adds to the sense of diminished opportunities. Is it any wonder, in the face of these daunting material conditions, that young Latino and Latina faces are filling the lowest ranks of the military in the lowest-tech occupations? As they do so, the pipeline of Latino and Latina teachers, doctors, and other professionals continues to dry up, a fact that will have devastating consequences for our communities for decades to come.

So Latino blood now flows in the ancient waters of the Tigris and Euphrates. A historical irony of stunning proportions—that the spirits of the descendants of the great indigenous civilizations of Mesoamerica now mingle with those of the heirs of ancient Mesopotamia.

What can we say of the young Latino men who sacrificed their lives in Iraq? That they fought without knowing their enemy, played their role as pawns in a geopolitical chess game devised by arrogant bureaucrats, and died simply trying to get an education; trying to have a fair shot at the American Dream that has eluded the vast majority of Latinos for over a century and a half; dying as soldiers who just wanted to be students.

Source: Jorge Mariscal, "They Died Trying to Become Students—The Future for Latinos in an Era of War and Occupation," *CounterPoint*, Hispanic Vista, April 28, 2003.

Index

About the Editors

RODOLFO F. ACUÑA is Professor of Chicano Studies at California State University, Northridge.

GUADALUPE COMPEÁN is an independent scholar.